THE SEVEN DEADLY SINS

nakaba suzuki presents

35

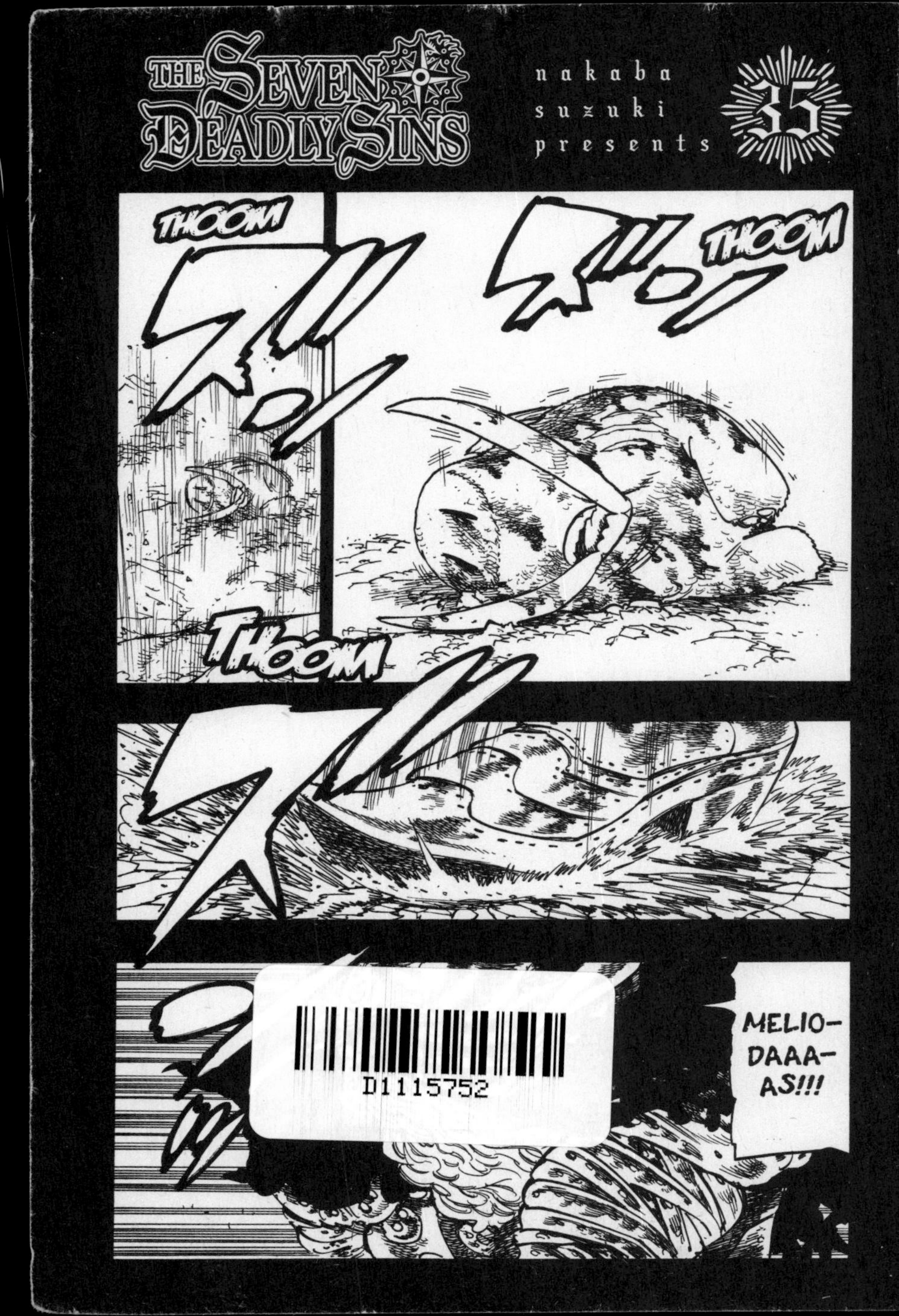
THOOM
THOOM
THOOM
MELIO-DAAA-AS!!!

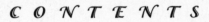

CONTENTS

The Seven Deadly Sins

THE SEVEN DEADLY SINS

Chapter 285 - What Lies Ahead

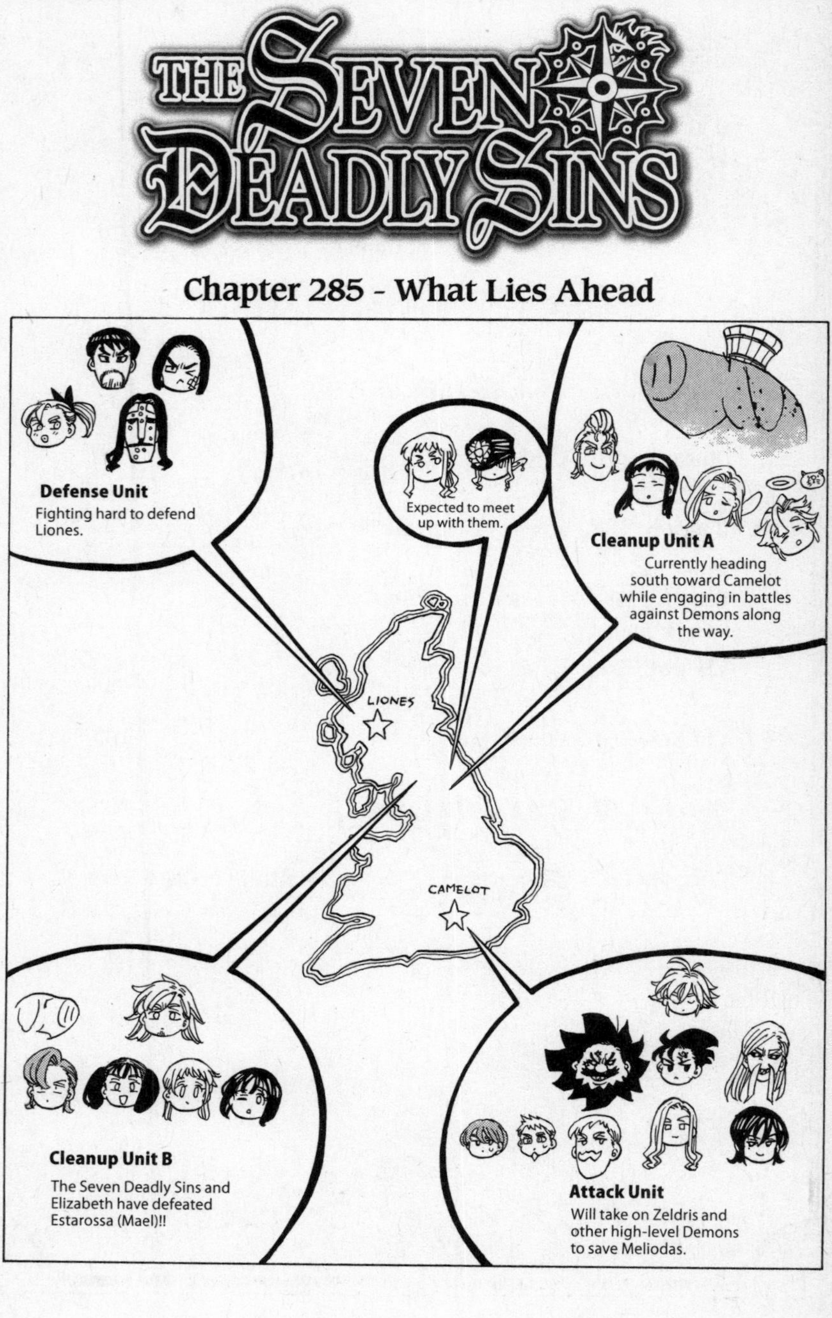
Defense Unit
Fighting hard to defend Liones.
Expected to meet up with them.
Cleanup Unit A
Currently heading south toward Camelot while engaging in battles against Demons along the way.
LIONES
CAMELOT
Cleanup Unit B
The Seven Deadly Sins and Elizabeth have defeated Estarossa (Mael)!!
Attack Unit
Will take on Zeldris and other high-level Demons to save Meliodas.

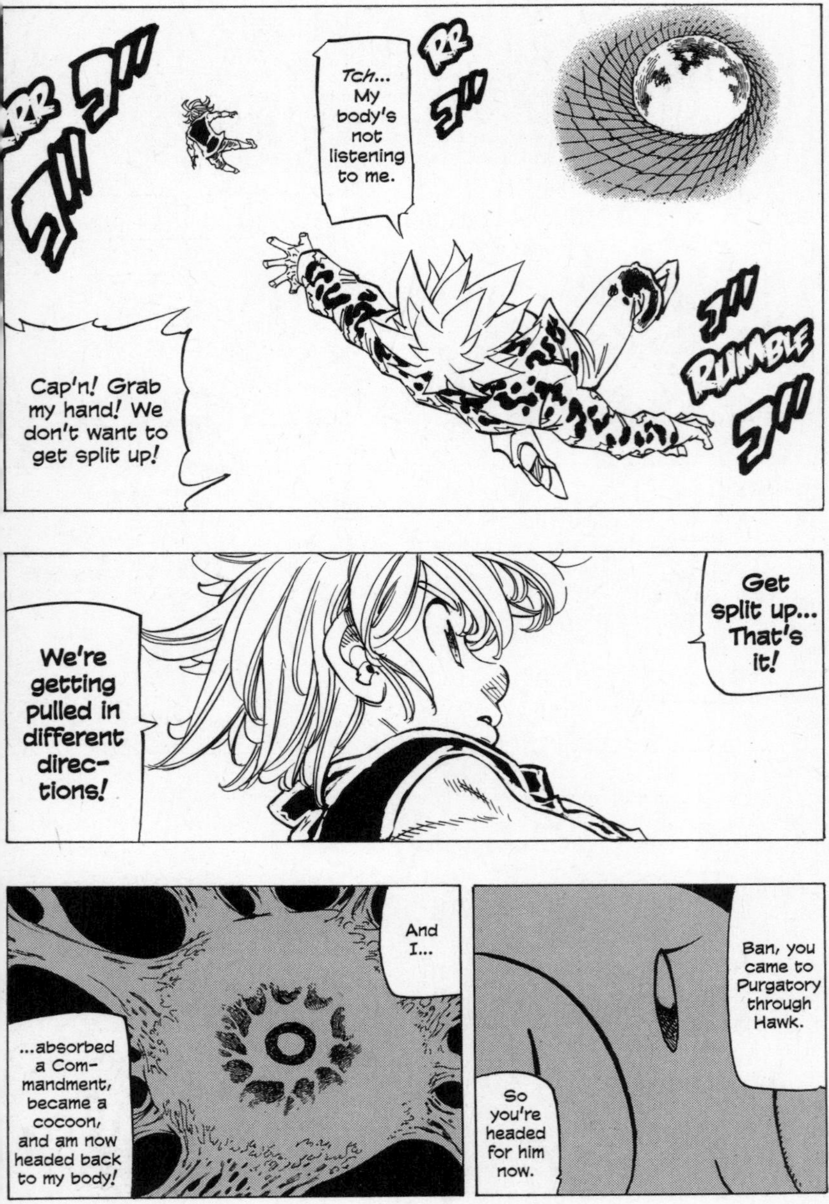
RR
RUMBLE
Tch... My body's not listening to me.
Cap'n! Grab my hand! We don't want to get split up!
Get split up... That's it!
We're getting pulled in different directions!
Ban, you came to Purgatory through Hawk.
So you're headed for him now.
And I...
...absorbed a Commandment, became a cocoon, and am now headed back to my body!

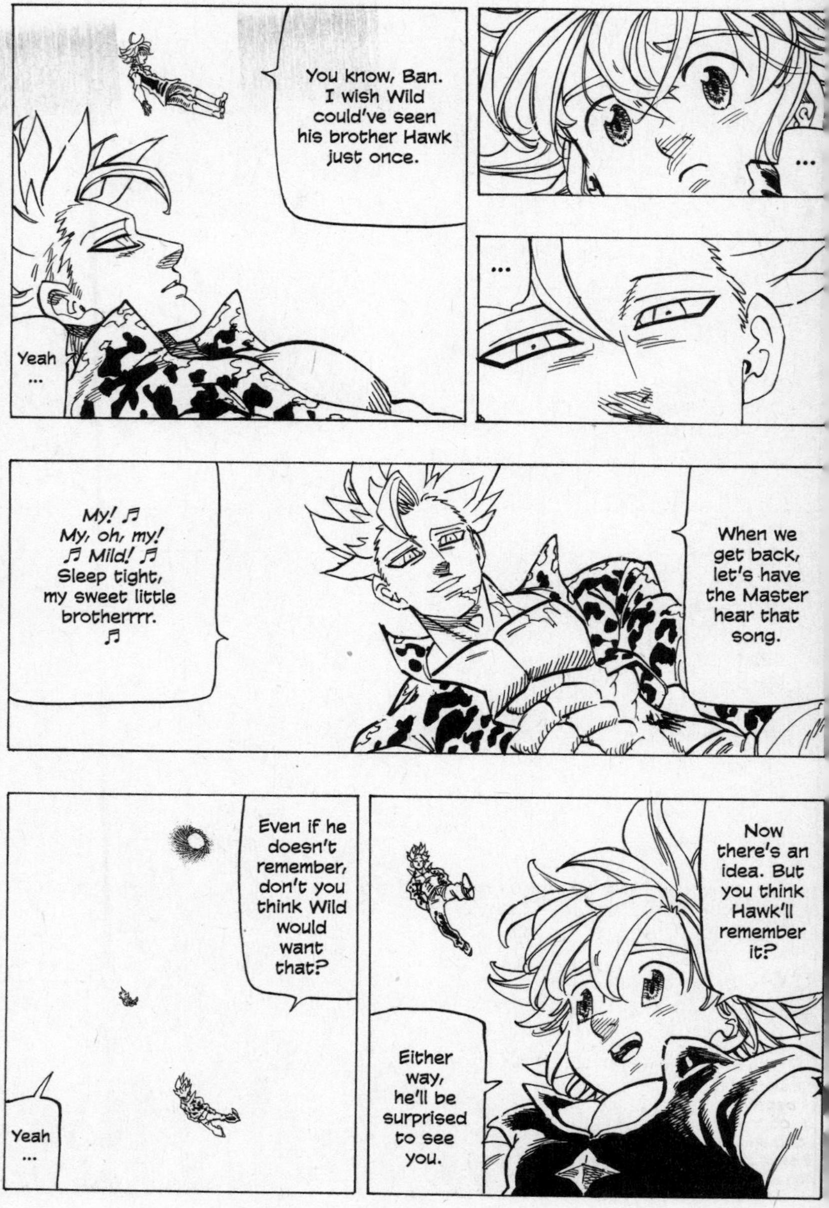
...
...
You know, Ban. I wish Wild could've seen his brother Hawk just once.
Yeah ...
When we get back, let's have the Master hear that song.
My! ♬ My, oh, my! ♬ Mild! ♬ Sleep tight, my sweet little brotherrrr. ♬
Now there's an idea. But you think Hawk'll remember it?
Either way, he'll be surprised to see you.
Even if he doesn't remember, don't you think Wild would want that?
Yeah ...

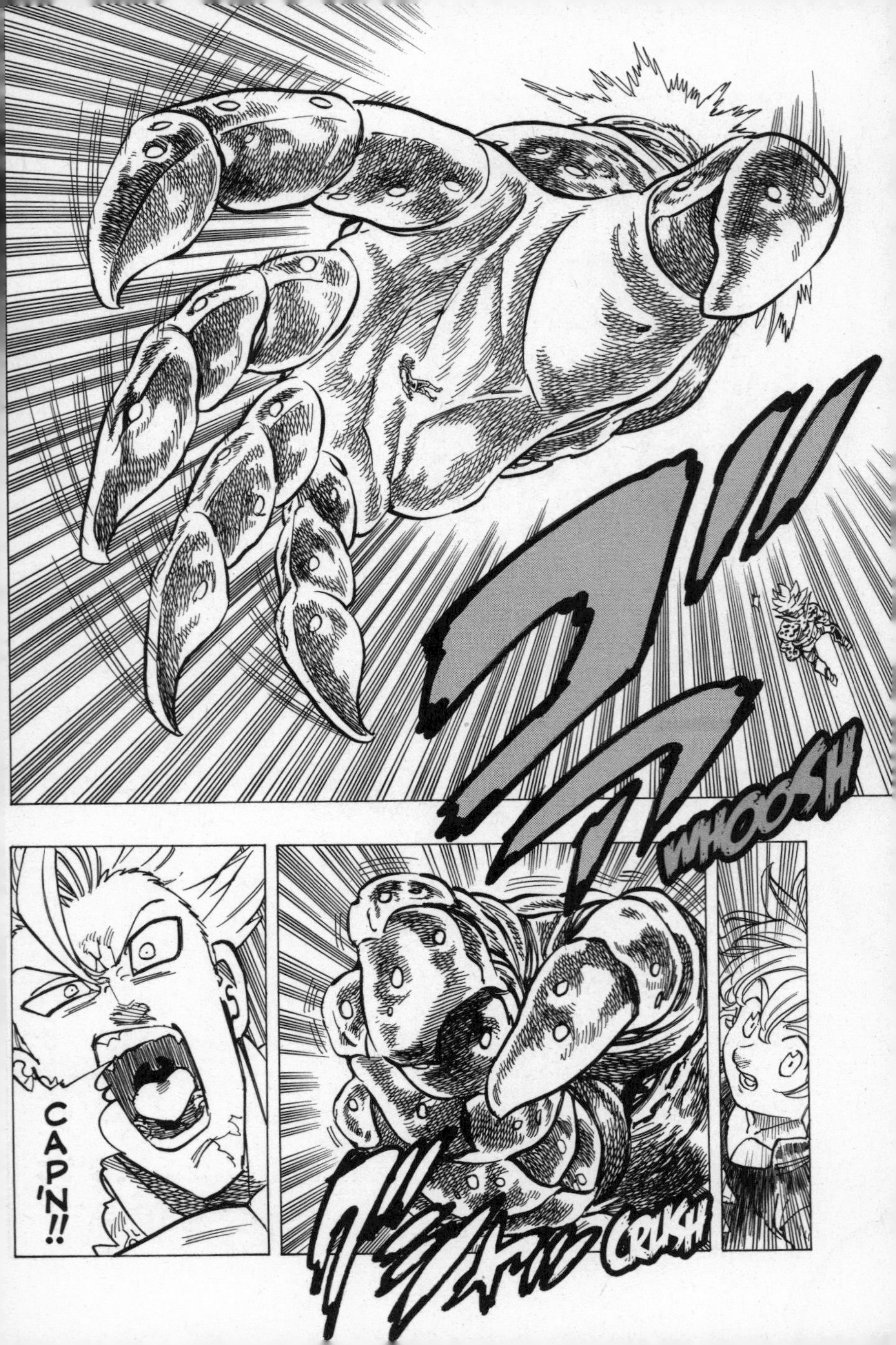
WHOOSH
CRUSH
CAP'N!!

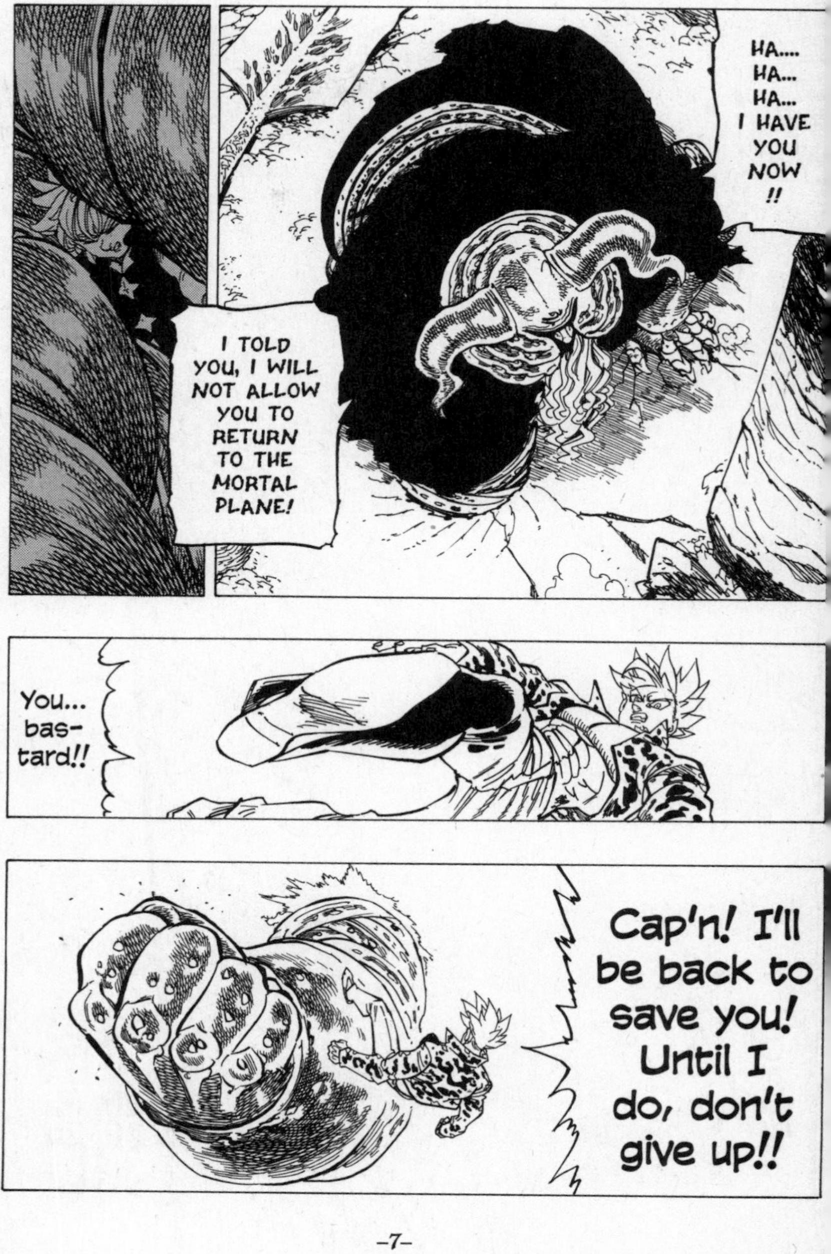
HA.... HA... HA... I HAVE YOU NOW!!
I TOLD YOU, I WILL NOT ALLOW YOU TO RETURN TO THE MORTAL PLANE!
You... bas-tard!!
Cap'n! I'll be back to save you! Until I do, don't give up!!

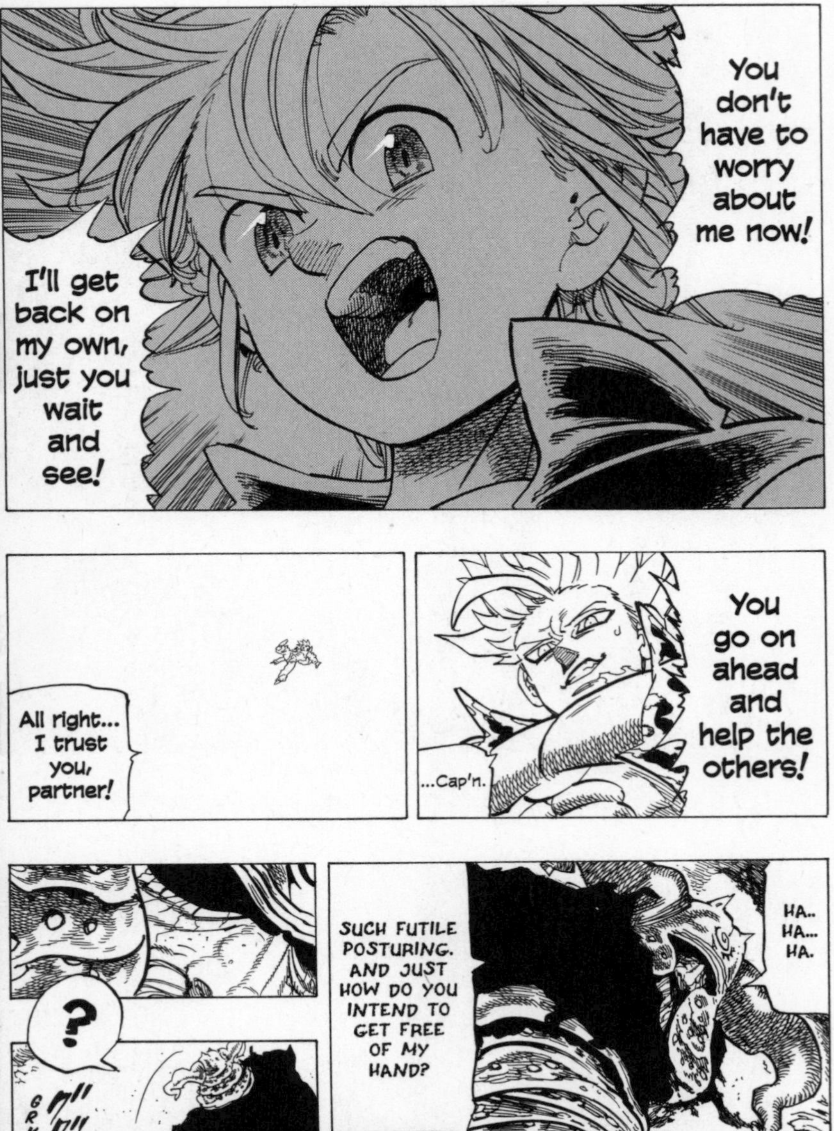
You don't have to worry about me now!
I'll get back on my own, just you wait and see!
You go on ahead and help the others!
...Cap'n.
All right... I trust you, partner!
HA.. HA... HA.
SUCH FUTILE POSTURING. AND JUST HOW DO YOU INTEND TO GET FREE OF MY HAND?
?
GRK

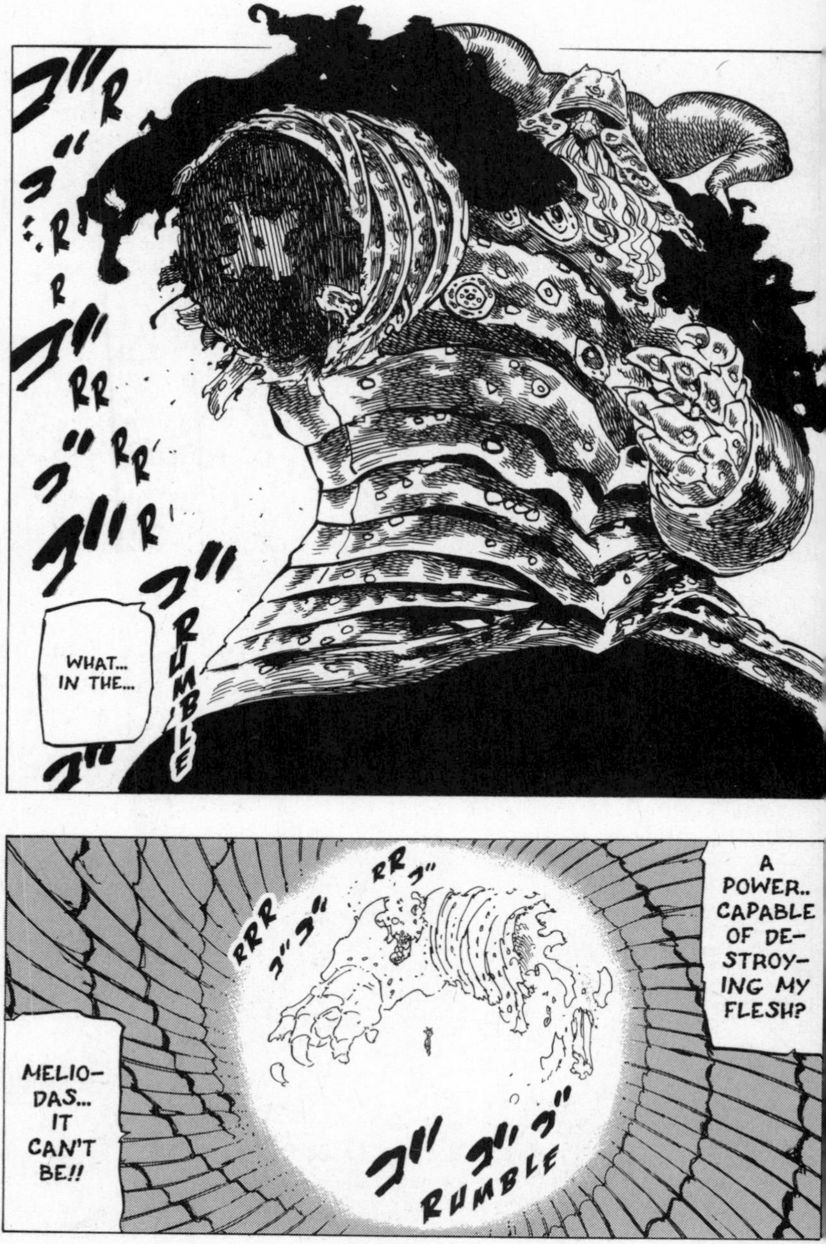
R
R
R
RR
RR
R
RUMBLE
WHAT... IN THE...
A POWER.. CAPABLE OF DE-STROYING MY FLESH?
RR
RRR
RUMBLE
MELIO-DAS... IT CAN'T BE!!

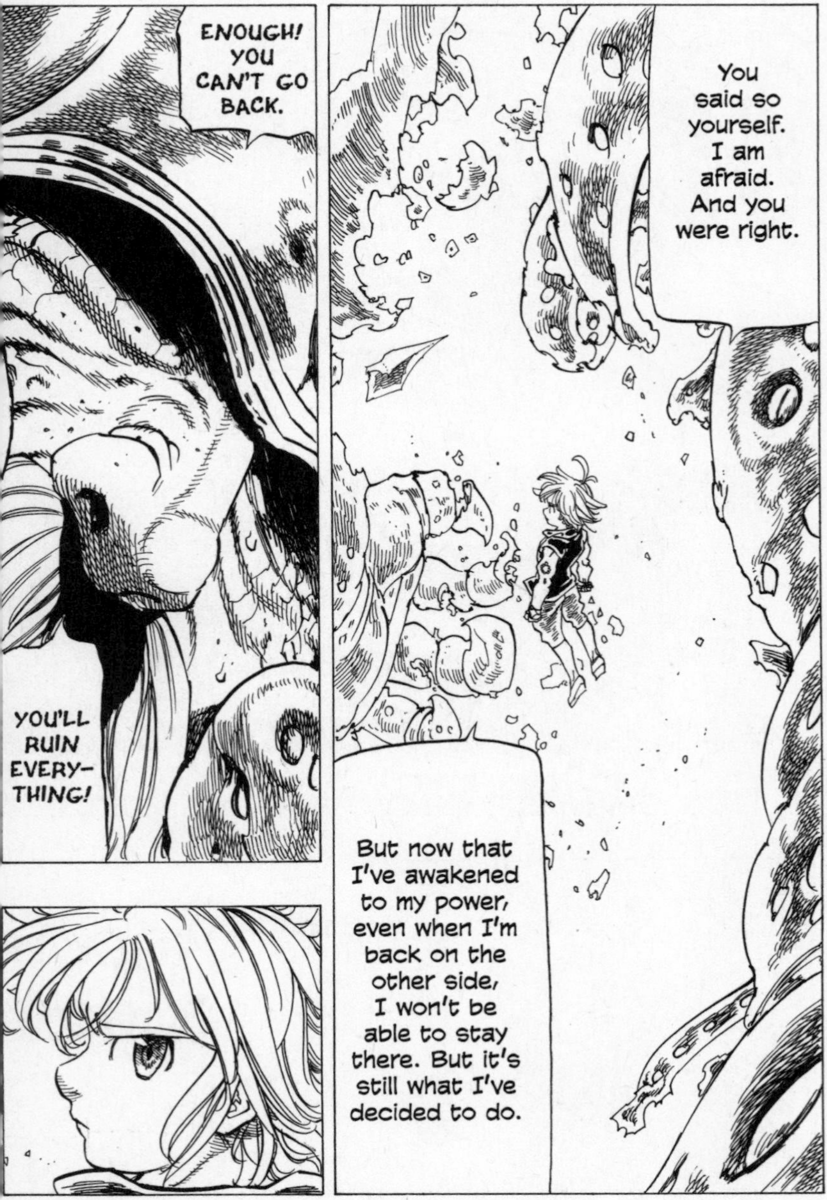
You said so yourself. I am afraid. And you were right.
But now that I've awakened to my power, even when I'm back on the other side, I won't be able to stay there. But it's still what I've decided to do.
ENOUGH! YOU CAN'T GO BACK.
YOU'LL RUIN EVERY-THING!

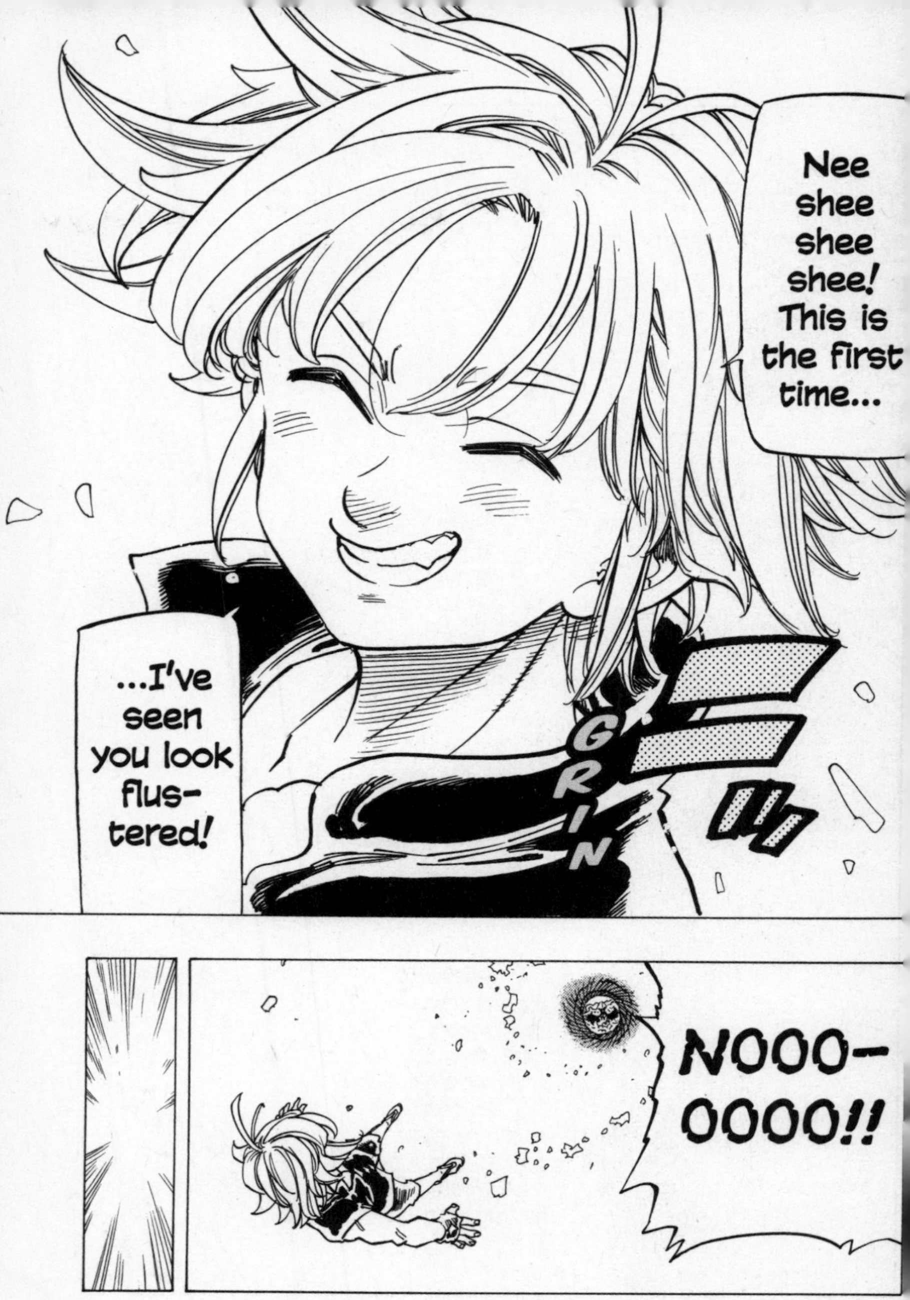
Nee shee shee shee! This is the first time...
...I've seen you look flus-tered!
GRIN
NOOO-OOOO!!

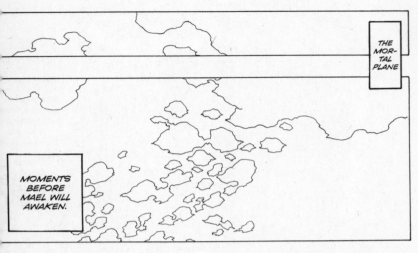

THE MORTAL PLANE

MOMENTS BEFORE MAEL WILL AWAKEN.

M-Merlin... What is this thing?

It's a powerful, high-density dark zone birthed from Meliodas. It's fusing with the Commandment.

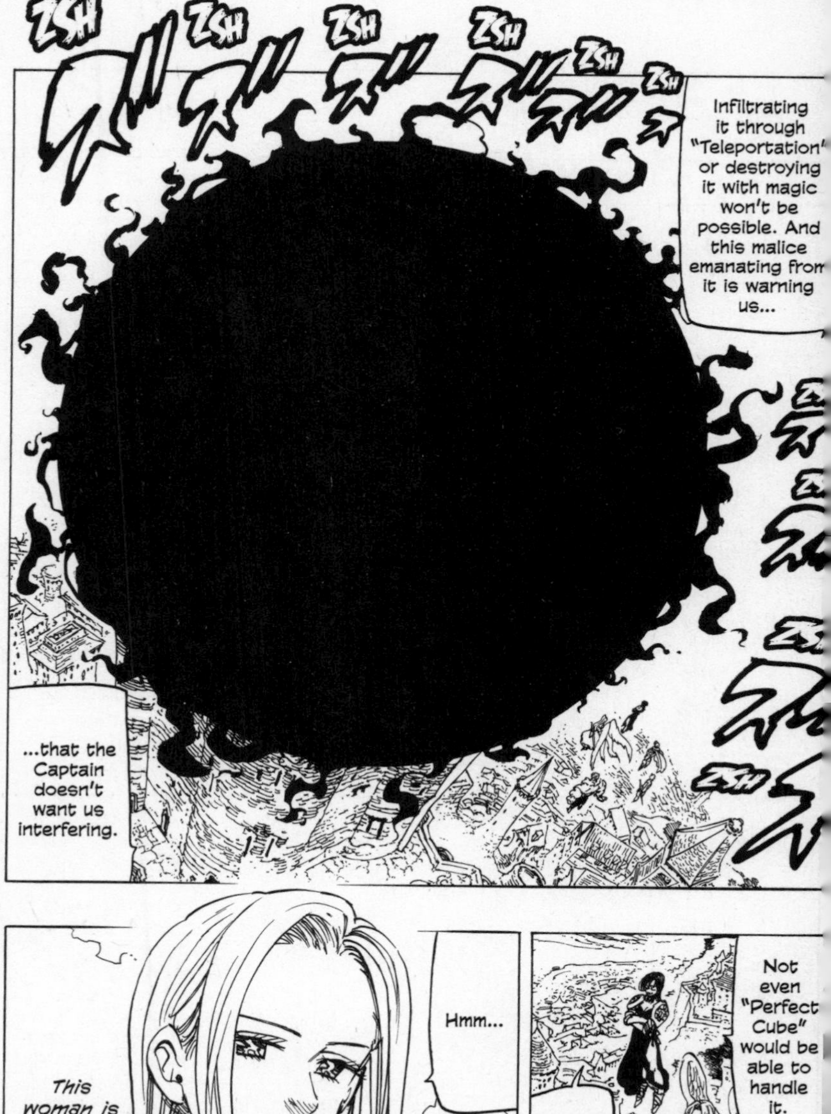
ZSH
ZSH
ZSH
ZSH
ZSH
ZSH
Infiltrating it through "Teleportation" or destroying it with magic won't be possible. And this malice emanating from it is warning us...
ZSH
...that the Captain doesn't want us interfering.
Not even "Perfect Cube" would be able to handle it.
Do you have any ideas, Sir Ludoshel?
Hmm...
This woman is not to be underestimated.

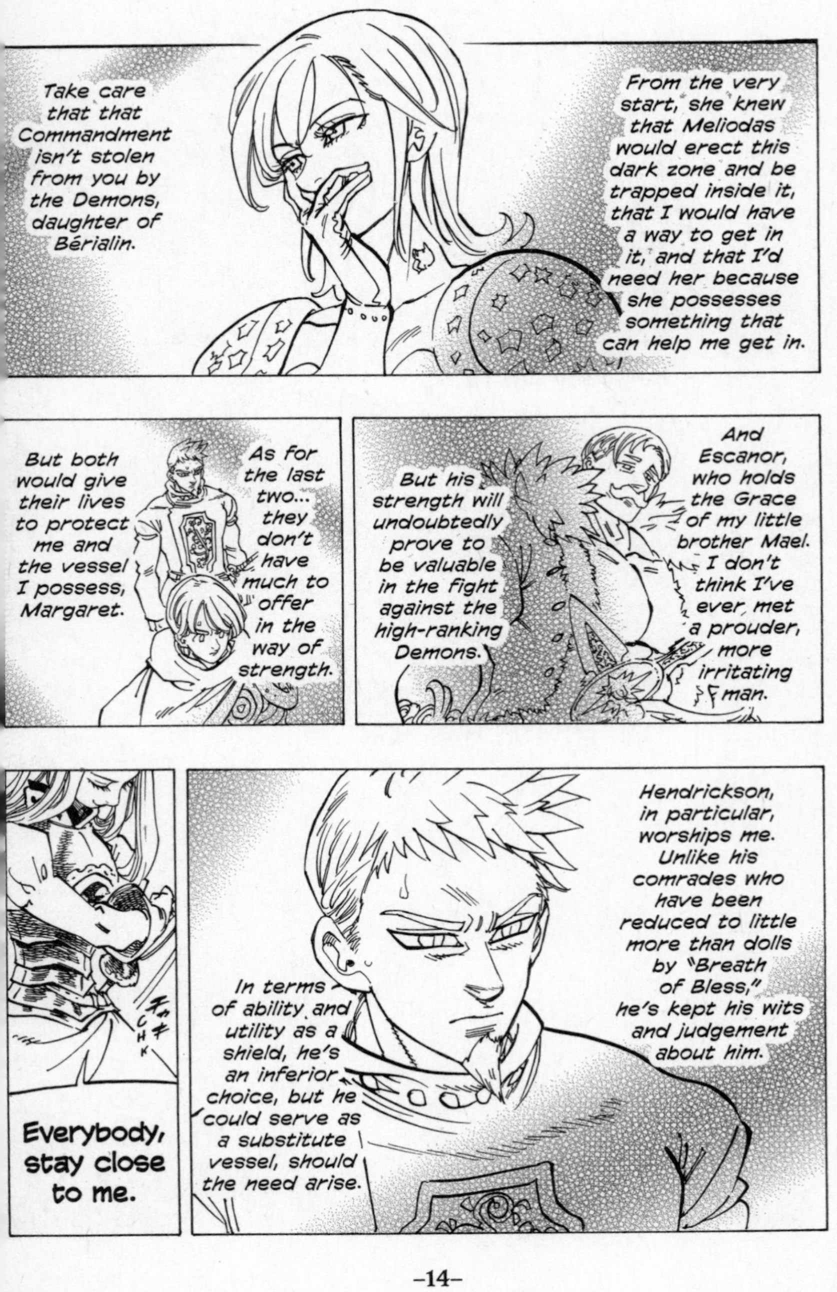

From the very start, she knew that Meliodas would erect this dark zone and be trapped inside it, that I would have a way to get in it, and that I'd need her because she possesses something that can help me get in.
Take care that that Commandment isn't stolen from you by the Demons, daughter of Bérialin.
And Escanor, who holds the Grace of my little brother Mael. I don't think I've ever met a prouder, more irritating man.
But his strength will undoubtedly prove to be valuable in the fight against the high-ranking Demons.
As for the last two... they don't have much to offer in the way of strength.
But both would give their lives to protect me and the vessel I possess, Margaret.
Hendrickson, in particular, worships me. Unlike his comrades who have been reduced to little more than dolls by "Breath of Bless," he's kept his wits and judgement about him.
In terms of ability and utility as a shield, he's an inferior choice, but he could serve as a substitute vessel, should the need arise.
CHK
Everybody, stay close to me.

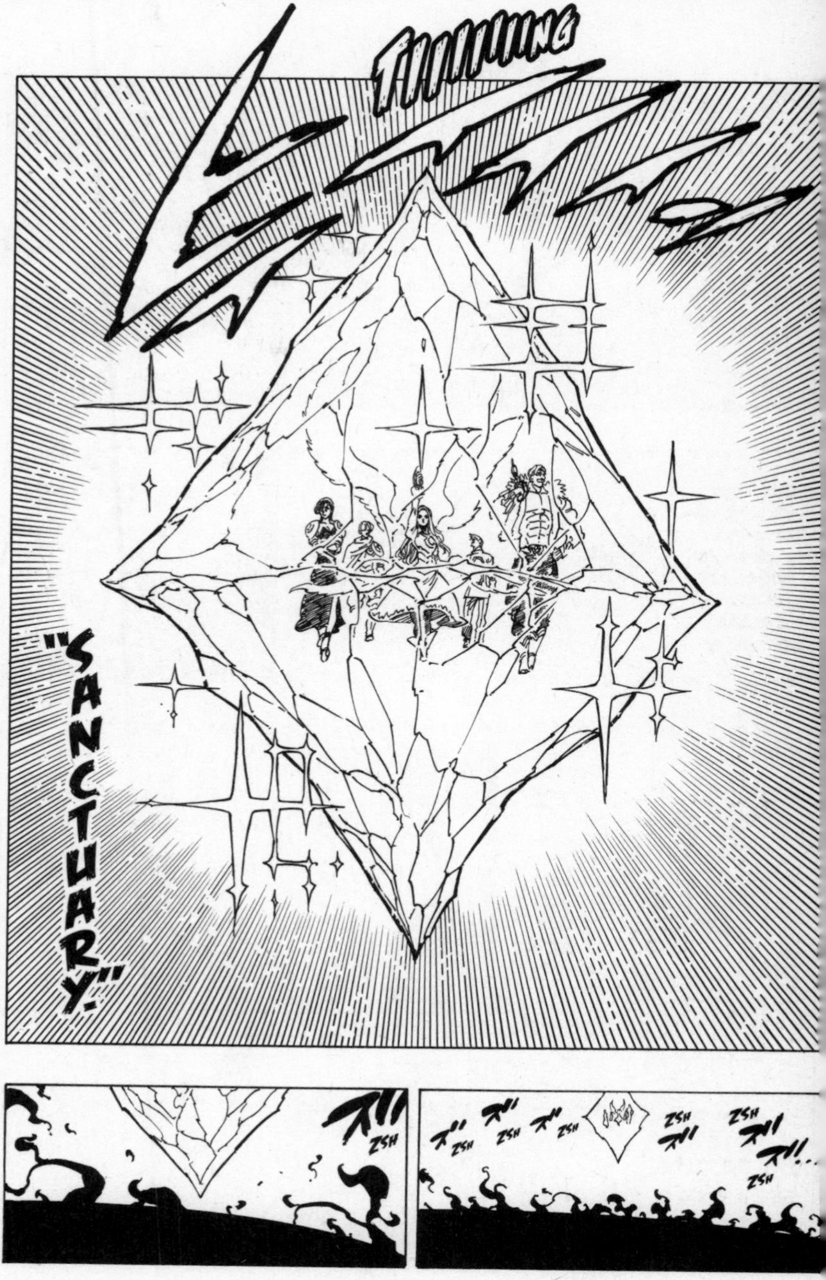
TIIIIIING
"SANCTUARY."
ZSH
ZSH
ZSH
ZSH
ZSH
ZSH
ZSH

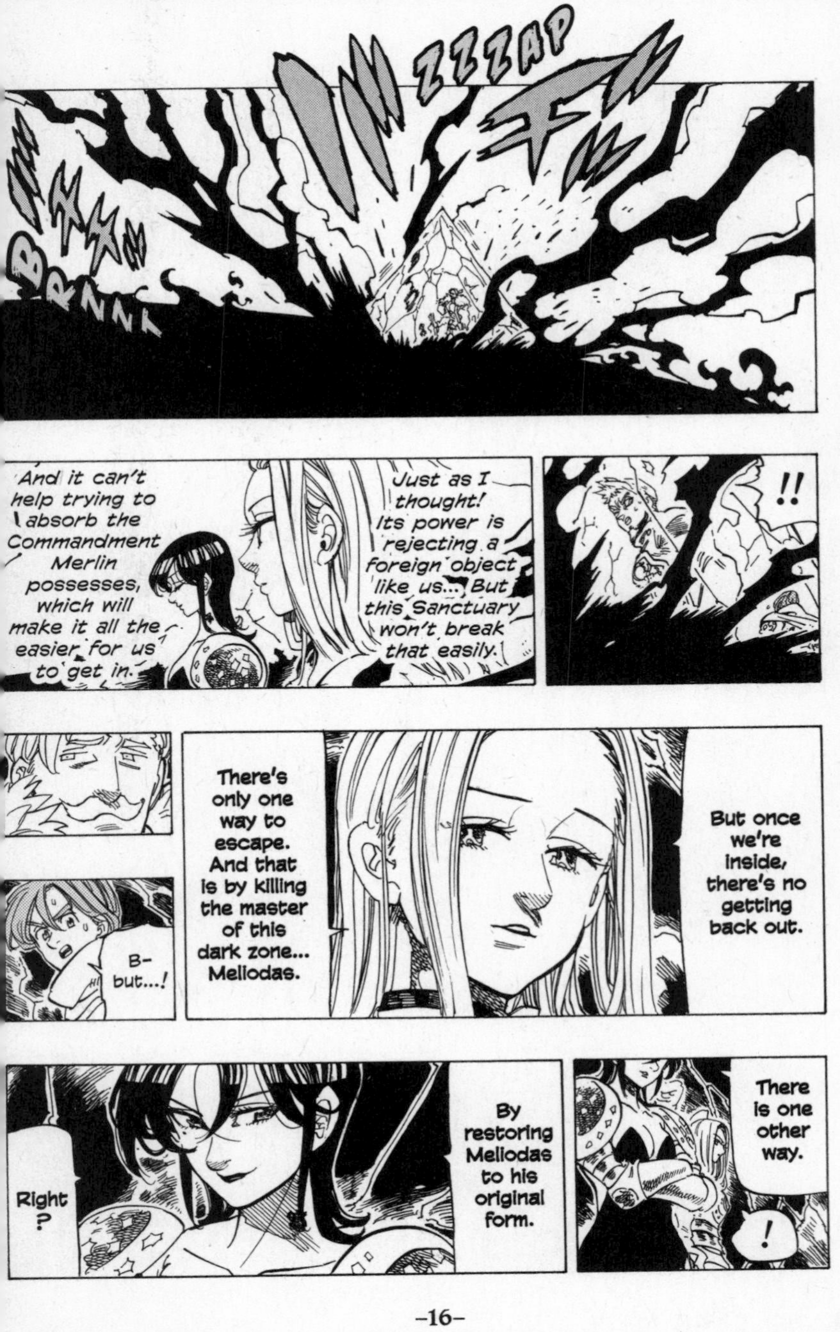
ZZZAP
BRNNT
!!
Just as I thought! Its power is rejecting a foreign object like us... But this Sanctuary won't break that easily.
And it can't help trying to absorb the Commandment Merlin possesses, which will make it all the easier for us to get in.
But once we're inside, there's no getting back out.
There's only one way to escape. And that is by killing the master of this dark zone... Meliodas.
B-but...!
There is one other way.
!
By restoring Meliodas to his original form.
Right?

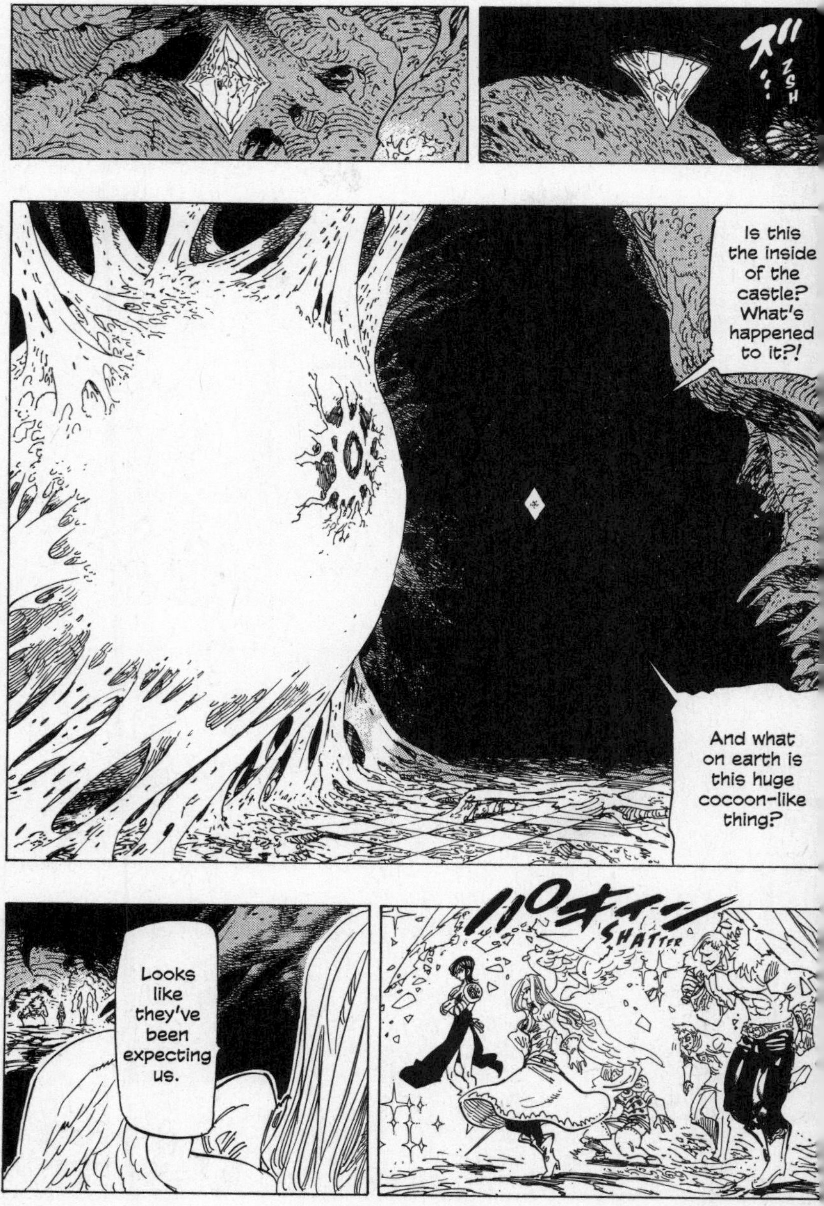
ZSH
Is this the inside of the castle? What's happened to it?!
And what on earth is this huge cocoon-like thing?
SHATTER
Looks like they've been expecting us.

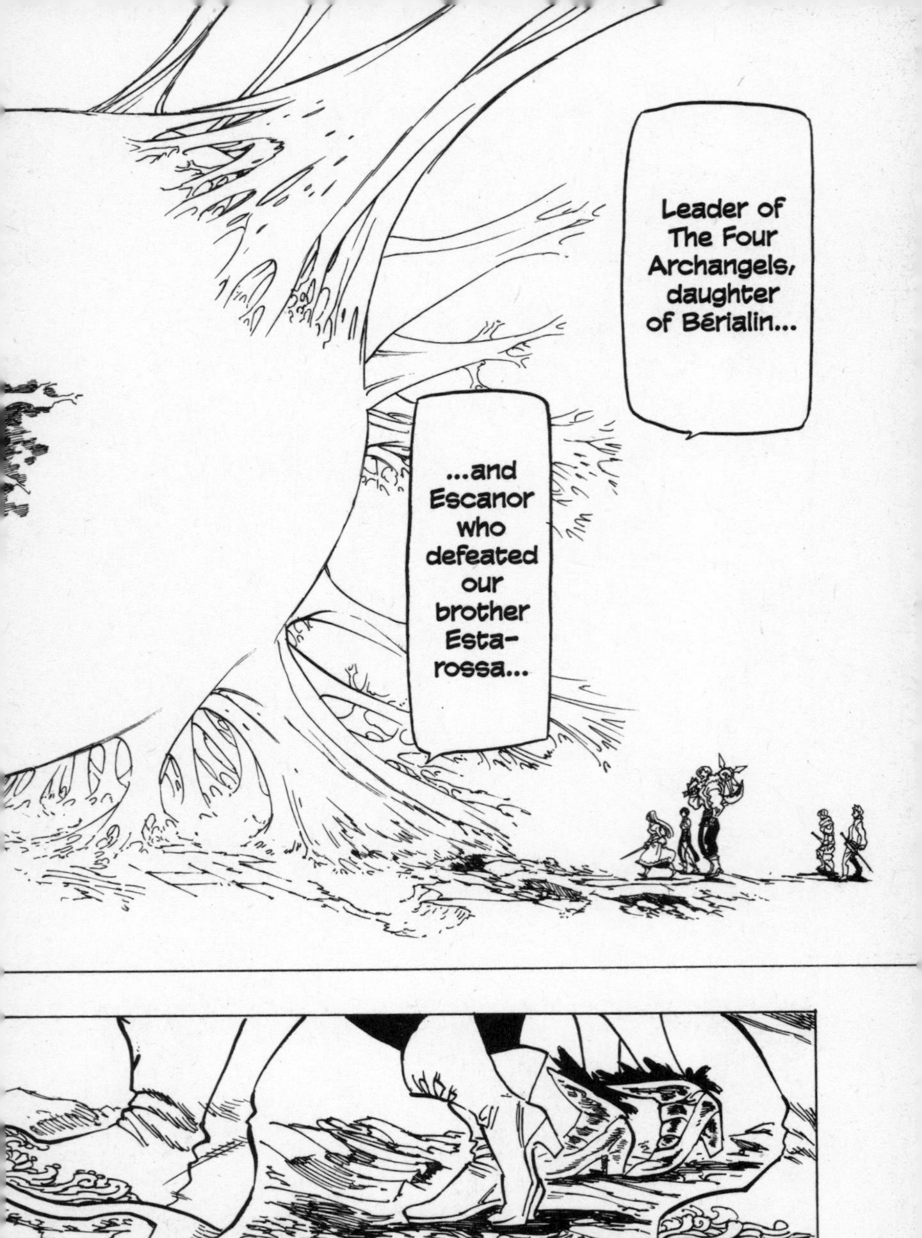
Leader of The Four Archangels, daughter of Bérialin...
...and Escanor who defeated our brother Esta-rossa...

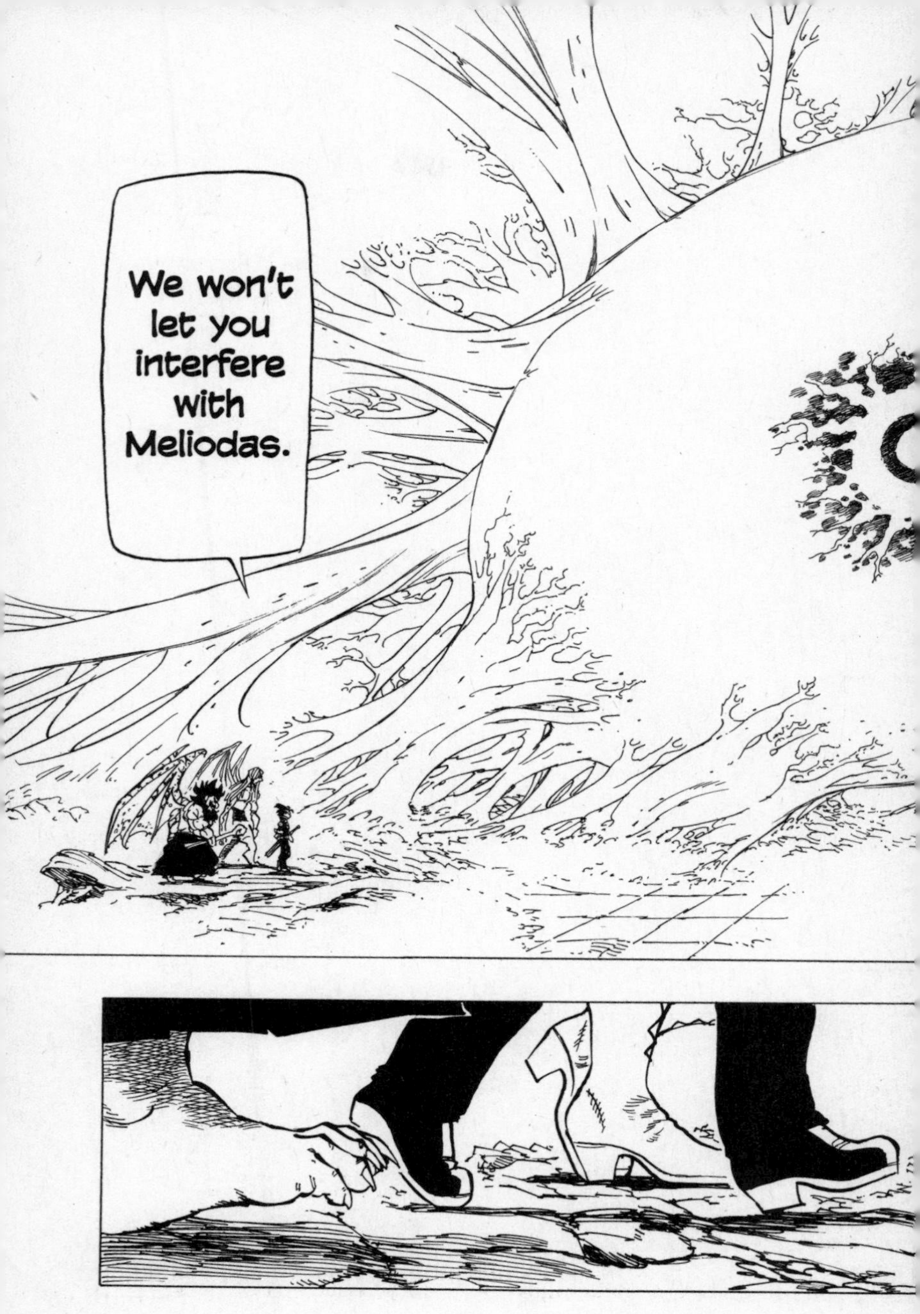
We won't let you interfere with Meliodas.

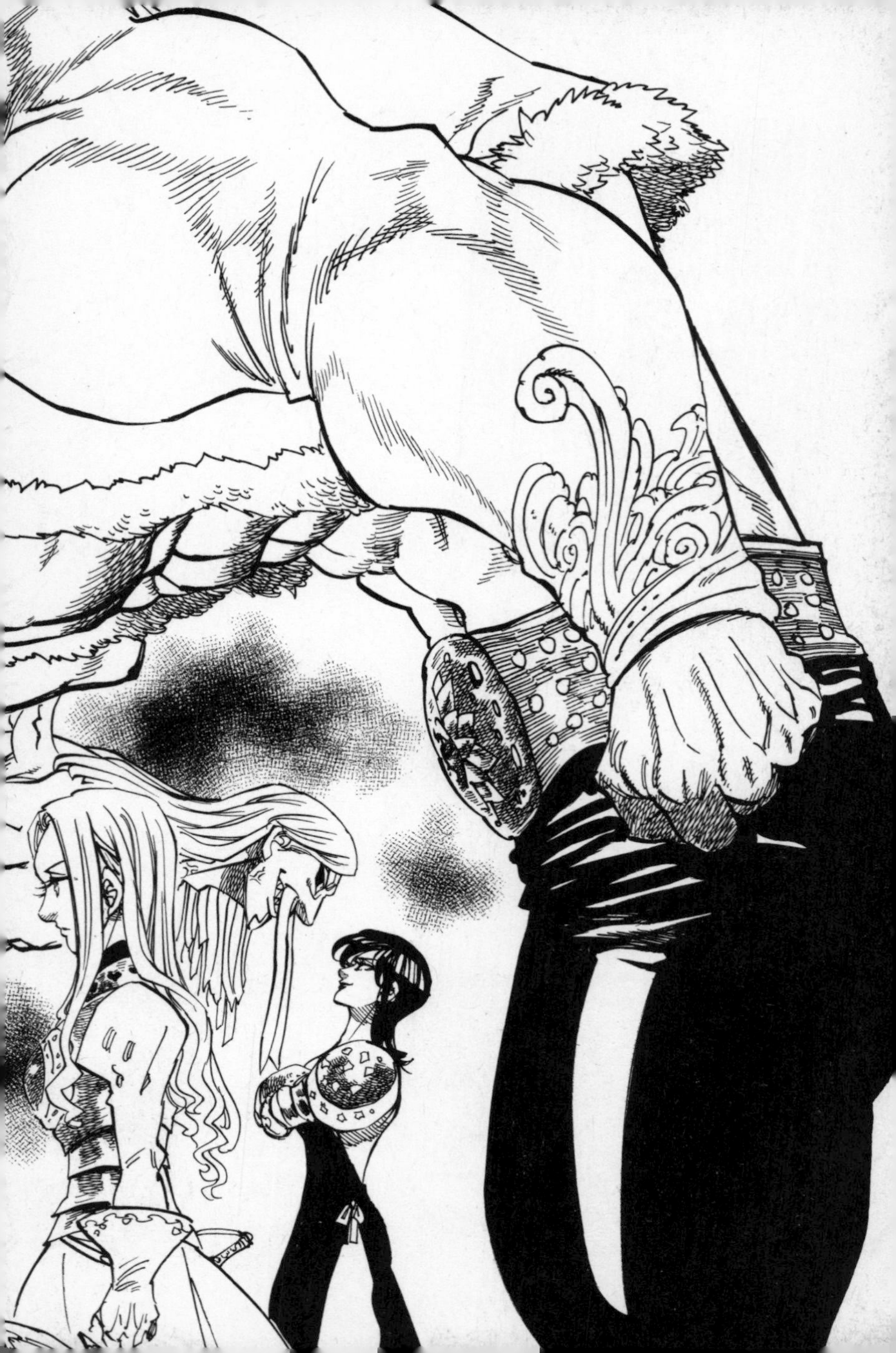

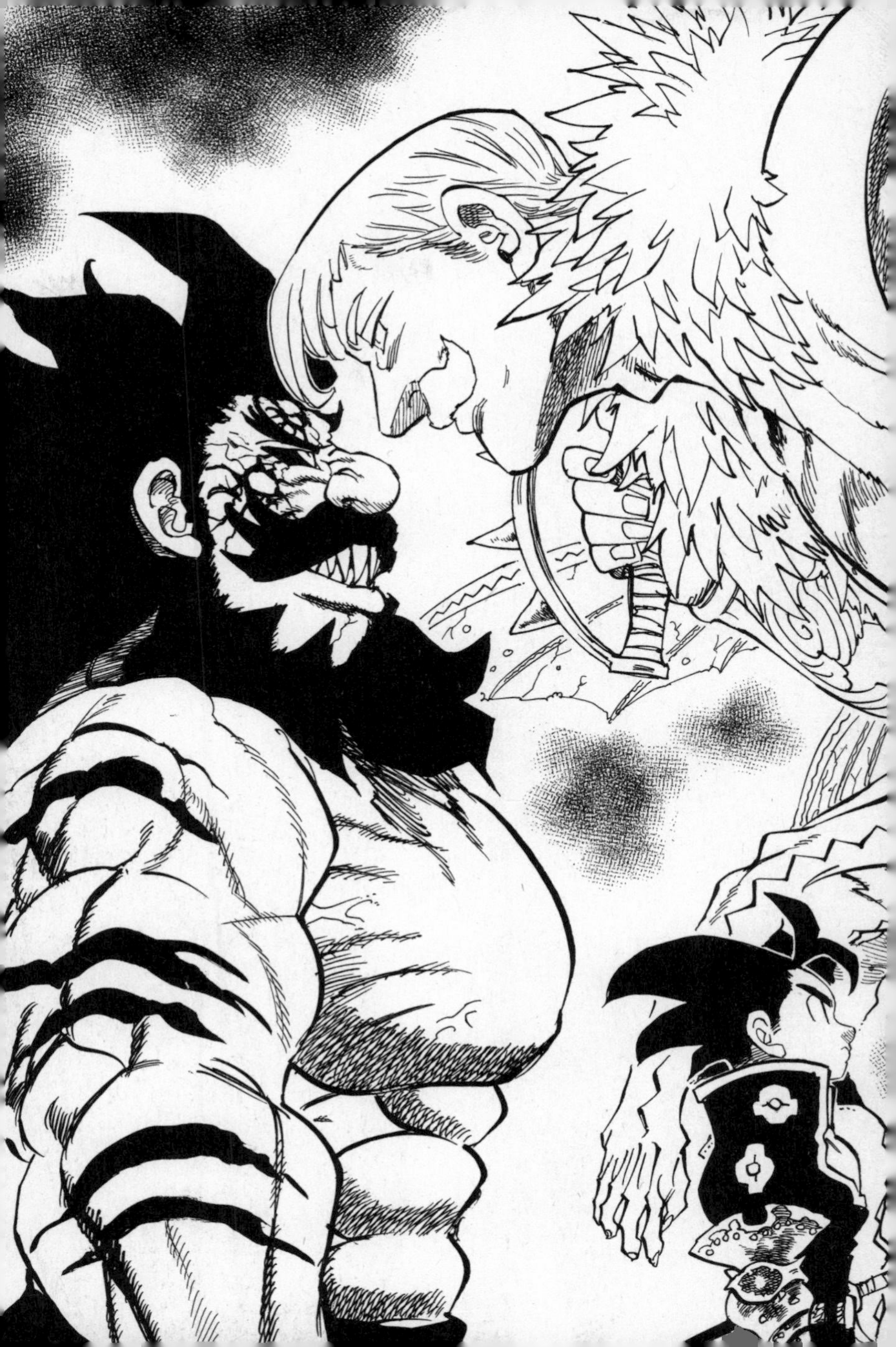

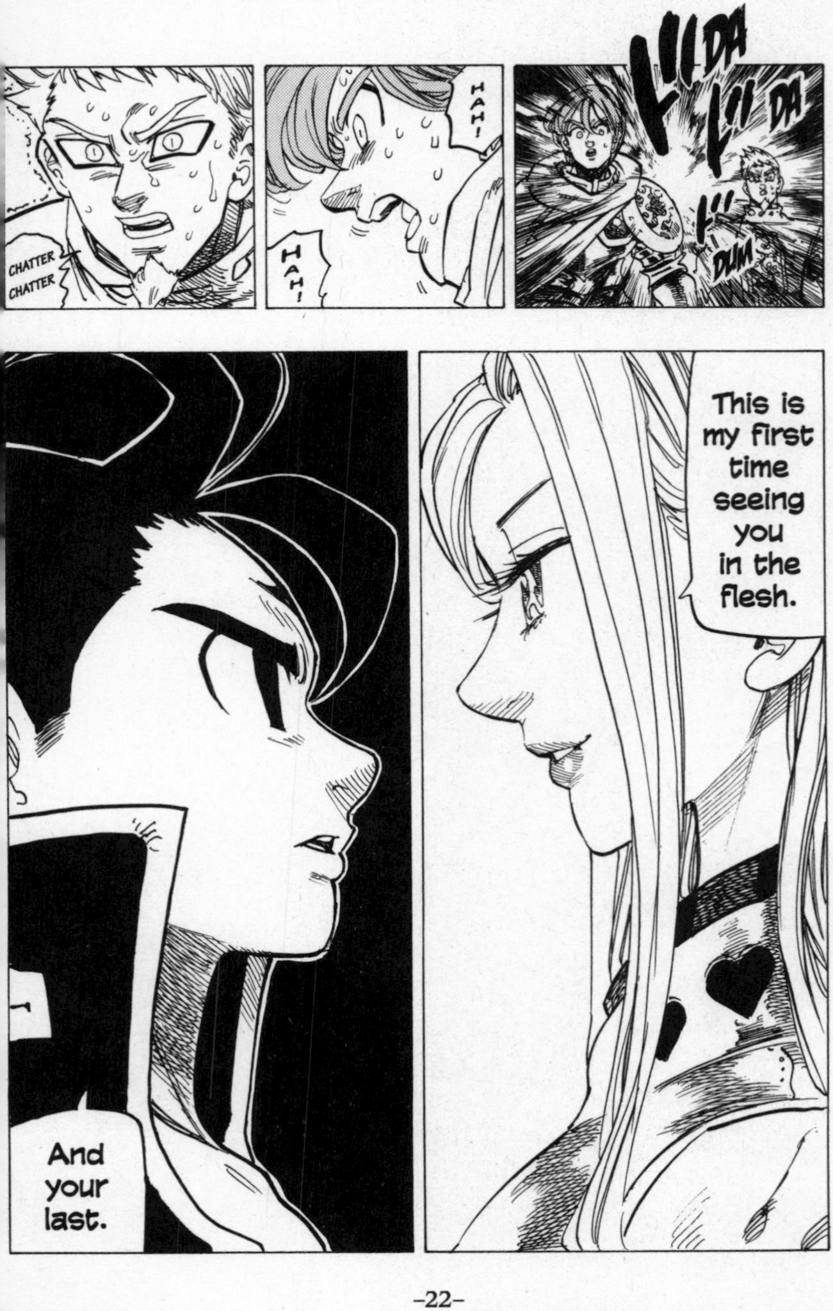
DA
DA
DUM
HAH!
HAH!
CHATTER
CHATTER
This is my first time seeing you in the flesh.
And your last.

Chapter 286 - Flash

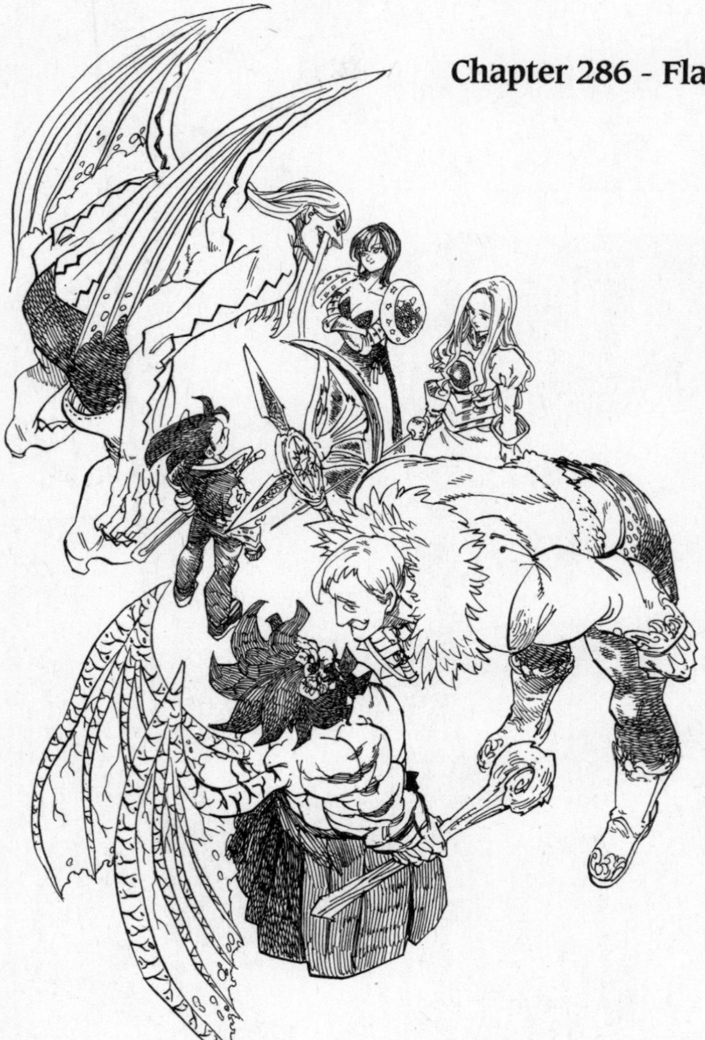

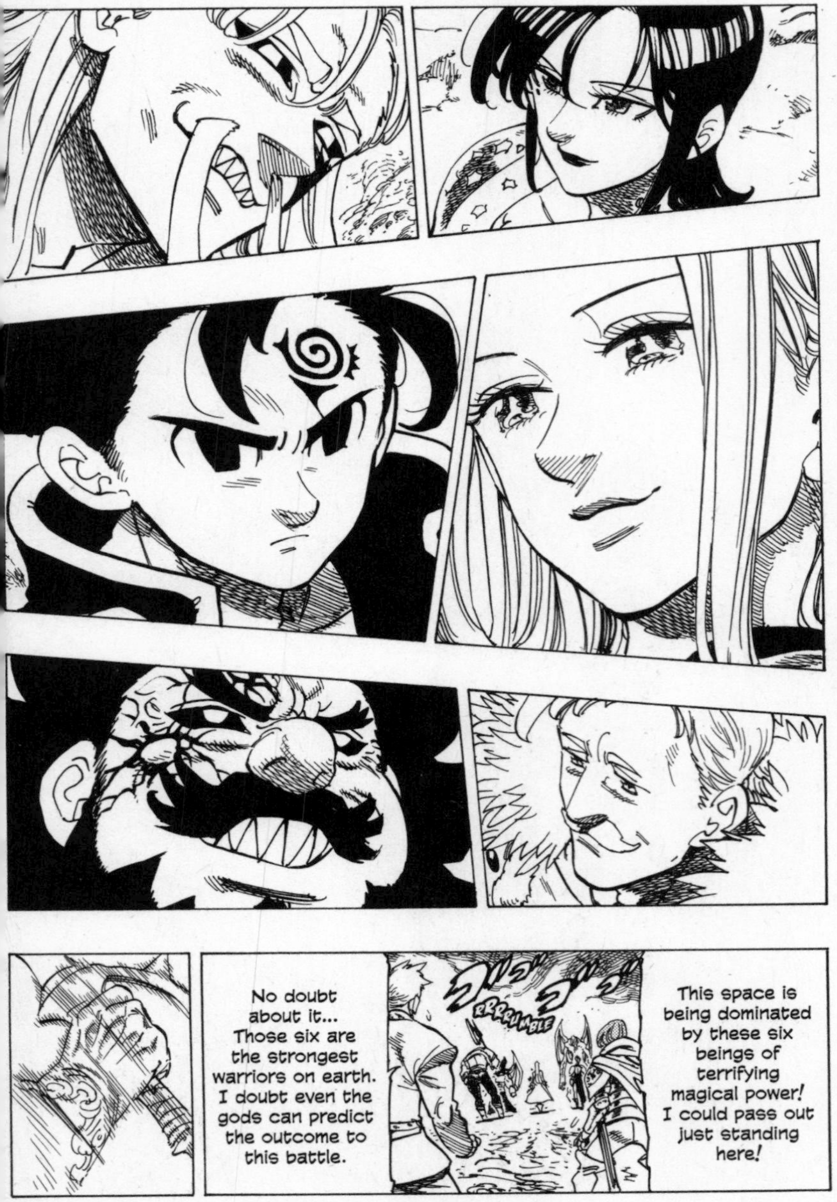
This space is being dominated by these six beings of terrifying magical power! I could pass out just standing here!
RRRUMBLE
No doubt about it... Those six are the strongest warriors on earth. I doubt even the gods can predict the outcome to this battle.

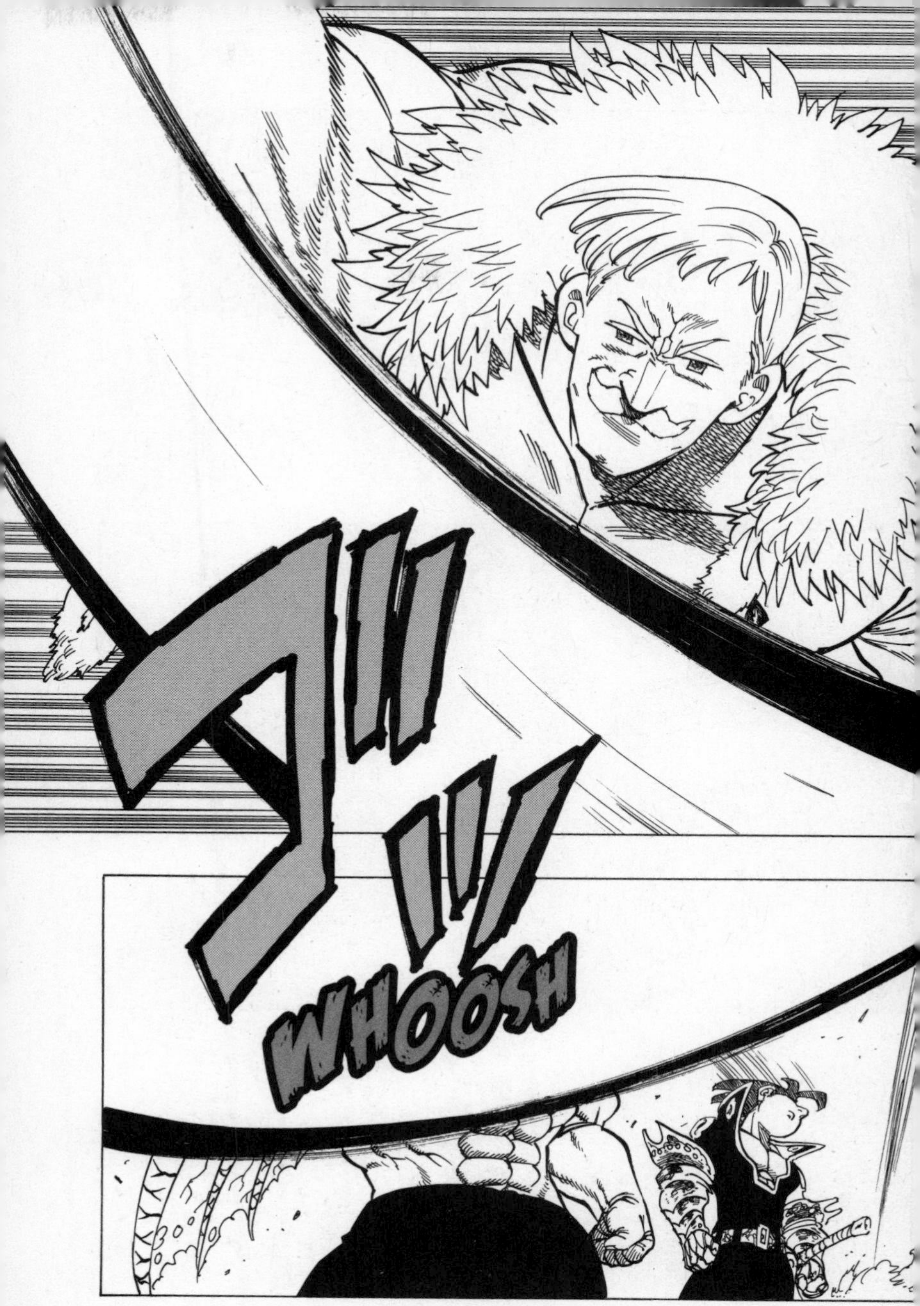
ゴッ
WHOOSH

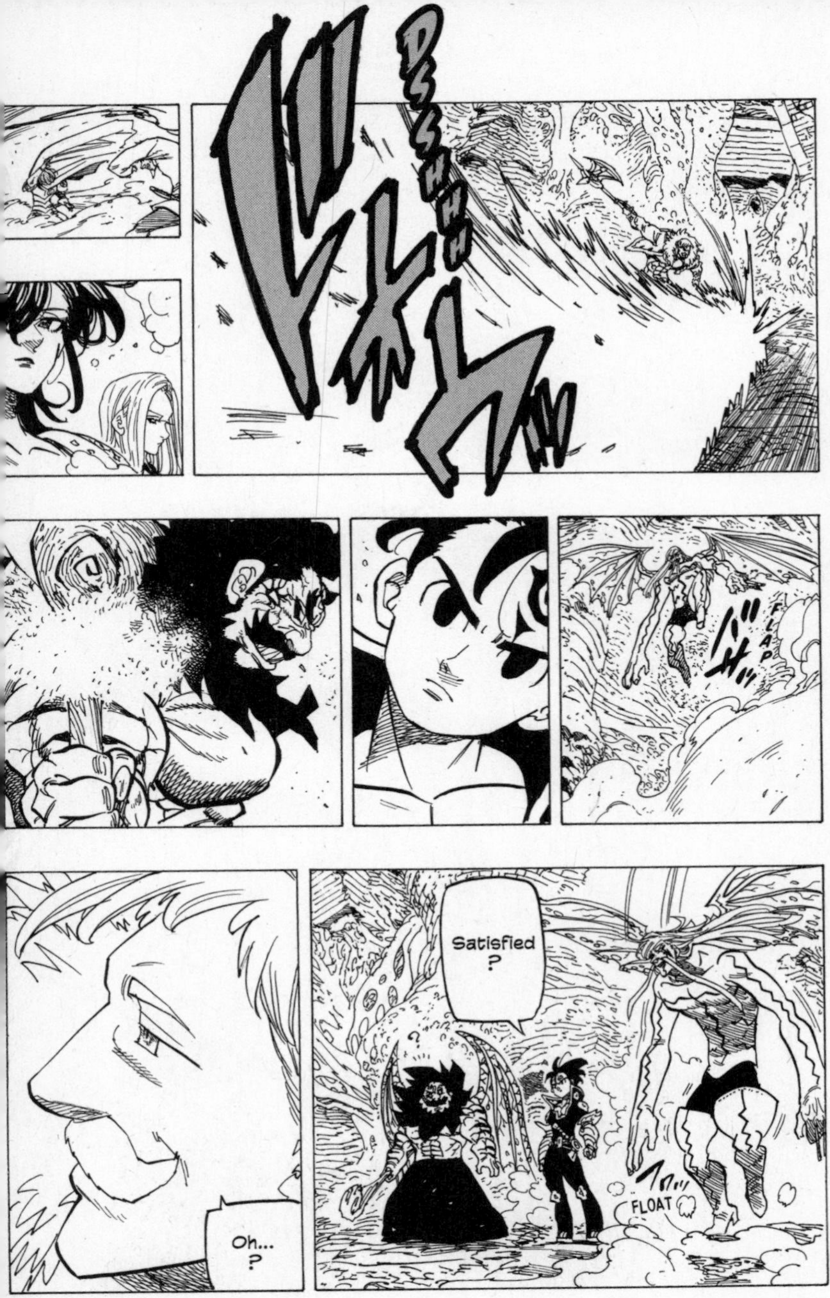
DSSHHHH
FLAP
Satisfied ?
FLOAT
Oh... ?

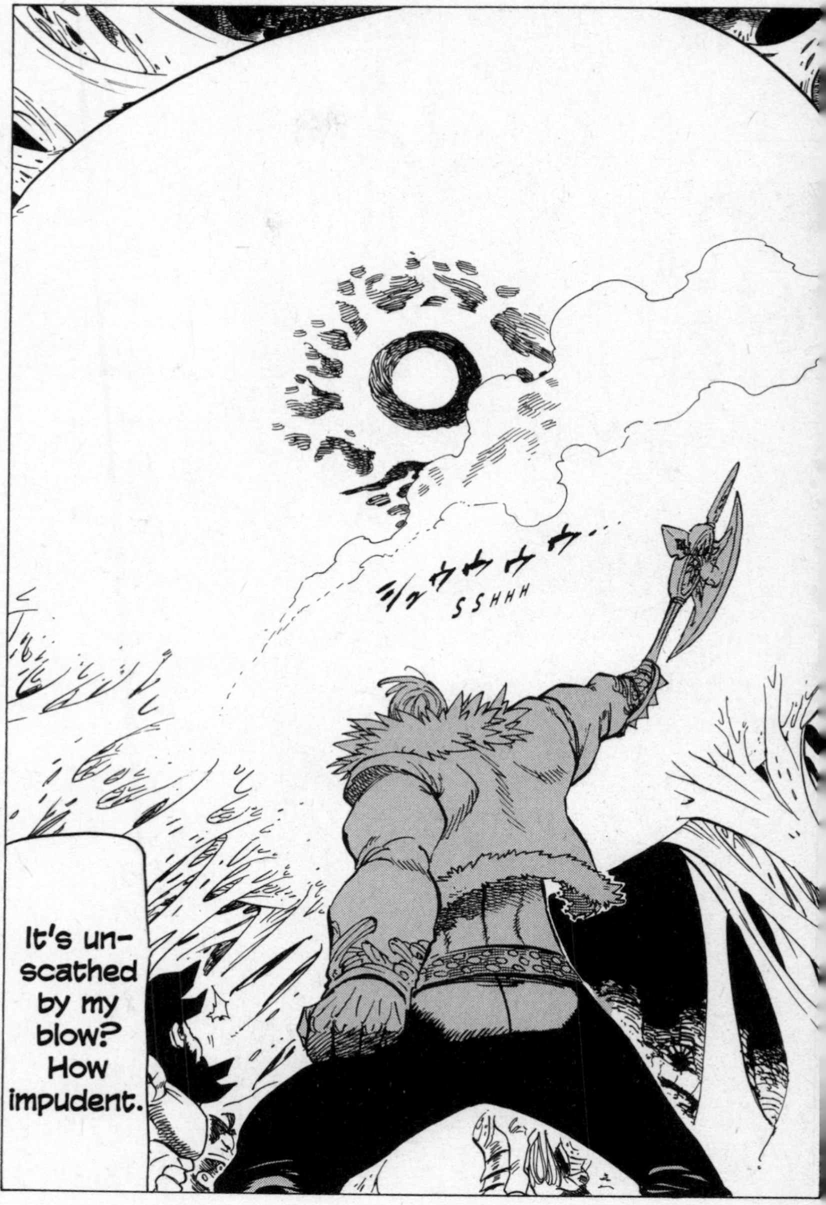
シュウウウウ…
SSHHH
It's un-scathed by my blow? How impudent.

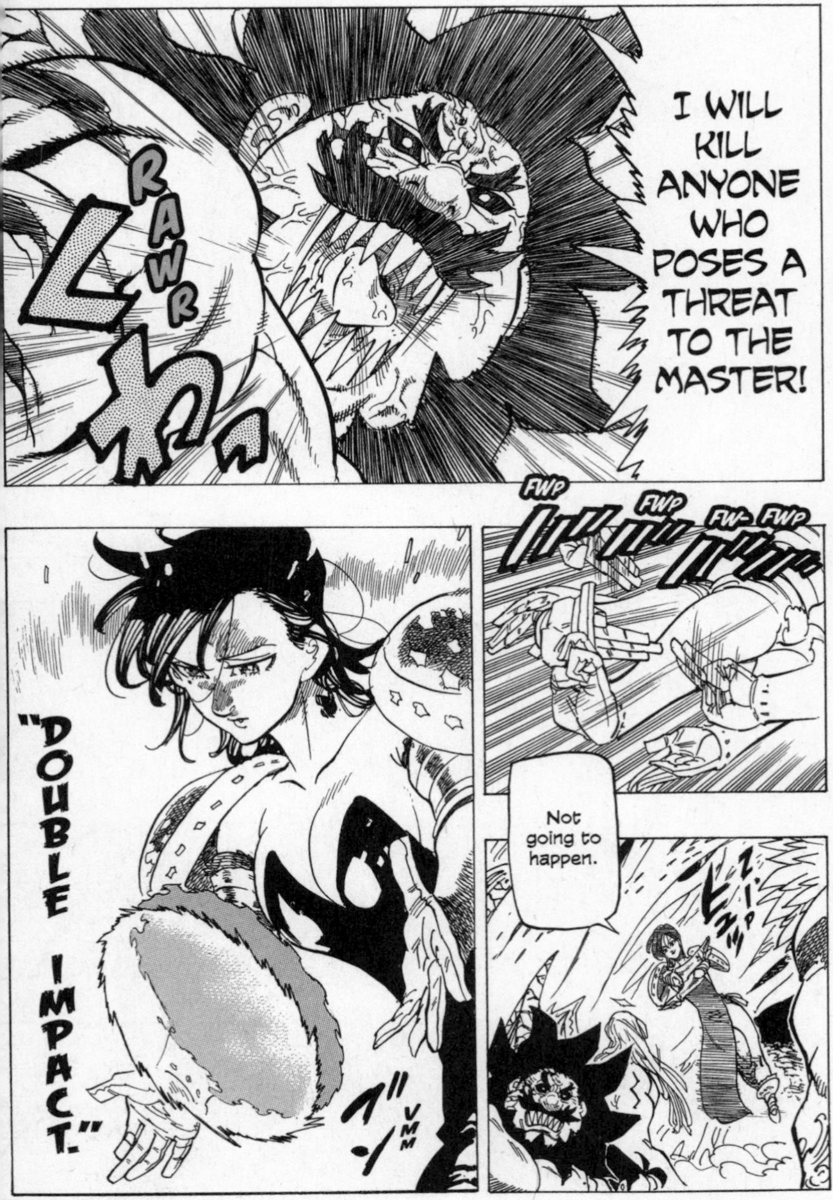
I WILL KILL ANYONE WHO POSES A THREAT TO THE MASTER!
RAWR
FWP
FWP
FW-
FWP
Not going to happen.
ZIP
"DOUBLE IMPACT."
VMM

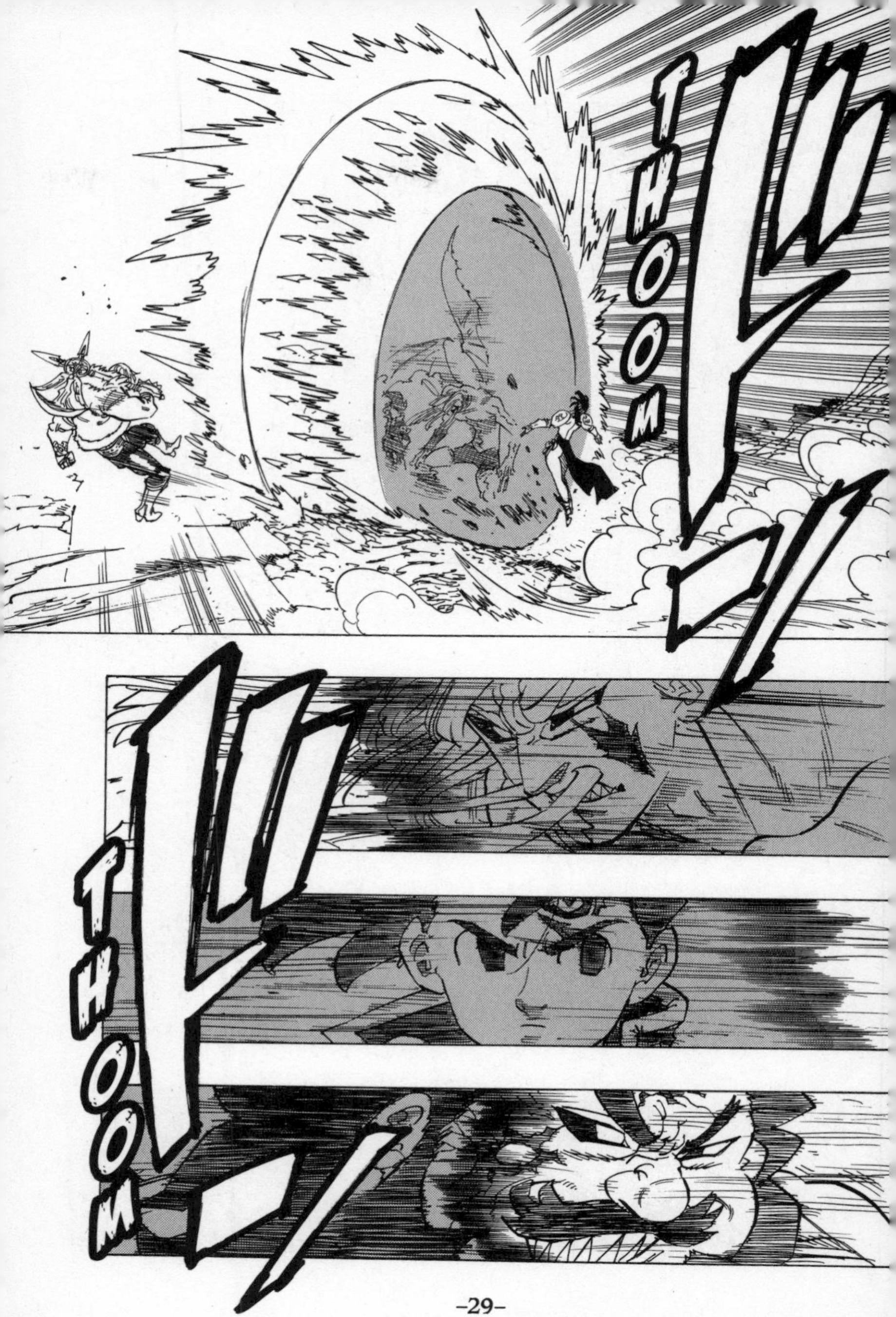
THOOM
THOOM

Could this be the genius problem child who deceived both our lord and the Supreme Deity alike?!

RRRRRRUMBLE

TMP

GRGRGRGR

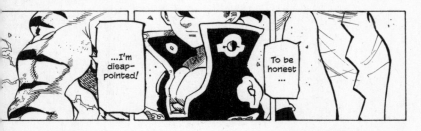

...I'm disappointed!

To be honest...

These monsters surpass even The Ten Commandments...

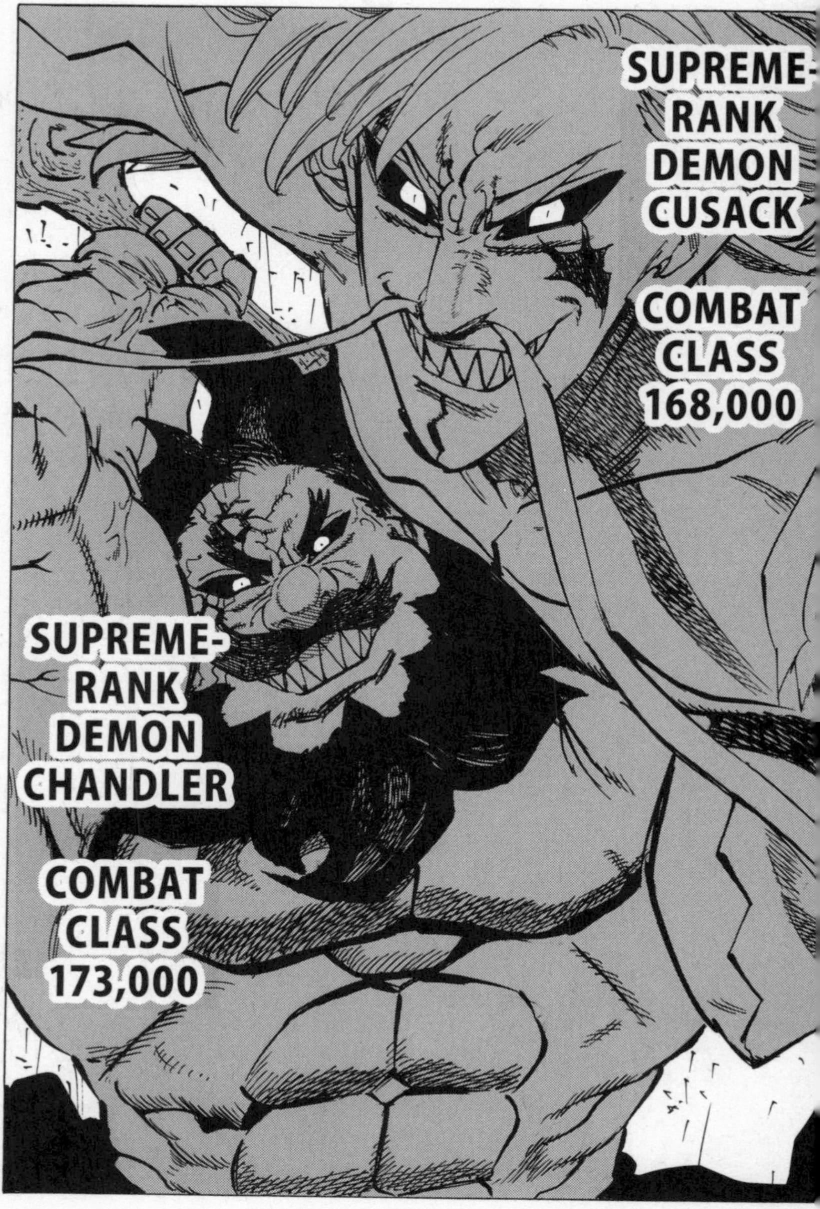
SUPREME-RANK DEMON CUSACK
COMBAT CLASS 168,000
SUPREME-RANK DEMON CHANDLER
COMBAT CLASS 173,000

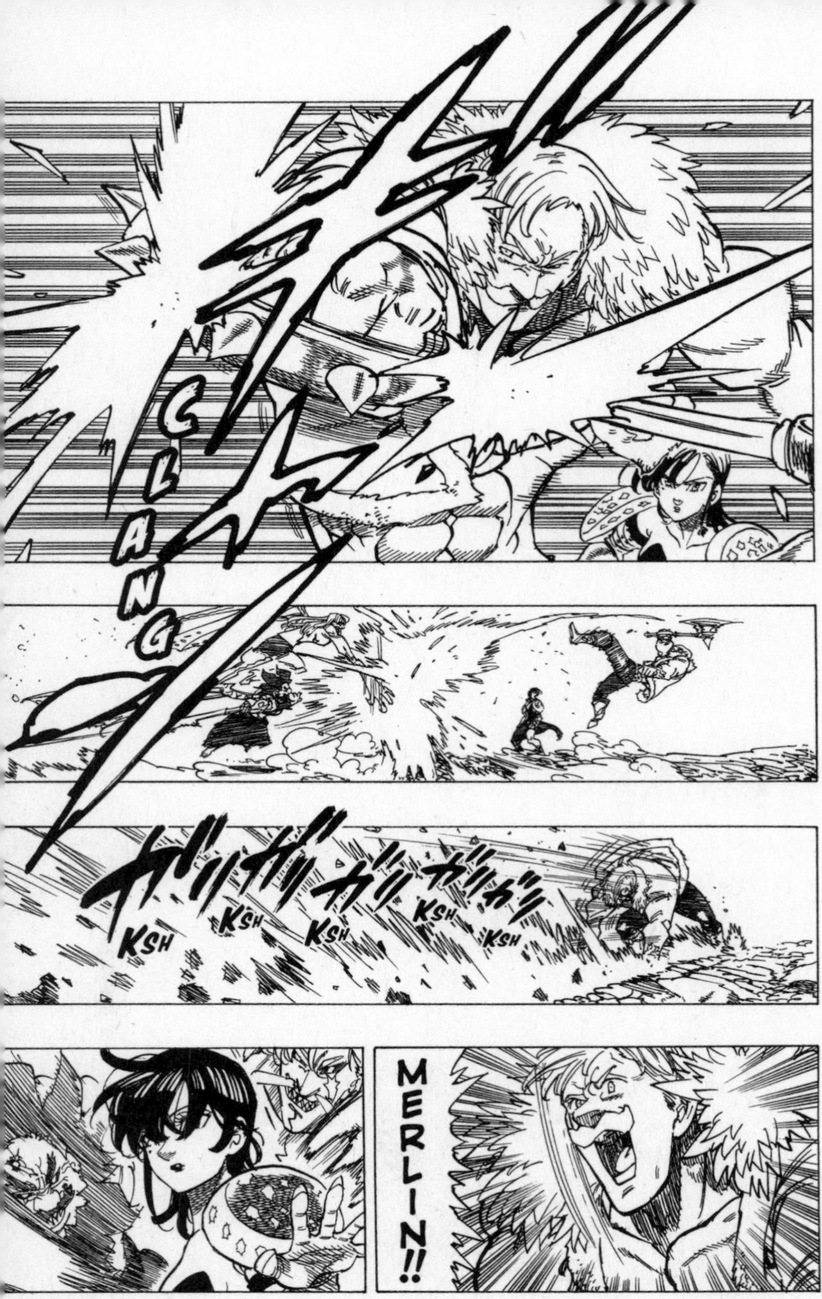
CLANG
KSH
KSH
KSH
KSH
KSH
MERLIN!!

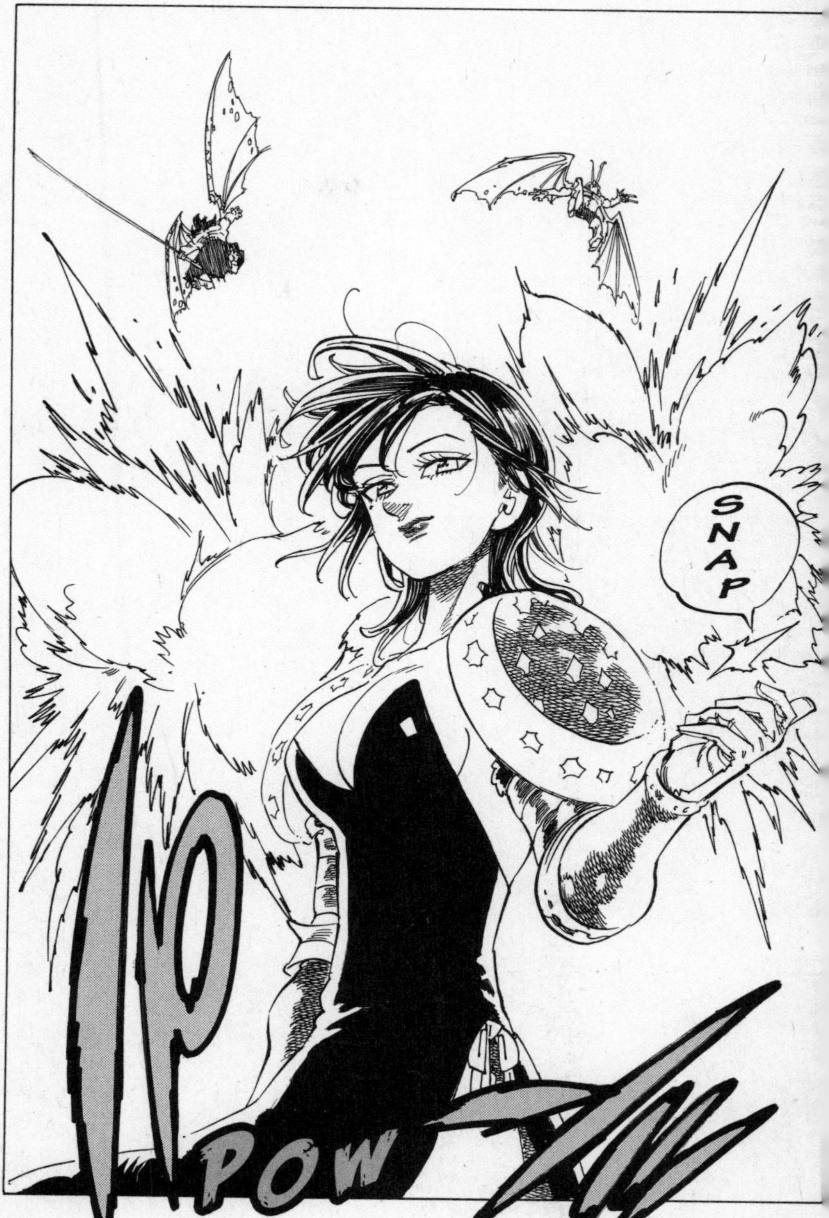
SNAP
POW

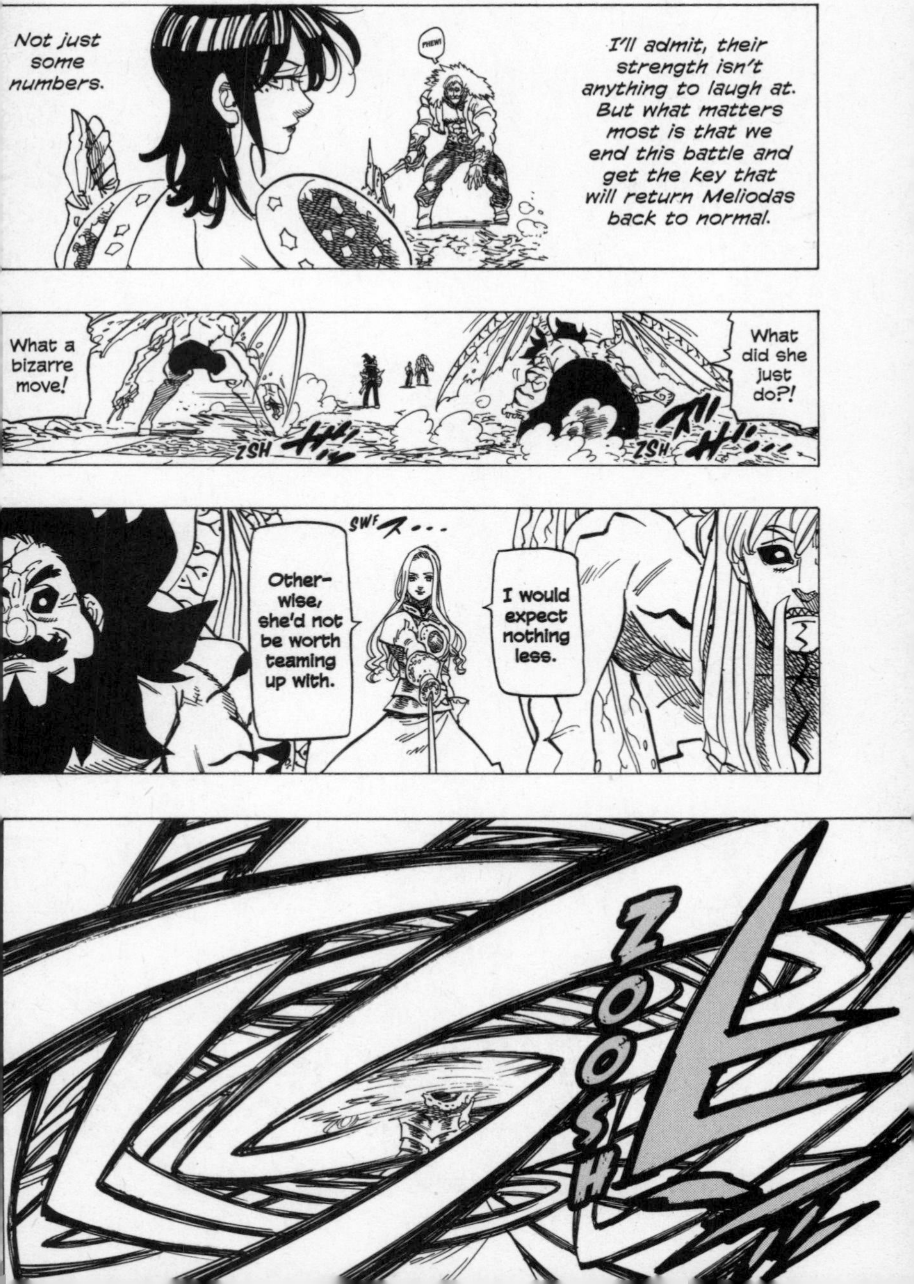
I'll admit, their strength isn't anything to laugh at. But what matters most is that we end this battle and get the key that will return Meliodas back to normal.
PHEW!
Not just some numbers.
What did she just do?!
ZSH
What a bizarre move!
ZSH
I would expect nothing less.
SWF
Other-wise, she'd not be worth teaming up with.
ZOOOSH

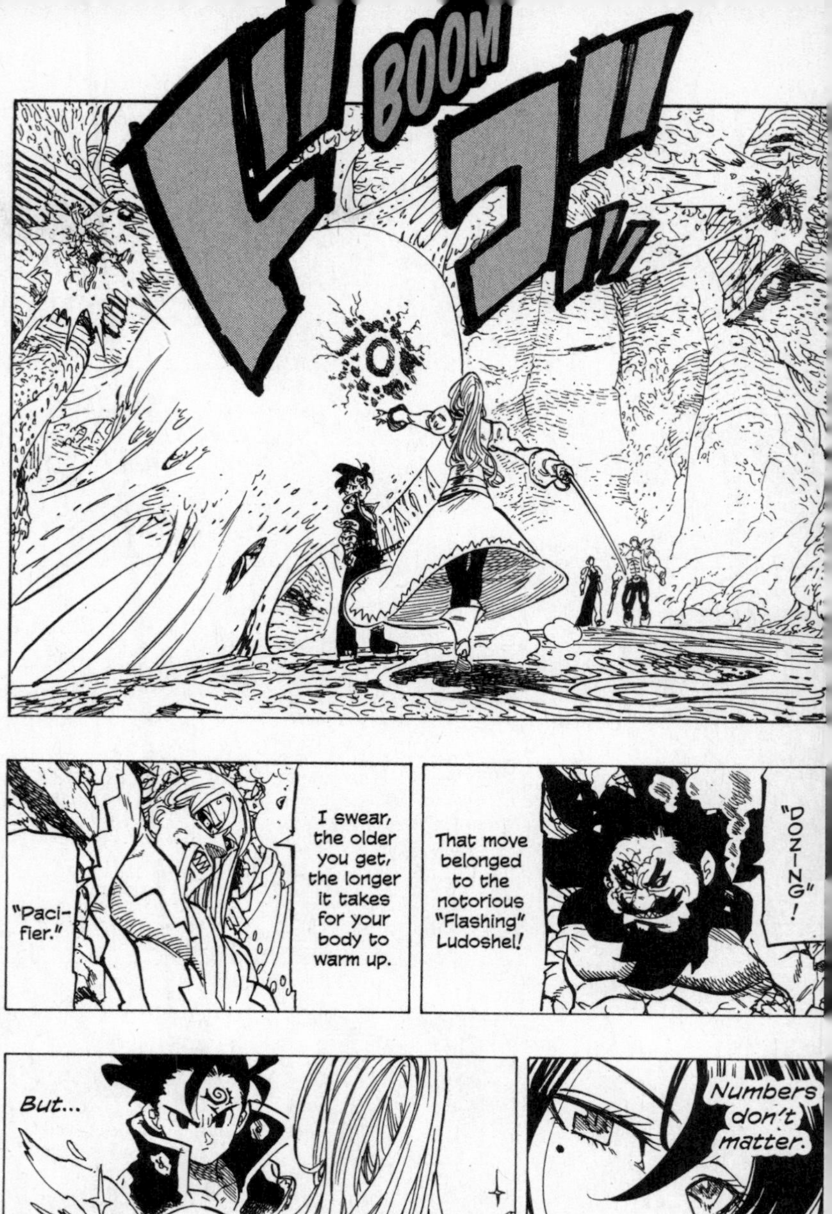
BOOM
"DOZING"!
That move belonged to the notorious "Flashing" Ludoshel!
I swear, the older you get, the longer it takes for your body to warm up.
"Paci-fier."
Numbers don't matter.
But...

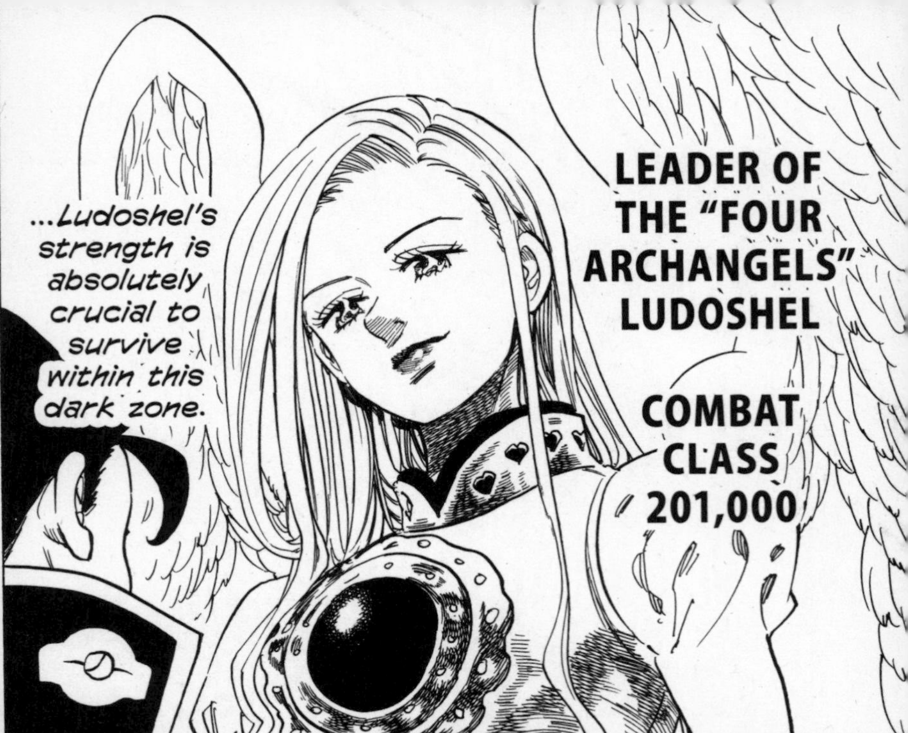
LEADER OF THE "FOUR ARCHANGELS" LUDOSHEL
COMBAT CLASS 201,000
...Ludoshel's strength is absolutely crucial to survive within this dark zone.

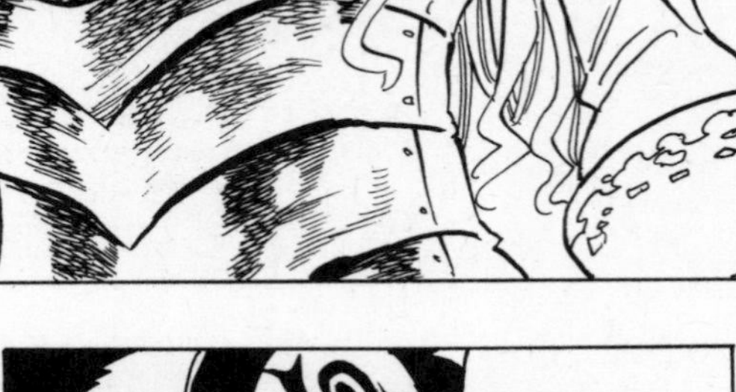
Zeldris... They say your sword is the fastest in the Demon World. is that true?

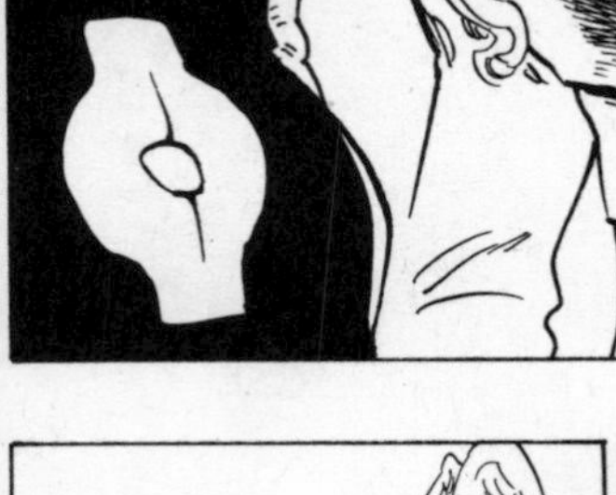

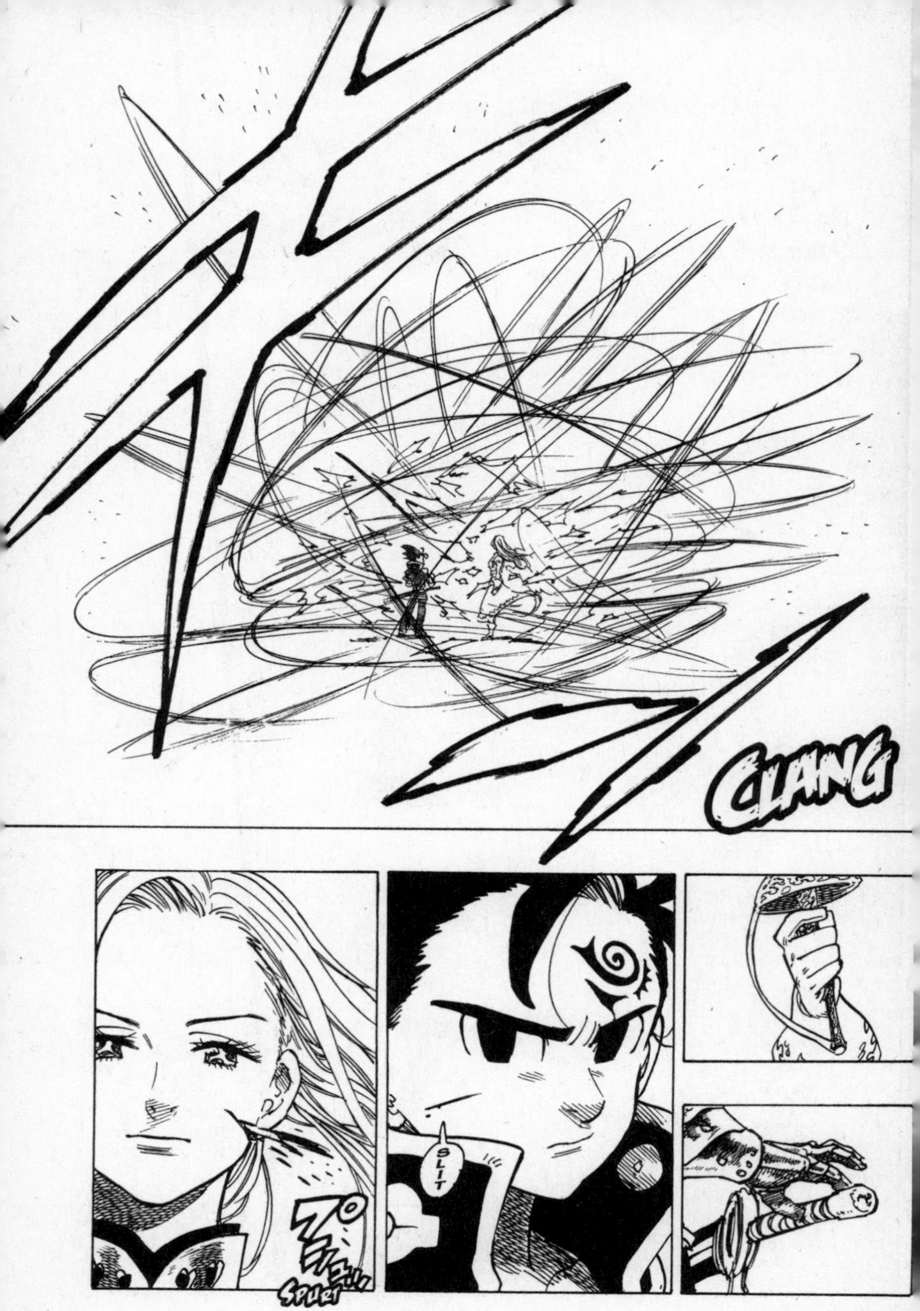
CLANG
SLIT
SPURT

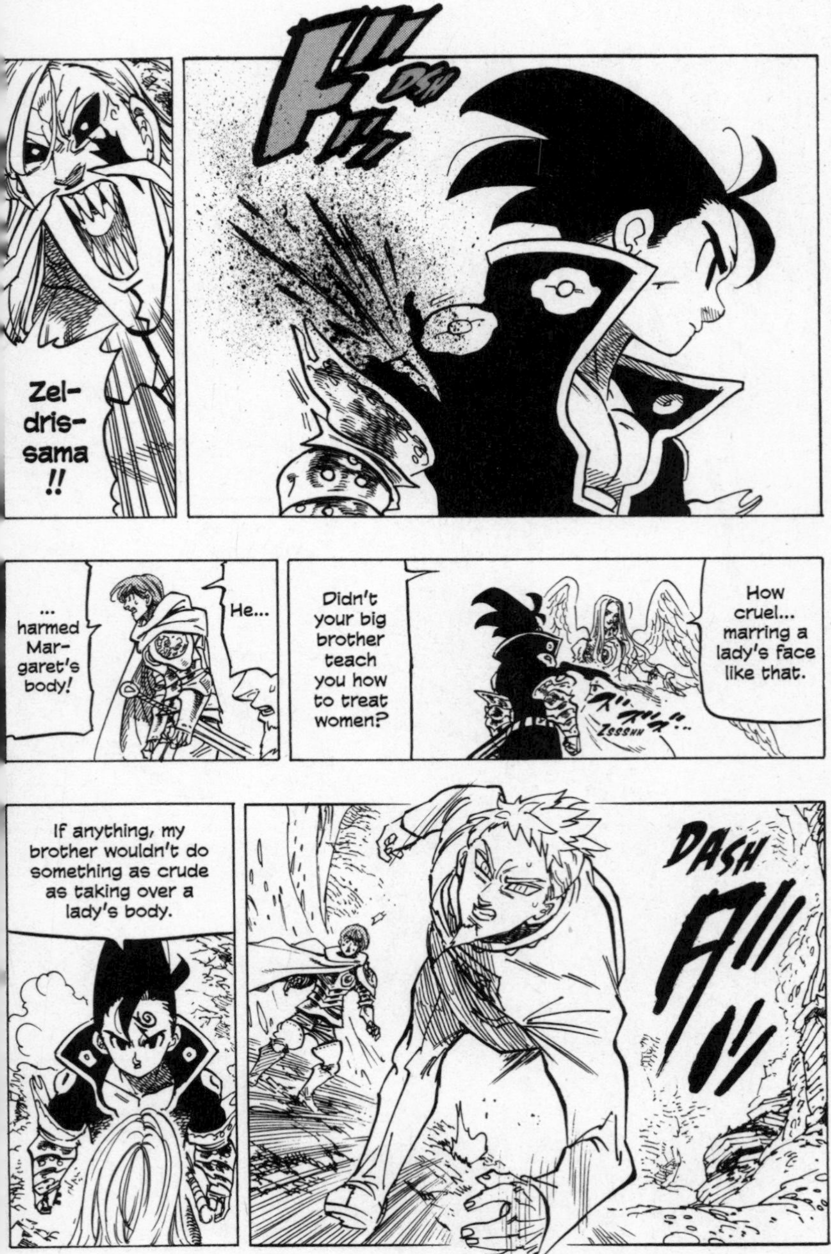
DASH
Zel-dris-sama!!
How cruel... marring a lady's face like that.
ZSSSHN
Didn't your big brother teach you how to treat women?
He...
... harmed Margaret's body!
DASH
If anything, my brother wouldn't do something as crude as taking over a lady's body.

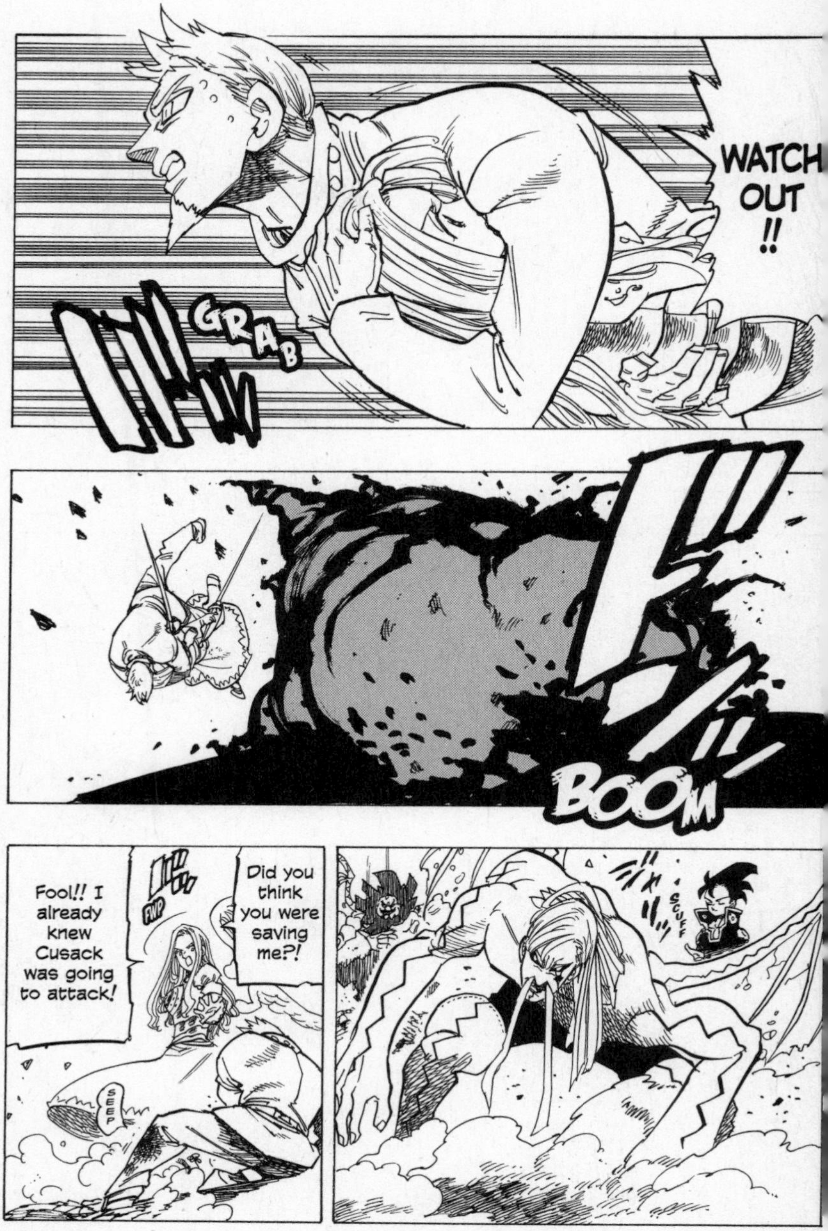
WATCH OUT!!
GRAB
BOOM
SCUFF
Did you think you were saving me?!
FWP
Fool!! I already knew Cusack was going to attack!
SEEP

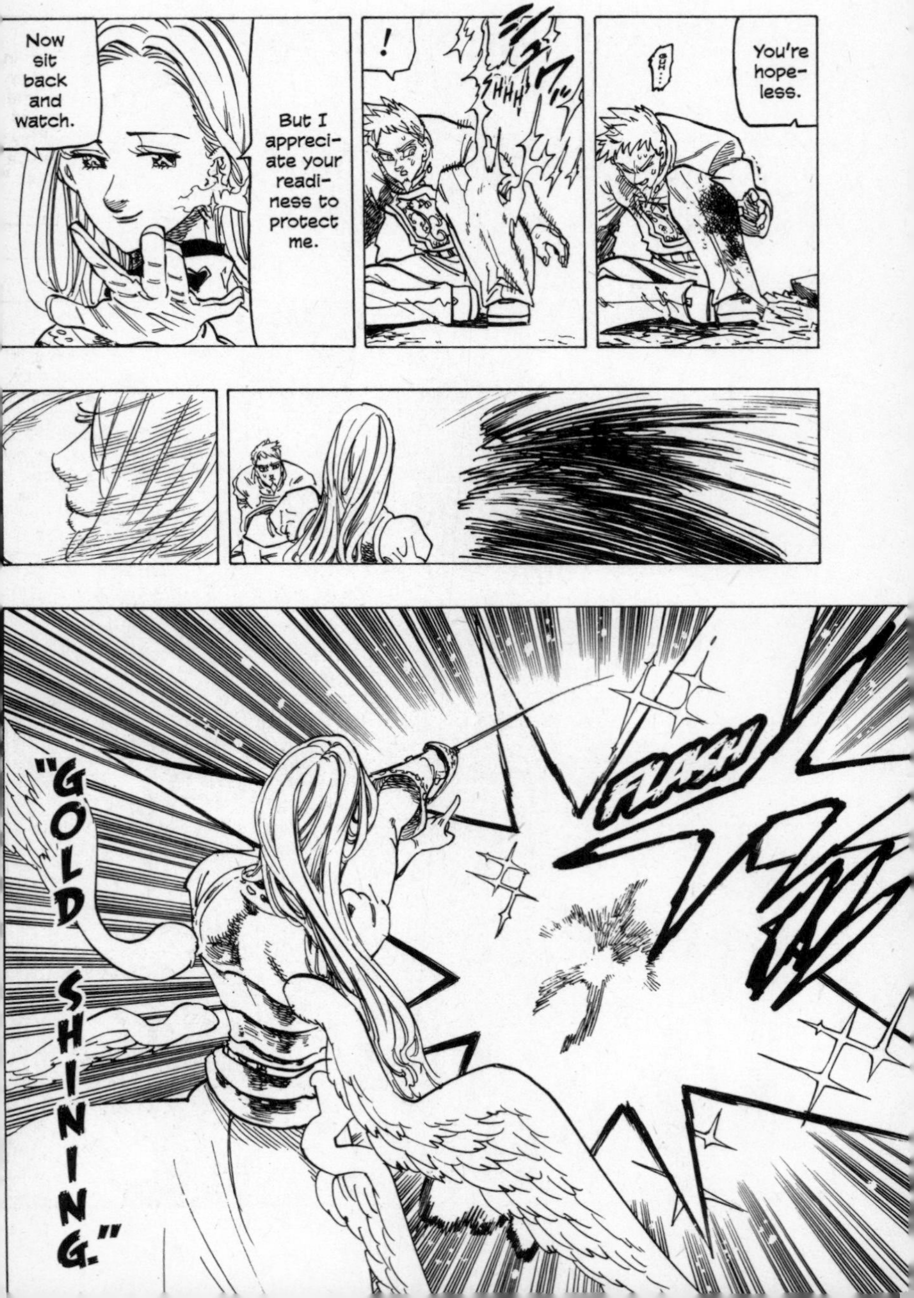
You're hopeless.
GH...
!
SHHH
But I appreciate your readiness to protect me.
Now sit back and watch.
FLASH
"GOLD SHINING."

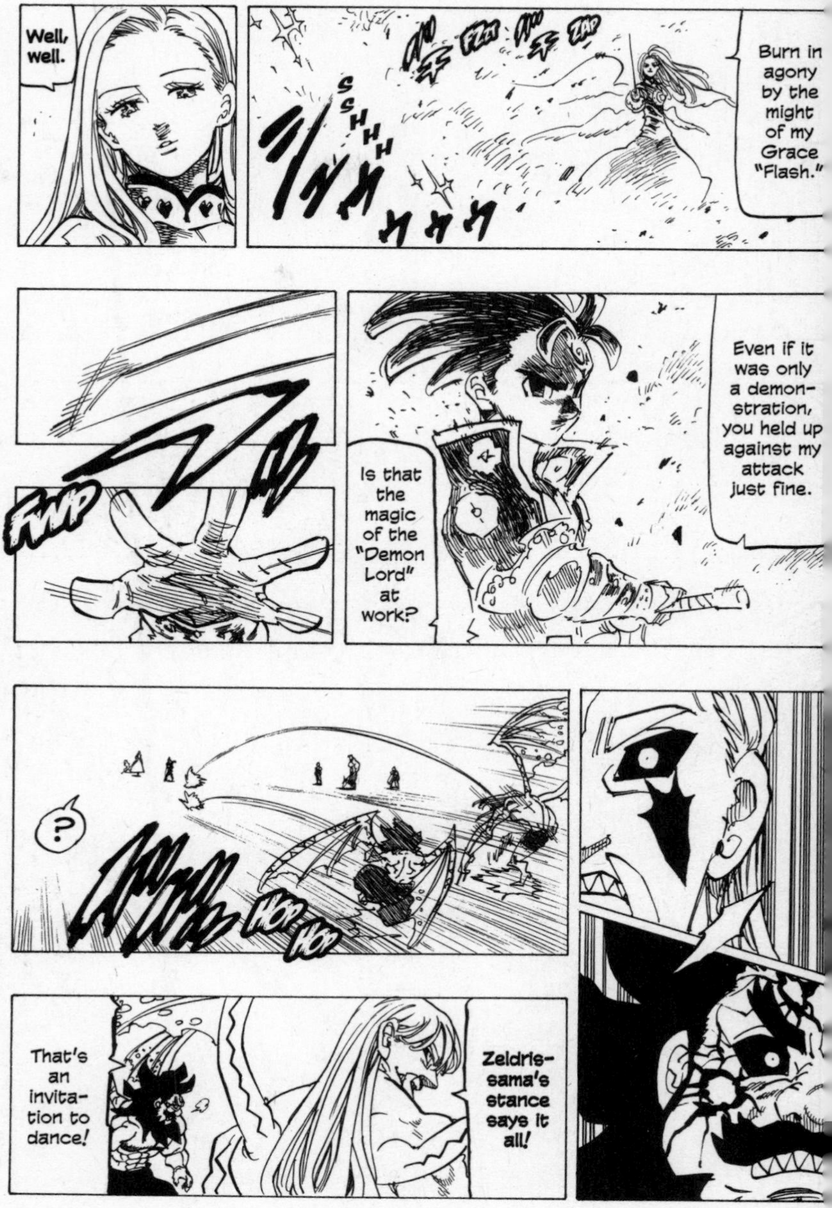
Burn in agony by the might of my Grace "Flash."
ZAP
FZZT
SSHHH
Well, well.
Even if it was only a demonstration, you held up against my attack just fine.
Is that the magic of the "Demon Lord" at work?
FWP
?
HOP HOP
Zeldris-sama's stance says it all!
That's an invitation to dance!

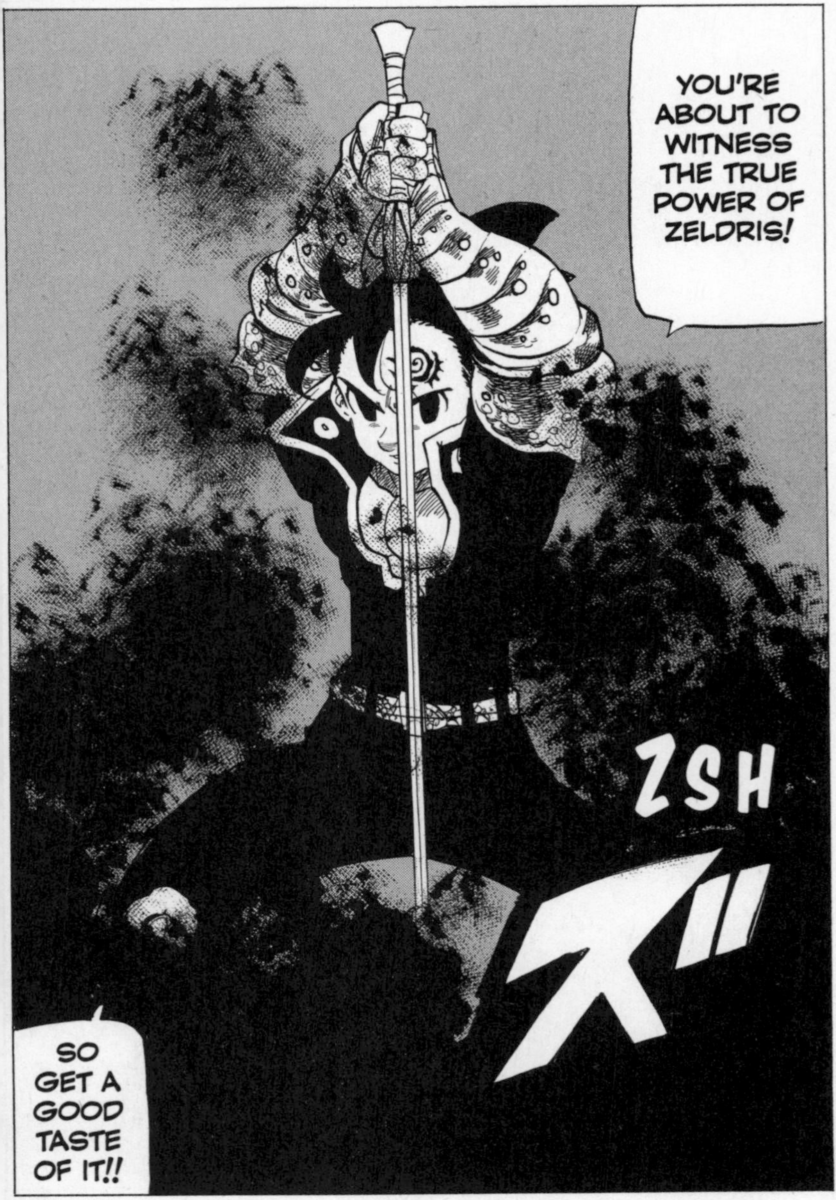
YOU'RE ABOUT TO WITNESS THE TRUE POWER OF ZELDRIS!
ZSH
ズ
SO GET A GOOD TASTE OF IT!!

Chapter 287 - The Prince of Darkness

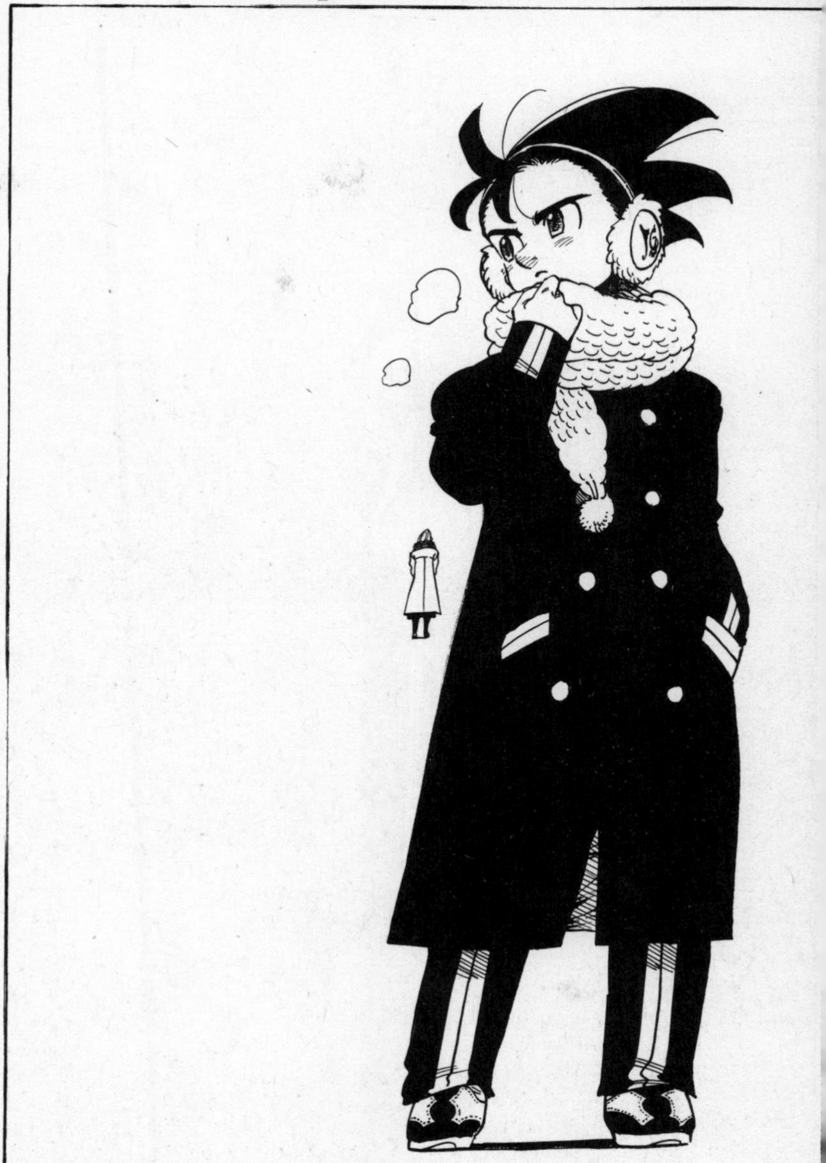

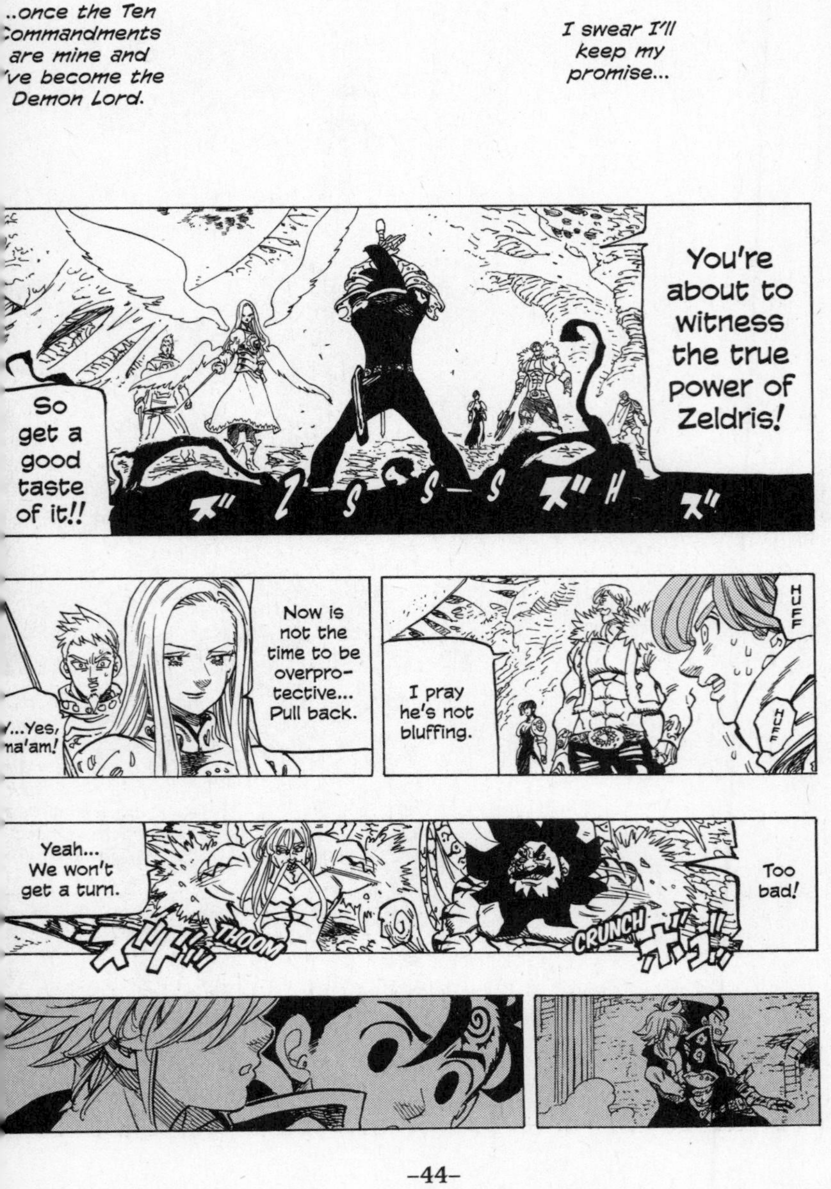
I swear I'll keep my promise...
..once the Ten Commandments are mine and I've become the Demon Lord.
You're about to witness the true power of Zeldris!
So get a good taste of it!!
ZSSSSH
HUFF
HUFF
I pray he's not bluffing.
Now is not the time to be overprotective... Pull back.
...Yes, ma'am!
Too bad!
CRUNCH
THOOM
Yeah... We won't get a turn.

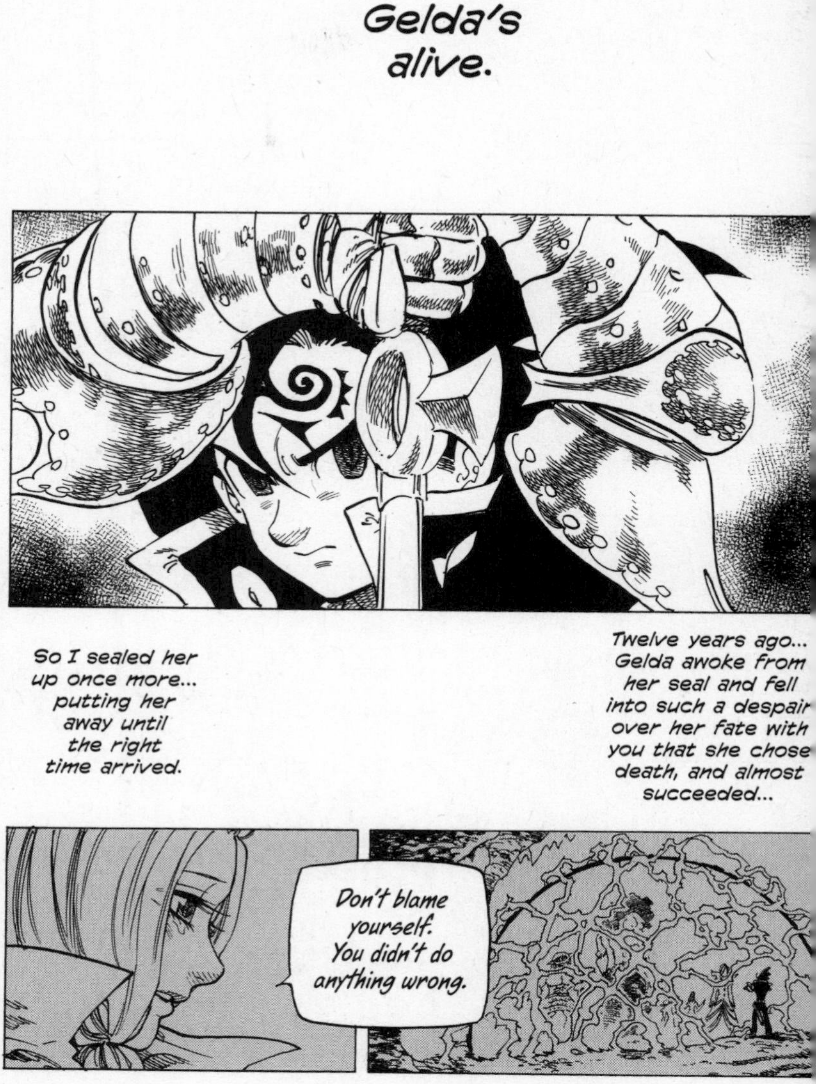
Gelda's alive.
Twelve years ago... Gelda awoke from her seal and fell into such a despair over her fate with you that she chose death, and almost succeeded...
So I sealed her up once more... putting her away until the right time arrived.
Don't blame yourself. You didn't do anything wrong.

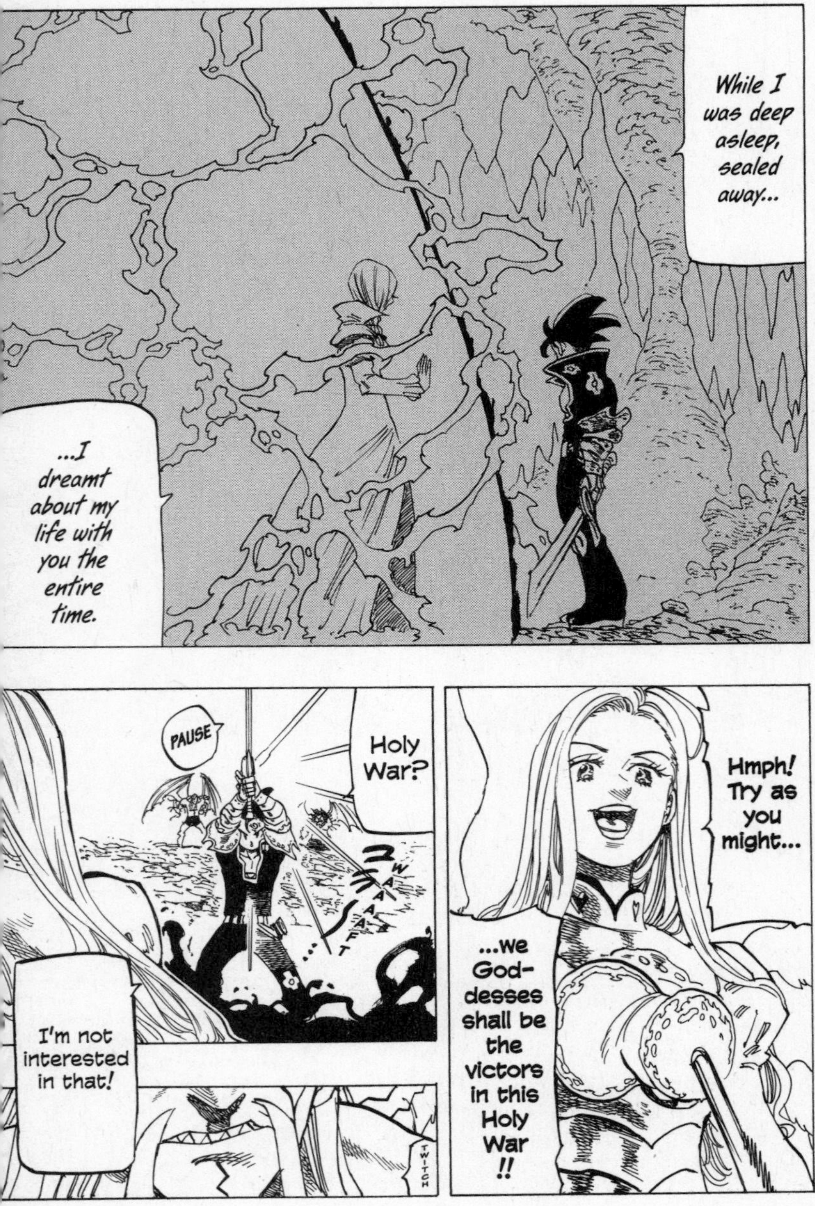

While I was deep asleep, sealed away...
...I dreamt about my life with you the entire time.
Hmph! Try as you might...
...we Goddesses shall be the victors in this Holy War!!
Holy War?
PAUSE
WAAAAFFT
...
I'm not interested in that!
TWITCH

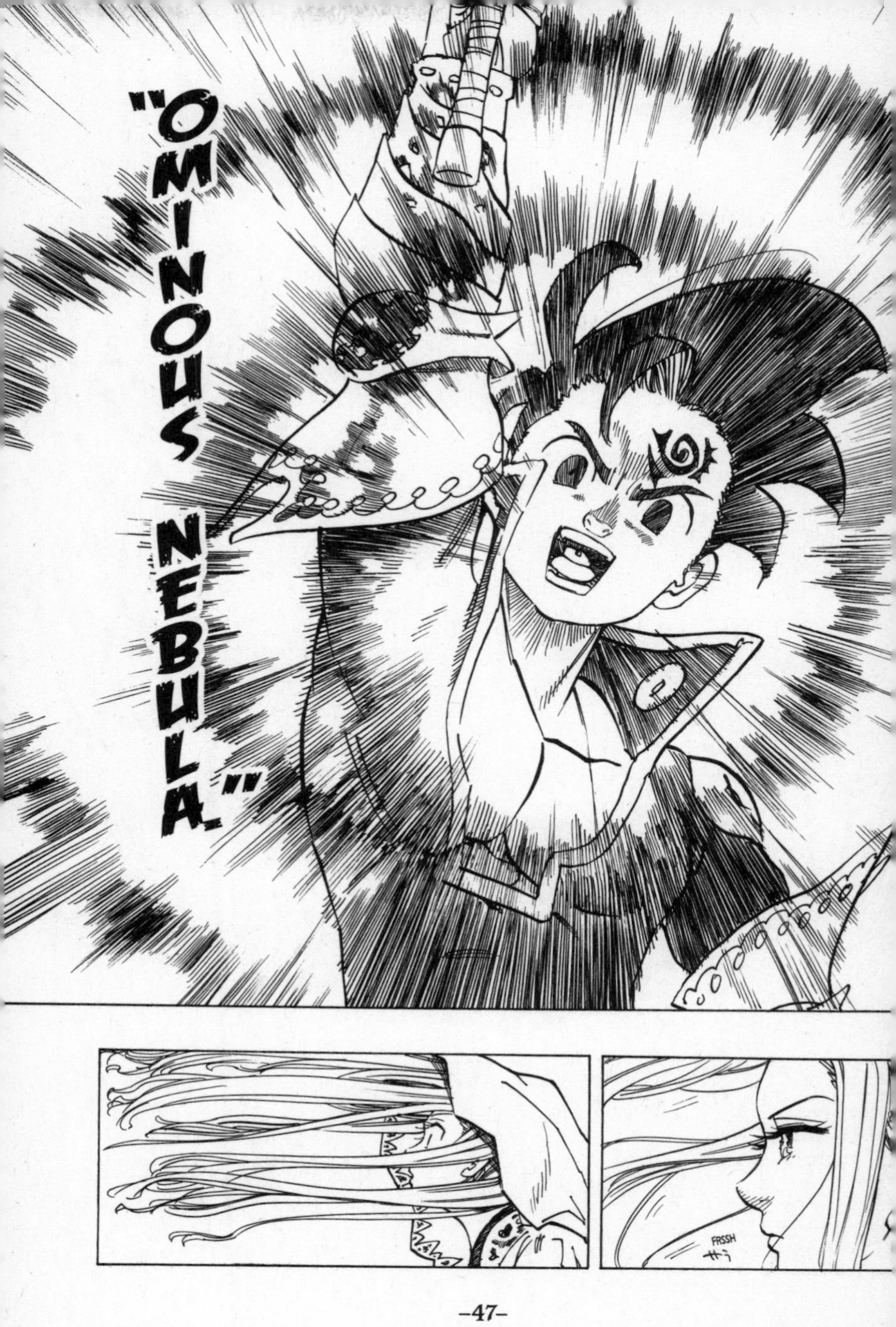
"OMINOUS NEBULA"
FRSSH

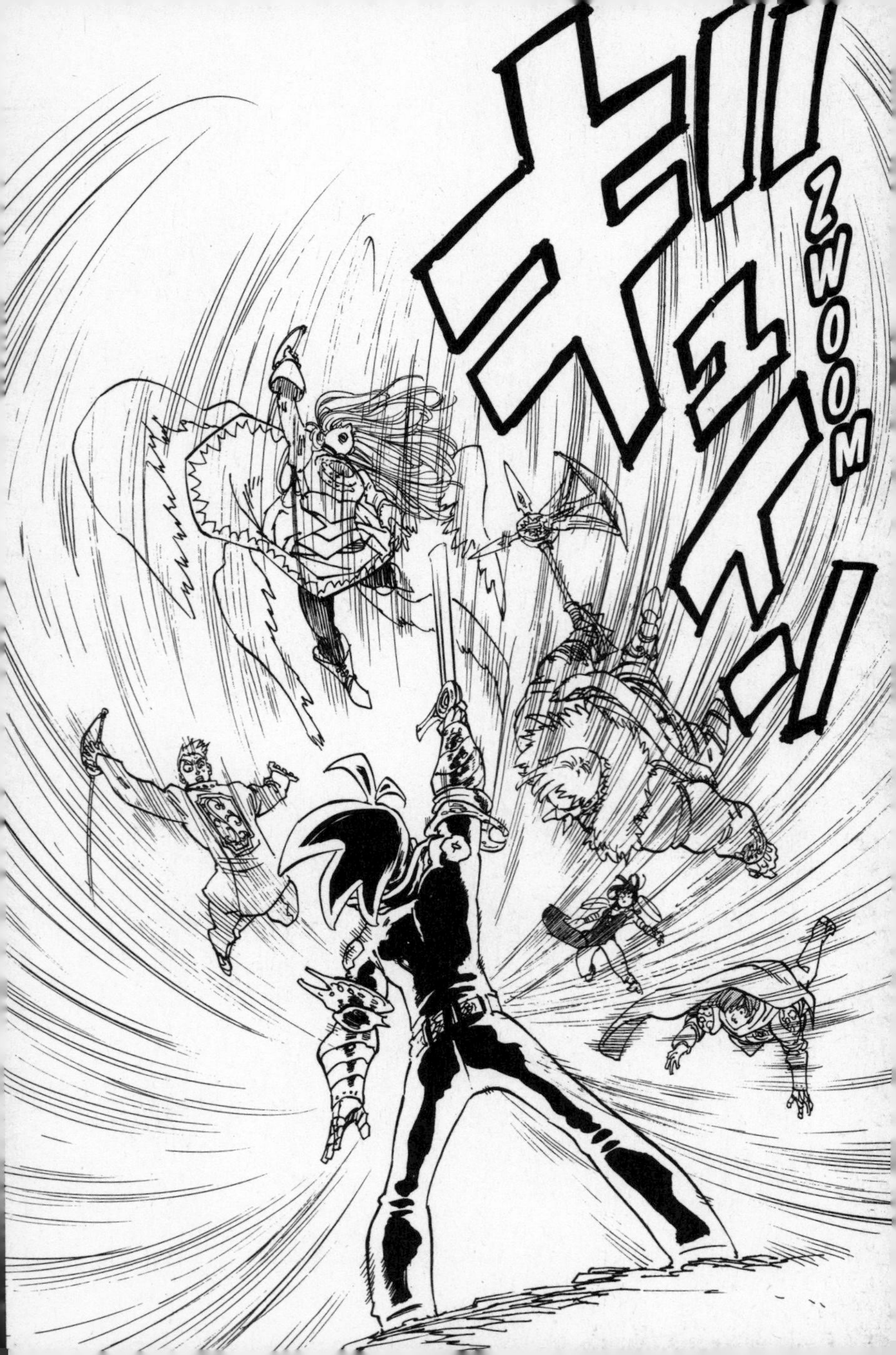
ZWOOM

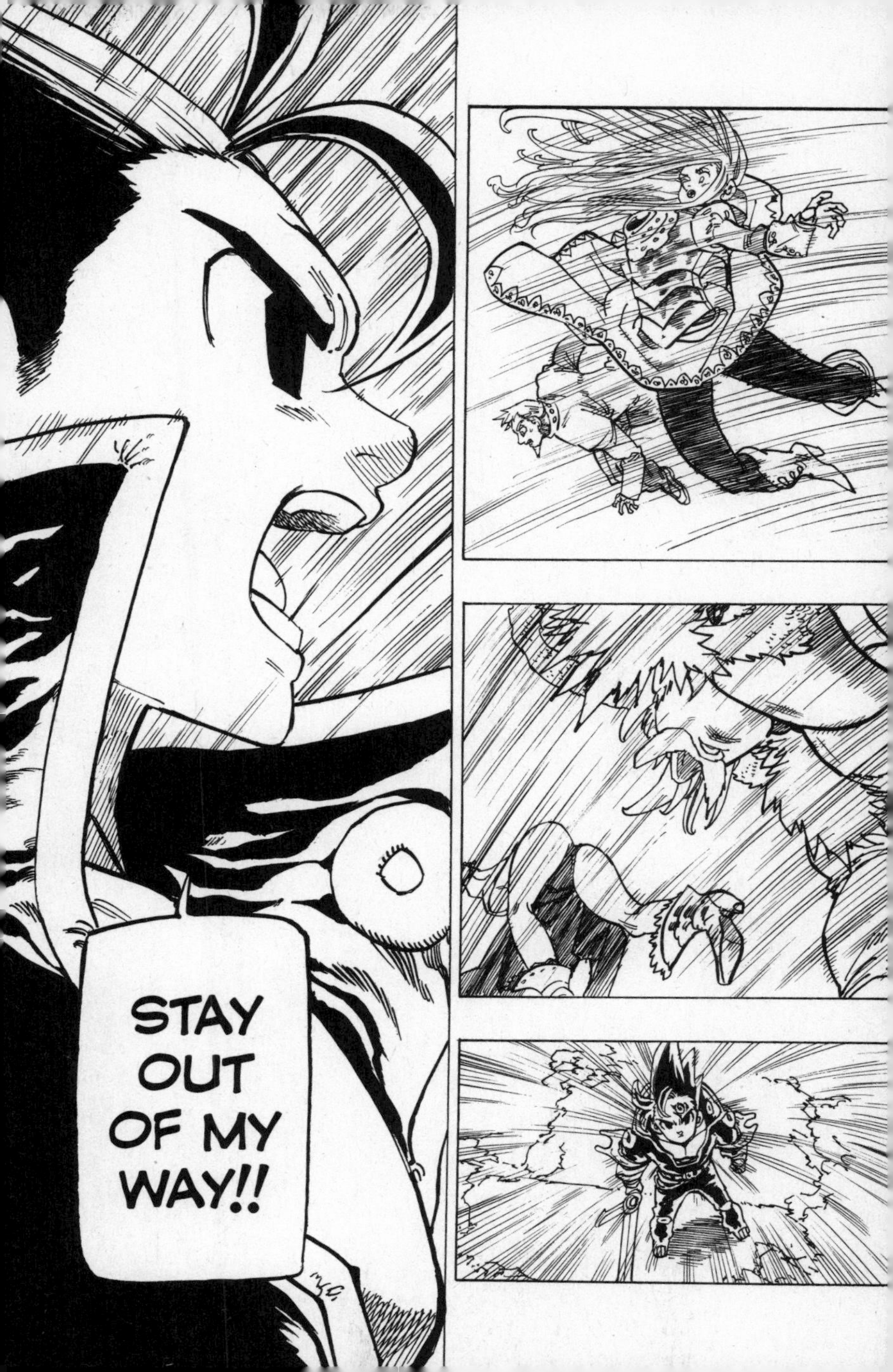
STAY OUT OF MY WAY!!

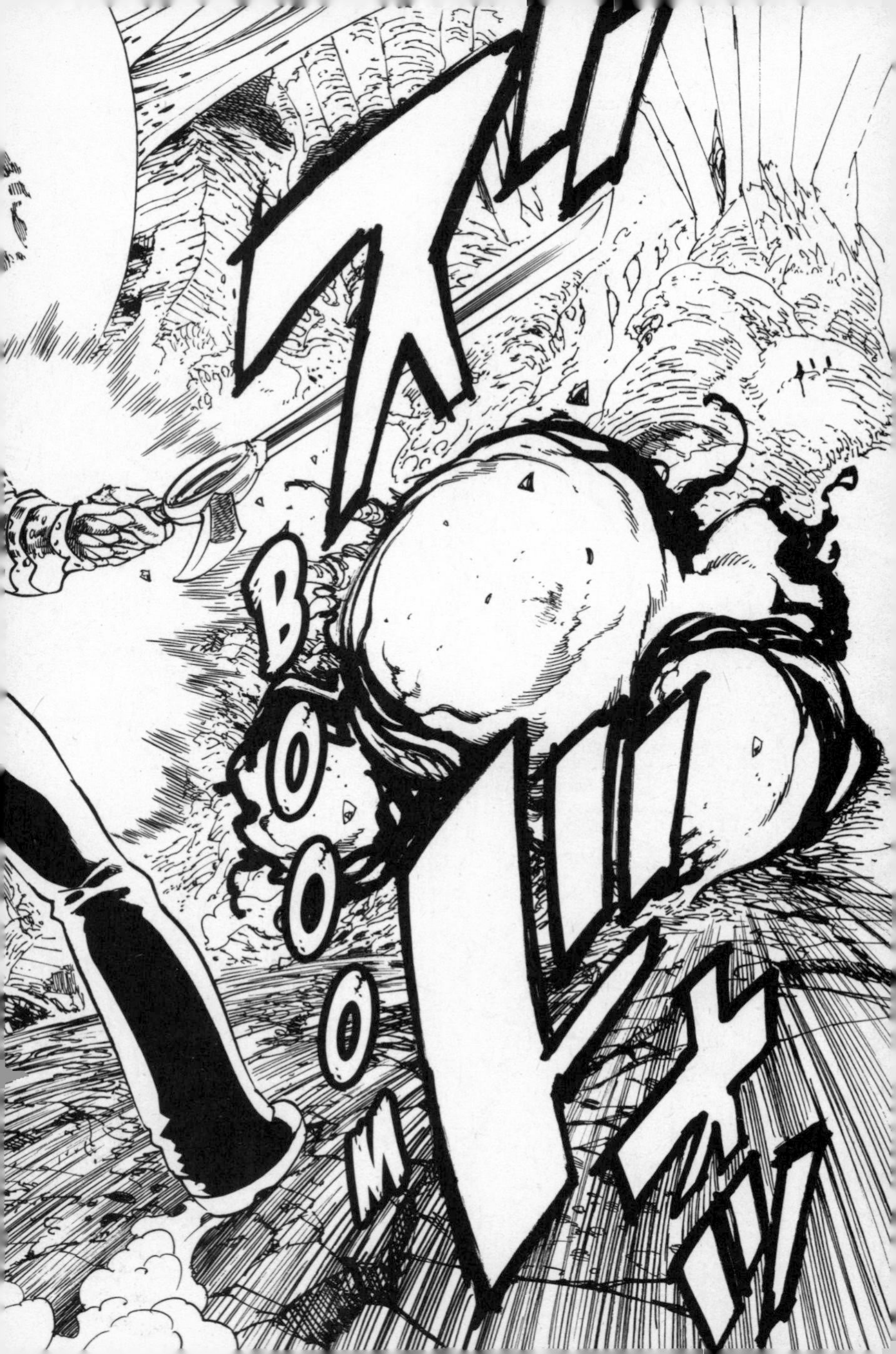
BOOOM

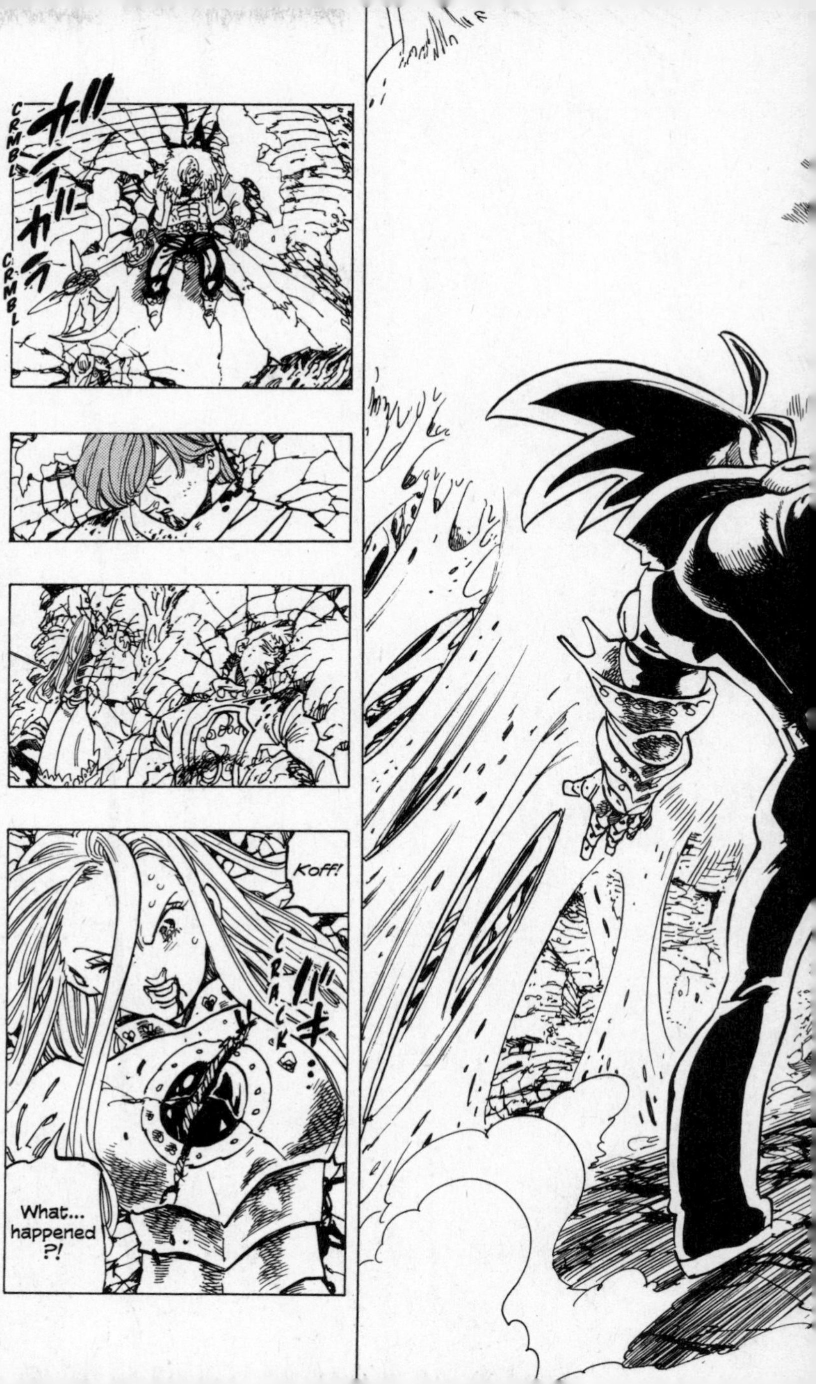
CRMBL
CRMBL
Koff!
CRACK
What... happened?!

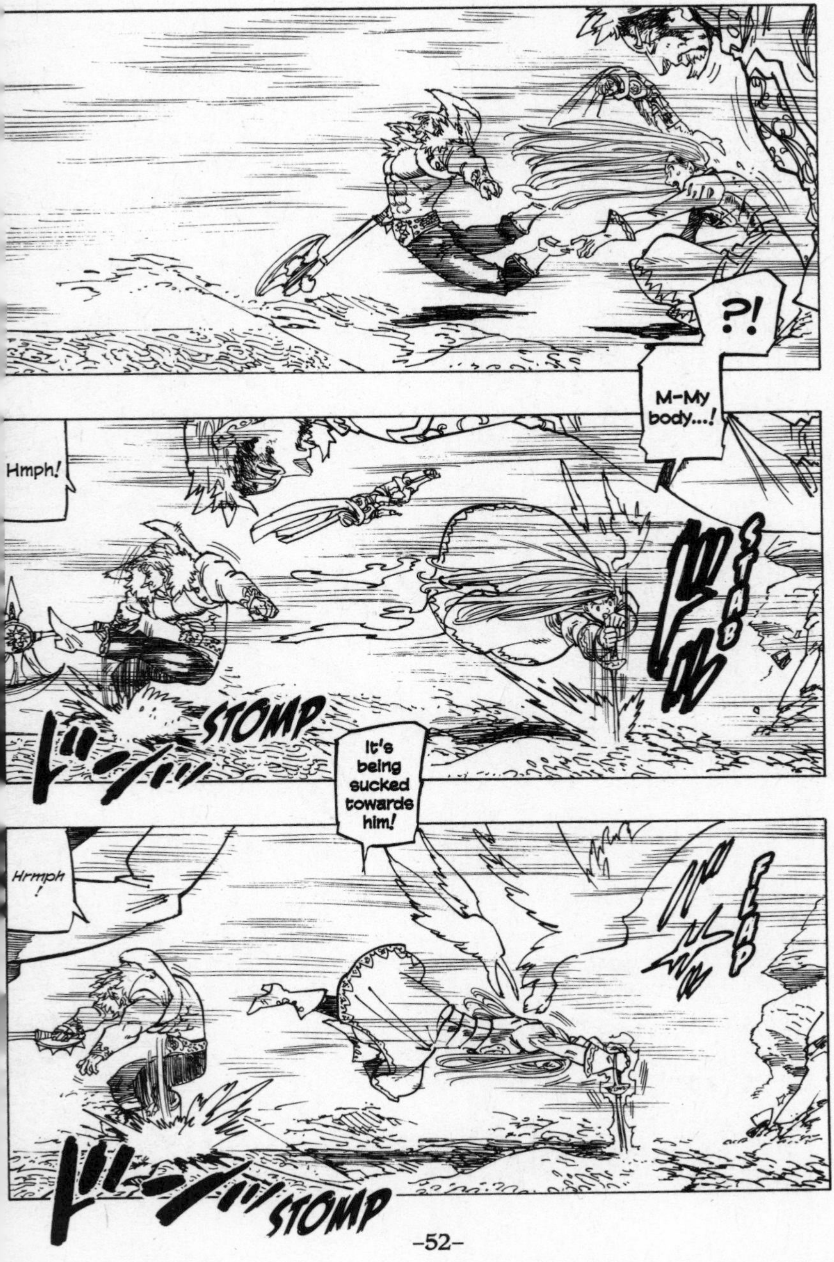
?!
M-My body...!
STAB
Hmph!
STOMP
It's being sucked towards him!
FLAP
Hrmph!
STOMP

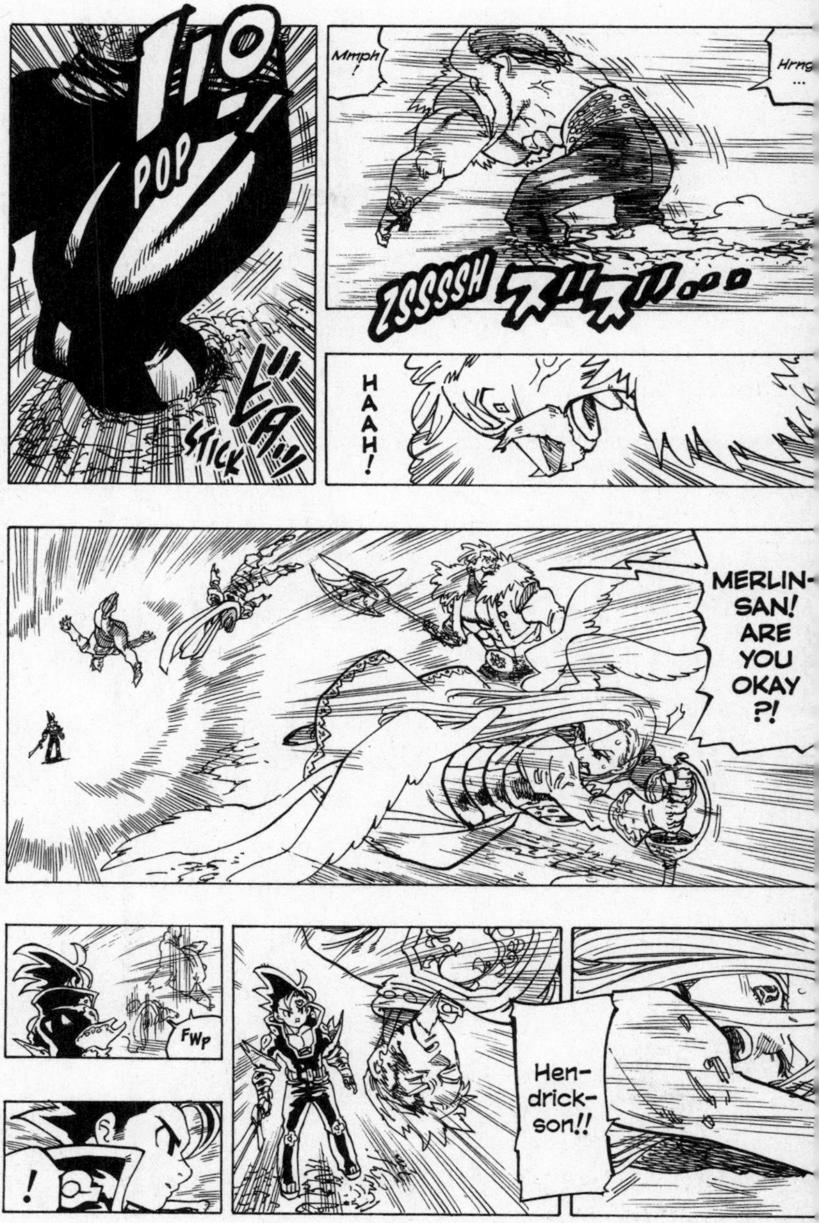
Hrng...
Mmph!
ZSSSSH
HAAH!
POP
STICK
MERLIN-SAN! ARE YOU OKAY?!
Hen-drick-son!!
FWp
!

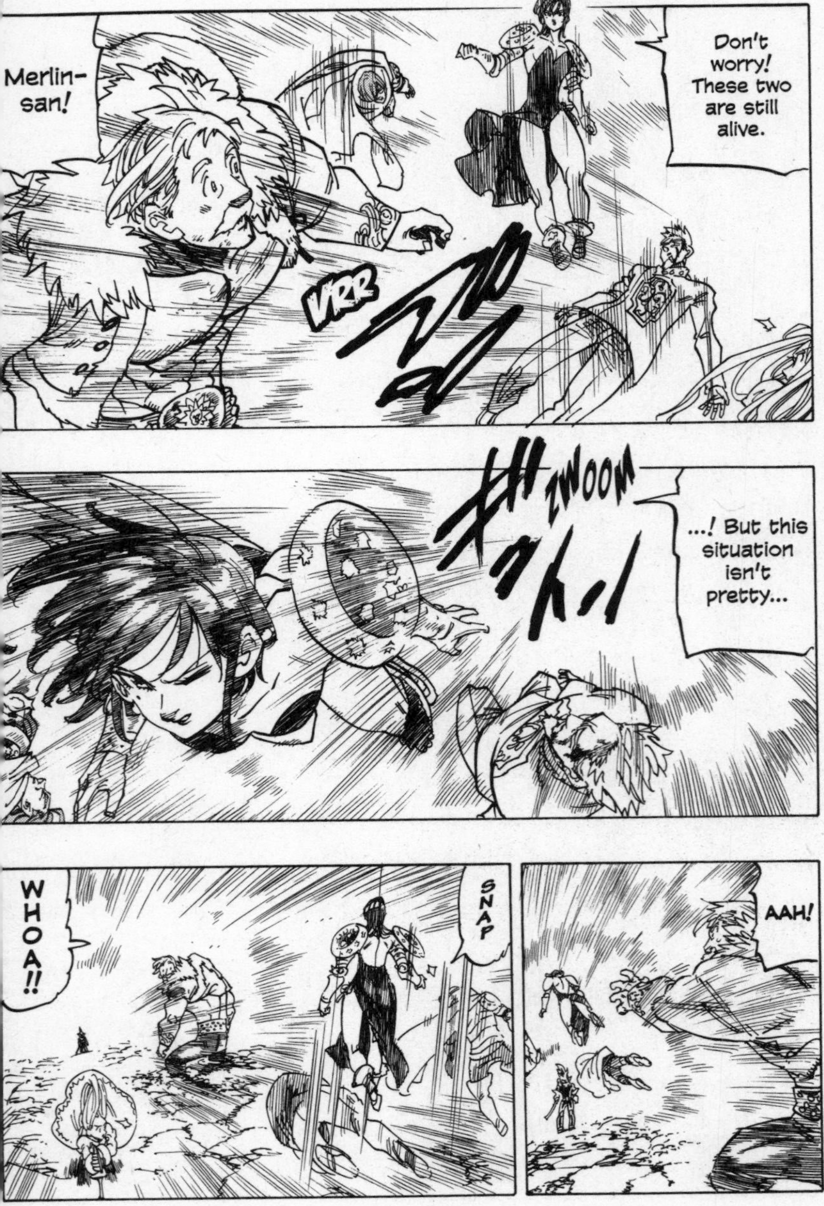
Don't worry! These two are still alive.
Merlin-san!
VRR
ZWOOM
...! But this situation isn't pretty...
AAH!
SNAP
WHOA!!

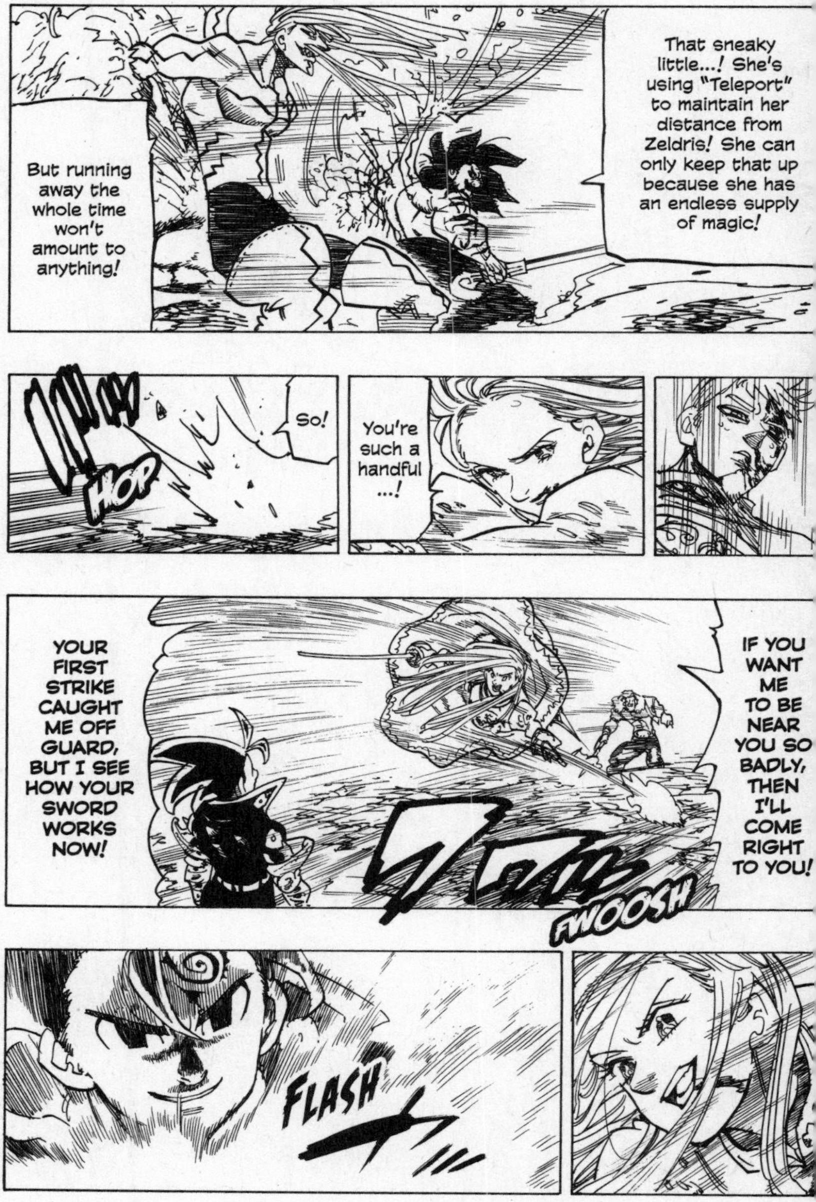
That sneaky little...! She's using "Teleport" to maintain her distance from Zeldris! She can only keep that up because she has an endless supply of magic!
But running away the whole time won't amount to anything!
You're such a handful ...!
So!
HOP
IF YOU WANT ME TO BE NEAR YOU SO BADLY, THEN I'LL COME RIGHT TO YOU!
YOUR FIRST STRIKE CAUGHT ME OFF GUARD, BUT I SEE HOW YOUR SWORD WORKS NOW!
FWOOSH
FLASH

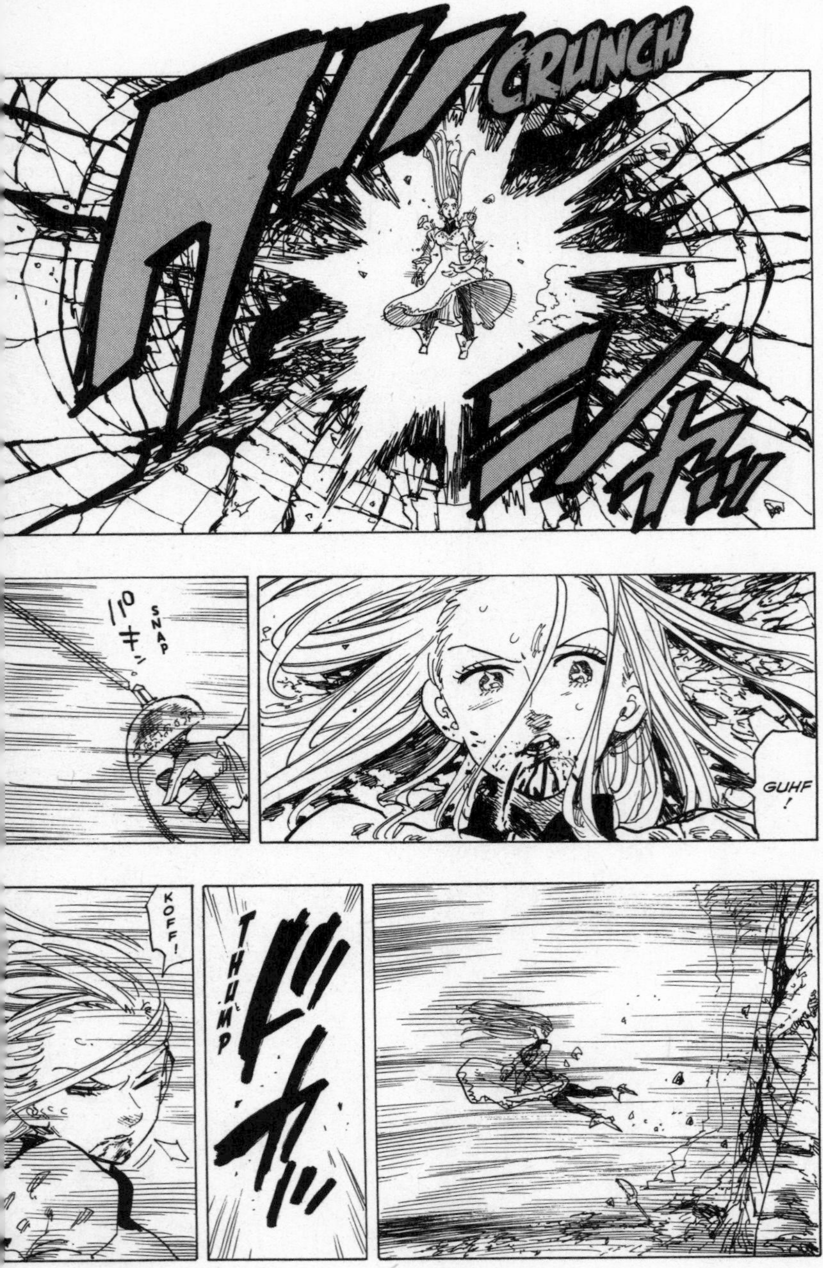
CRUNCH
GUHF!
SNAP
THUMP
KOFF!

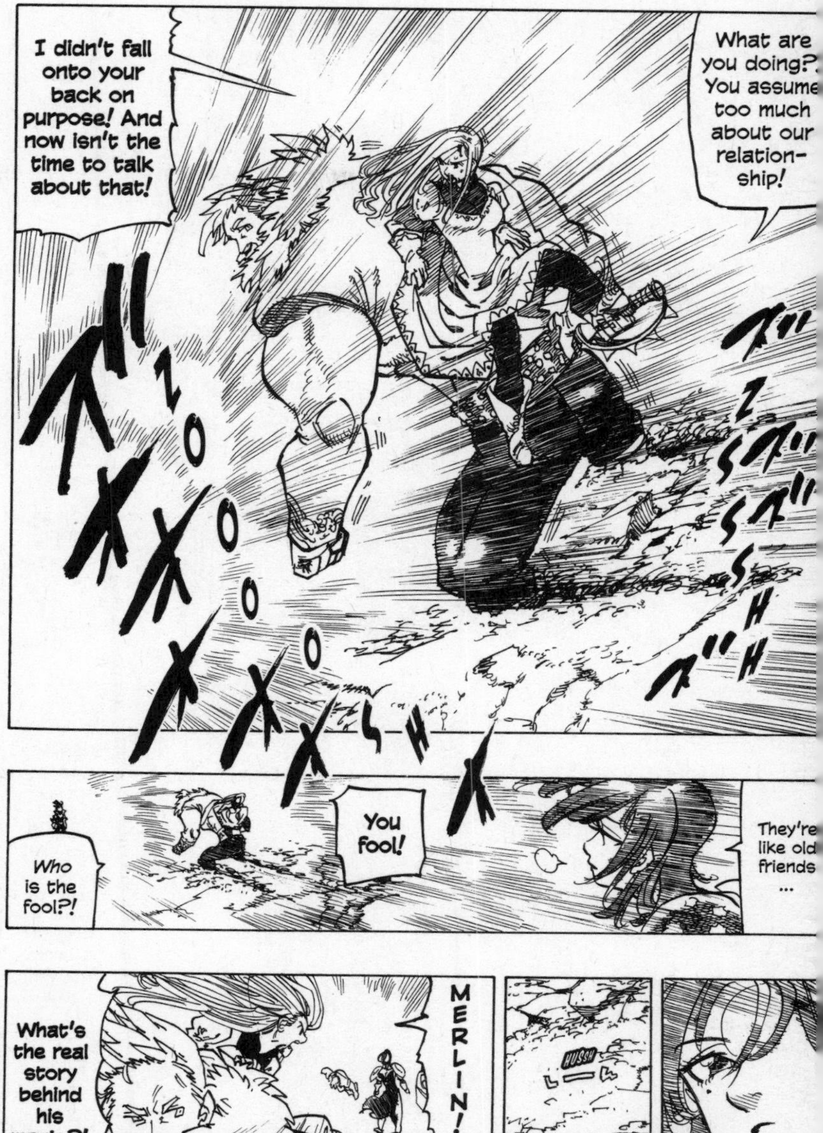
What are you doing?! You assume too much about our relationship!
I didn't fall onto your back on purpose! And now isn't the time to talk about that!
ZSSSHHH
ZOOOOSH
They're like old friends...
You fool!
Who is the fool?!
!
HUSSH
MERLIN!
What's the real story behind his magic?!

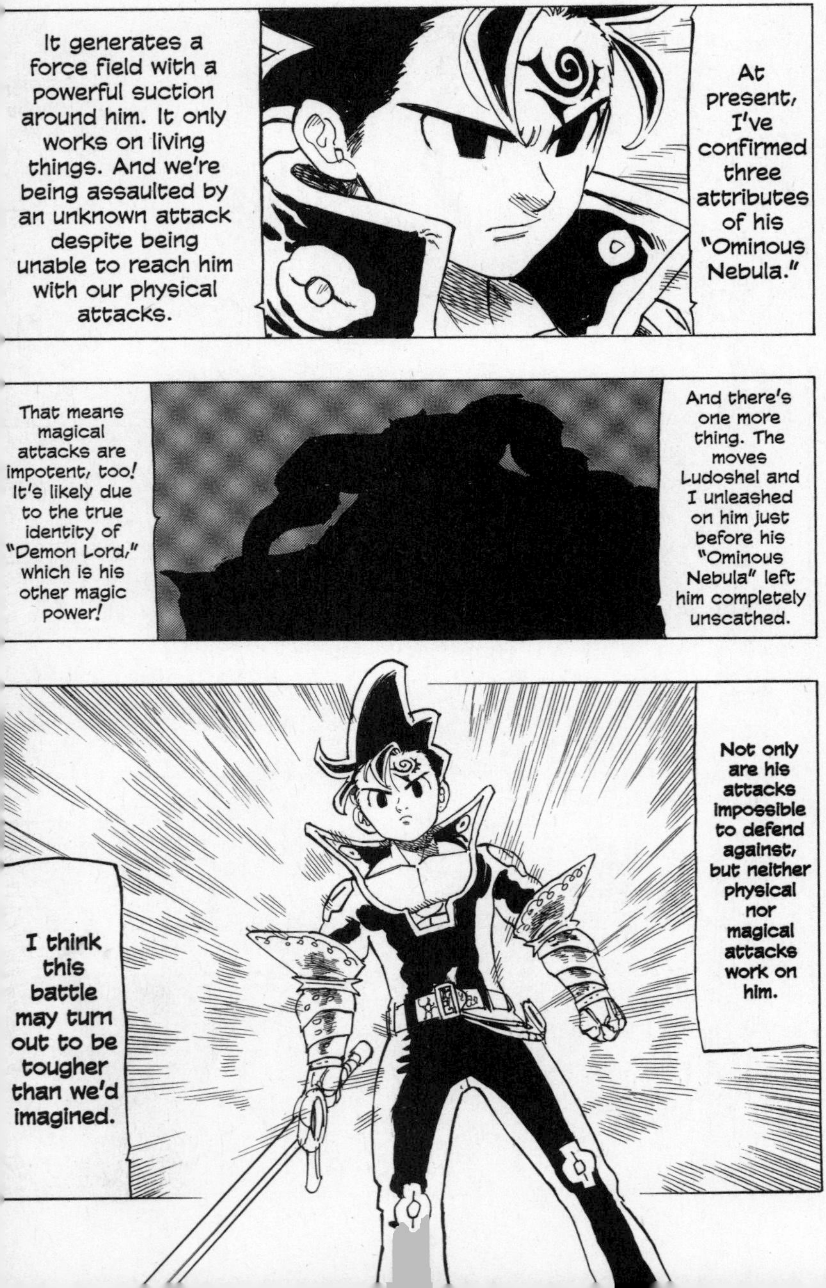

At present, I've confirmed three attributes of his "Ominous Nebula."
It generates a force field with a powerful suction around him. It only works on living things. And we're being assaulted by an unknown attack despite being unable to reach him with our physical attacks.
And there's one more thing. The moves Ludoshel and I unleashed on him just before his "Ominous Nebula" left him completely unscathed.
That means magical attacks are impotent, too! It's likely due to the true identity of "Demon Lord," which is his other magic power!
Not only are his attacks impossible to defend against, but neither physical nor magical attacks work on him.
I think this battle may turn out to be tougher than we'd imagined.

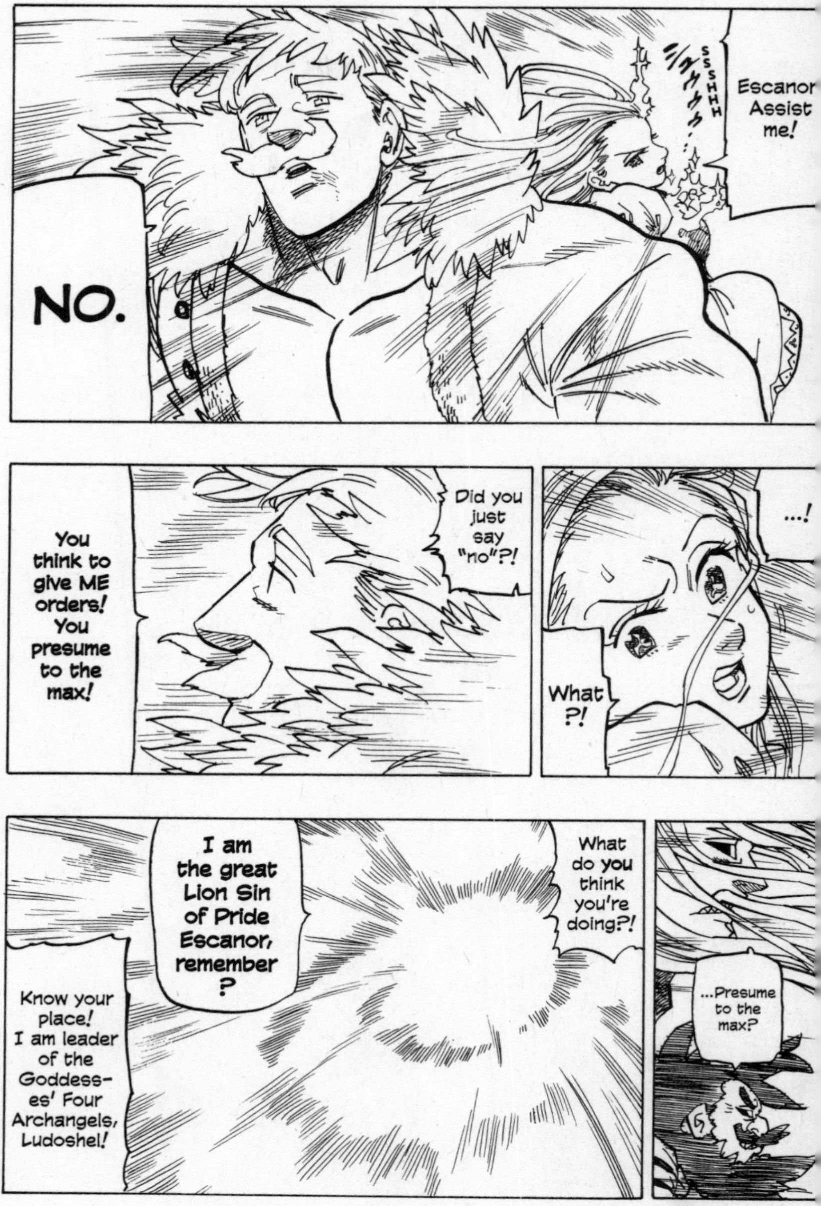
Escanor Assist me!
SSSHHH
NO.
...!
What?!
Did you just say "no"?!
You think to give ME orders! You presume to the max!
...Presume to the max?
What do you think you're doing?!
I am the great Lion Sin of Pride Escanor, remember?
Know your place! I am leader of the Goddess-es' Four Archangels, Ludoshel!

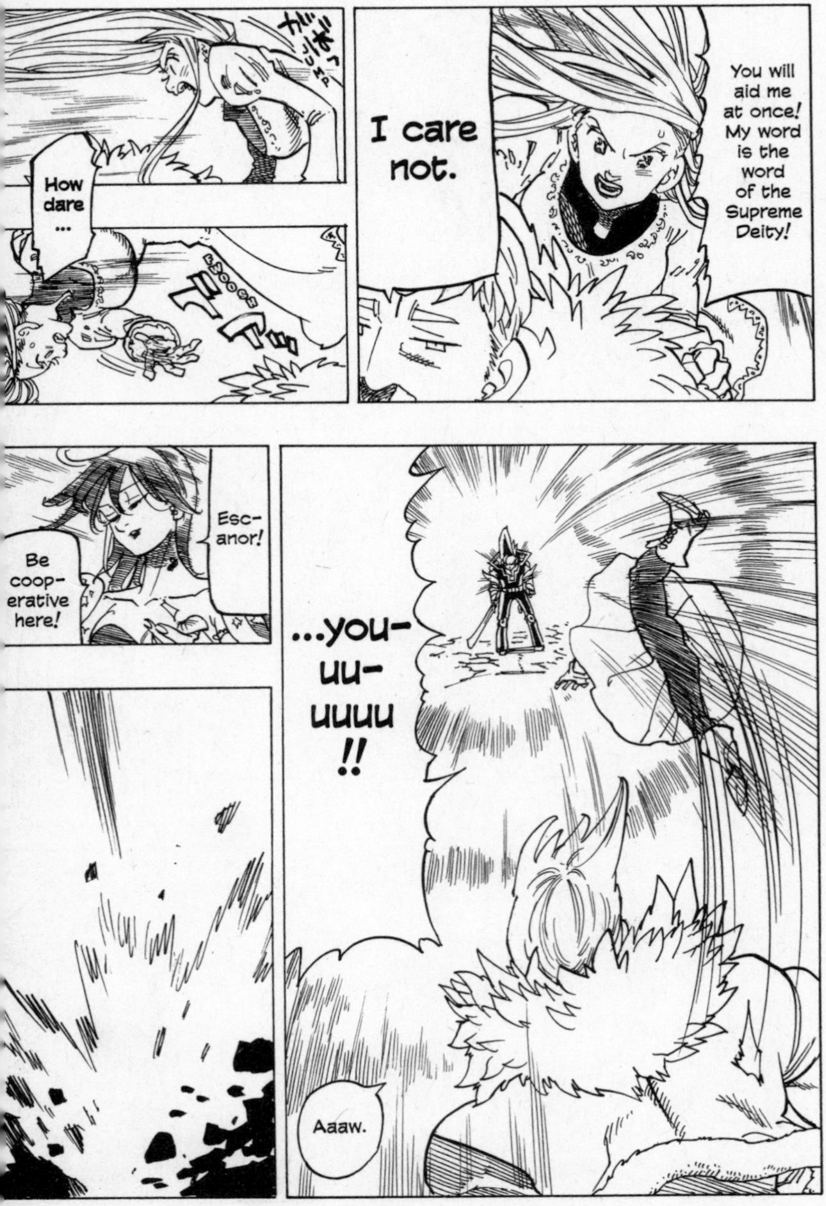
You will aid me at once! My word is the word of the Supreme Deity!
I care not.
JUMP
How dare ...
FWOOSH
...you-uu-uuuu!!
Aaaw.
Escanor!
Be cooperative here!

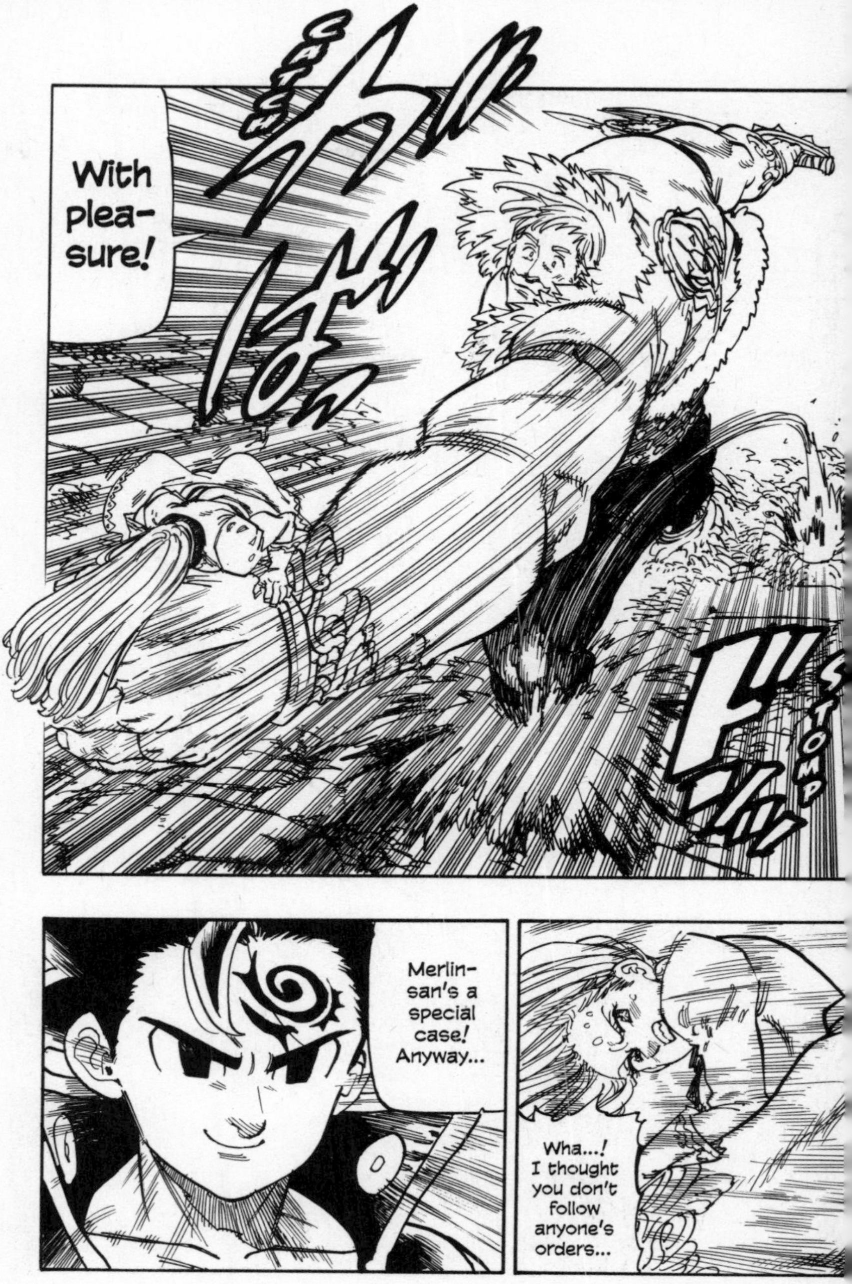
CATCH
With plea-sure!
STOMP
Wha...! I thought you don't follow anyone's orders...
Merlin-san's a special case! Anyway...

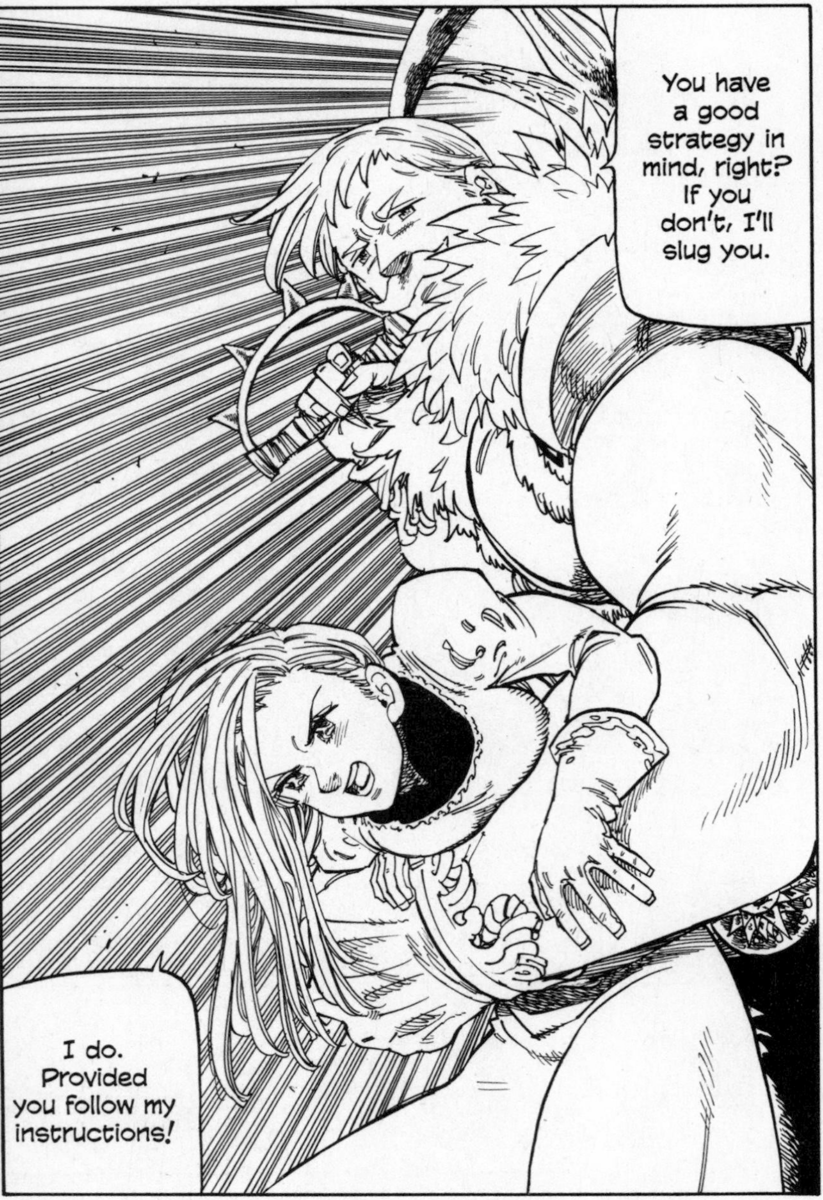
You have a good strategy in mind, right? If you don't, I'll slug you.
I do. Provided you follow my instructions!

THE SEVEN DEADLY SINS

"THE DOZING GOD OF DEATH."

A Former Chief Holy Knight.

Head of "The Four Archangels."

Agent of the Demon Lord.

Daughter of Bérialin.

"THE PACIFIER DEMON."

"The Lion Sin of Pride."

"The Diamond Class" Holy Knight.

Chapter 288 - "Ominous Nebula"

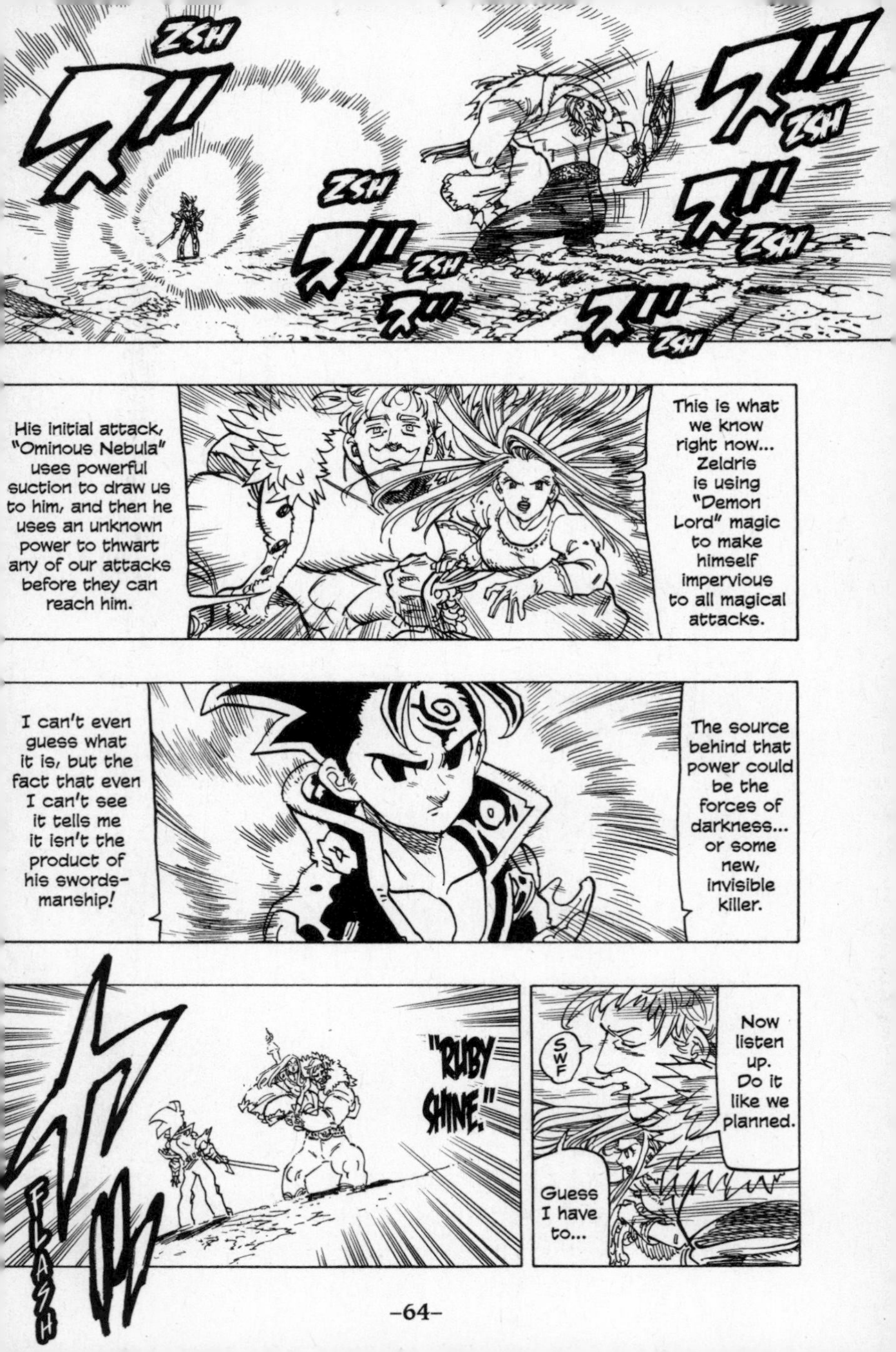
ZSH
ZSH
ZSH
ZSH
ZSH
ZSH
This is what we know right now... Zeldris is using "Demon Lord" magic to make himself impervious to all magical attacks.
His initial attack, "Ominous Nebula" uses powerful suction to draw us to him, and then he uses an unknown power to thwart any of our attacks before they can reach him.
The source behind that power could be the forces of darkness... or some new, invisible killer.
I can't even guess what it is, but the fact that even I can't see it tells me it isn't the product of his swords-manship!
Now listen up. Do it like we planned.
SWF
Guess I have to...
"RUBY SHINE."
FLASH

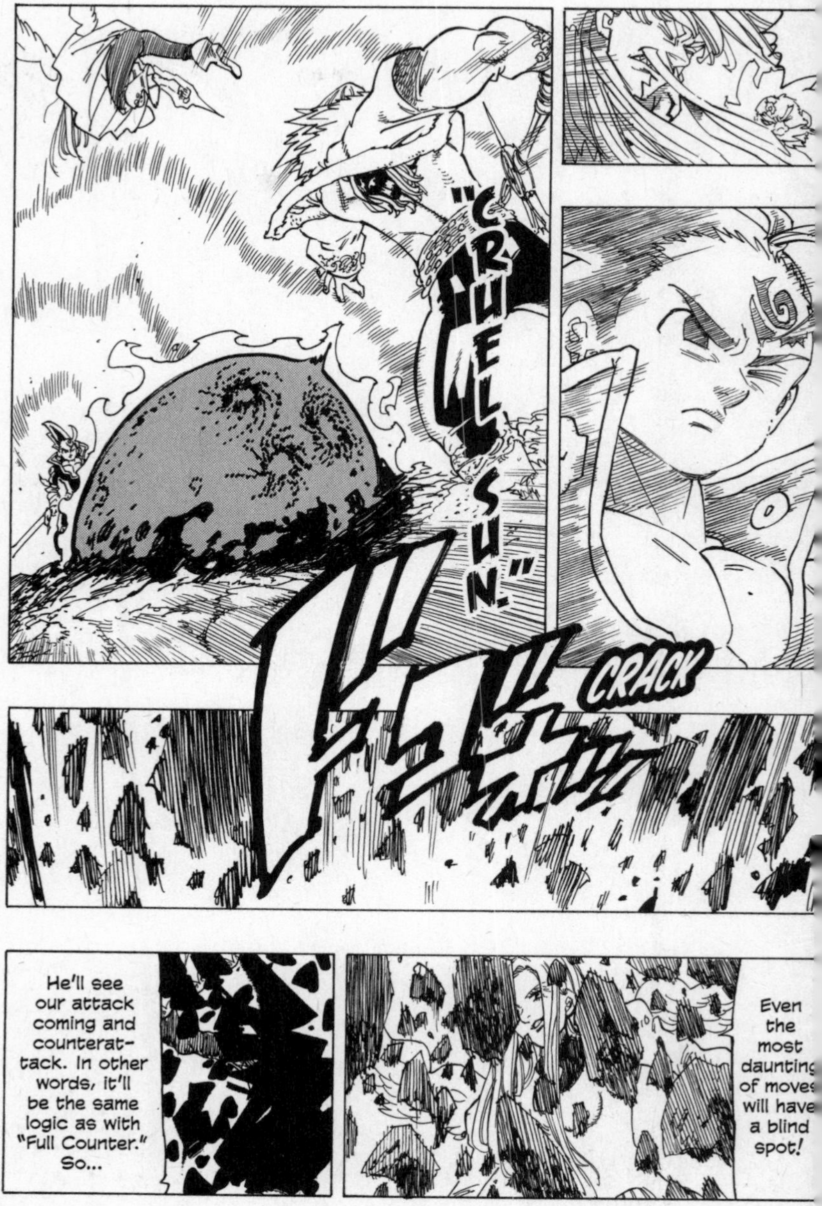
"CRUEL SUN."
CRACK
Even the most daunting of moves will have a blind spot!
He'll see our attack coming and counterat-tack. In other words, it'll be the same logic as with "Full Counter." So...

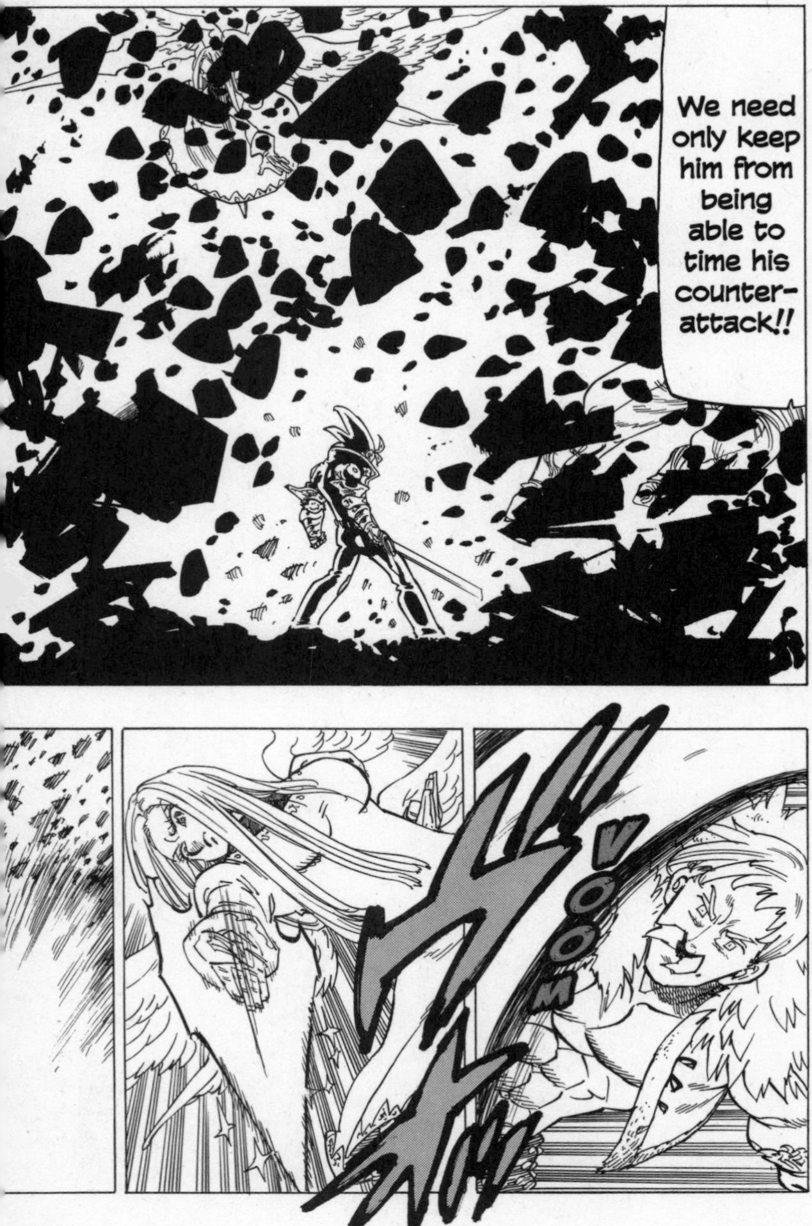
We need only keep him from being able to time his counter-attack!!
VOOOM

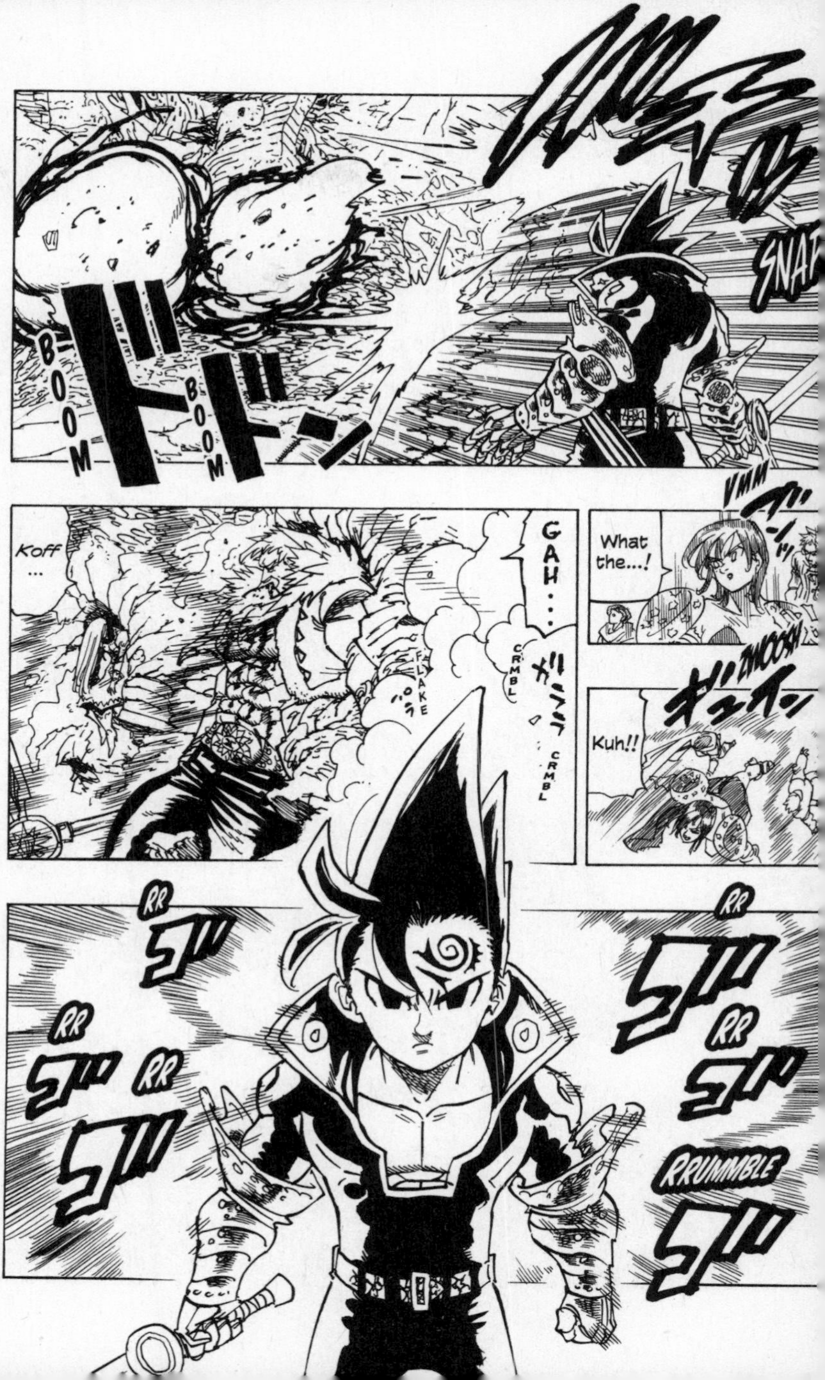
SNAP
BOOM
BOOM
VMMM
What the...!
WHOOSH
Kuh!!
GAH...
CRMBL
FLAKE
CRMBL
Koff ...
RR
RR
RR
RRUMMBLE
RR
RR
RR

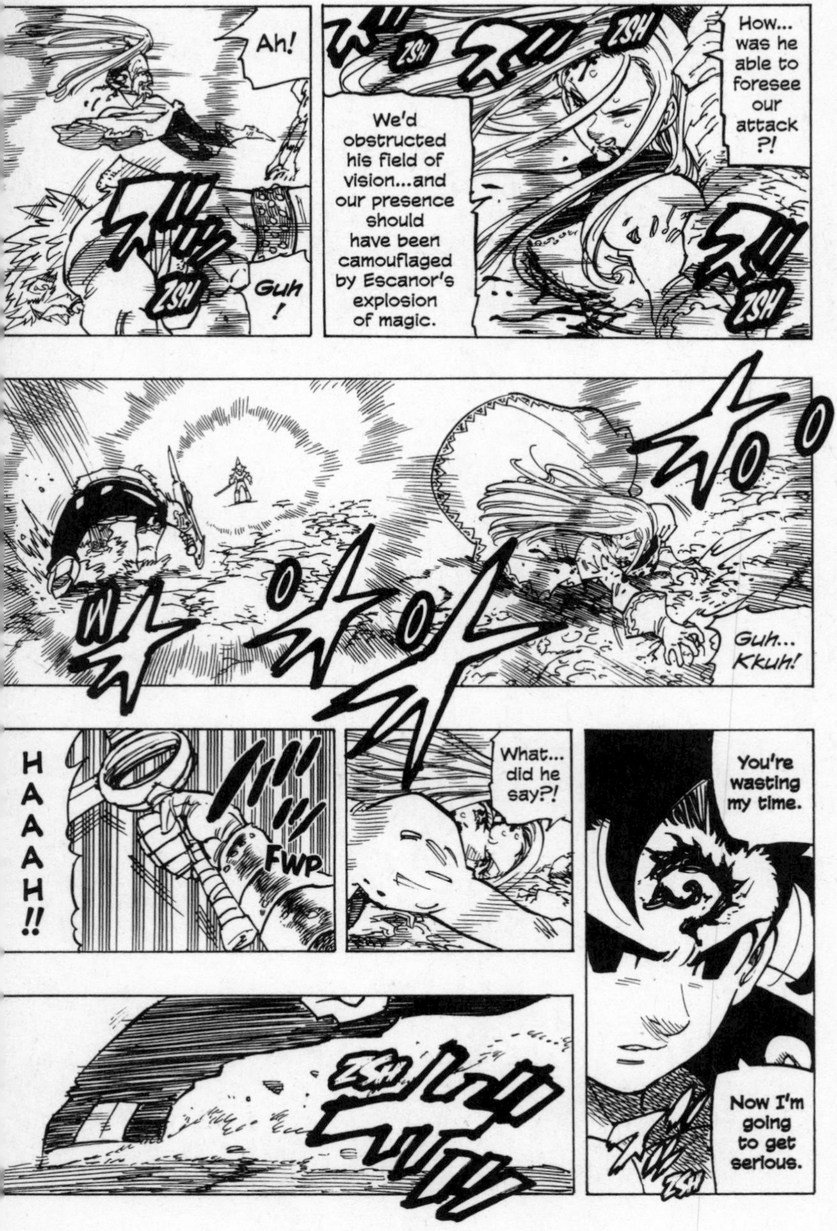

How... was he able to foresee our attack?!
We'd obstructed his field of vision...and our presence should have been camouflaged by Escanor's explosion of magic.
ZSH
ZSH
ZSH
Ah!
ZSH
Guh!
Guh... Kkuh!
You're wasting my time.
Now I'm going to get serious.
ZSH
What... did he say?!
FWP
HAAAAH!!
ZSH

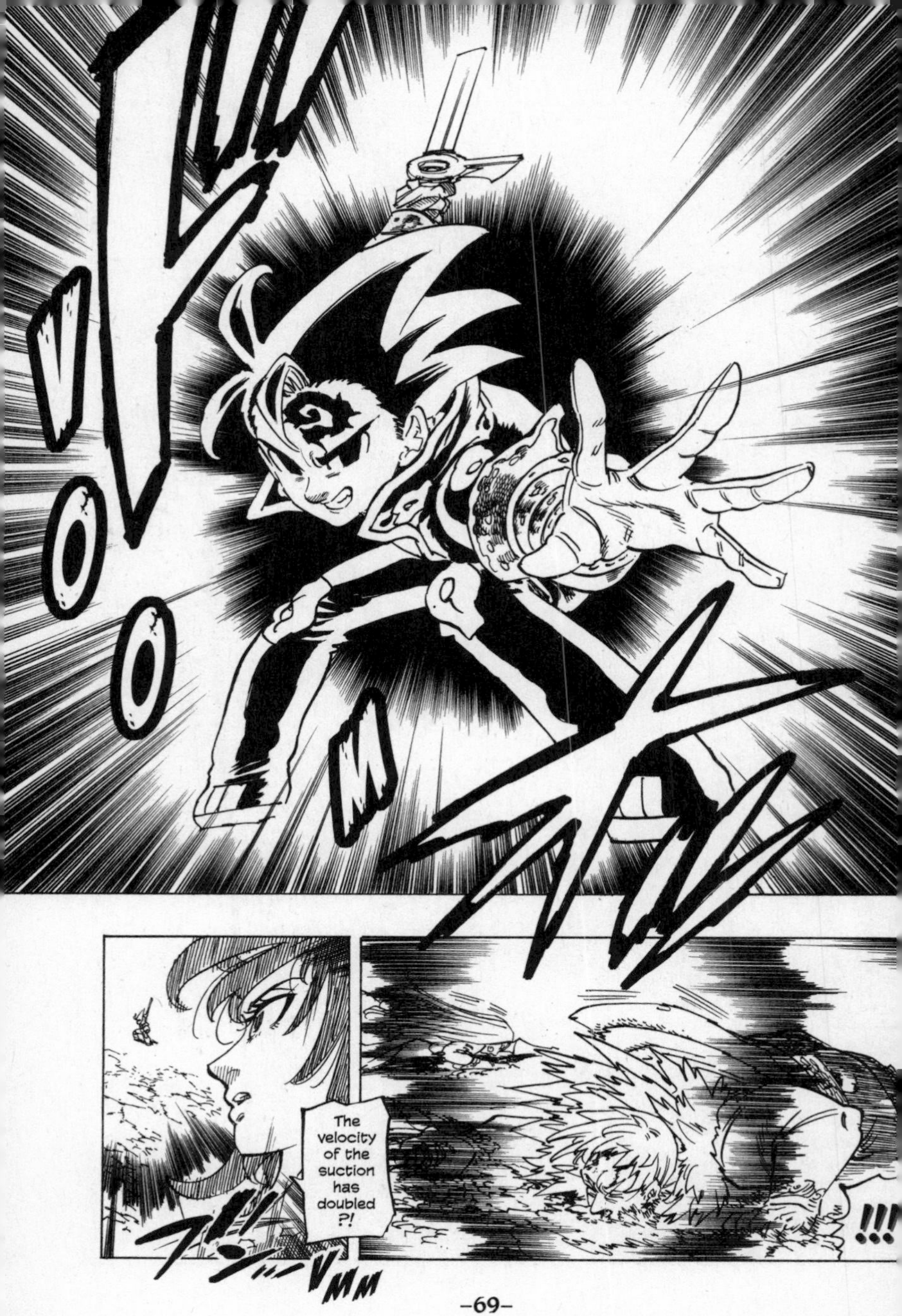
!!!
The velocity of the suction has doubled ?!

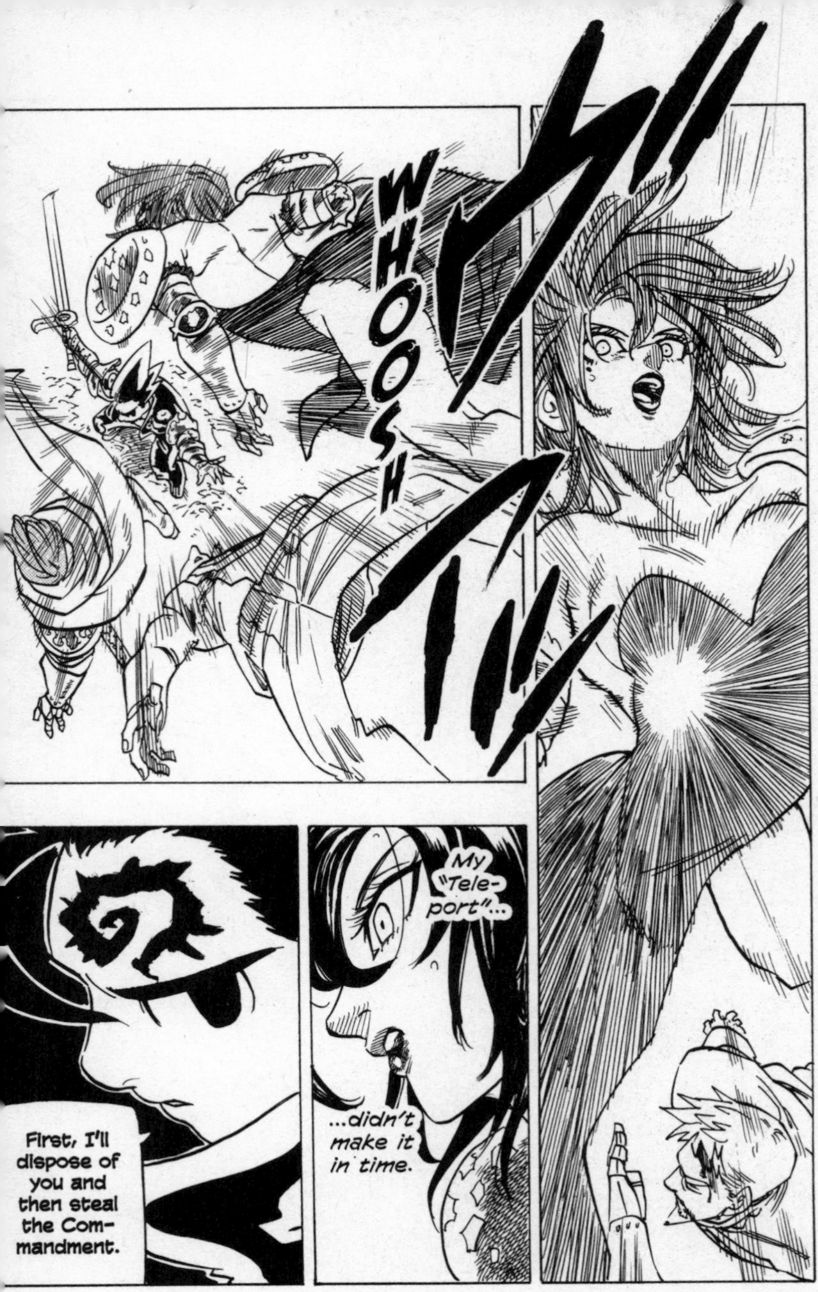
WHOOSH
My "Teleport"...
...didn't make it in time.
First, I'll dispose of you and then steal the Commandment.

BOOOOM

I'm sorry...!

ESCANOR...

Kah!

!!

...!
Merlin?

I was only... following my heart...

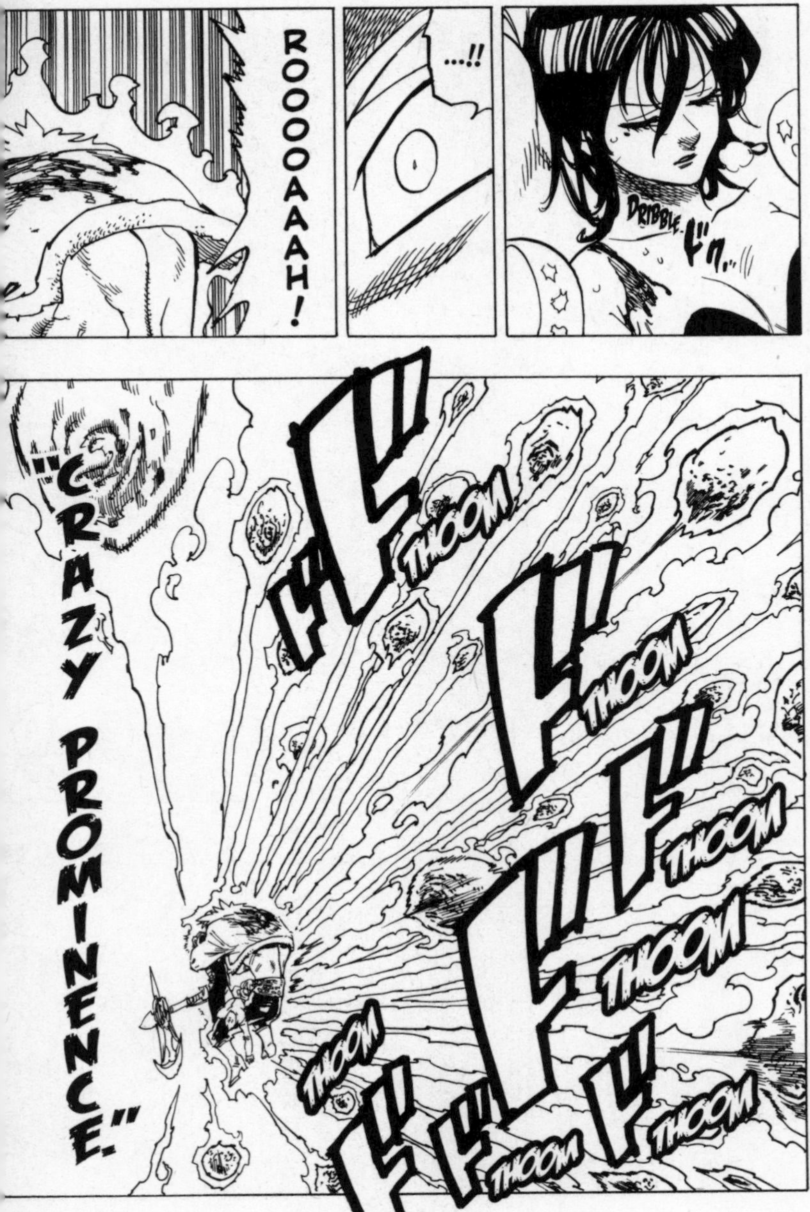
DRIBBLE
...!!
ROOOOOAAAAH!
"CRAZY PROMINENCE."
THOOM
THOOM
THOOM
THOOM
THOOM
THOOM
THOOM

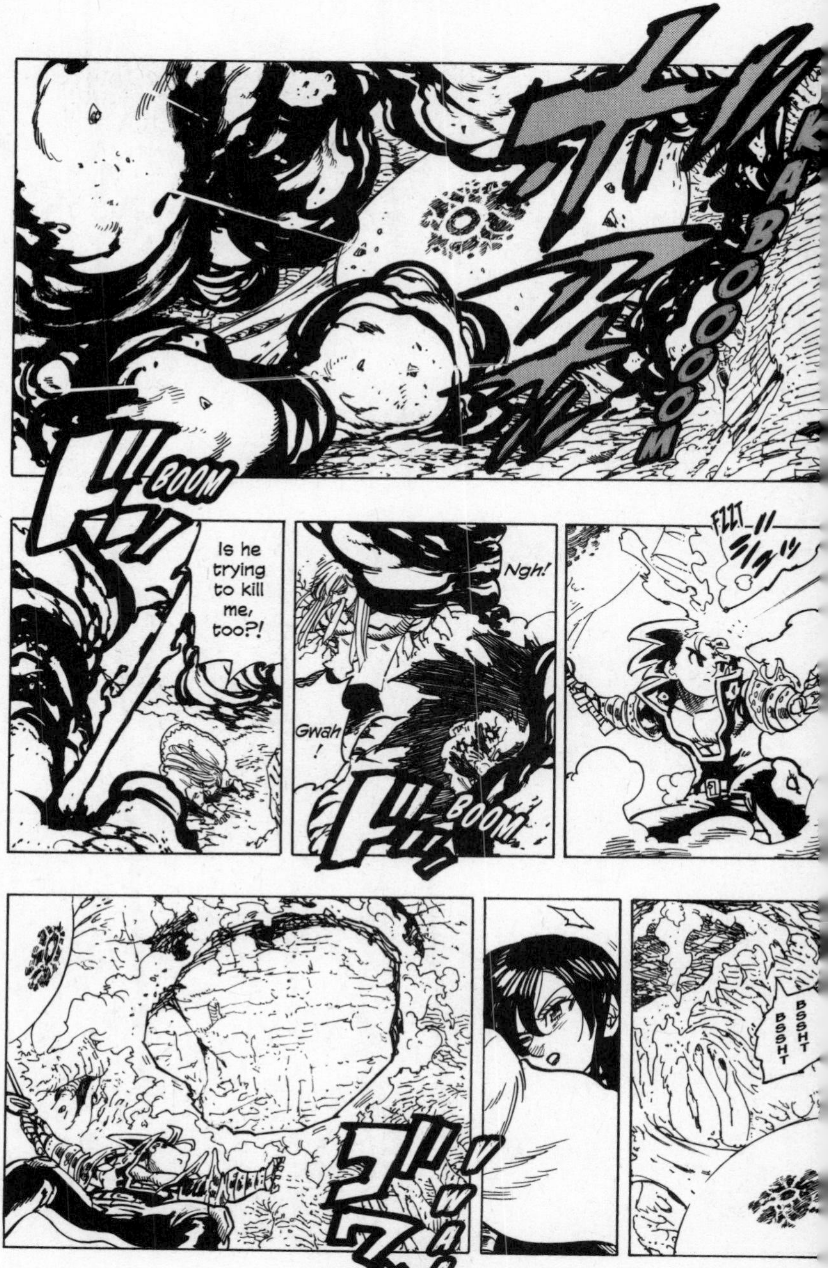
KABOOOOOM
BOOM
FZZT
Ngh!
Gwah!
BOOM
Is he trying to kill me, too?!
BSSHT
BSSHT
VWAA

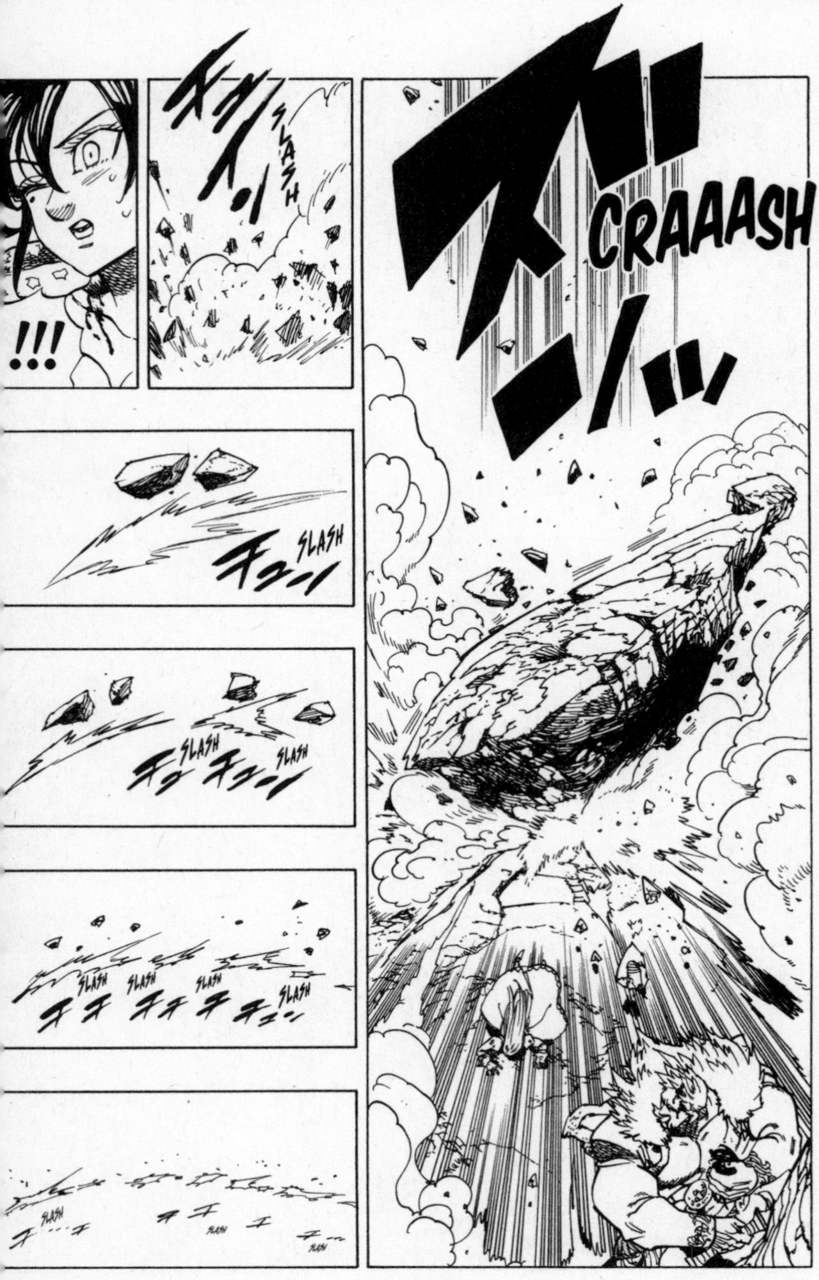
CRAASH
SLASH
!!!
SLASH
SLASH
SLASH
SLASH
SLASH
SLASH
SLASH
SLASH
SLASH
SLASH
SLASH

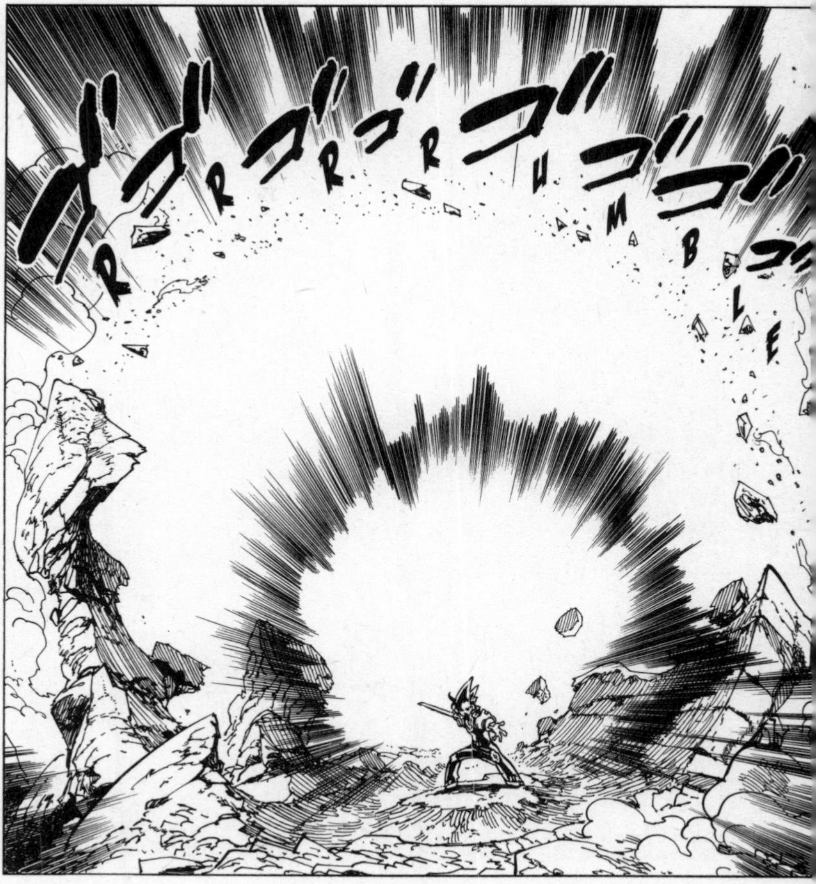
RRRRUMBLE

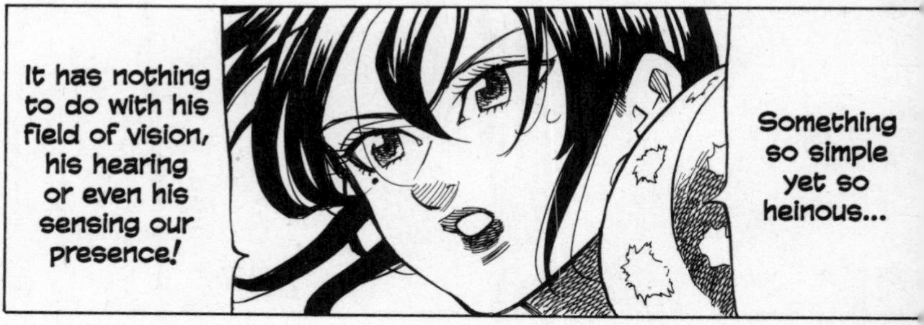
It has nothing to do with his field of vision, his hearing or even his sensing our presence!
Something so simple yet so heinous...

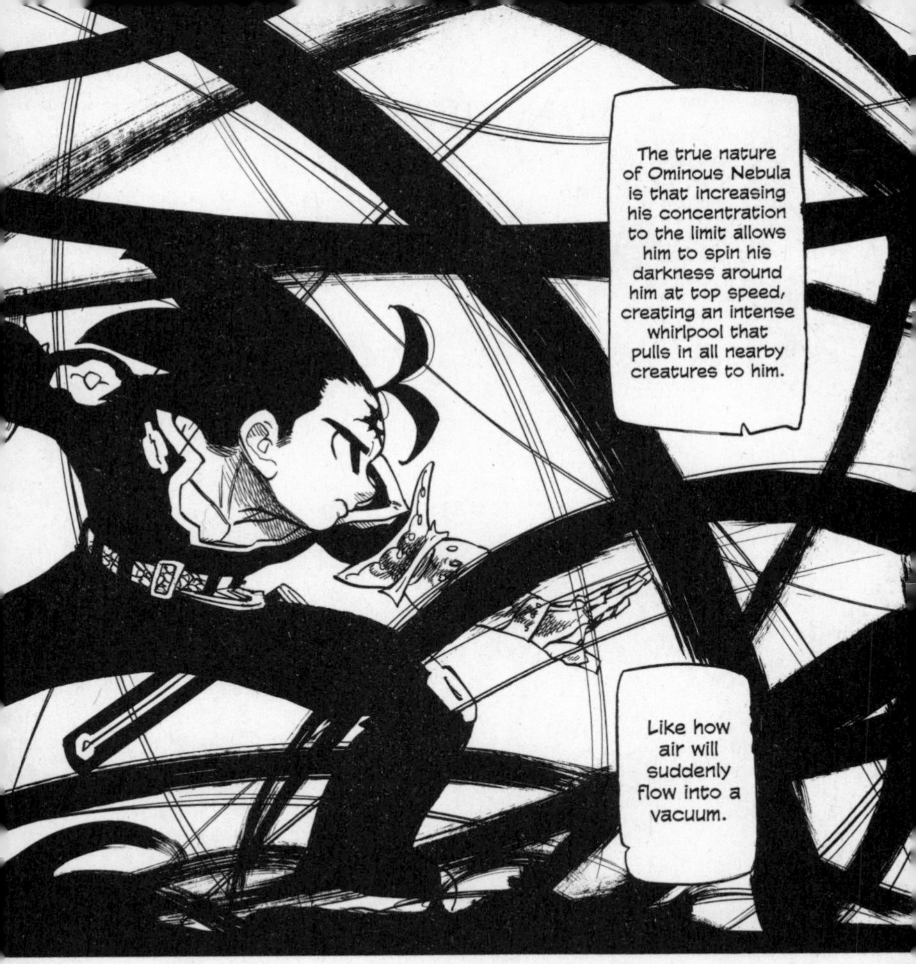
The true nature of Ominous Nebula is that increasing his concentration to the limit allows him to spin his darkness around him at top speed, creating an intense whirlpool that pulls in all nearby creatures to him.
Like how air will suddenly flow into a vacuum.

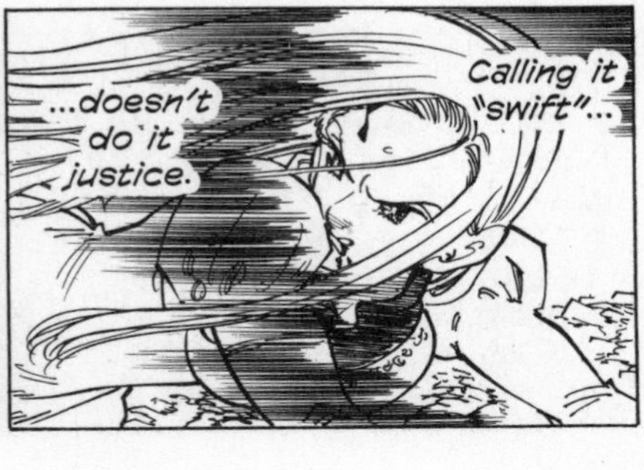
Calling it "swift"...
...doesn't do it justice.

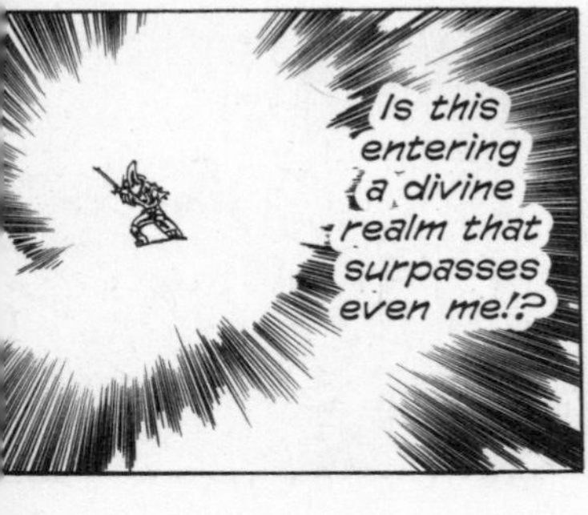
Is this entering a divine realm that surpasses even me!?

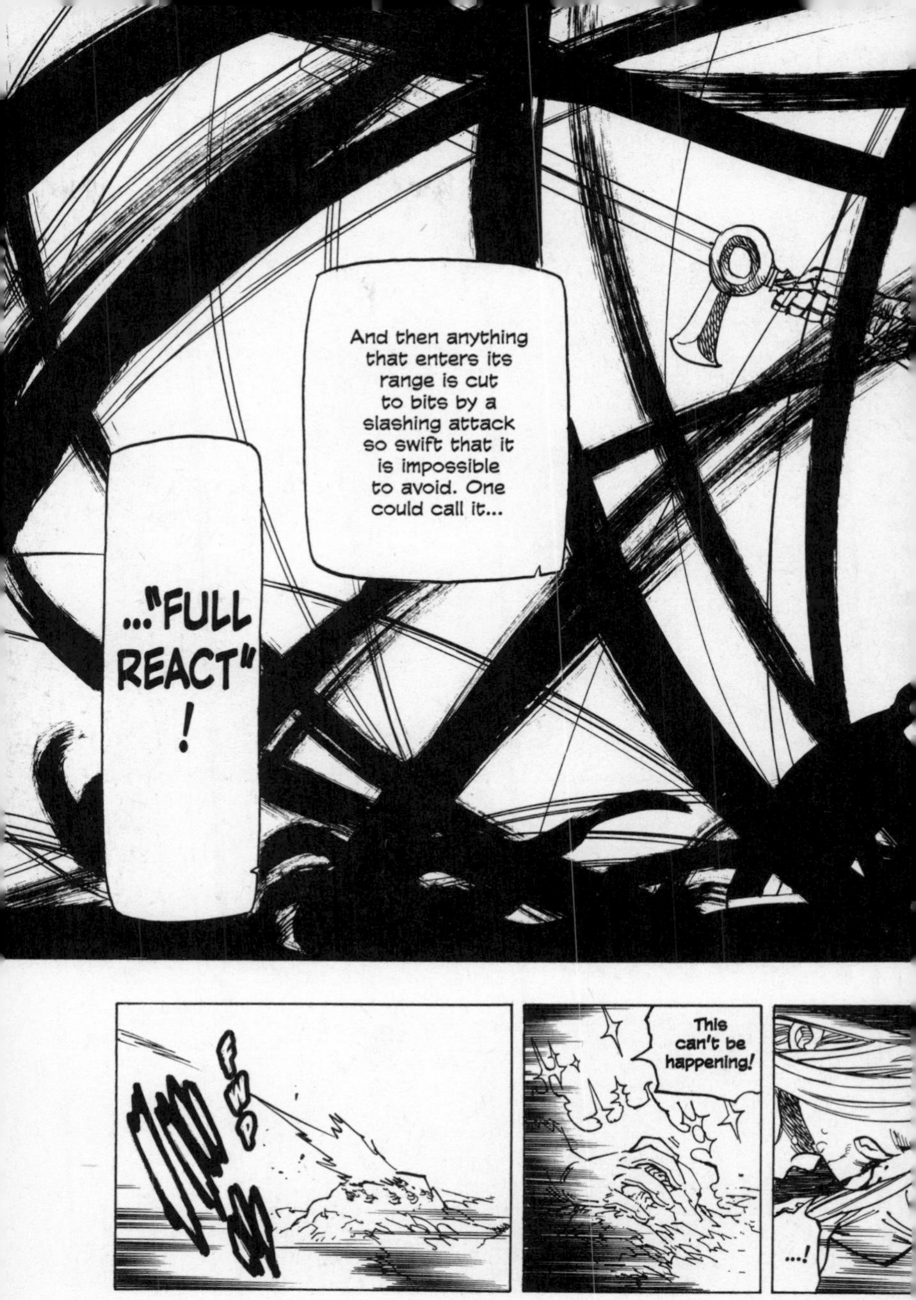
And then anything that enters its range is cut to bits by a slashing attack so swift that it is impossible to avoid. One could call it...
..."FULL REACT"!
...!
This can't be happening!
FWP

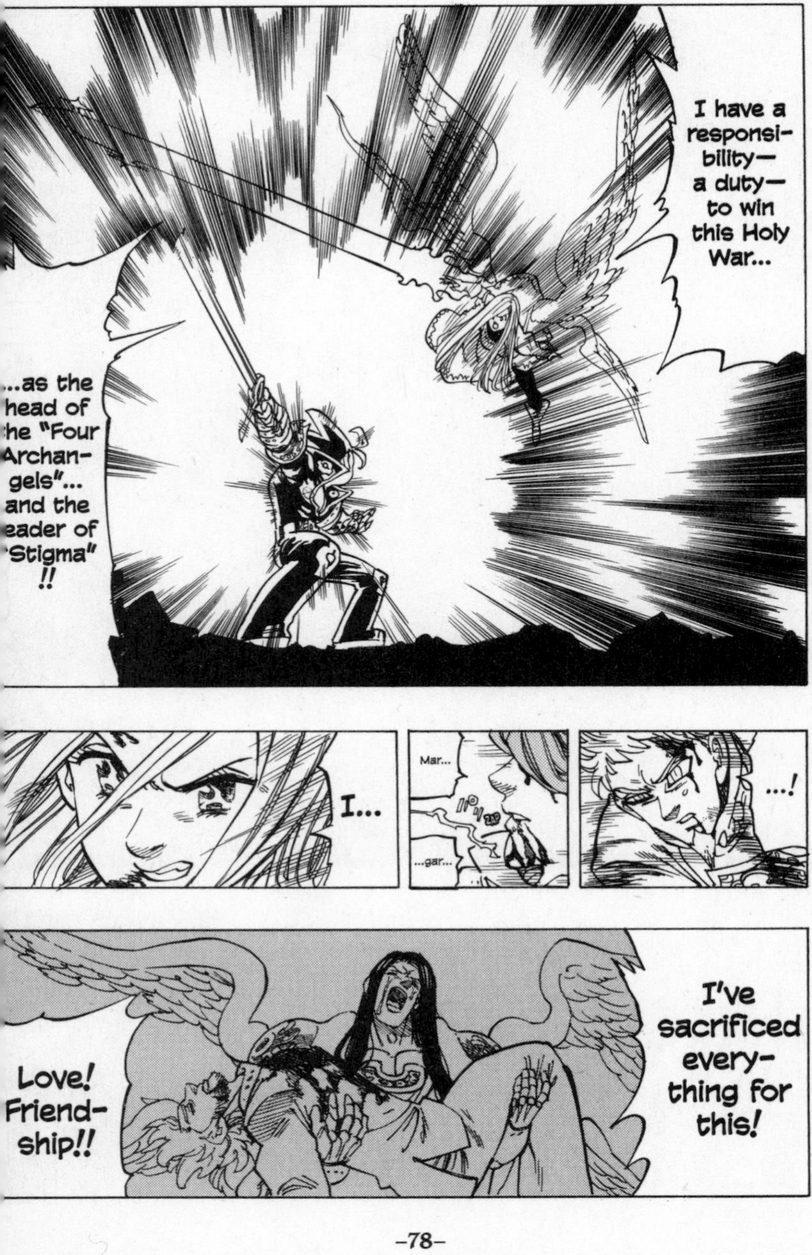
I have a responsibility—a duty—to win this Holy War...
...as the head of the "Four Archangels"... and the leader of "Stigma" !!
...!
Mar...
ZAP
...gar...
I...
I've sacrificed everything for this!
Love! Friendship!!

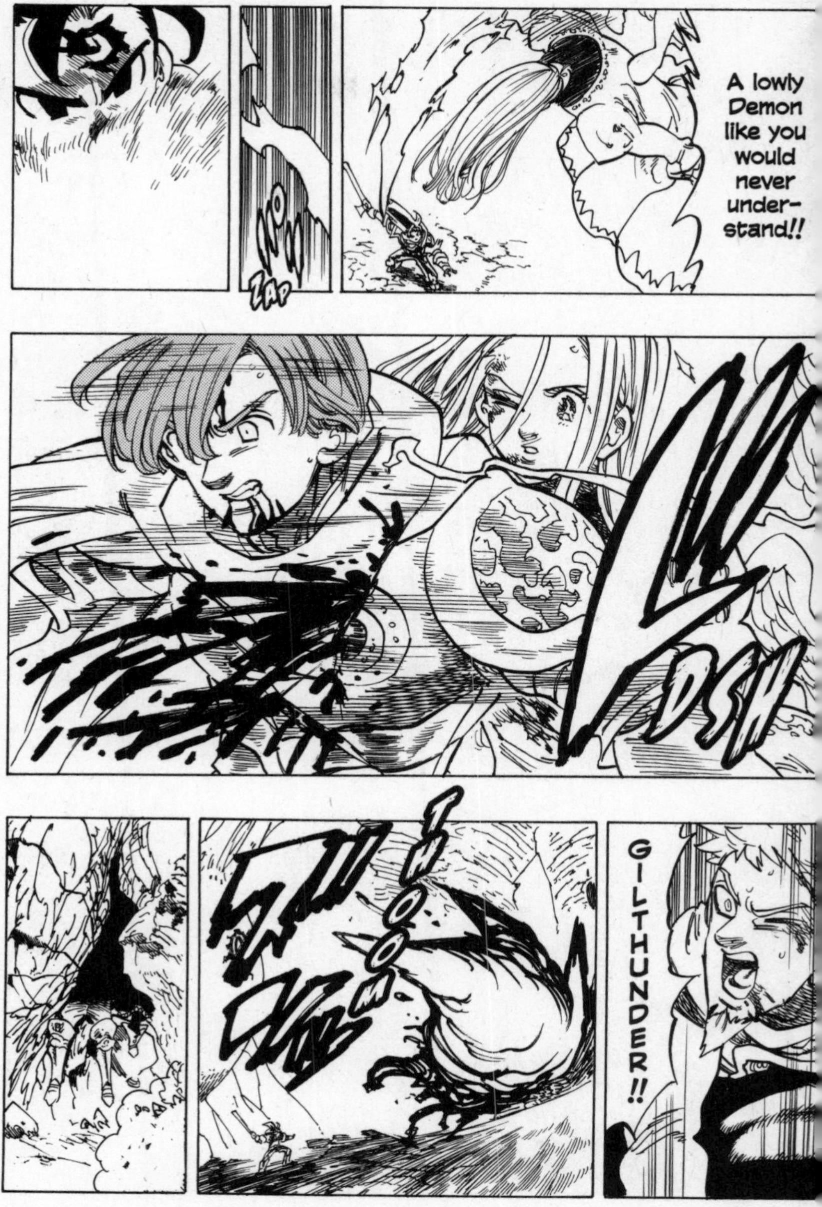
A lowly Demon like you would never under-stand!!
ZAP
DSH
GILTHUNDER!!
THOOM

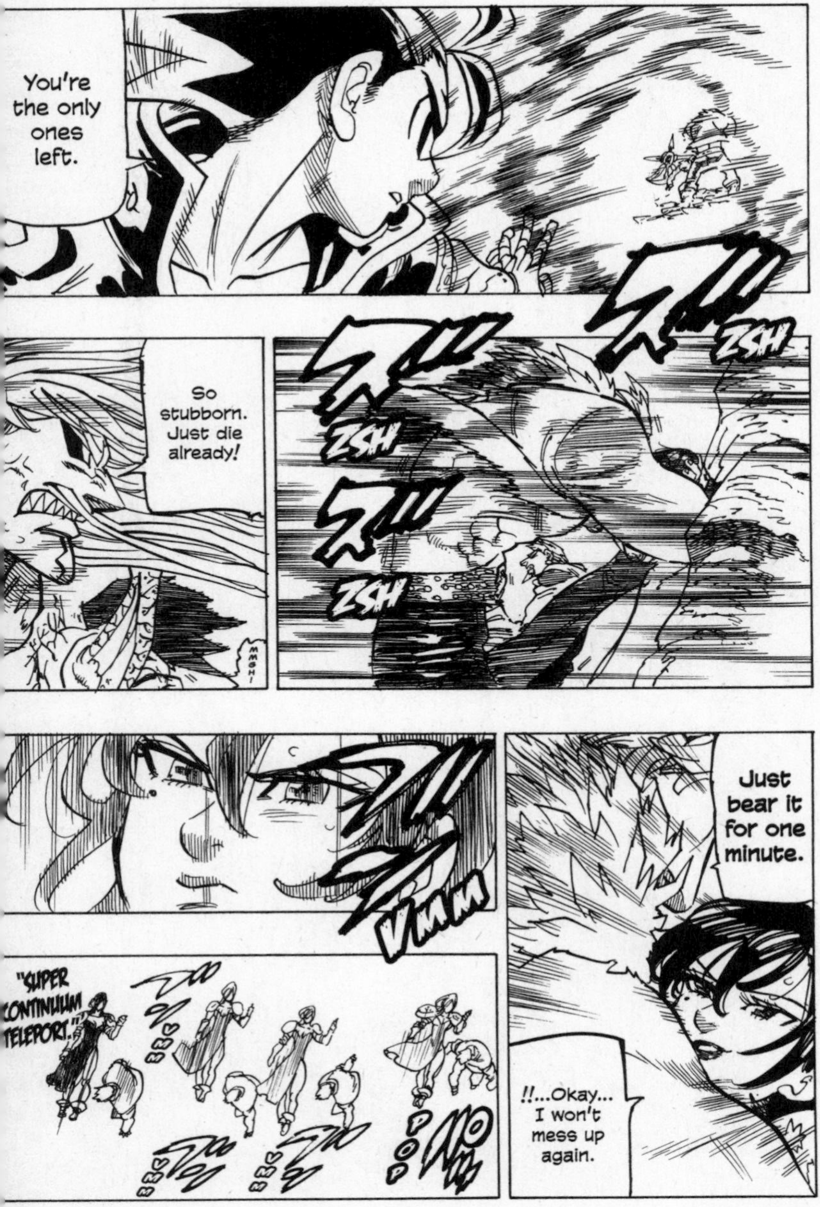
You're the only ones left.
ZSH
ZSH
ZSH
So stubborn. Just die already!
MMSH!
Just bear it for one minute.
!!...Okay... I won't mess up again.
VMM
"SUPER CONTINUUM TELEPORT."
POP
POP

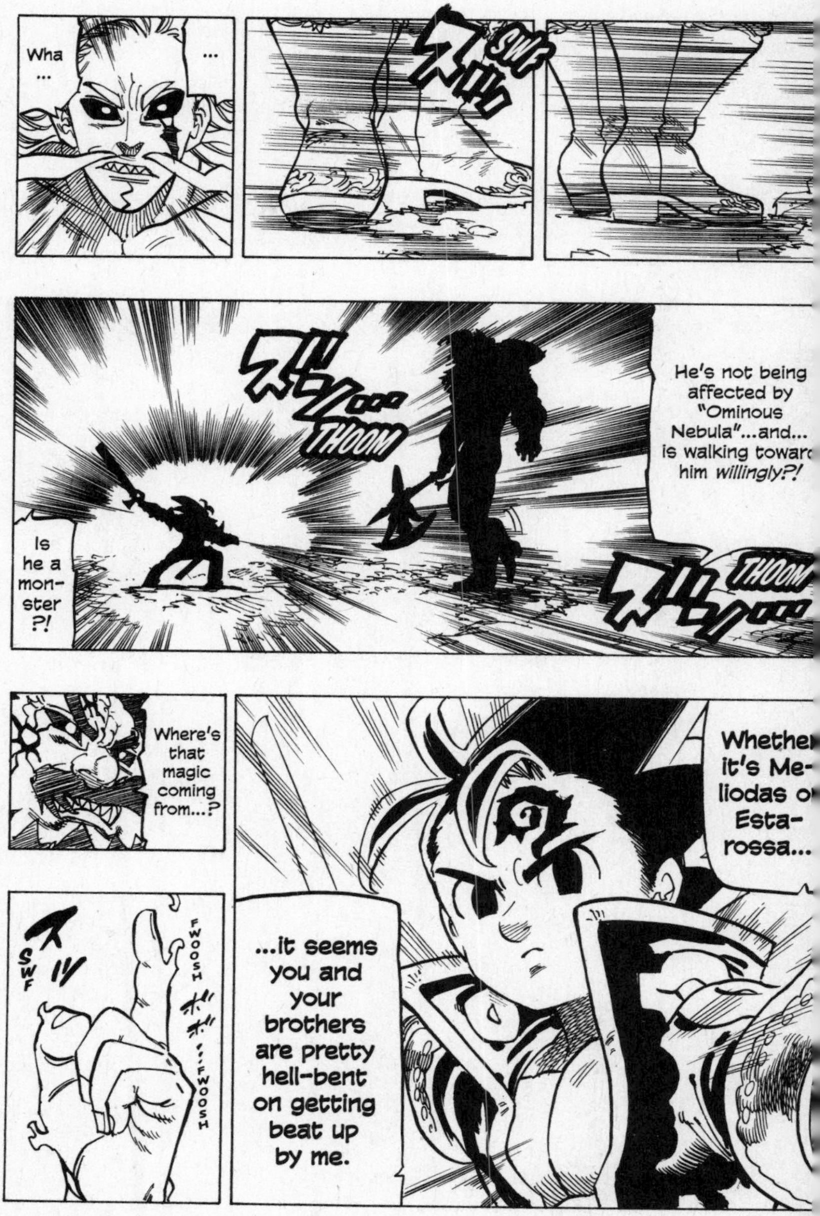
SWF
Wha ...
...
THOOM
He's not being affected by "Ominous Nebula"...and... is walking towar him *willingly?!*
THOOM
Is he a monster?!
Whethe it's Me-liodas o Esta-rossa...
...it seems you and your brothers are pretty hell-bent on getting beat up by me.
Where's that magic coming from...?
SWF
FWOOSH
...FWOOSH

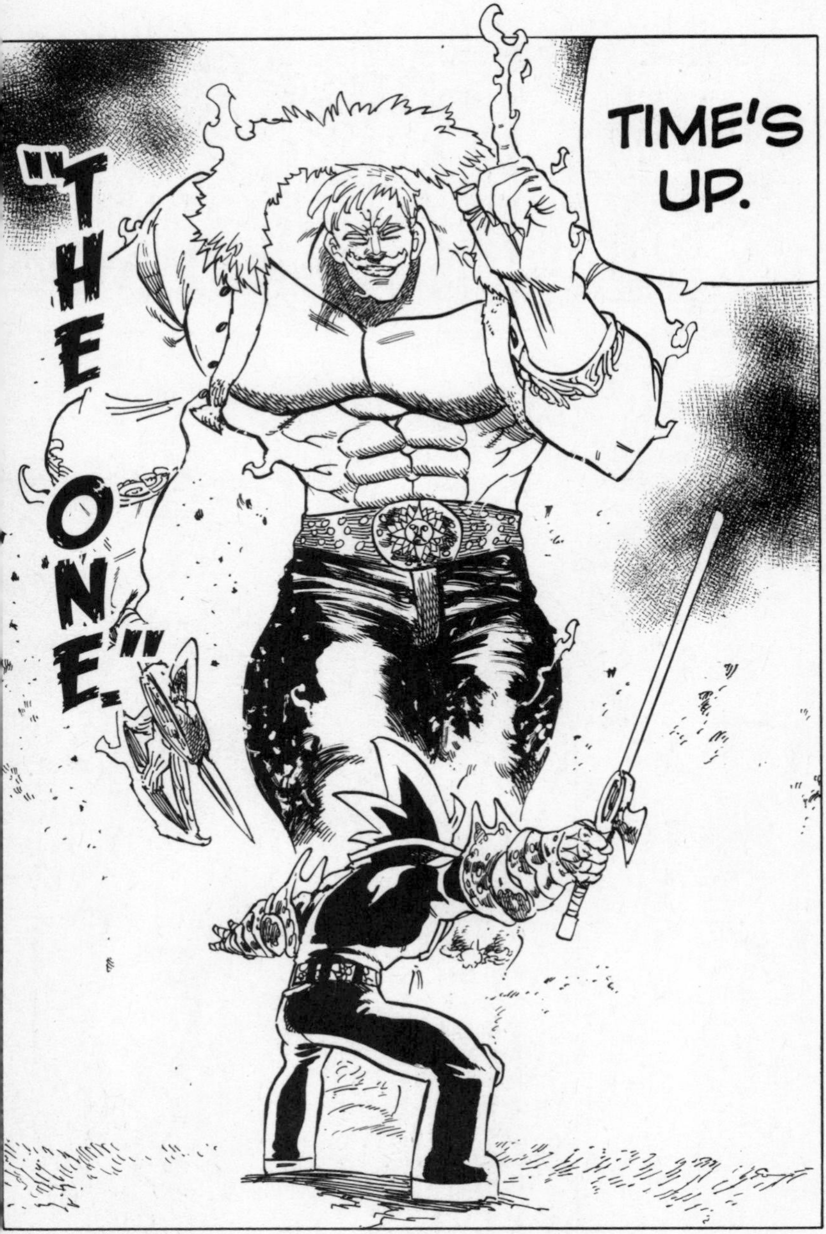
TIME'S UP.
"THE ONE"

THE SEVEN DEADLY SINS

Chapter 289 - Pride Vs. Piety

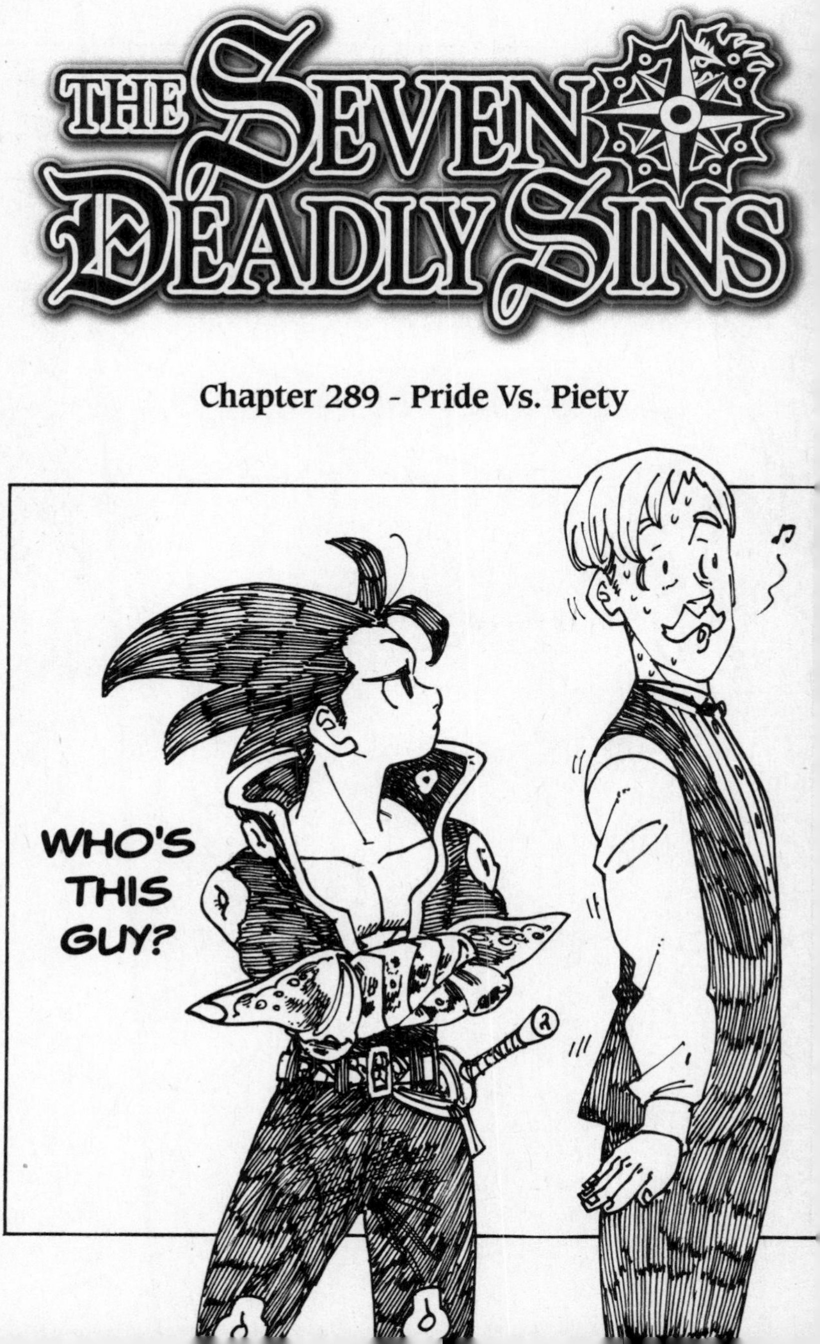
WHO'S THIS GUY?

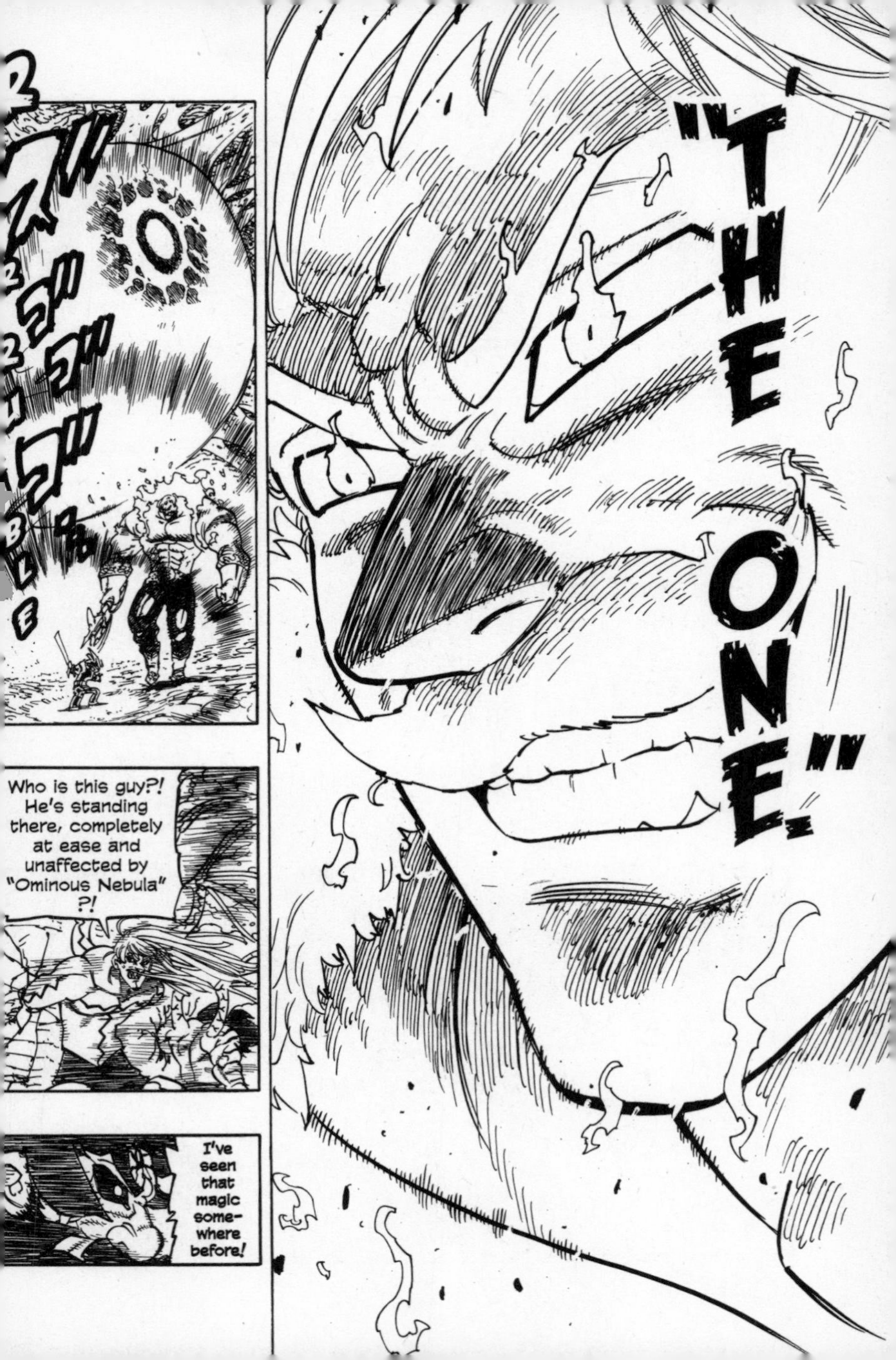
"THE ONE"
Who is this guy?! He's standing there, completely at ease and unaffected by "Ominous Nebula" ?!
I've seen that magic some-where before!

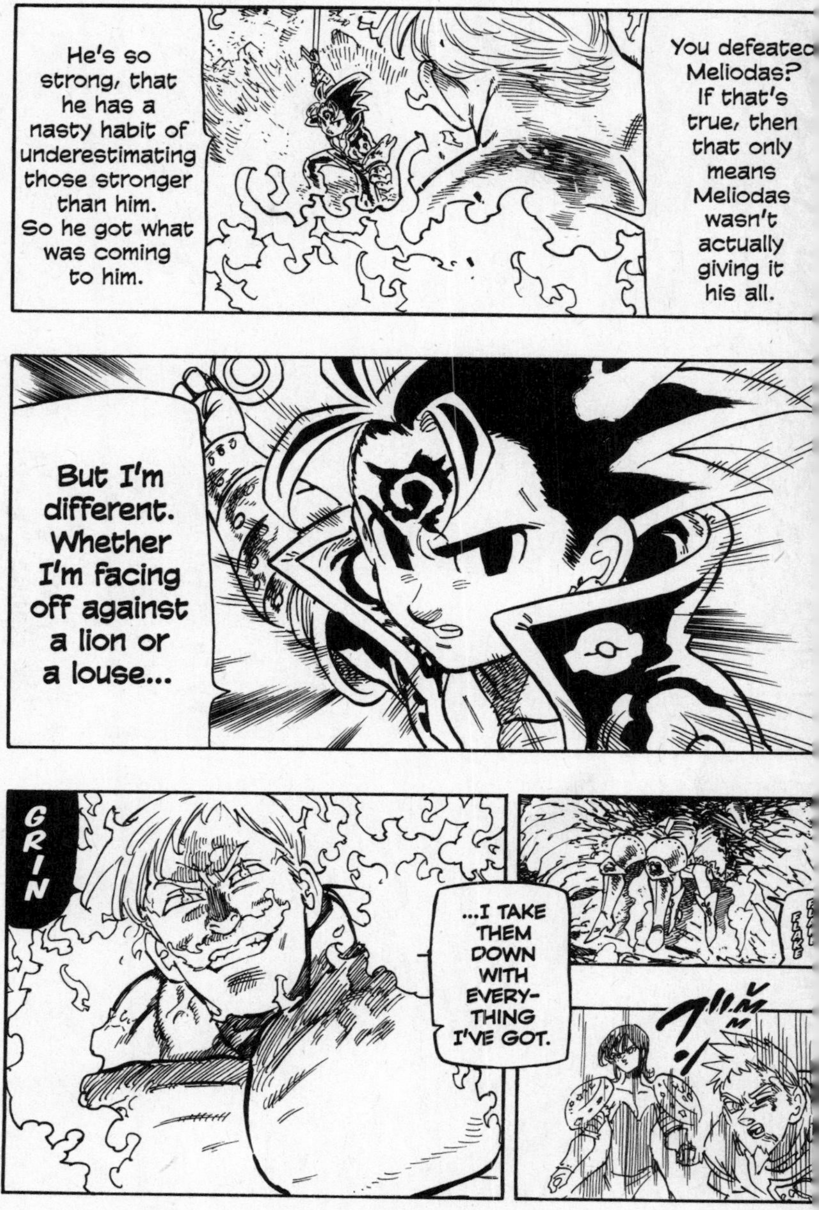
You defeated Meliodas? If that's true, then that only means Meliodas wasn't actually giving it his all.
He's so strong, that he has a nasty habit of underestimating those stronger than him. So he got what was coming to him.
But I'm different. Whether I'm facing off against a lion or a louse...
FLAKE
GRIN
...I TAKE THEM DOWN WITH EVERYTHING I'VE GOT.

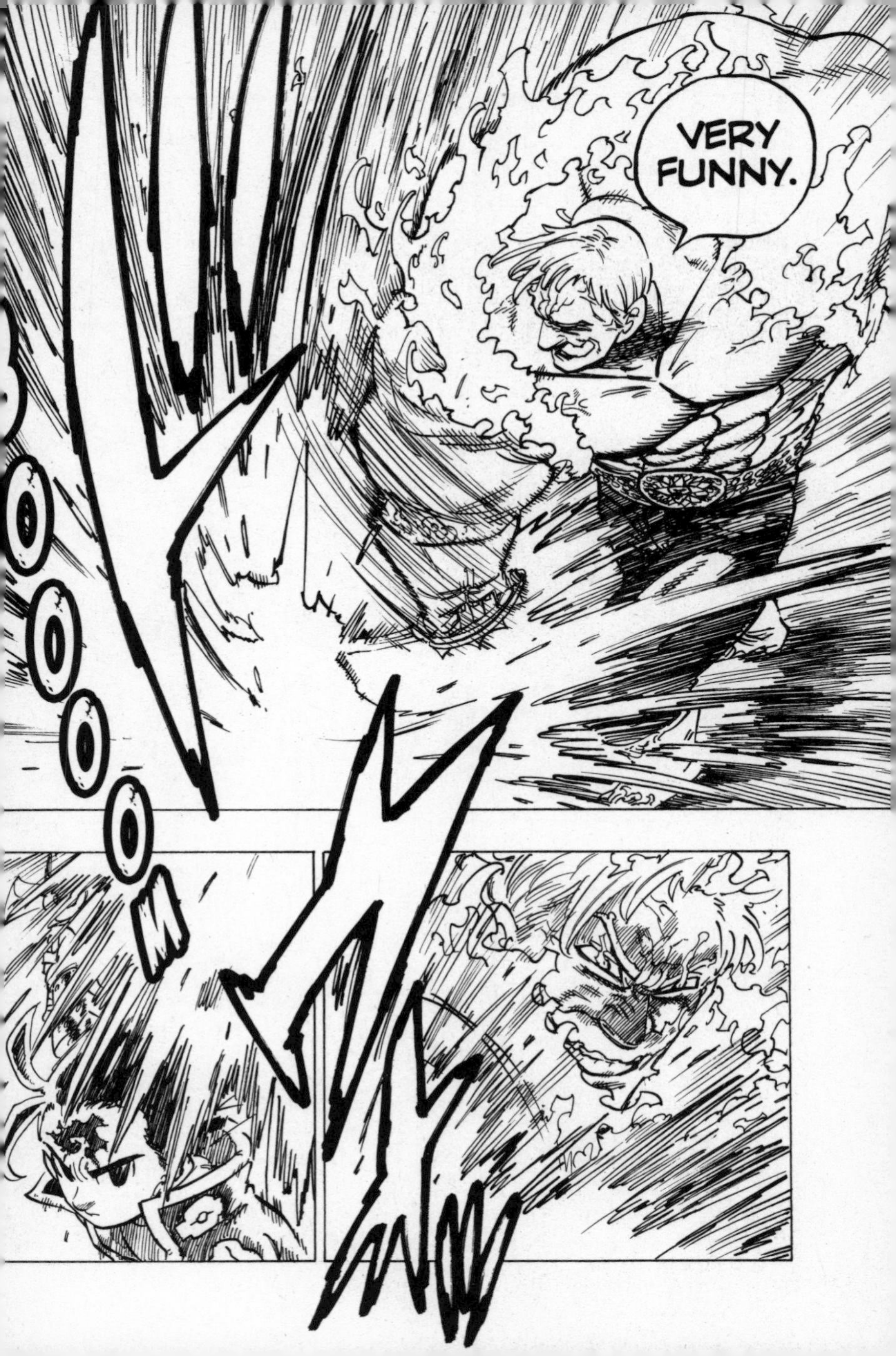
VERY FUNNY.

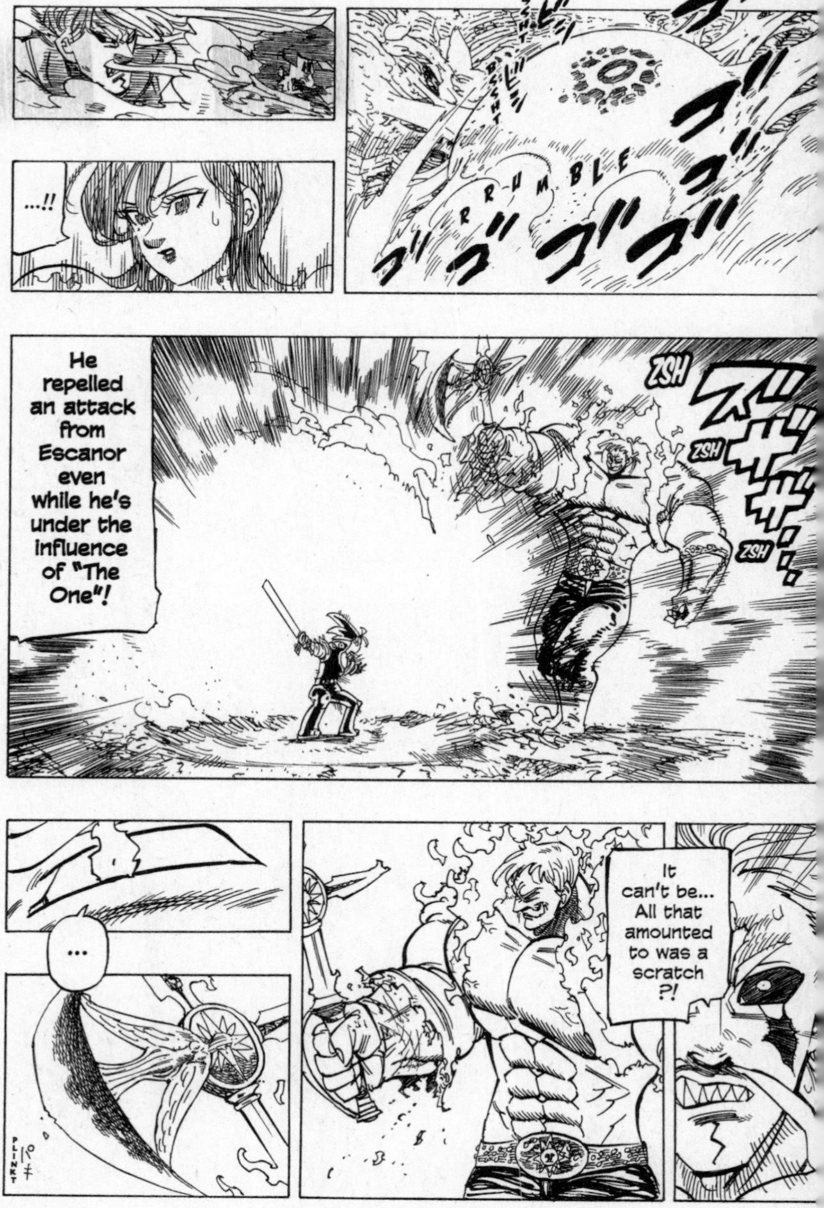
BISHT BISHT
RRUMBLE
...!!
ZSH ZSH ZSH
He repelled an attack from Escanor even while he's under the influence of "The One"!
It can't be... All that amounted to was a scratch?!
...
PLINKT

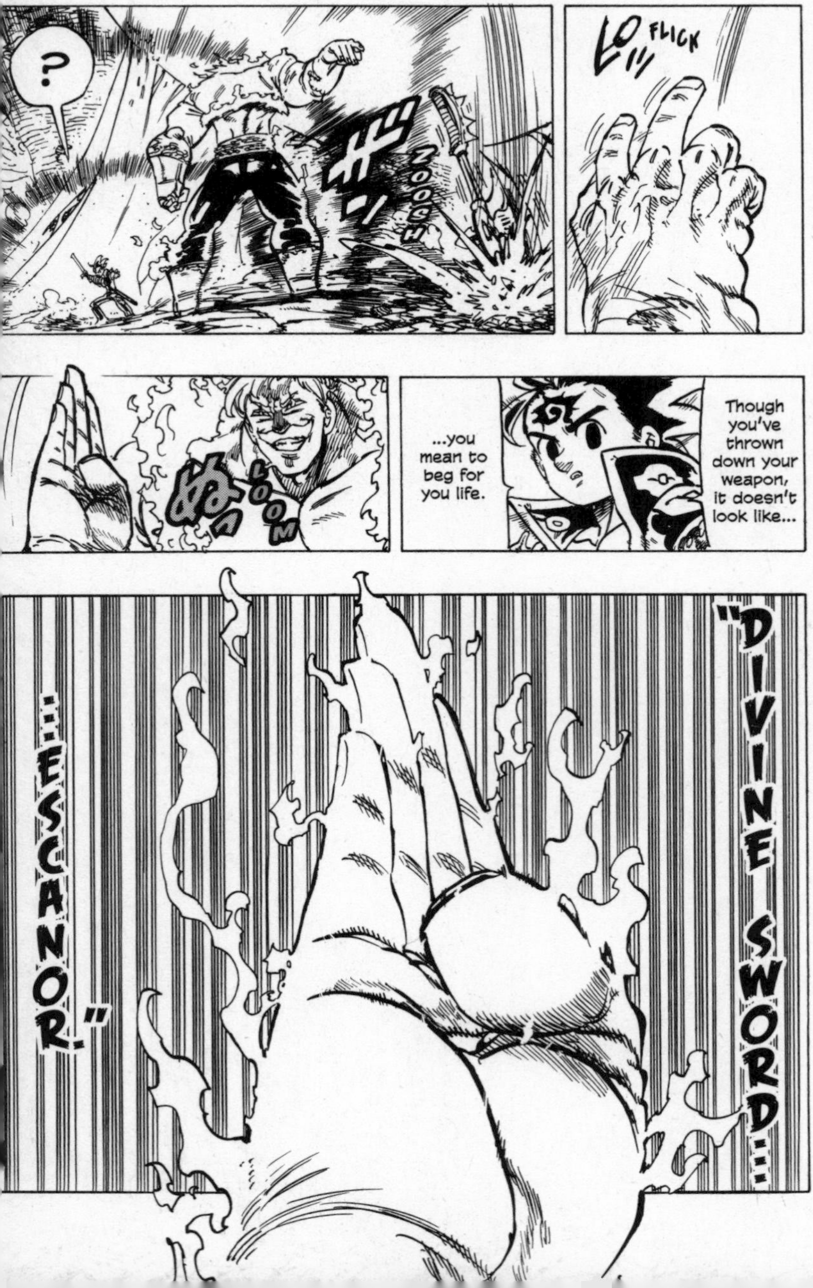
FLICK
?
ZOOSH
Though you've thrown down your weapon, it doesn't look like...
...you mean to beg for you life.
LOOOM
"DIVINE SWORD...
...ESCANOR."

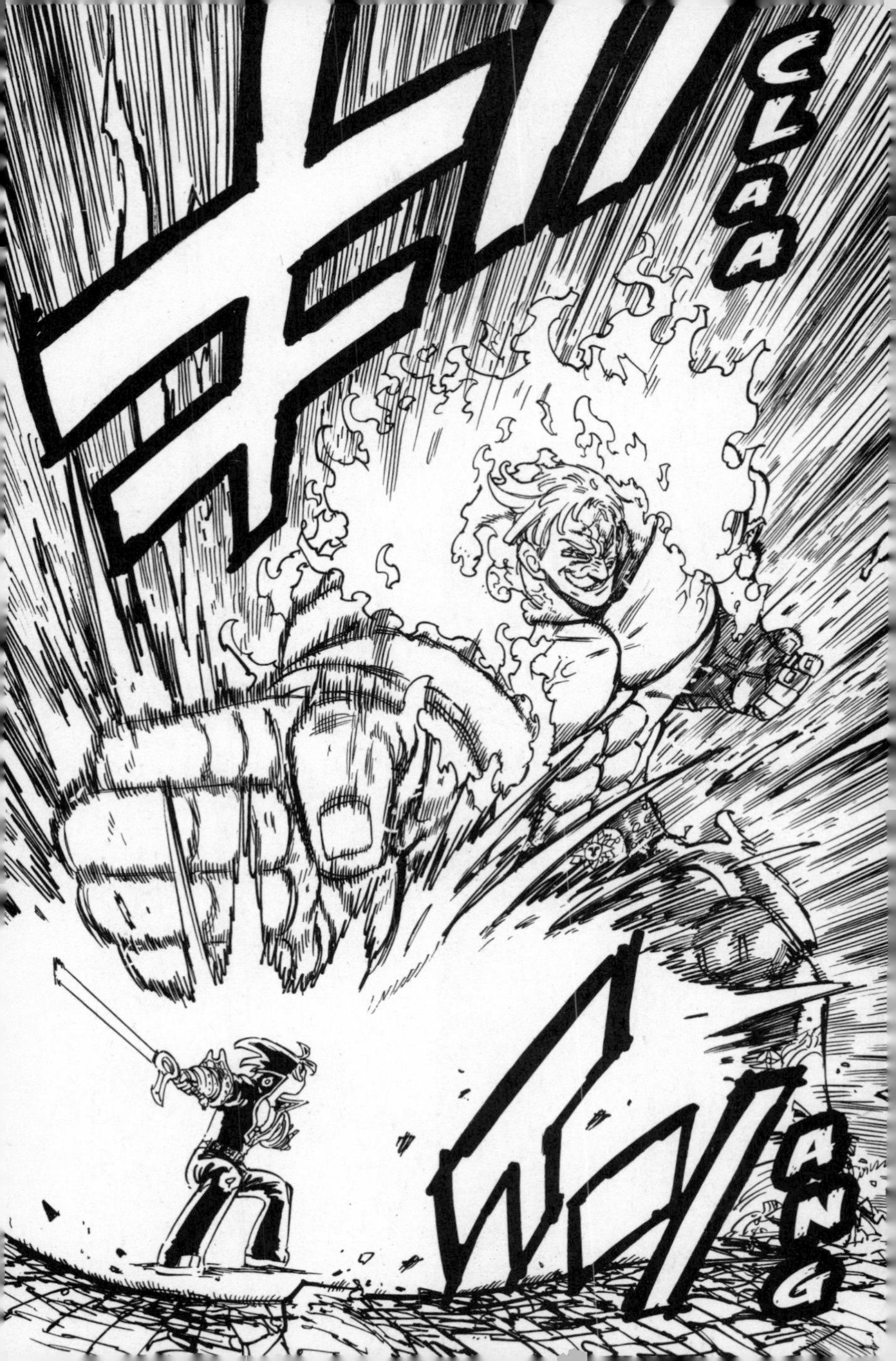
CLAA
ANG

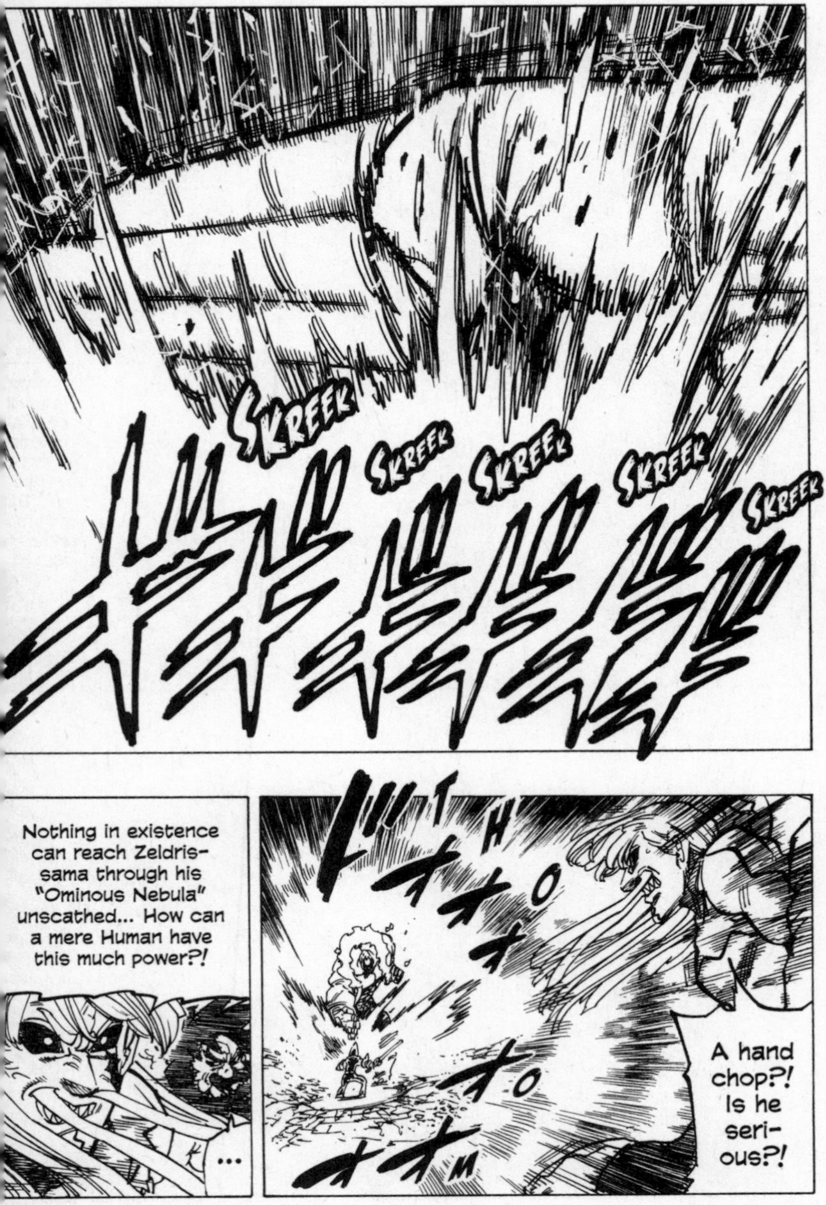
SKREEK
SKREEK
SKREEK
SKREEK
SKREEK
THOOM
A hand chop?! Is he seri-ous?!
Nothing in existence can reach Zeldris-sama through his "Ominous Nebula" unscathed... How can a mere Human have this much power?!
...

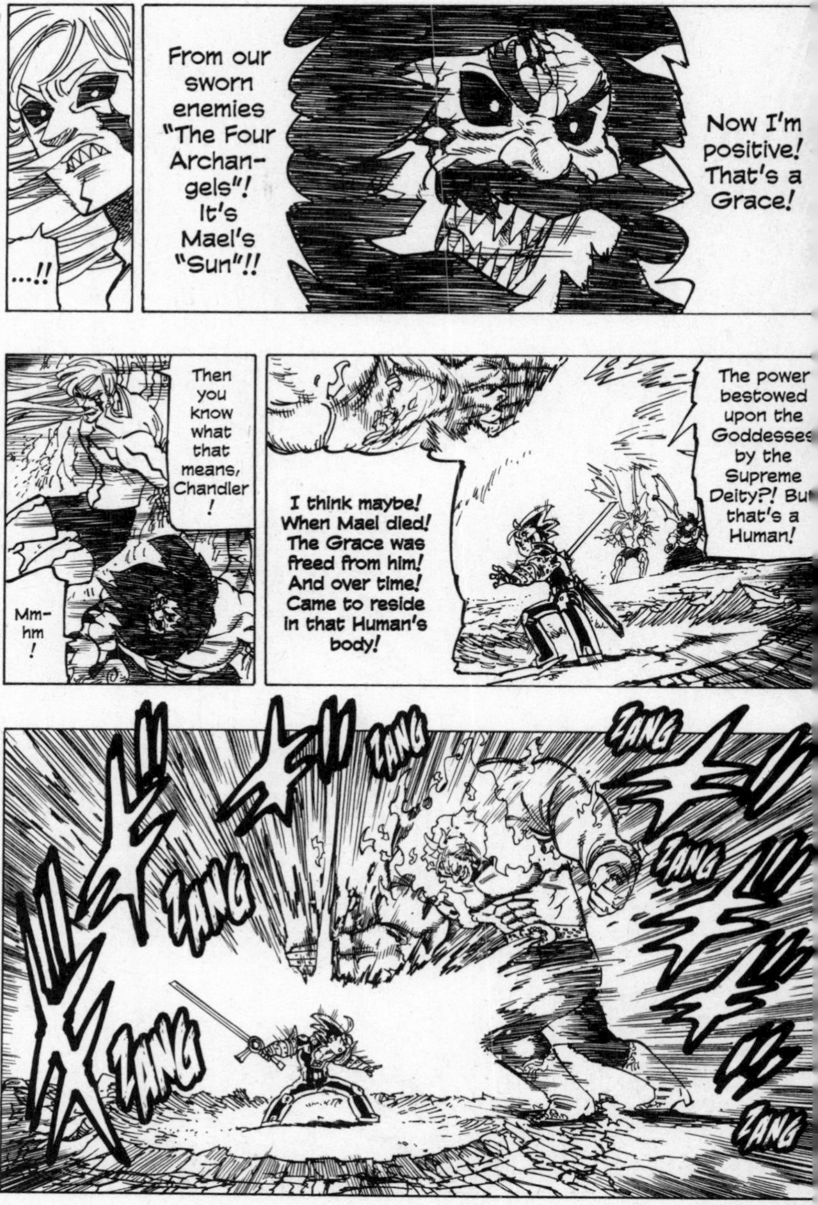
Now I'm positive! That's a Grace!
From our sworn enemies "The Four Archangels"! It's Mael's "Sun"!!
...!!
The power bestowed upon the Goddesses by the Supreme Deity?! Bu that's a Human!
I think maybe! When Mael died! The Grace was freed from him! And over time! Came to reside in that Human's body!
Then you know what that means, Chandler!
Mm-hm!
ZANG
ZANG
ZANG
ZANG
ZANG
ZANG

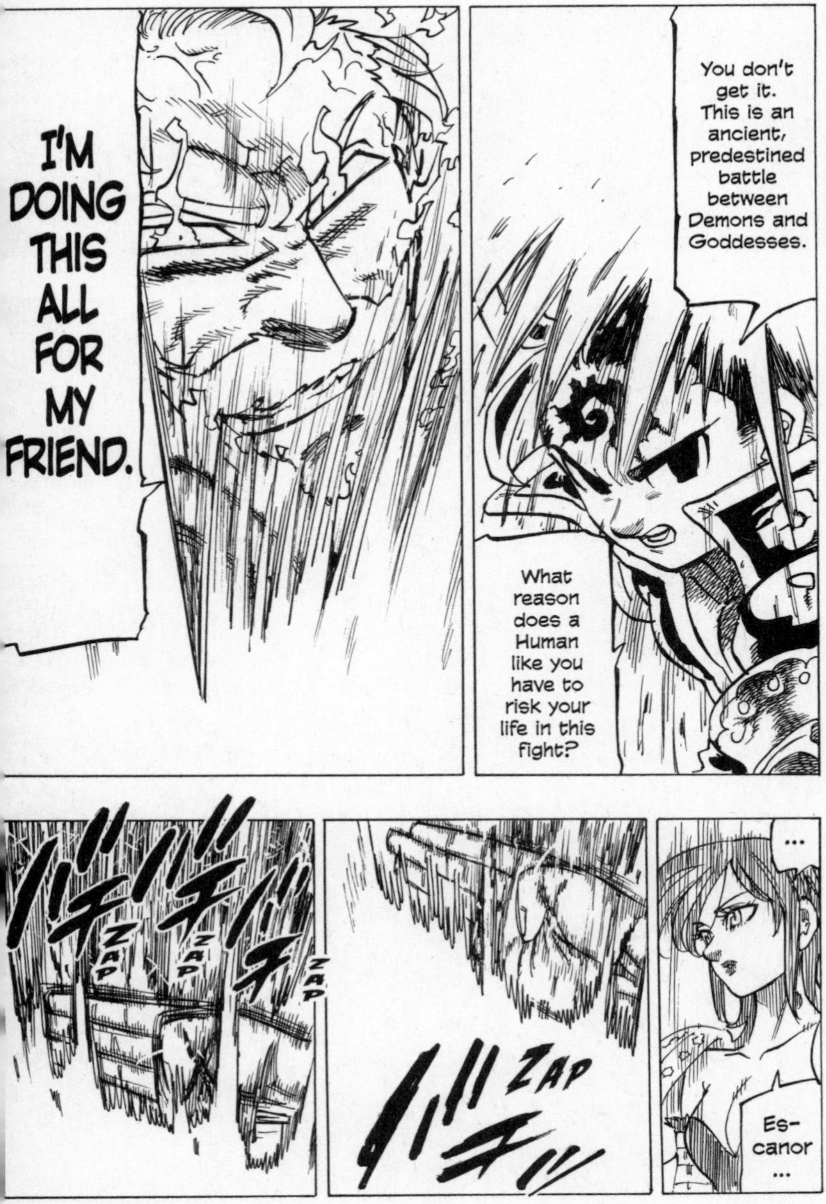
You don't get it. This is an ancient, predestined battle between Demons and Goddesses.
What reason does a Human like you have to risk your life in this fight?
I'M DOING THIS ALL FOR MY FRIEND.
...
Es-canor ...
ZAP
ZAP
ZAP
ZAP

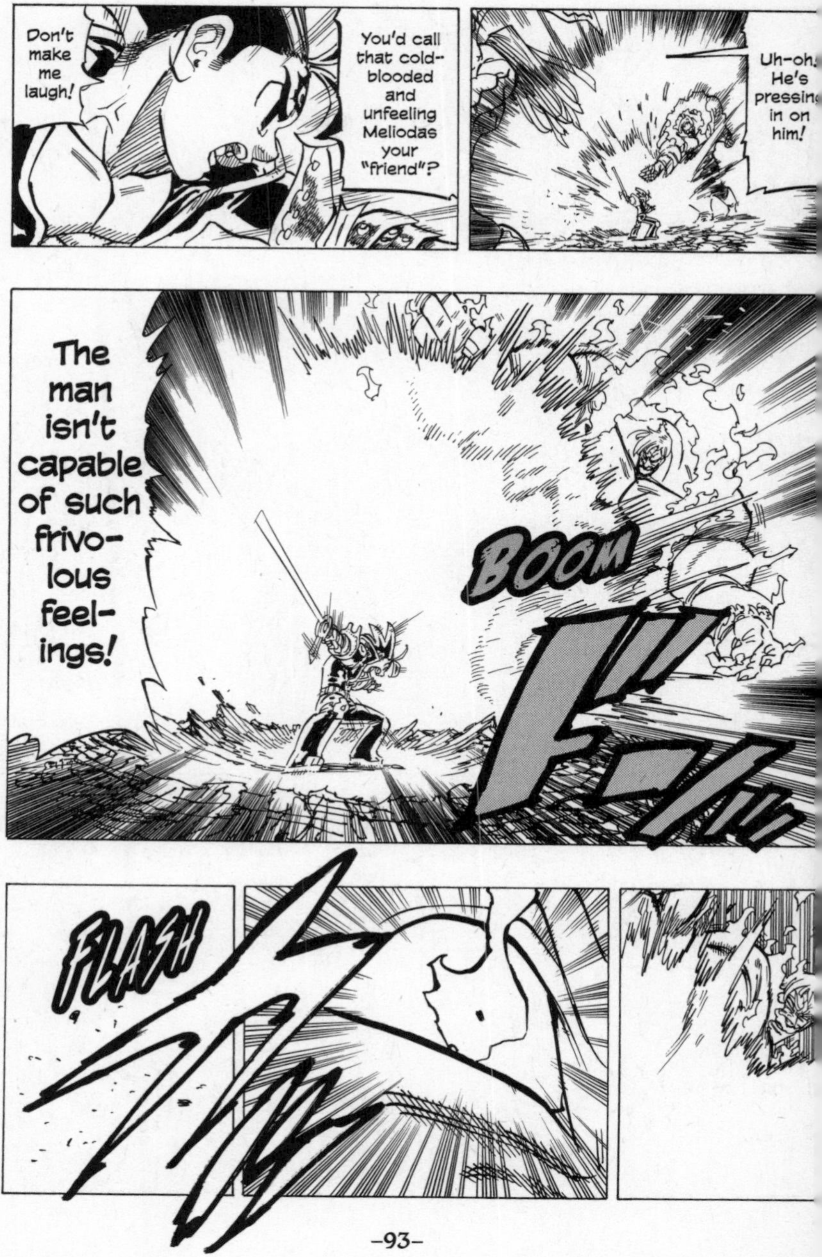
Uh-oh He's pressin in on him!
You'd call that cold-blooded and unfeeling Meliodas your "friend"?
Don't make me laugh!
The man isn't capable of such frivolous feelings!
BOOM
FLASH

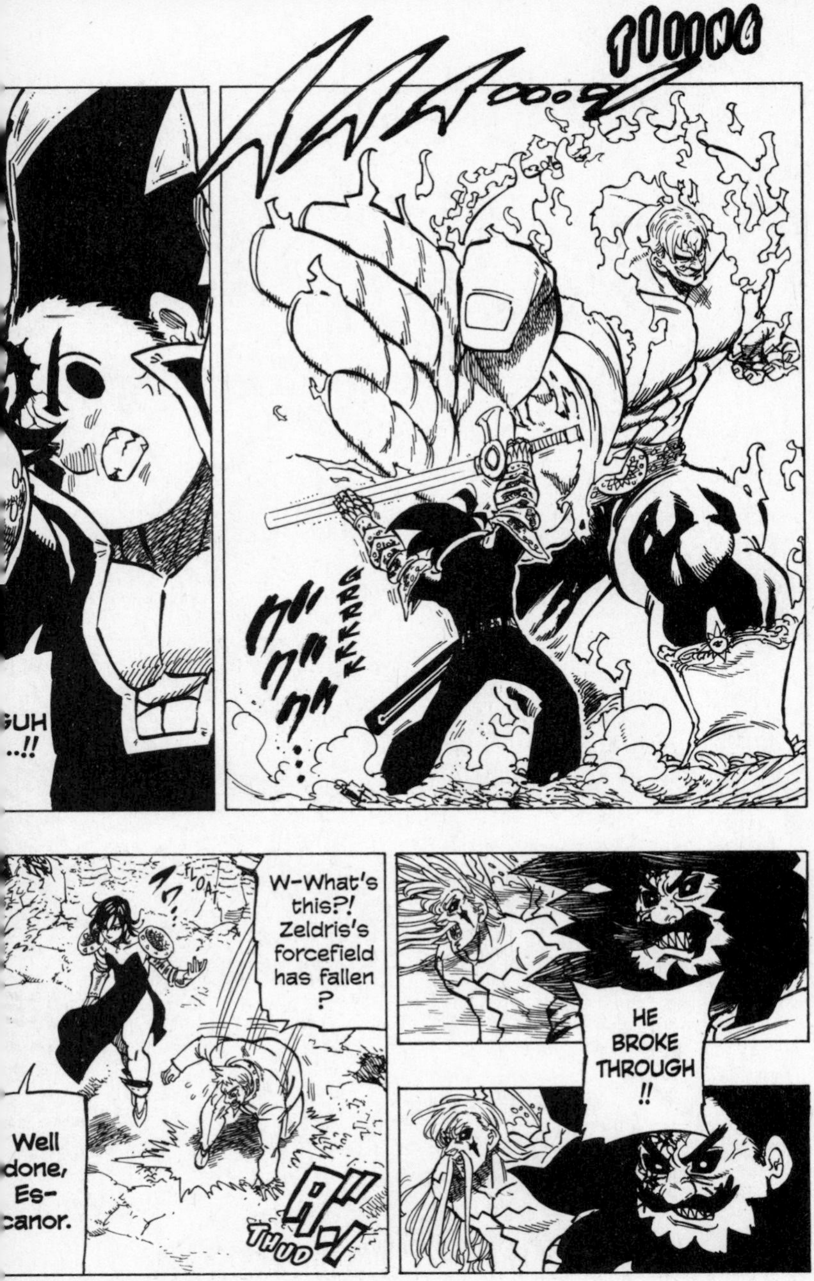
TIIING
KRRRRG
GUH ..!!
HE BROKE THROUGH !!
W-What's this?! Zeldris's forcefield has fallen ?
FLOAT
Well done, Es-canor.
THUD

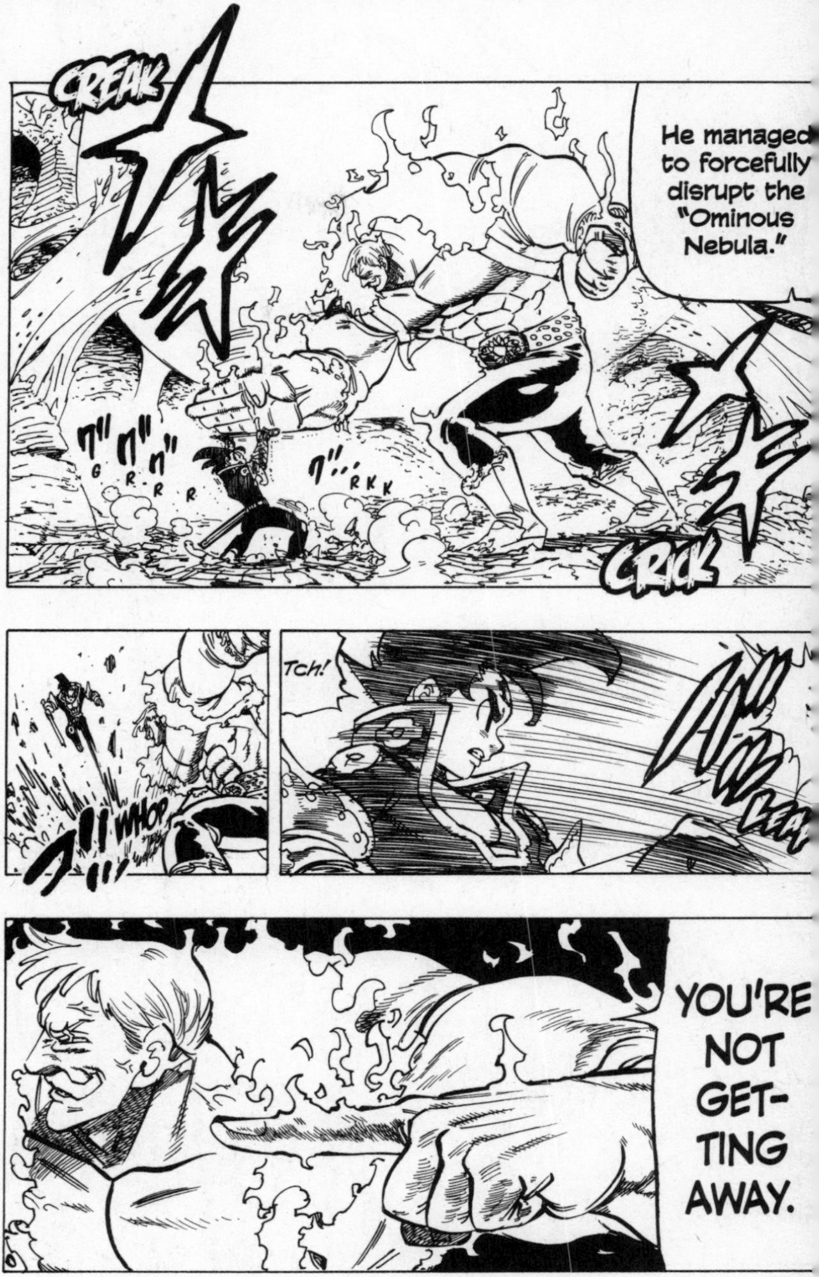
He managed to forcefully disrupt the "Ominous Nebula."
CREAK
CRICK
RKK
GRRR
Tch!
WHOP
YOU'RE NOT GET-TING AWAY.

"DIVINE SPEAR ESCANOR."

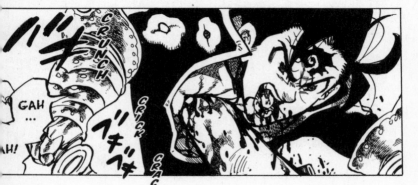

CRUNCH

GAH
...

AH!

CRICK

CRACK

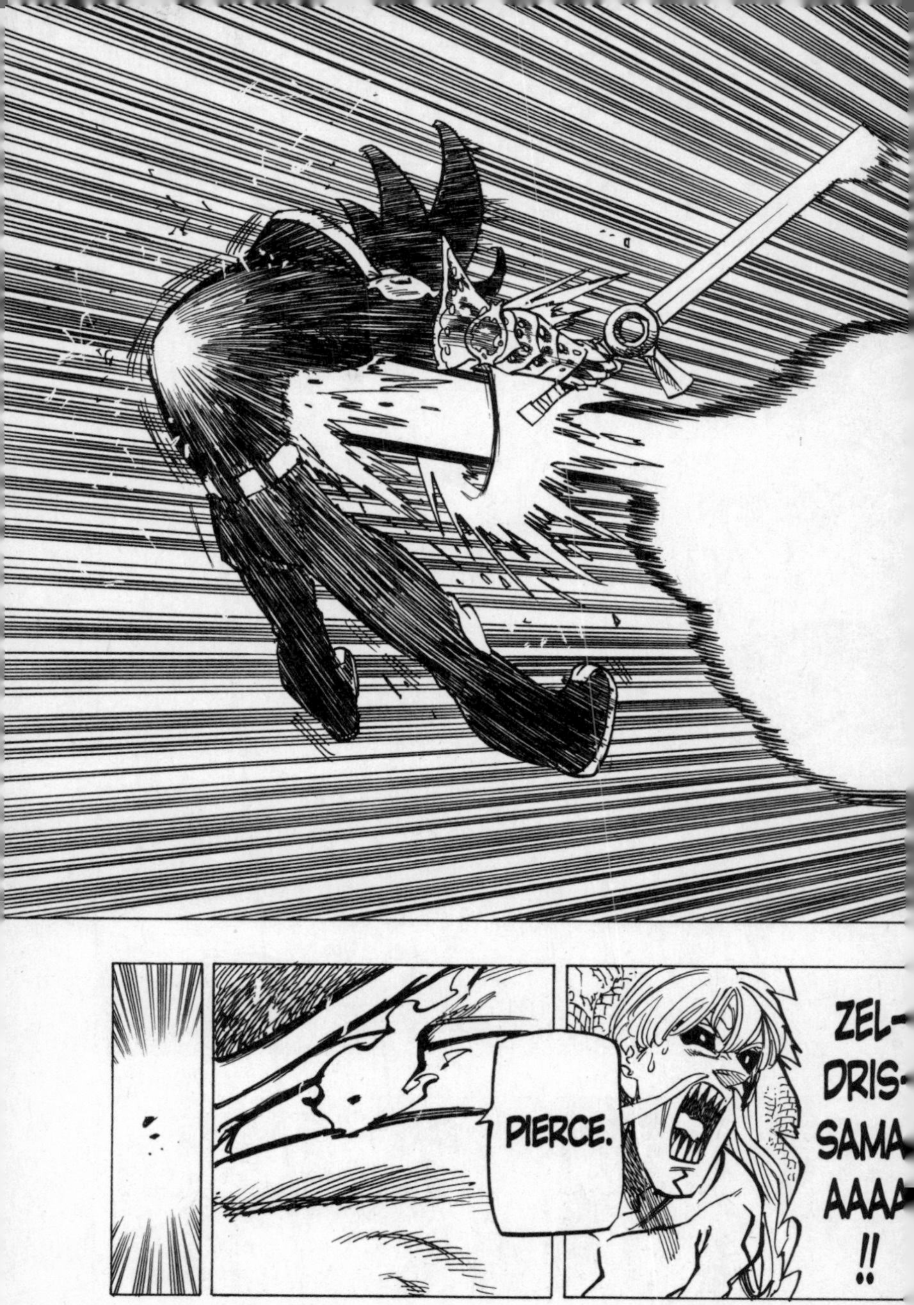
ZEL-DRIS-SAMAAAAA!!
PIERCE.

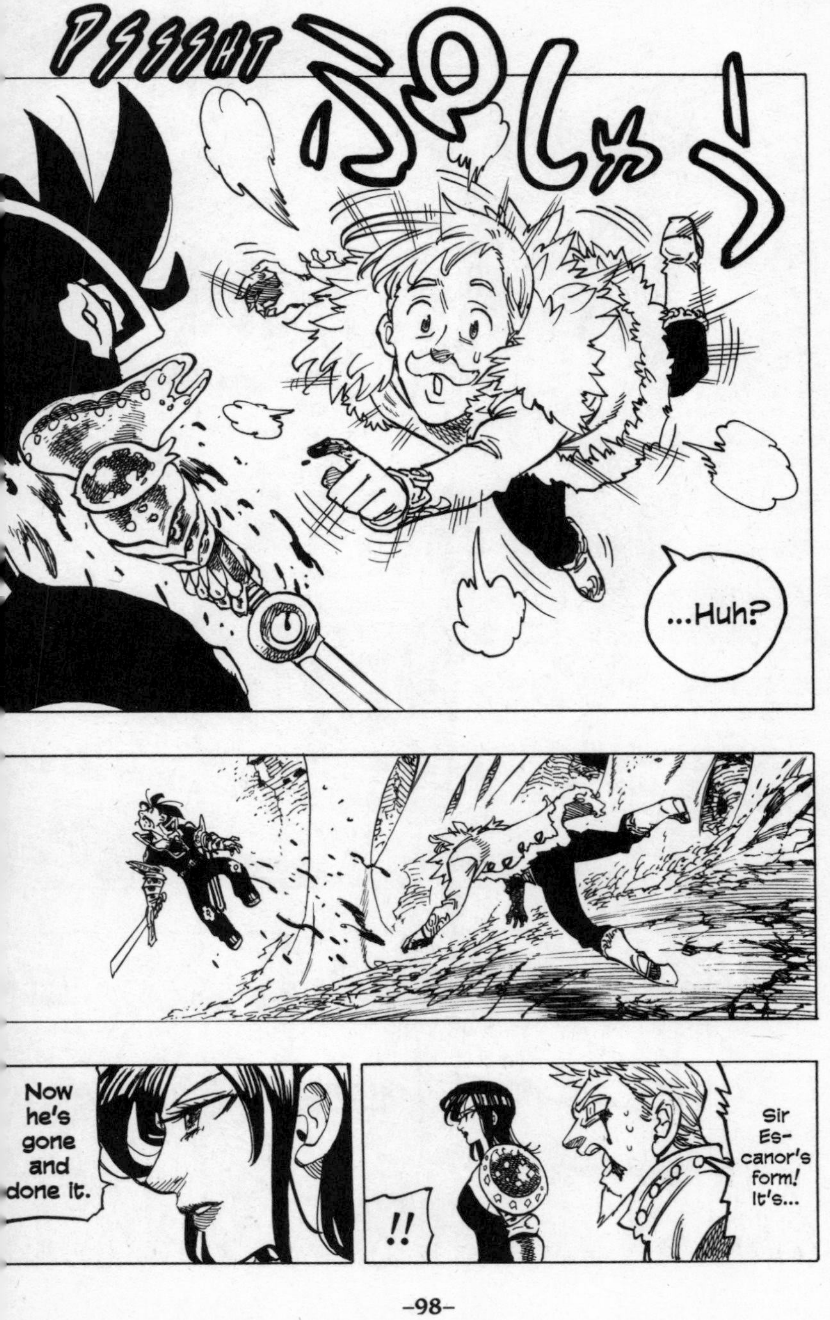
PSSSSHT
...Huh?
Sir Es-canor's form! It's...
!!
Now he's gone and done it.

GRIN

FLAP

"DARKNESS."

FSH

At that moment, Zeldris' two magic powers disappeared.

Because Escanor's one blow instantly knocked him out, forcing them to cease.

But the prince of the Demon World immediately came to.

It took a mere 0.8 seconds.

And from there...

...it'd take approximately one second for the "Demon Lord" to reactivate.

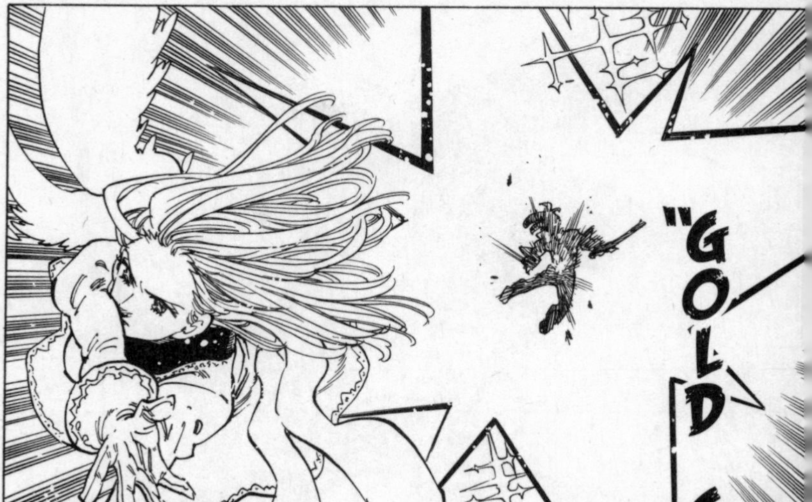
"GOLD SHINING."
FLASH
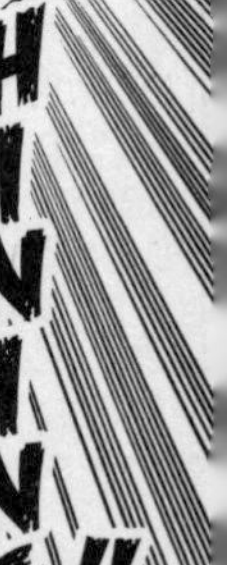
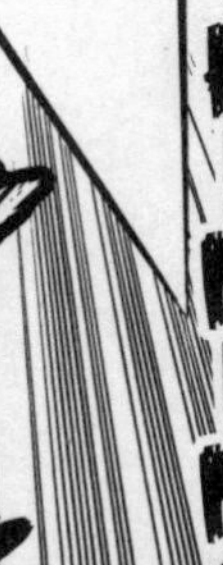
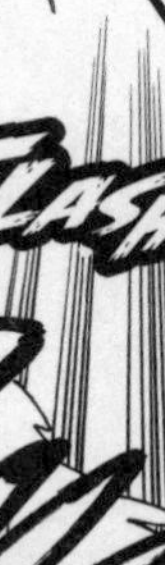
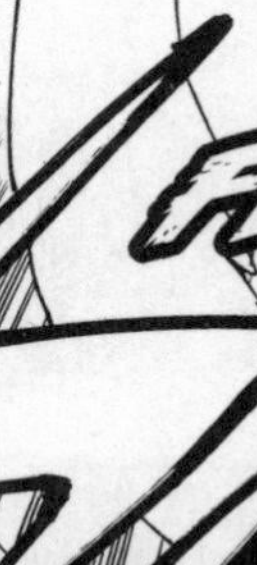
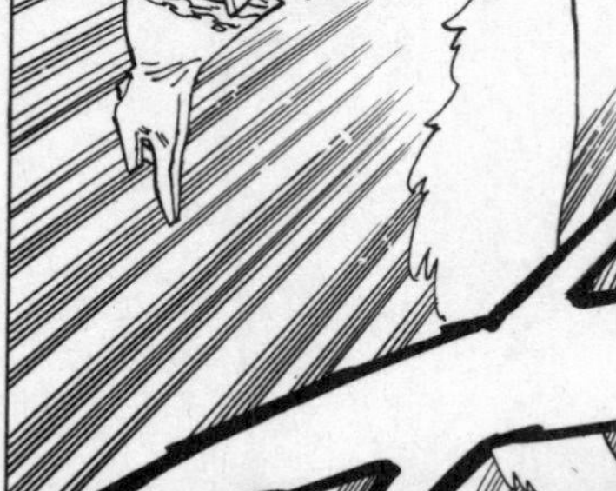

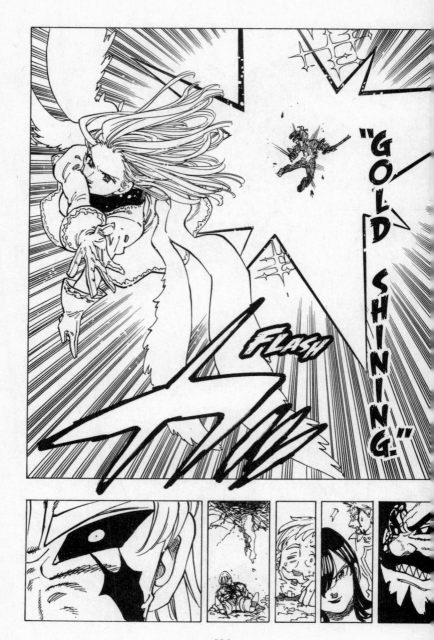

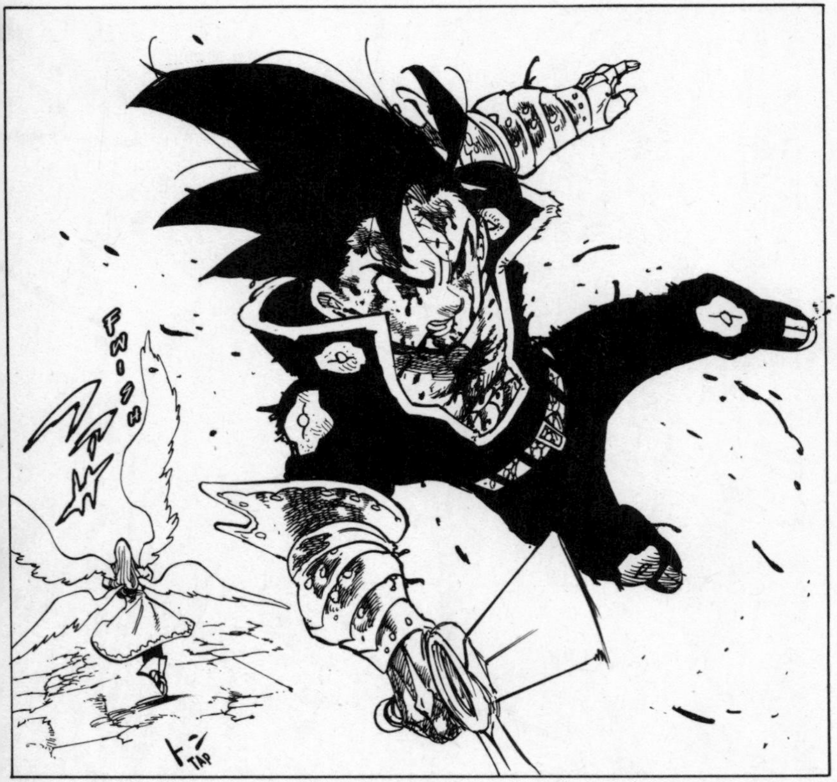
FWISH
TAP

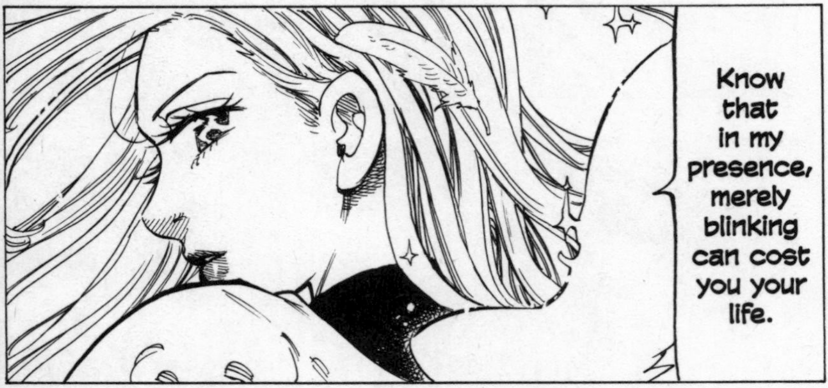
Know that in my presence, merely blinking can cost you your life.

Chapter 290 - Clever Little Grub

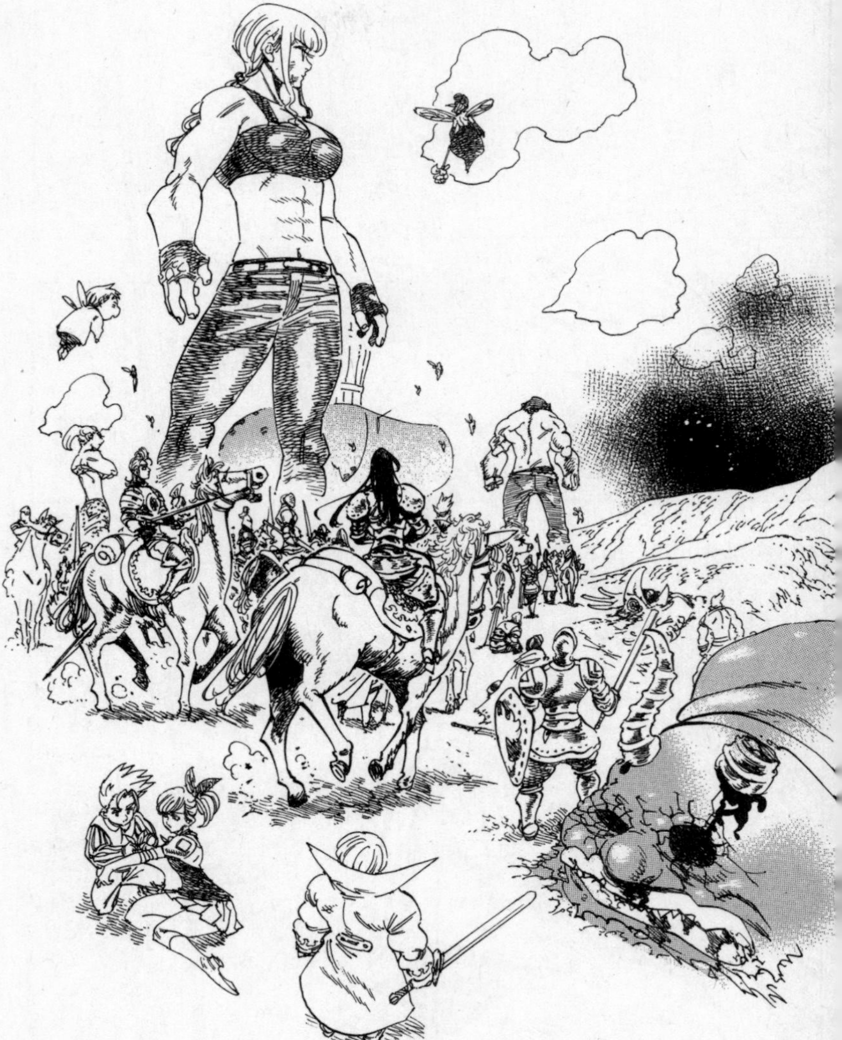

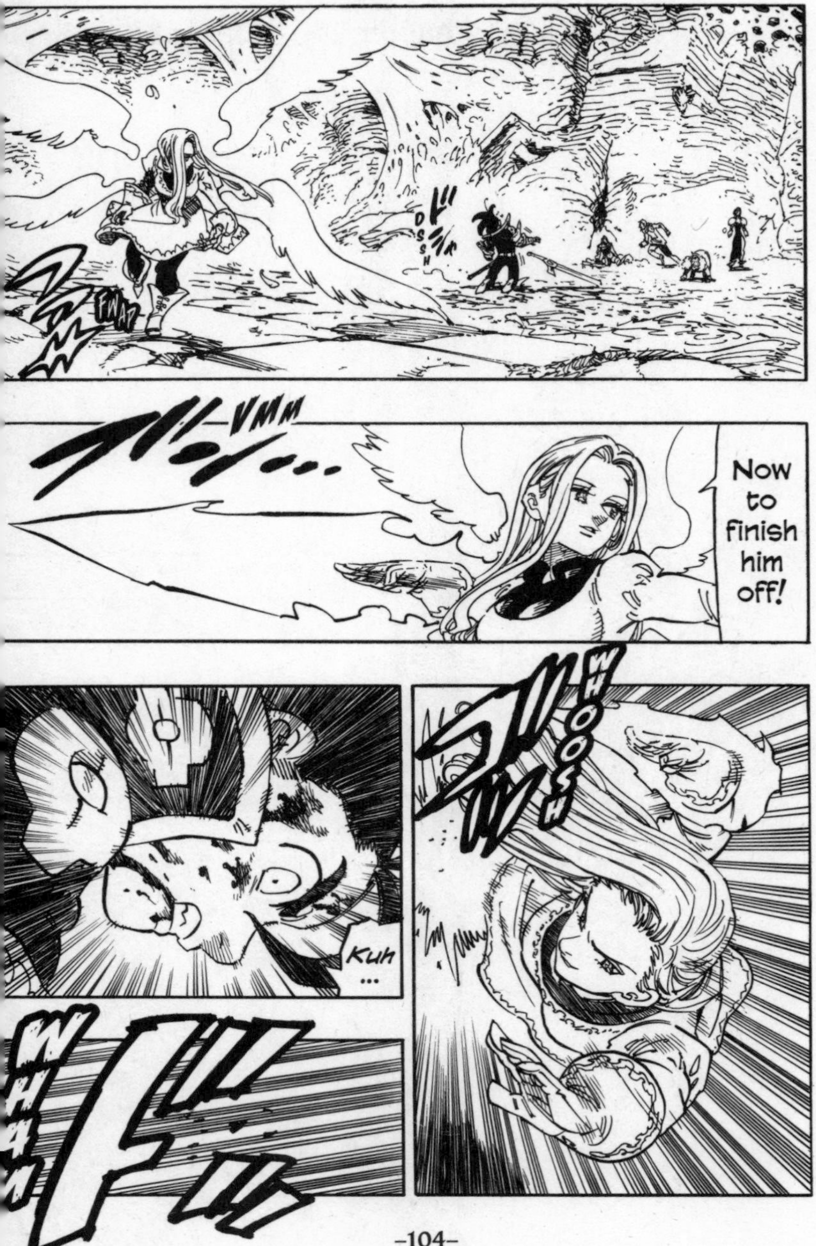
DSSH
FWAP
Now to finish him off!
VMM
WHOOOSH
Kuh...
WHAM

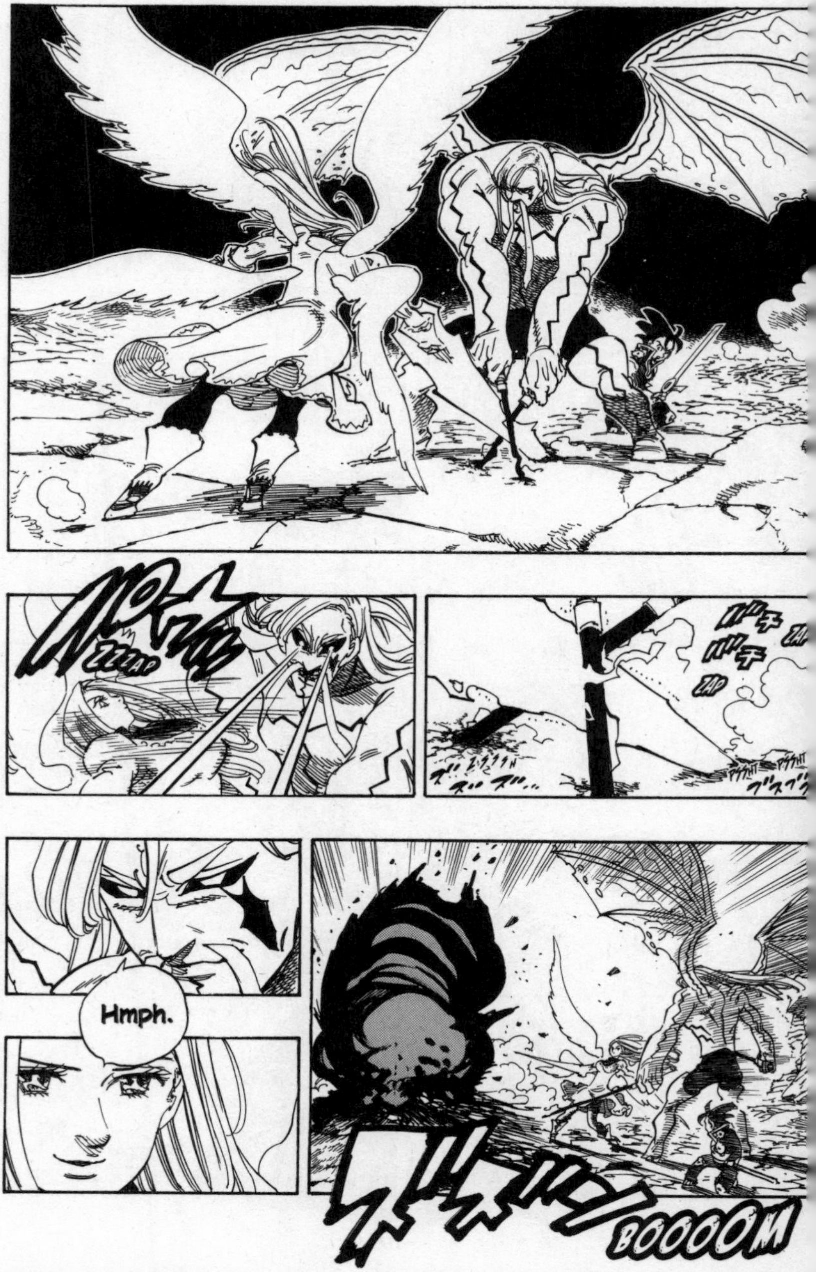
ZAP
ZAP
ZZZAP
BOOOOM
Hmph.

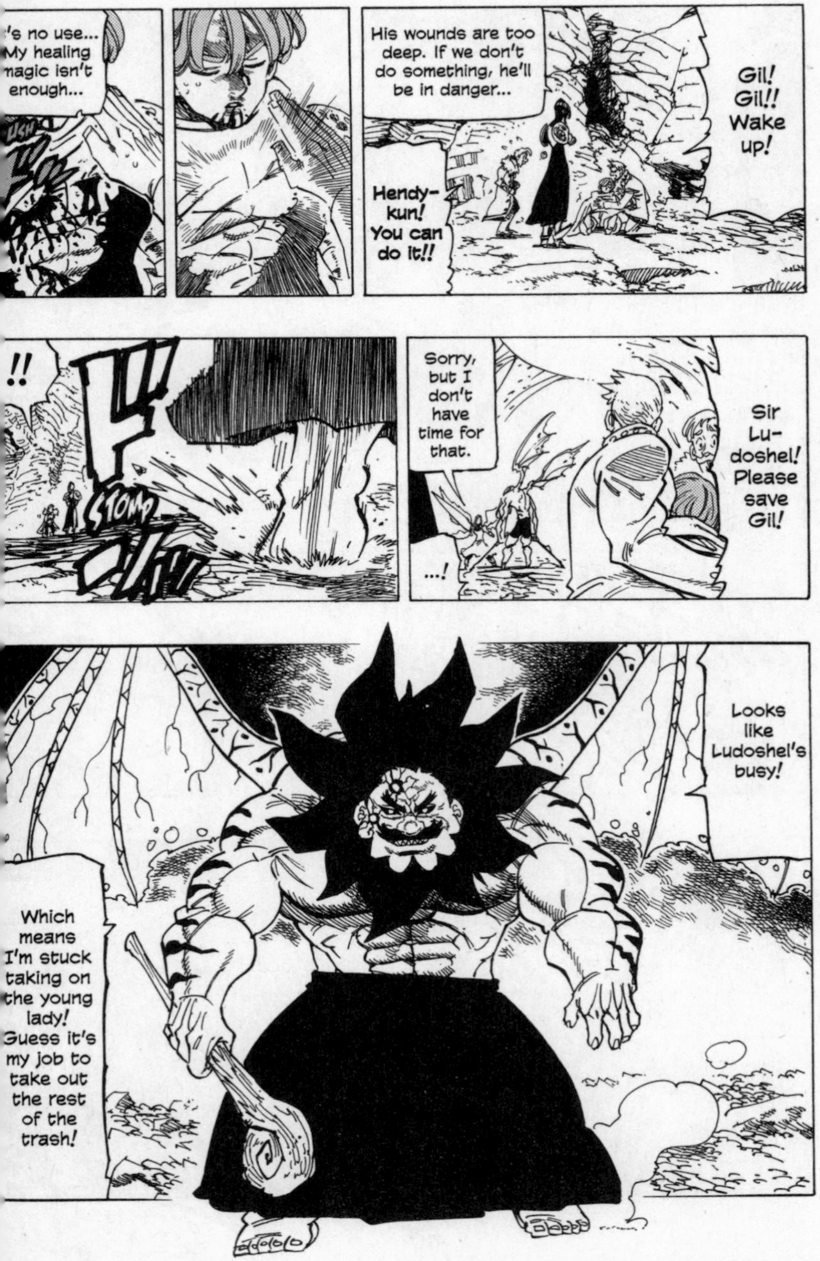
Gil! Gil!! Wake up!
His wounds are too deep. If we don't do something, he'll be in danger...
Hendy-kun! You can do it!!
's no use... My healing magic isn't enough...
Sir Ludoshel! Please save Gil!
Sorry, but I don't have time for that.
...!
!!
STOMP
Looks like Ludoshel's busy!
Which means I'm stuck taking on the young lady! Guess it's my job to take out the rest of the trash!

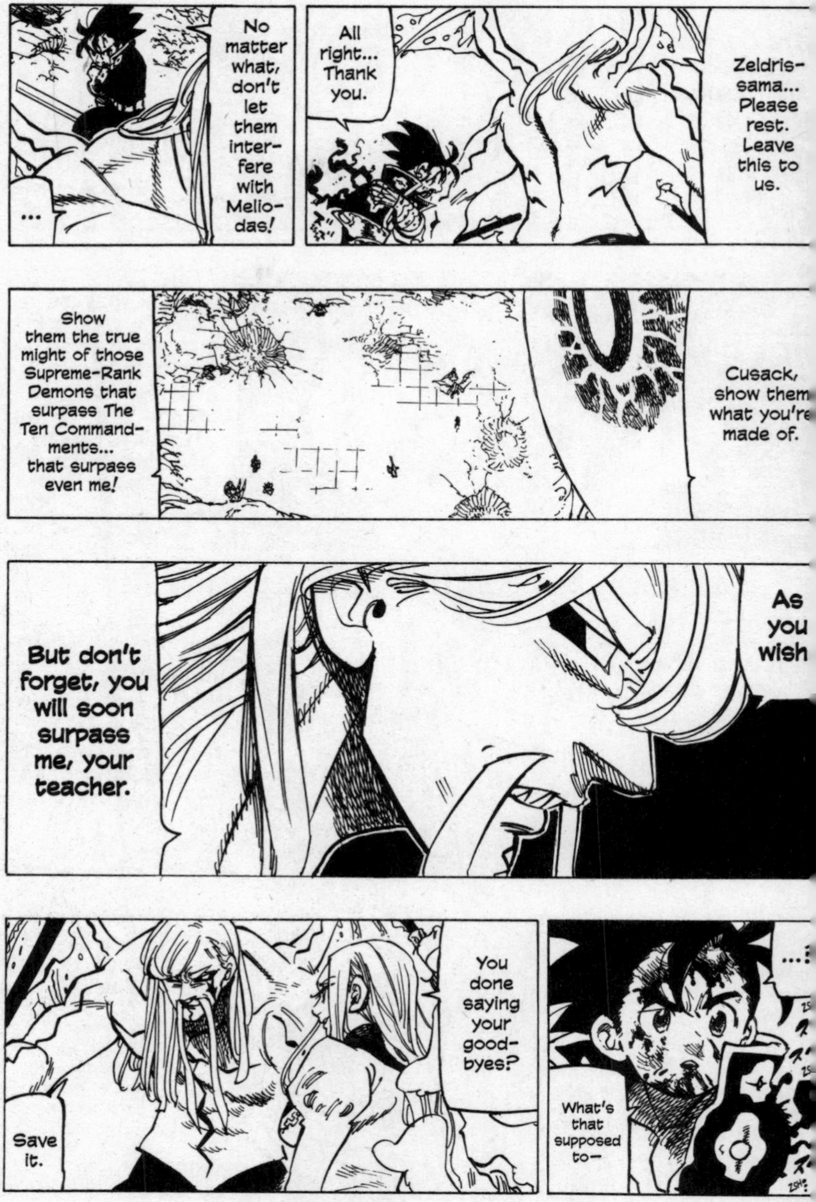
Zeldris-sama... Please rest. Leave this to us.
All right... Thank you.
No matter what, don't let them interfere with Meliodas!
...
Cusack, show them what you'r made of.
Show them the true might of those Supreme-Rank Demons that surpass The Ten Commandments... that surpass even me!
As you wish
But don't forget, you will soon surpass me, your teacher.
...!
What's that supposed to—
You done saying your goodbyes?
Save it.

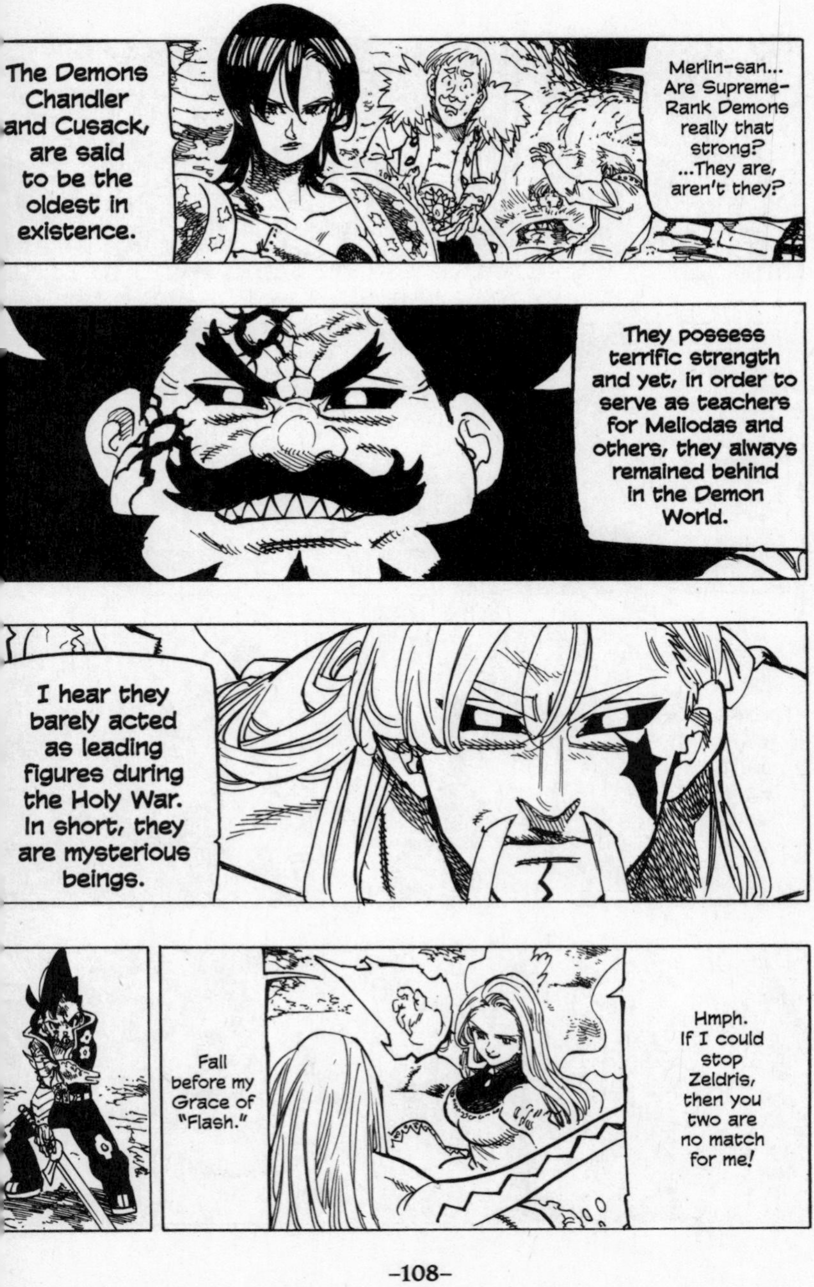
Merlin-san... Are Supreme-Rank Demons really that strong? ...They are, aren't they?
The Demons Chandler and Cusack, are said to be the oldest in existence.
They possess terrific strength and yet, in order to serve as teachers for Meliodas and others, they always remained behind in the Demon World.
I hear they barely acted as leading figures during the Holy War. In short, they are mysterious beings.
Hmph. If I could stop Zeldris, then you two are no match for me!
Fall before my Grace of "Flash."

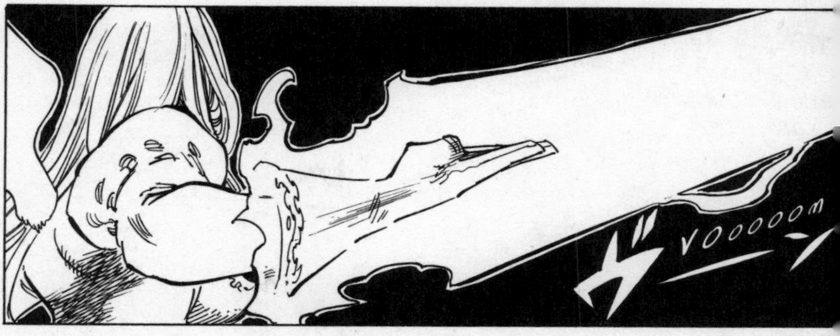
VOOOOOm
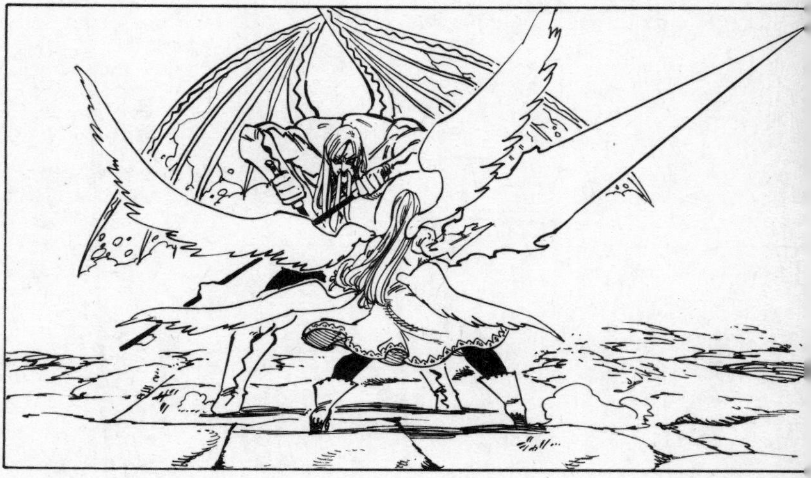
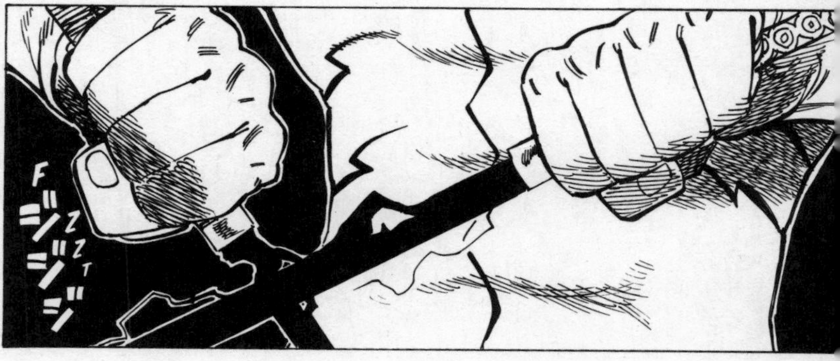
FZZZT

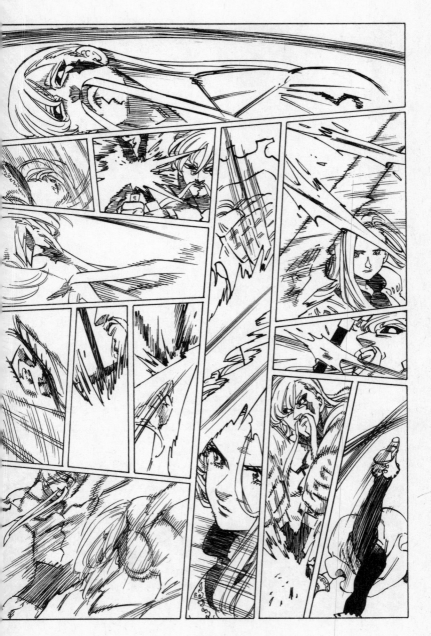

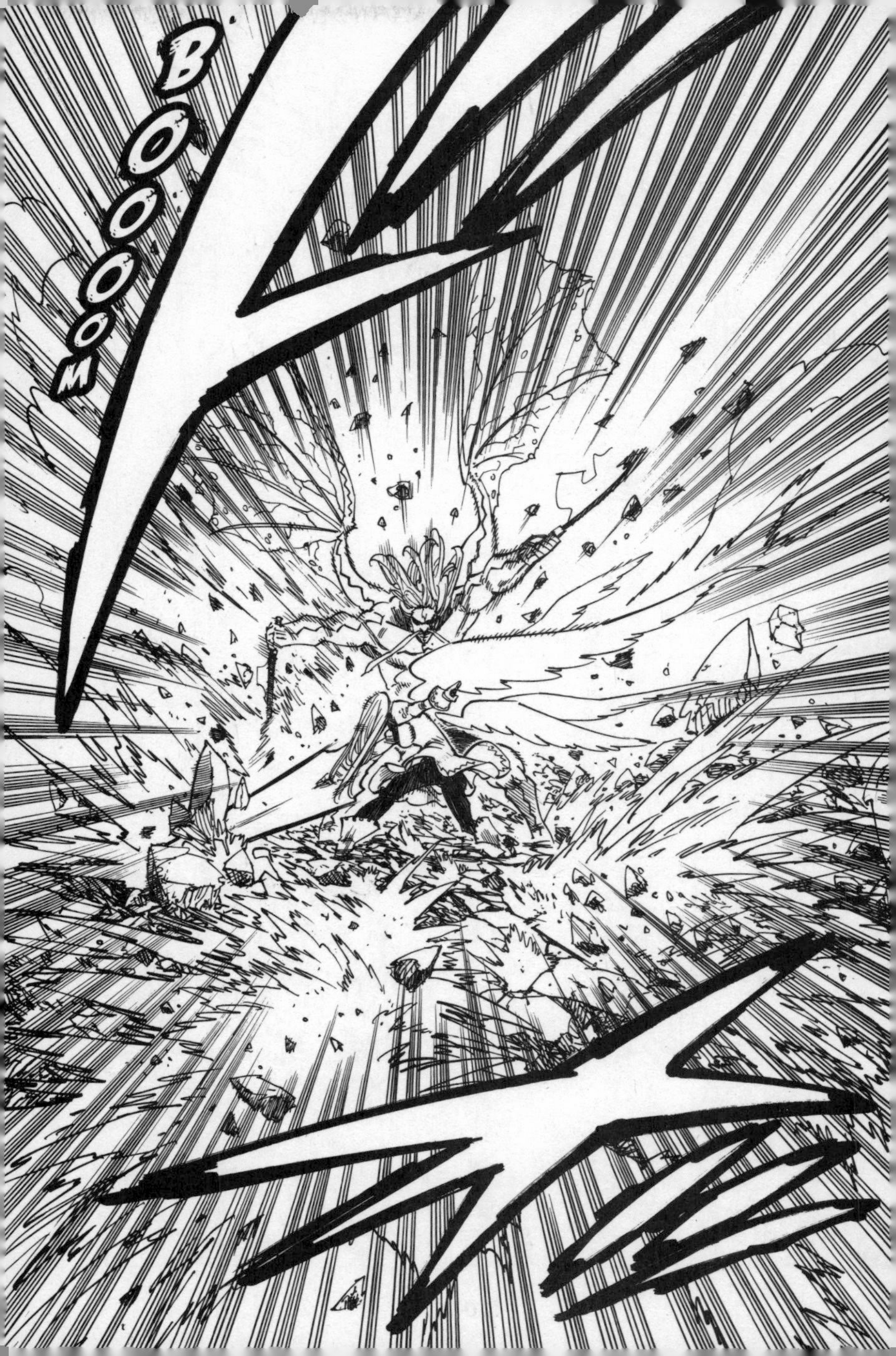
BOOOOOM

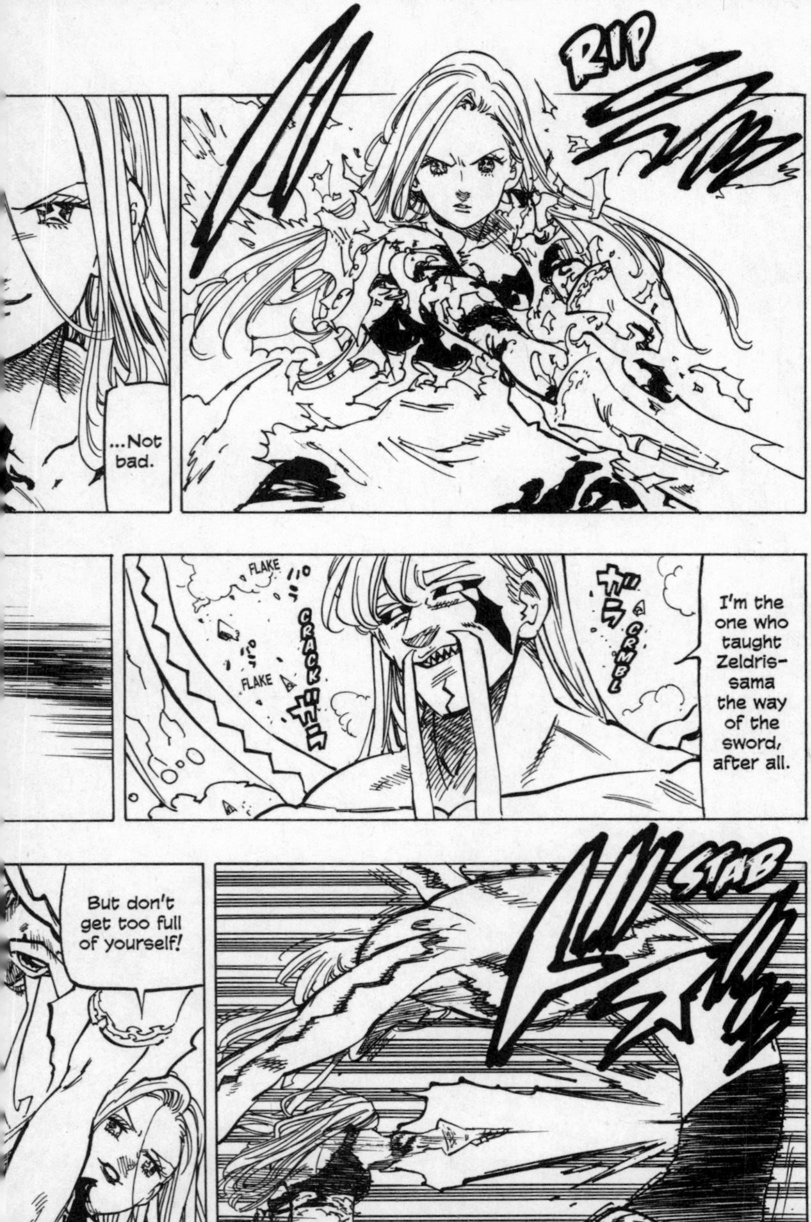
RIP
...Not bad.
I'm the one who taught Zeldris-sama the way of the sword, after all.
CRMBL
FLAKE
CRACK
FLAKE
STAB
But don't get too full of yourself!

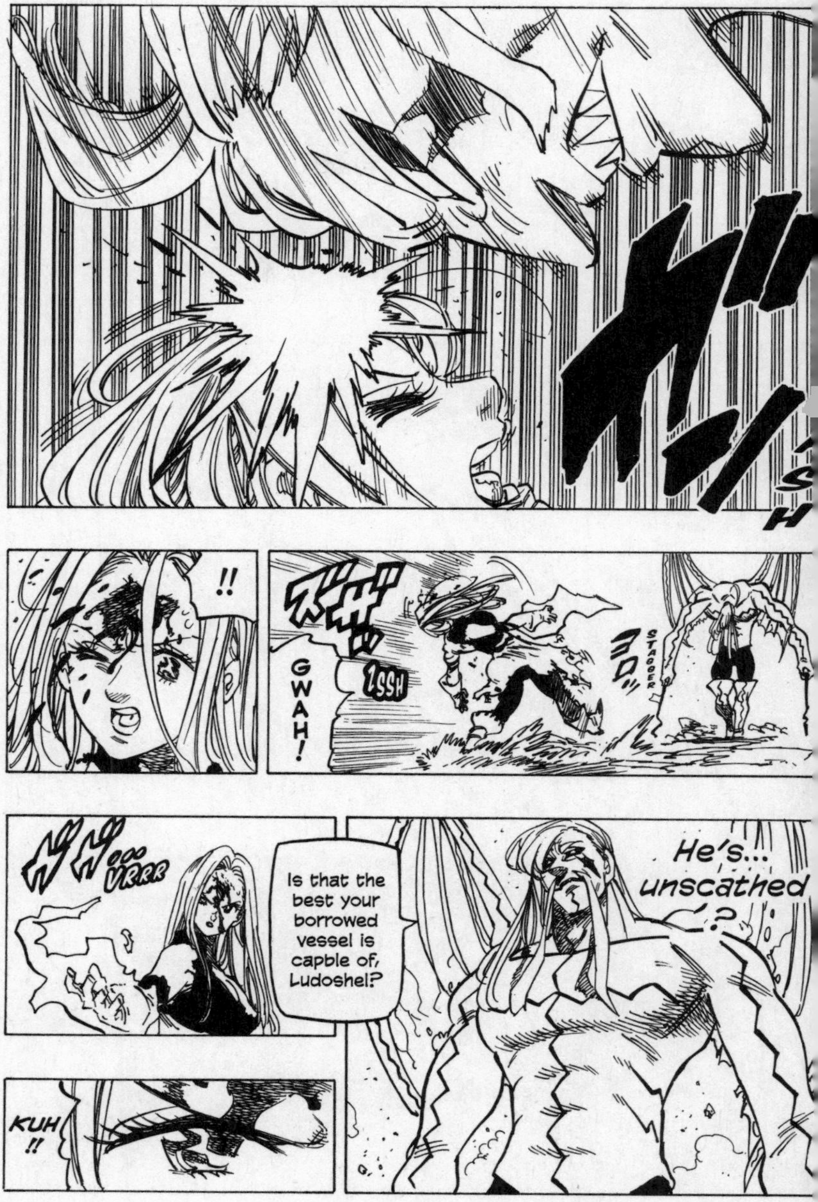
SH
STAGGER
ZSSH
GWAH!
!!
He's... unscathed...?
Is that the best your borrowed vessel is capble of, Ludoshel?
VRRR
KUH!!

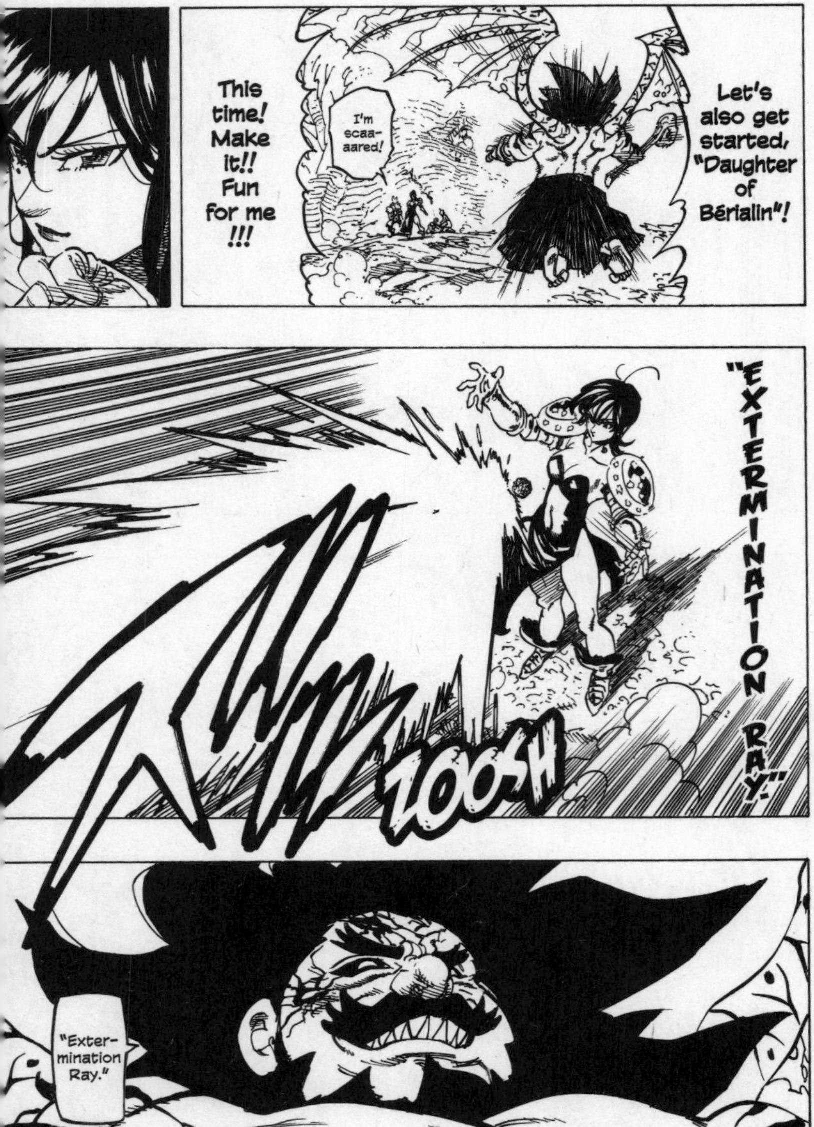
Let's also get started, "Daughter of Bérialin"!
I'm scaa-aared!
This time! Make it!! Fun for me!!!
"EXTERMINATION RAY."
ZOOSH
"Exter-mination Ray."

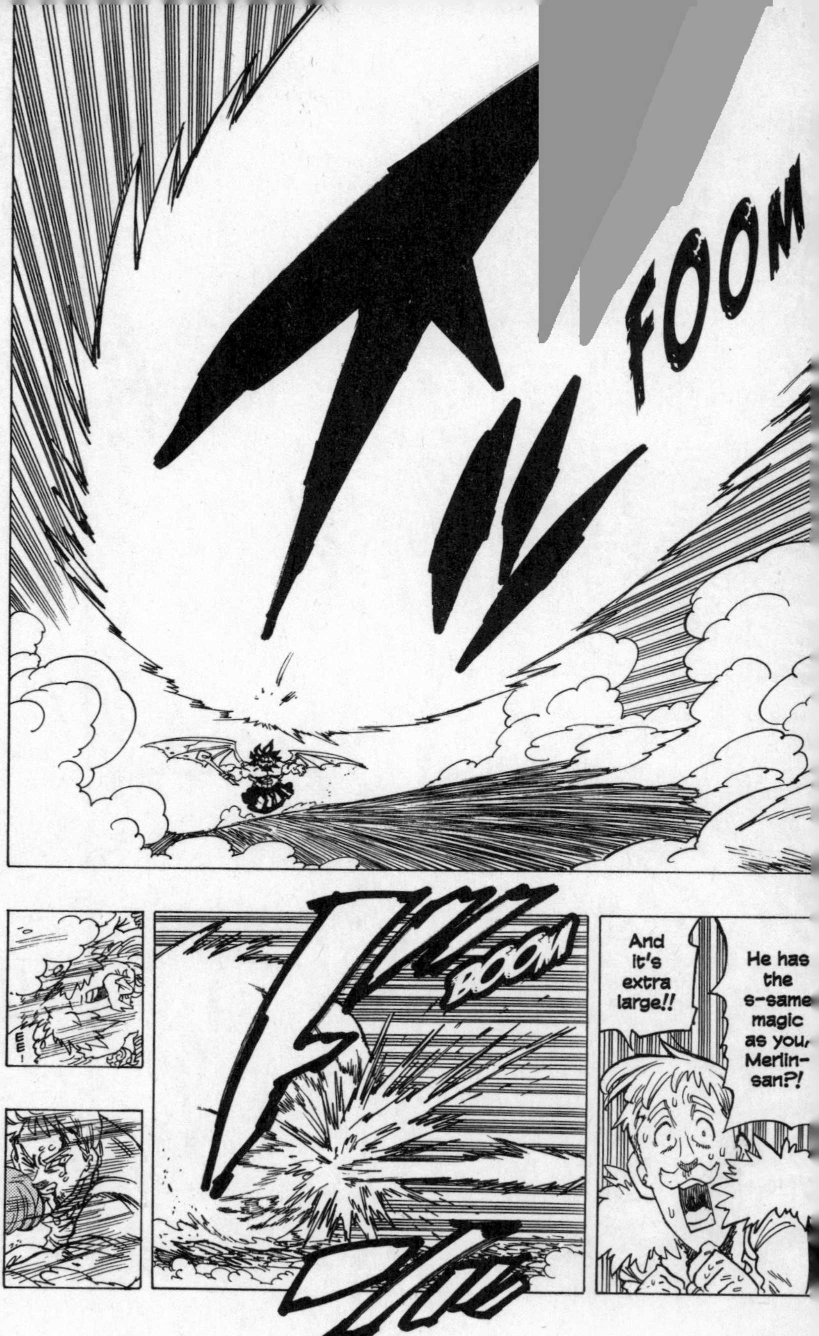
FOOM
He has the s-same magic as you, Merlin-san?!
And it's extra large!!
BOOM
EE!

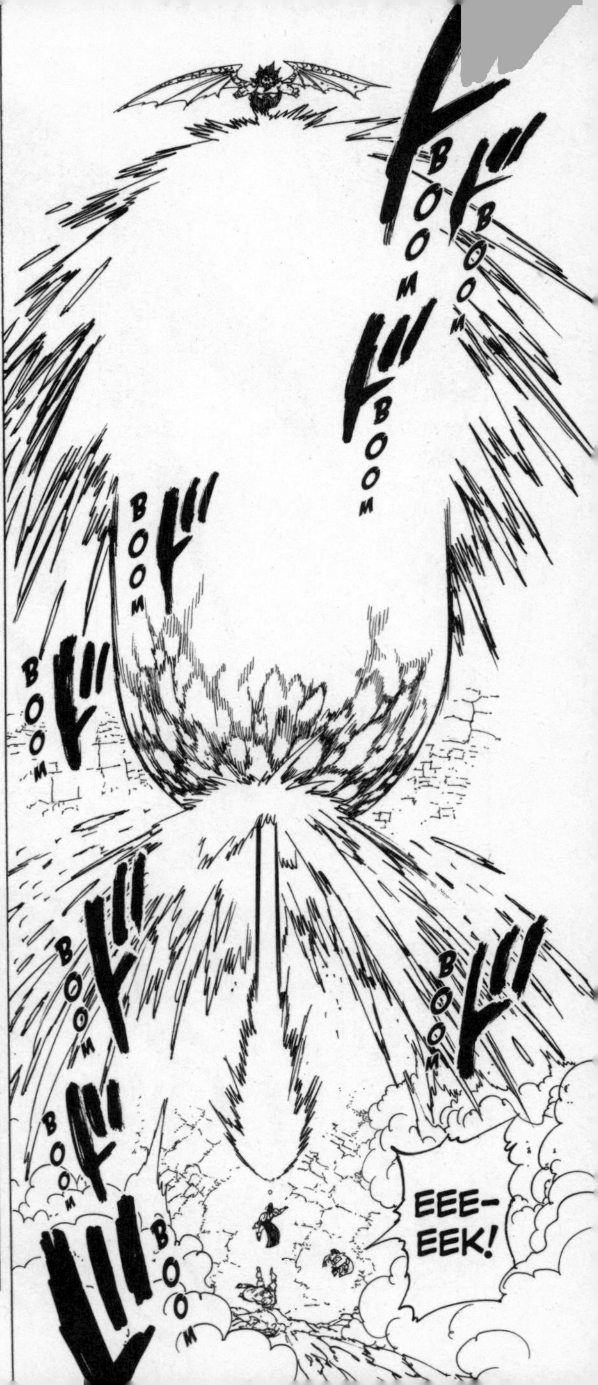
BOOM
BOOM
BOOM
BOOM
BOOM
BOOM
BOOM
BOOM
BOOM
EEE-EEK!

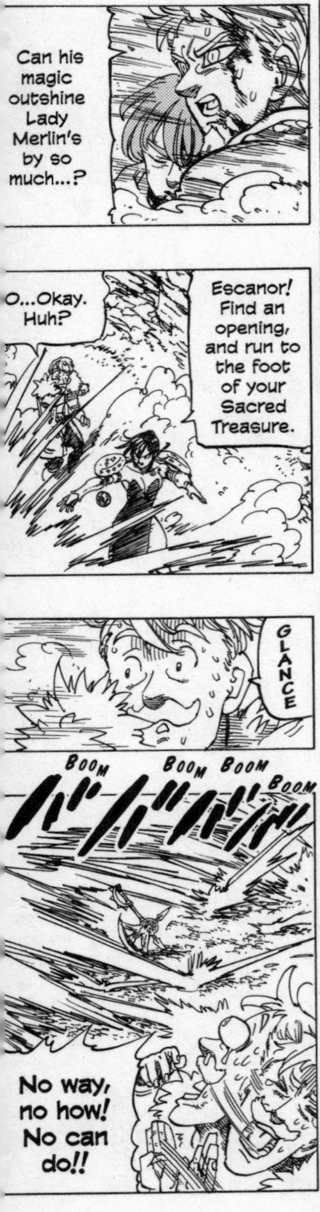
Can his magic outshine Lady Merlin's by so much...?
Escanor! Find an opening, and run to the foot of your Sacred Treasure.
O...Okay. Huh?
GLANCE
BOOM
BOOM
BOOM
BOOM
No way, no how! No can do!!

BOOM
BOOM
What's the matter? Huh?! Huh?!!
ZSH
"ENCHANT" INFINITY.
FWP
FWP
VWEEEE
VOOM
!!!!

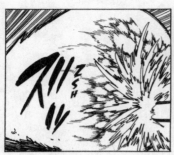

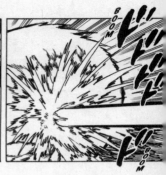

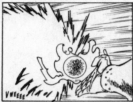

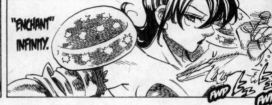

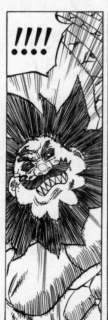

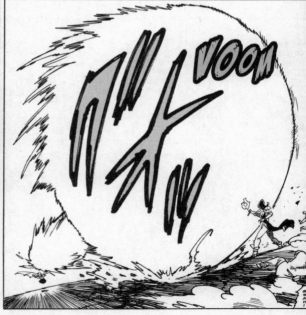

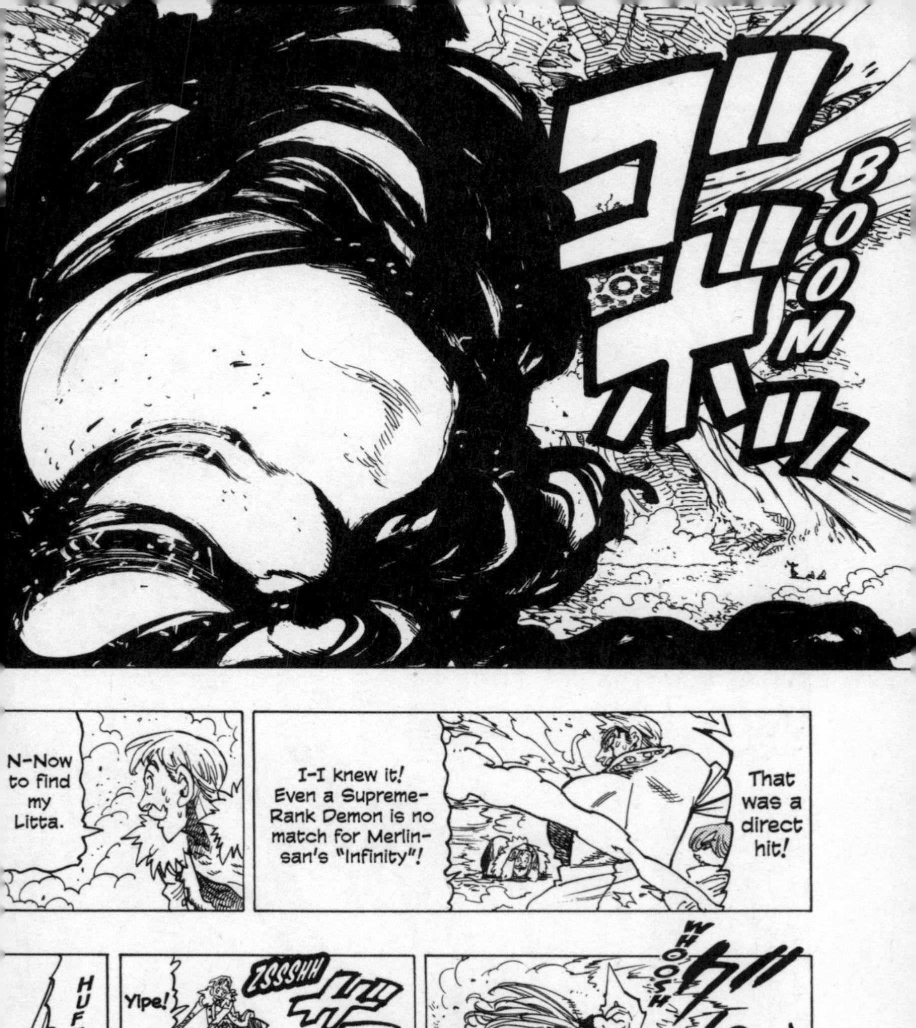
BOOM
That was a direct hit!
I-I knew it! Even a Supreme-Rank Demon is no match for Merlin-san's "Infinity"!
N-Now to find my Litta.
WHOOSH
JUMP
Ylpe!
ZSSSHH
HOP
HUFF
HUFF

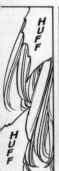

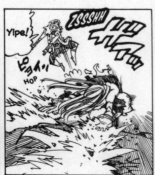

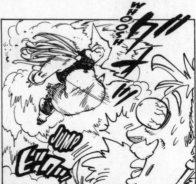

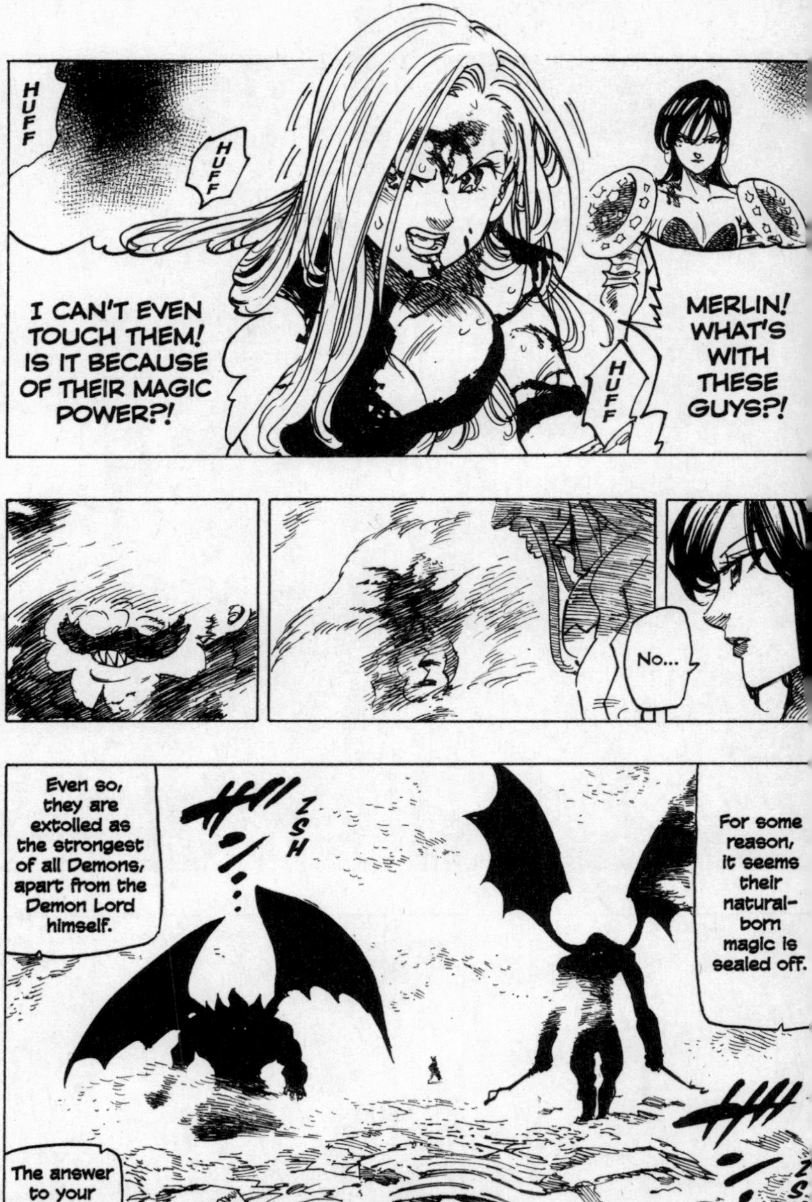
MERLIN! WHAT'S WITH THESE GUYS?!
HUFF
I CAN'T EVEN TOUCH THEM! IS IT BECAUSE OF THEIR MAGIC POWER?!
HUFF
HUFF
No...
For some reason, it seems their natural-born magic is sealed off.
ZSH
Even so, they are extolled as the strongest of all Demons, apart from the Demon Lord himself.
ZSH
The answer to your question's simple.

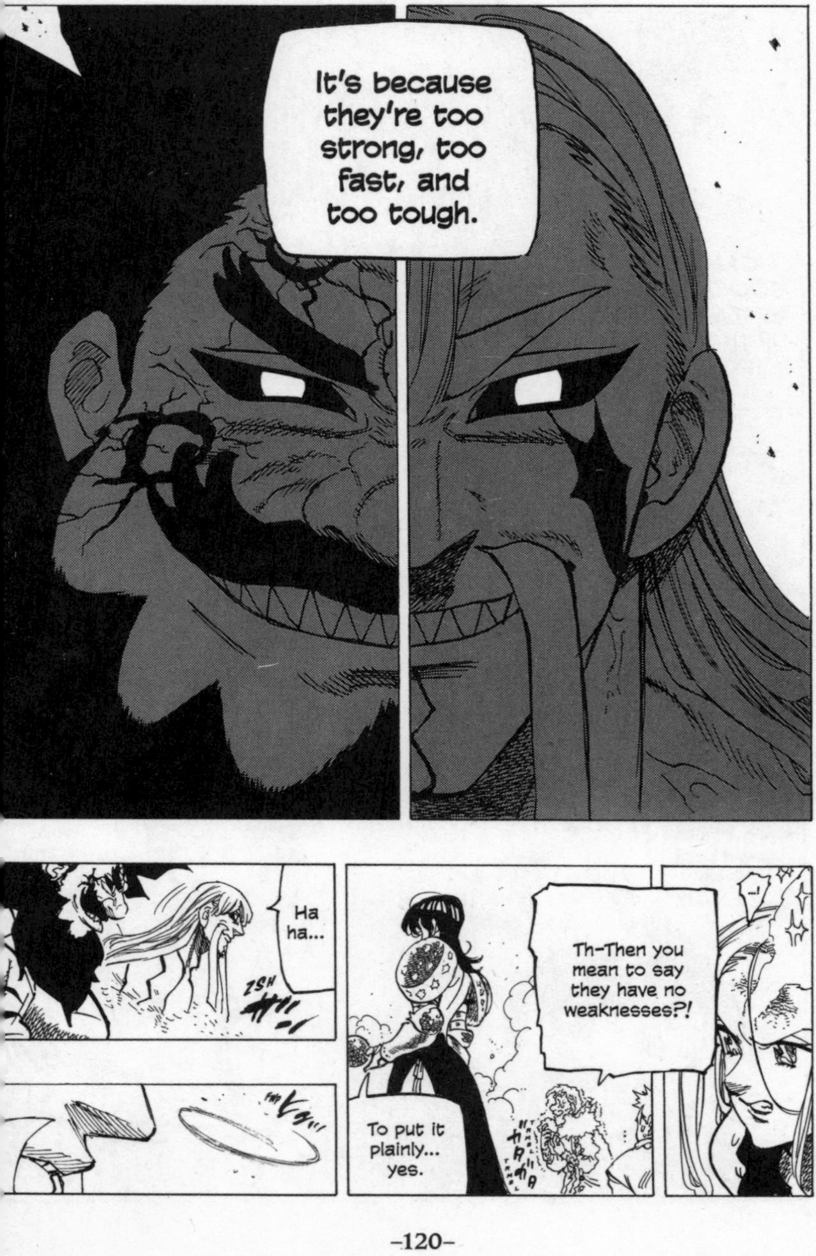
It's because they're too strong, too fast, and too tough.
...!
Th-Then you mean to say they have no weaknesses?!
To put it plainly... yes.
Ha ha...
ZSH

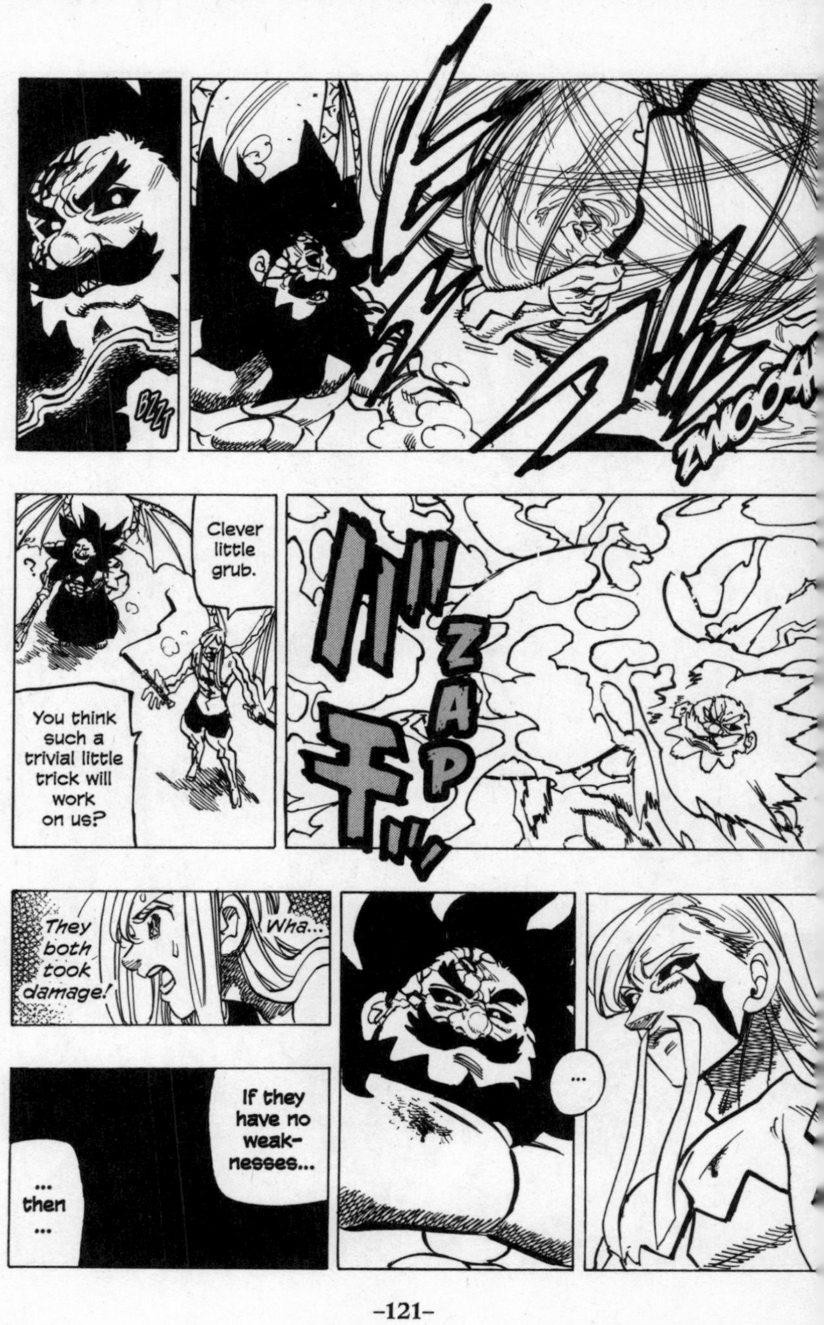
ZWOOA
BZZT
ZAP
Clever little grub.
You think such a trivial little trick will work on us?
...
Wha...
They both took damage!
If they have no weaknesses...
... then ...

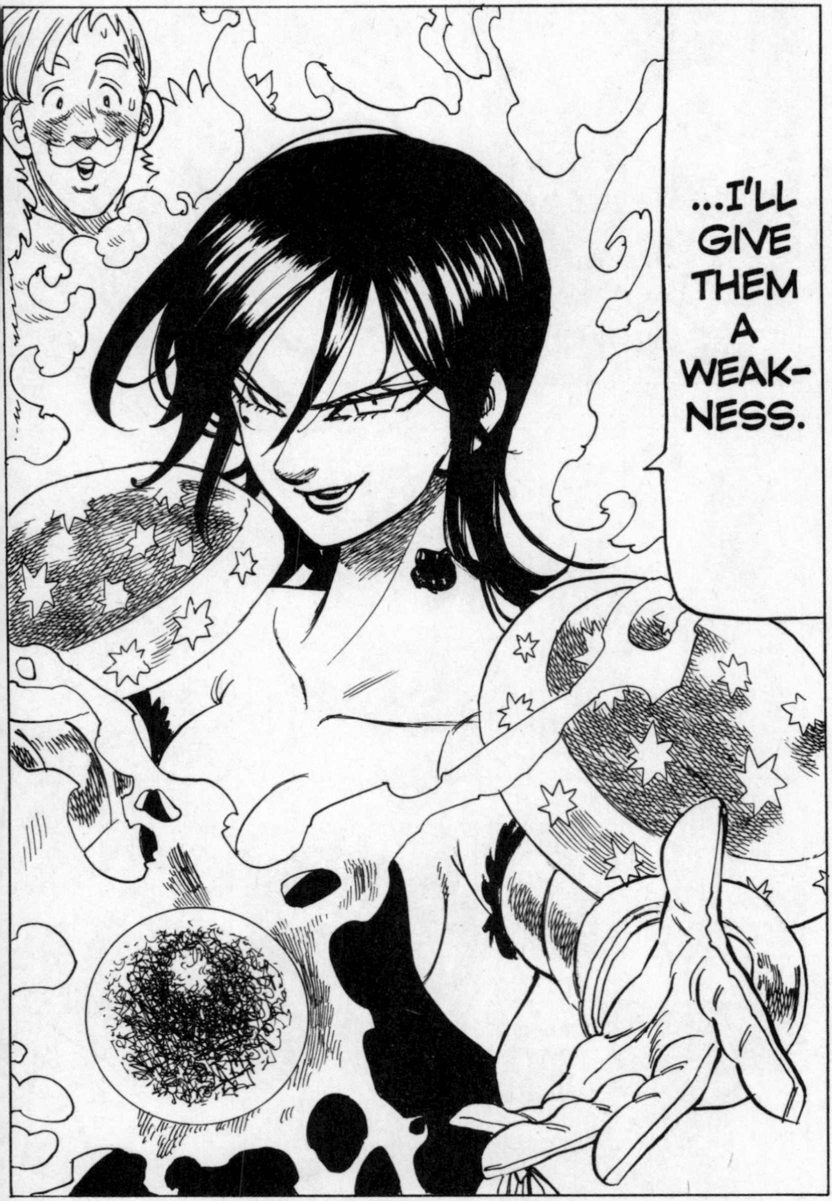
...I'LL GIVE THEM A WEAK-NESS.

Chapter 291 - The Witch's Feast

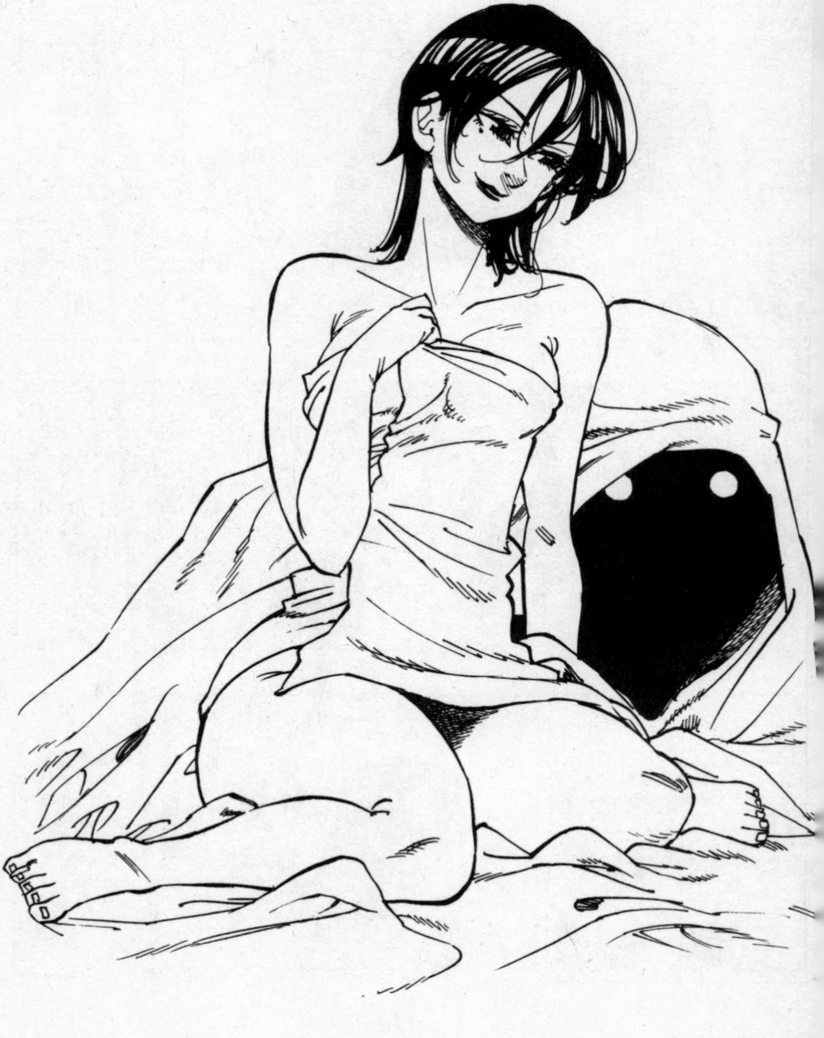

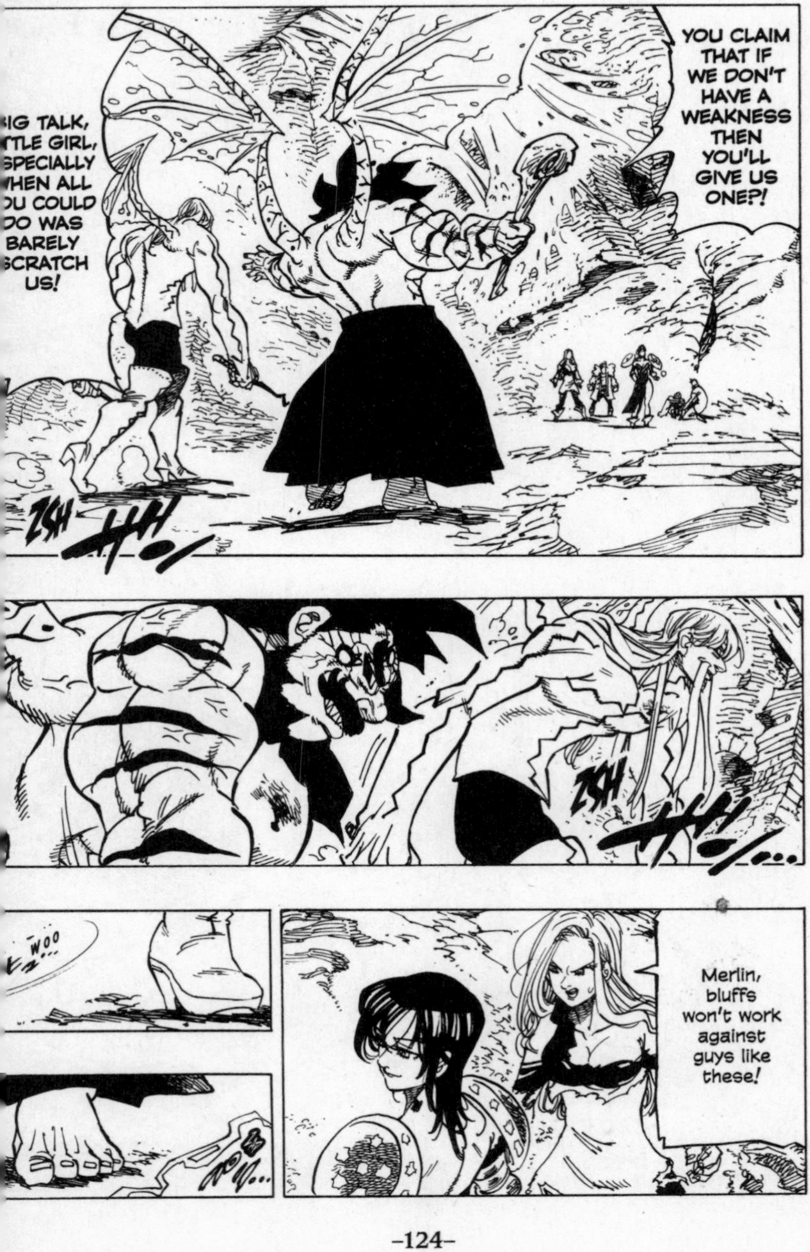
YOU CLAIM THAT IF WE DON'T HAVE A WEAKNESS THEN YOU'LL GIVE US ONE?!
IG TALK, TTLE GIRL, SPECIALLY HEN ALL OU COULD DO WAS BARELY CRATCH US!
ZSHHH!
ZSHHH!...
Merlin, bluffs won't work against guys like these!
WOO...

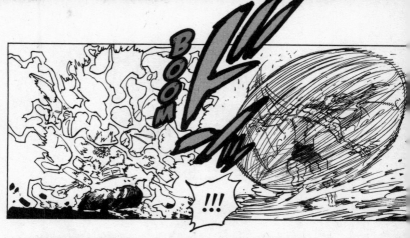

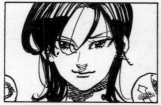

BOOM
!!!
!! Where did tha come from?.
ZSSSH
She didn't give us any sign that she was going to attack.
Wha the.
Our injuries have worsened?
It can't be!
It's some kind of dirty trick!

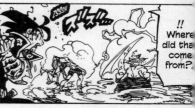

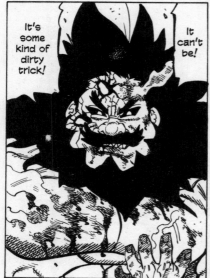

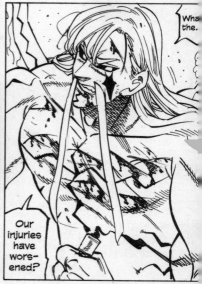

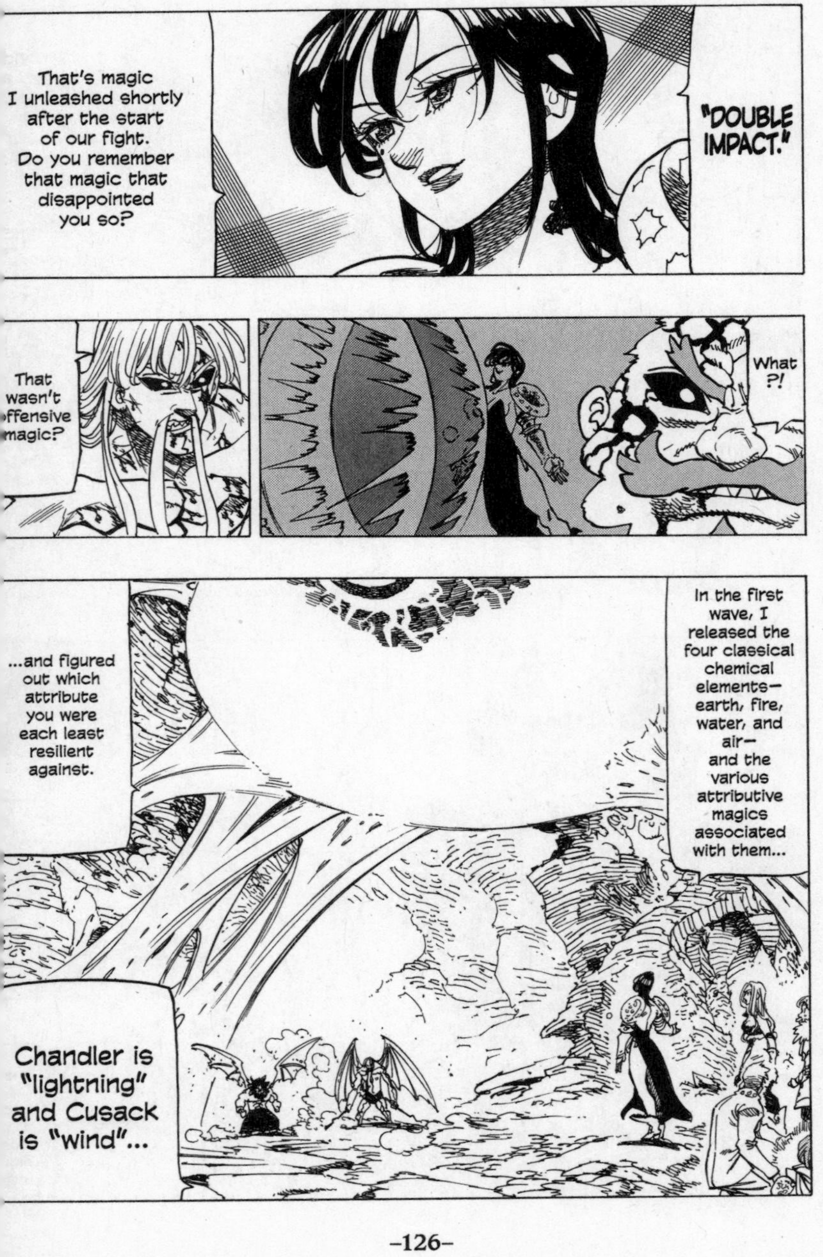
"DOUBLE IMPACT."
That's magic I unleashed shortly after the start of our fight. Do you remember that magic that disappointed you so?
What?!
That wasn't ffensive magic?
In the first wave, I released the four classical chemical elements— earth, fire, water, and air— and the various attributive magics associated with them...
...and figured out which attribute you were each least resilient against.
Chandler is "lightning" and Cusack is "wind"...

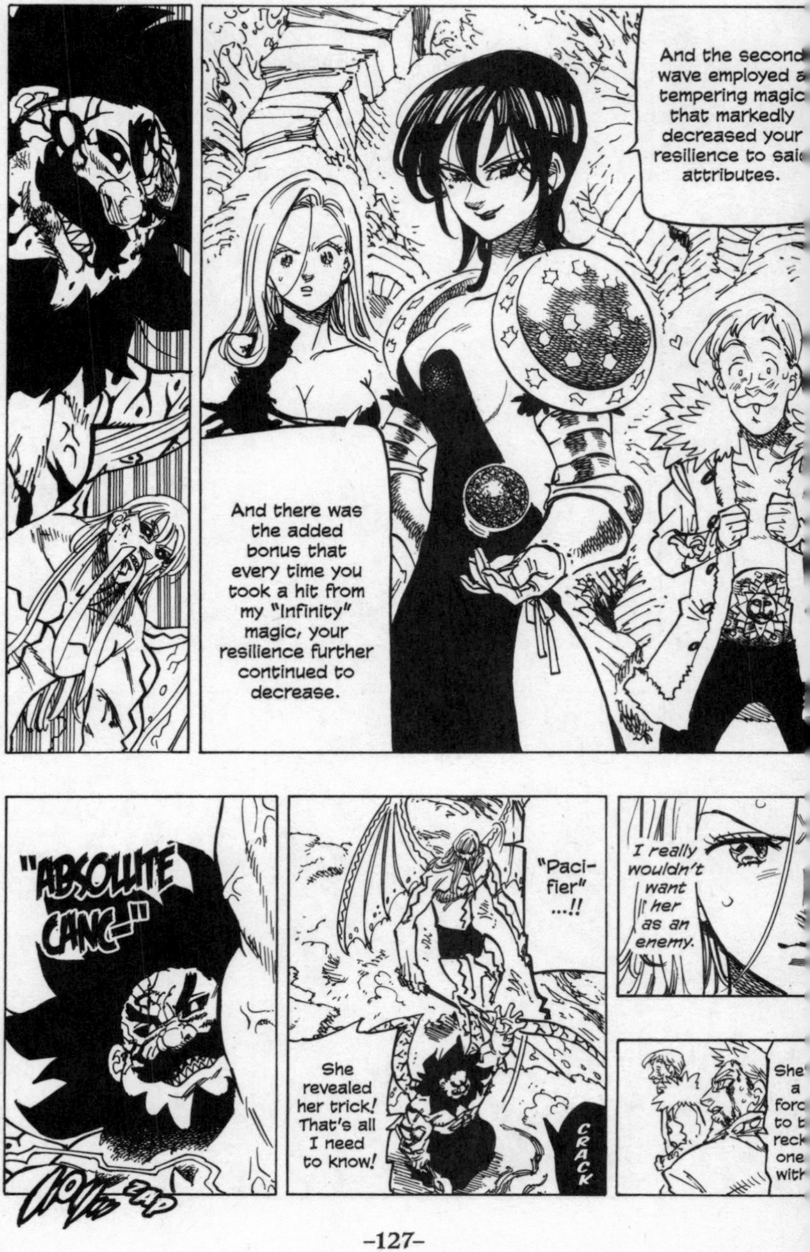
And the second wave employed a tempering magic that markedly decreased your resilience to sai attributes.
And there was the added bonus that every time you took a hit from my "Infinity" magic, your resilience further continued to decrease.
I really wouldn't want her as an enemy.
She a forc to b reck one with
"Pacifier" ...!!
She revealed her trick! That's all I need to know!
CRACK
"ABSOLUTE CANC--"
ZAP

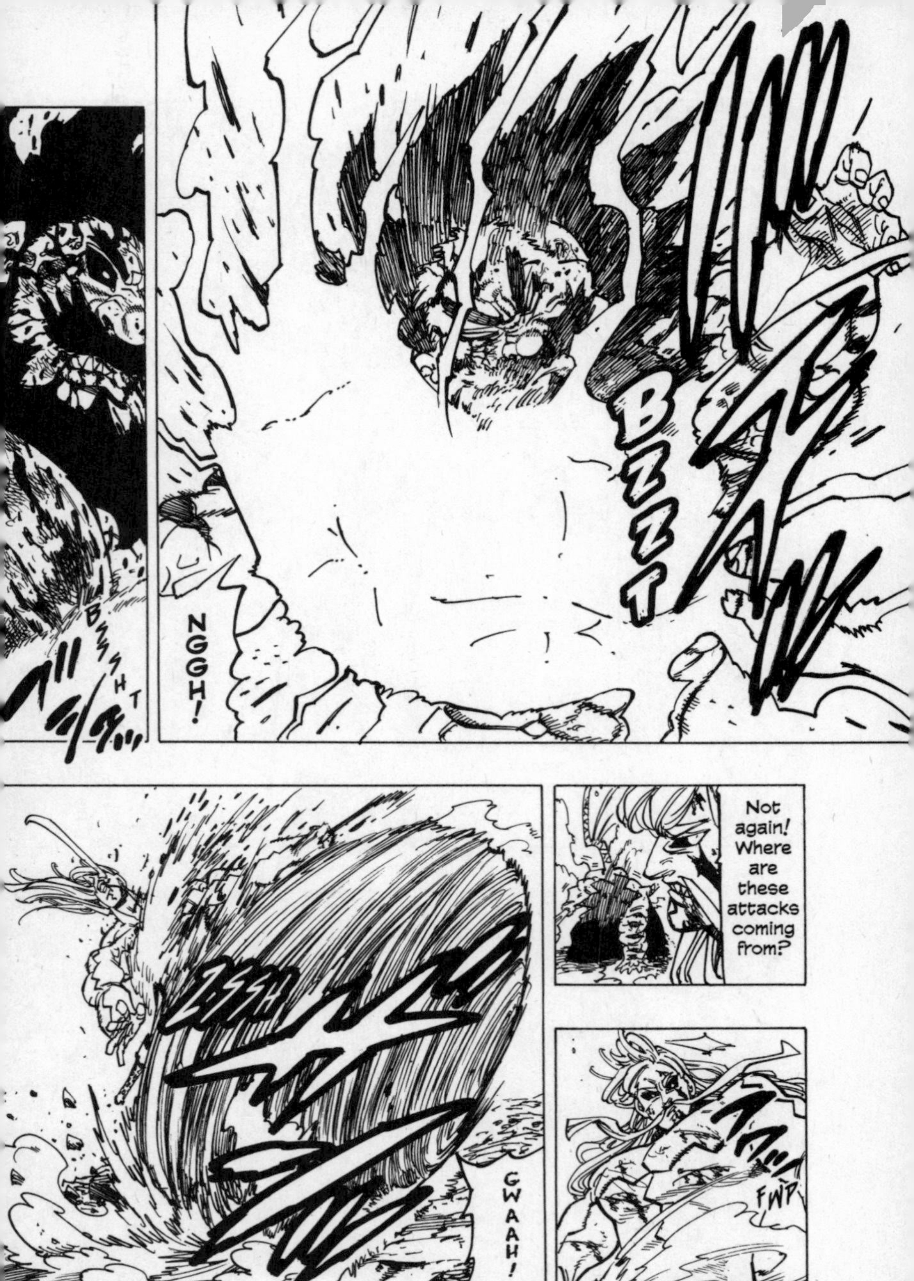
BZZZT
NGGH!
BSSHT
Not again! Where are these attacks coming from?
FWP
ZSSH
GWAAH!

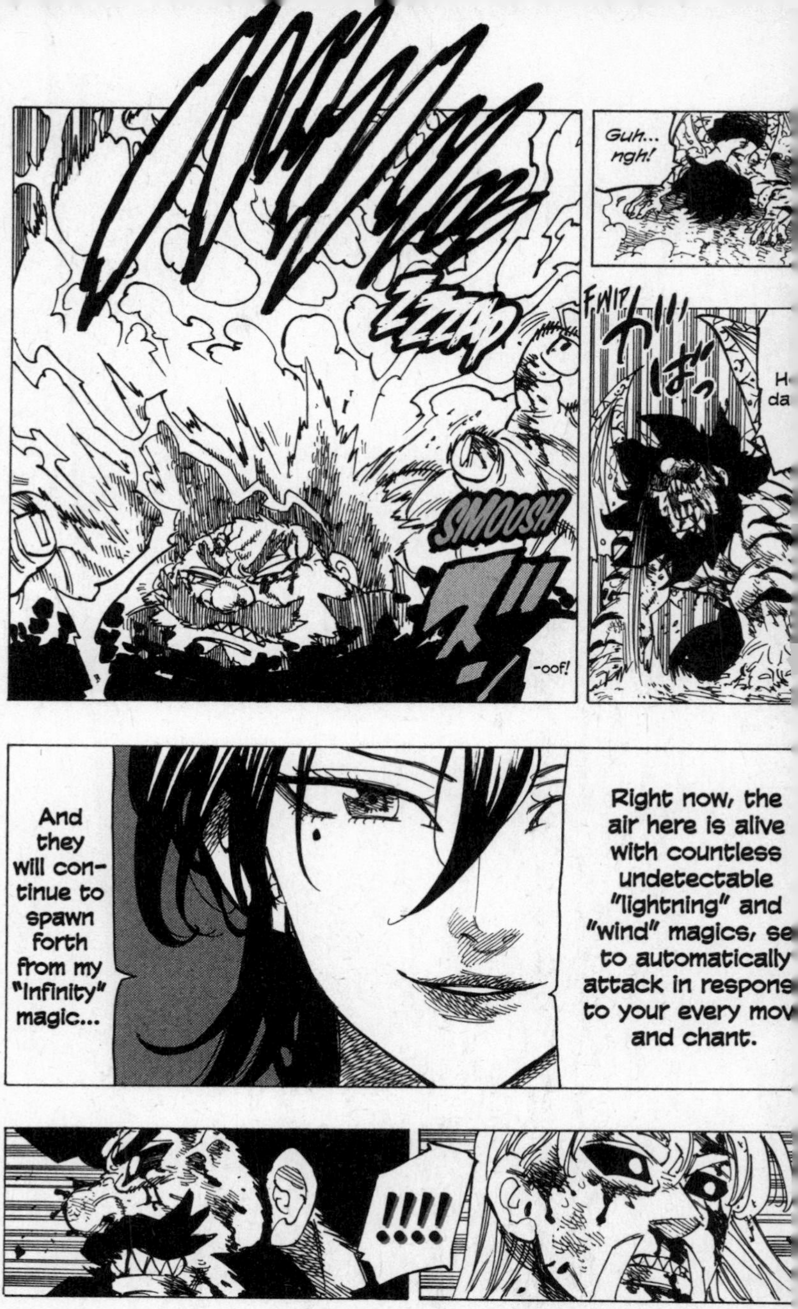

Guh... ngh!
FWIP
ZZZAP
SMOOSH
-oof!
Right now, the air here is alive with countless undetectable "lightning" and "wind" magics, se to automatically attack in respons to your every mov and chant.
And they will continue to spawn forth from my "Infinity" magic...
!!!!

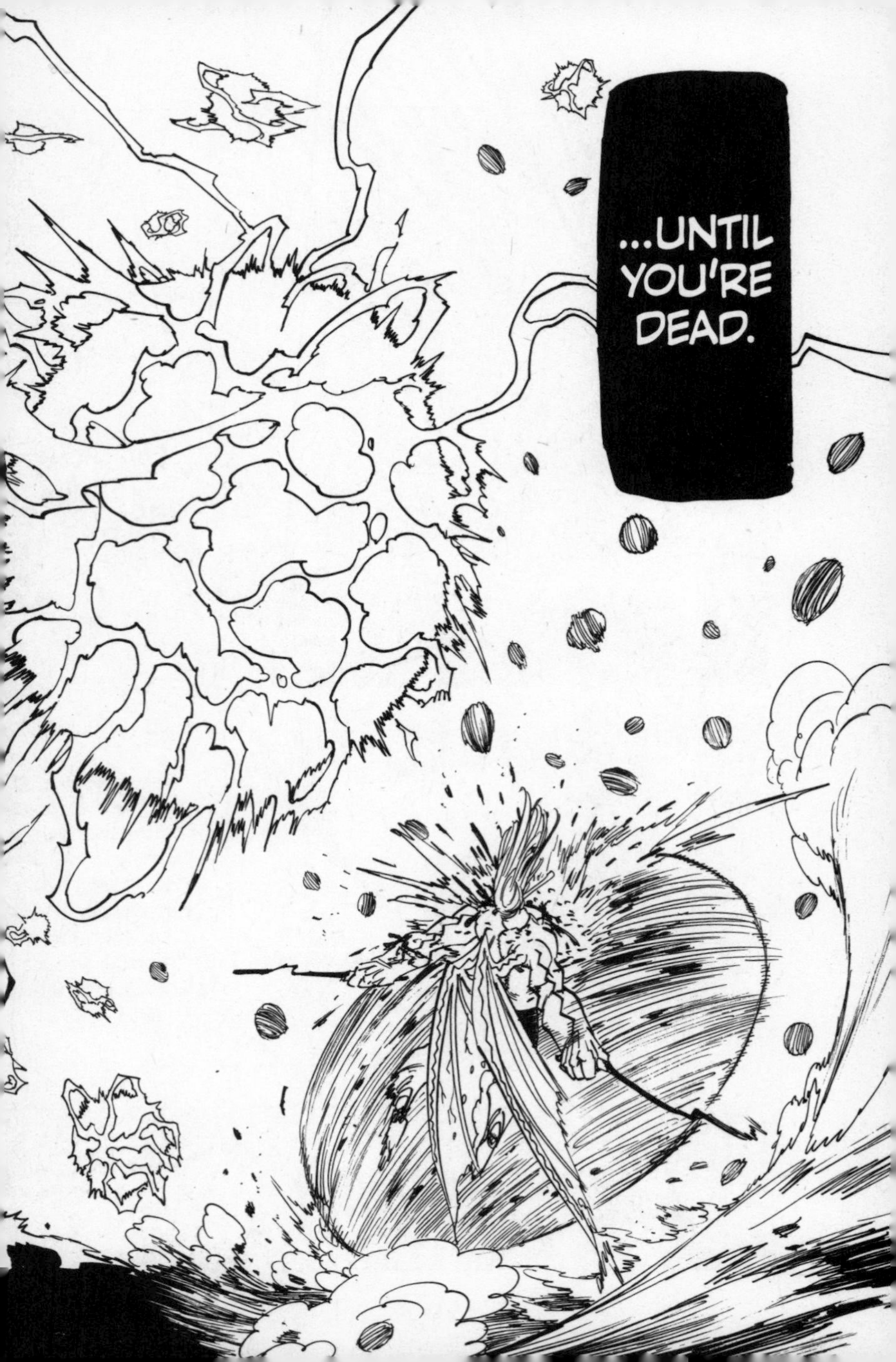
...UNTIL YOU'RE DEAD.

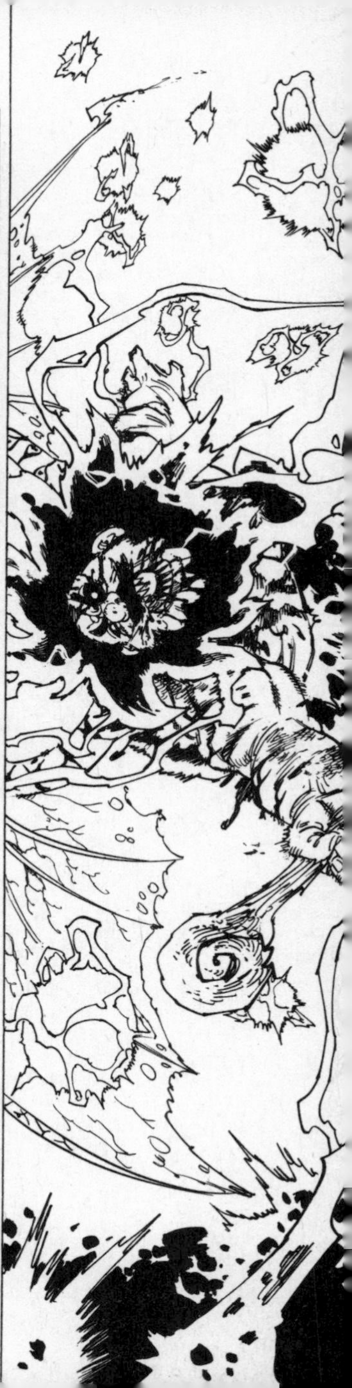

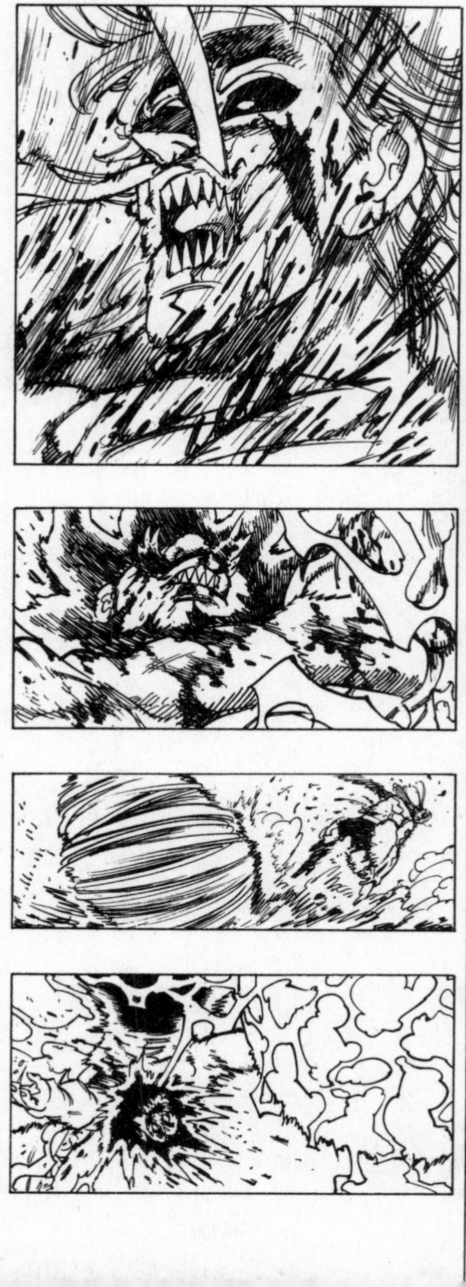

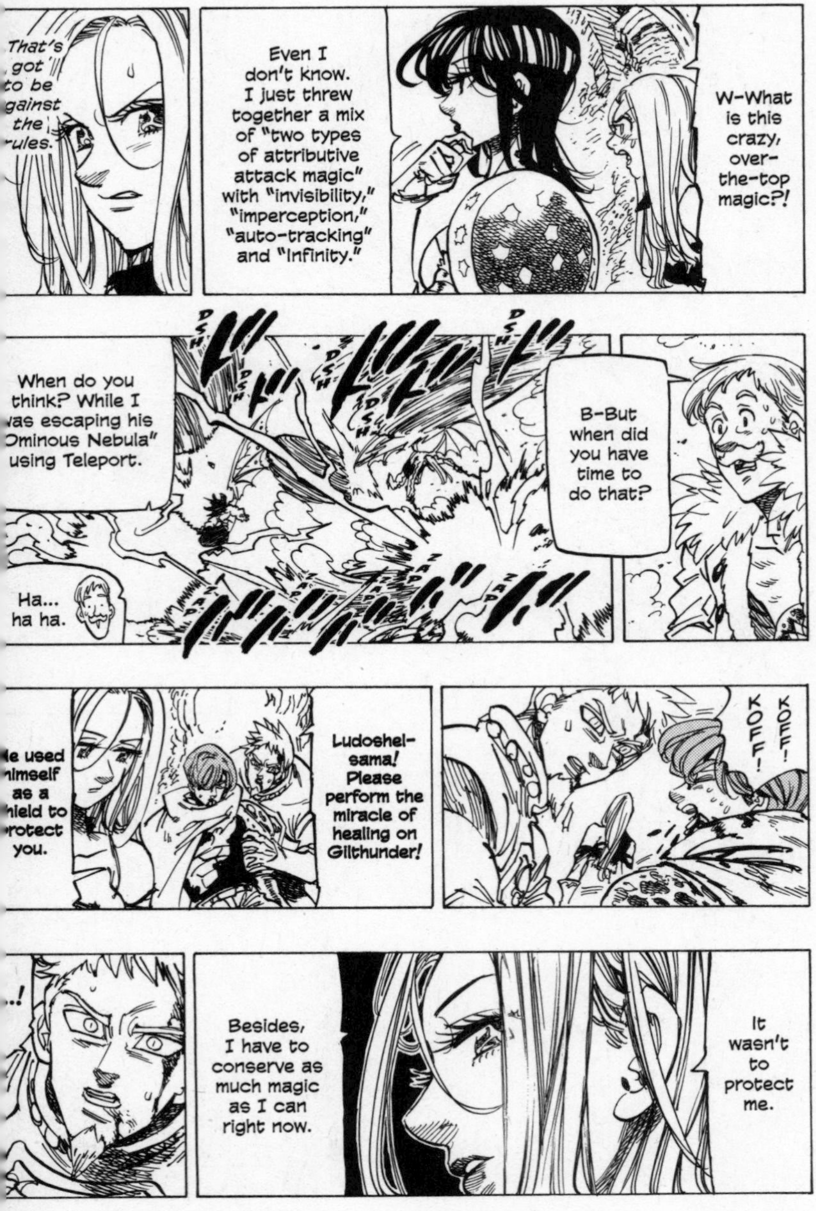
W-What is this crazy, over-the-top magic?!
Even I don't know. I just threw together a mix of "two types of attributive attack magic" with "invisibility," "imperception," "auto-tracking" and "Infinity."
That's got to be gainst the rules.
B-But when did you have time to do that?
DSH DSH DSH DSH DSH
ZAP ZAP ZAP ZAP ZAP
When do you think? While I vas escaping his Ominous Nebula" using Teleport.
Ha... ha ha.
KOFF! KOFF!
Ludoshel-sama! Please perform the miracle of healing on Gilthunder!
le used nimself as a hield to rotect you.
It wasn't to protect me.
Besides, I have to conserve as much magic as I can right now.
..!

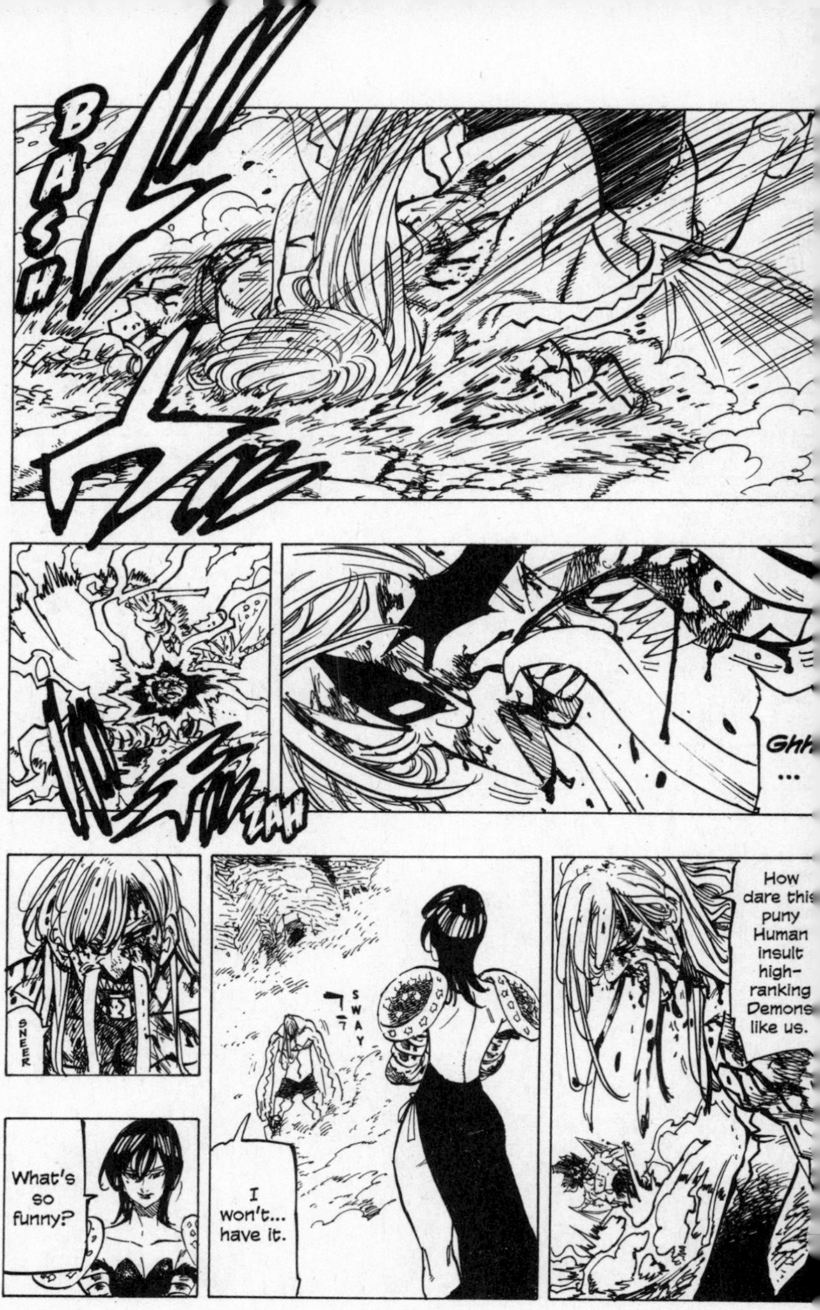
BASH
Ghh...
ZAH
How dare this puny Human insult high-ranking Demons like us.
SWAY
I won't... have it.
SNEER
What's so funny?

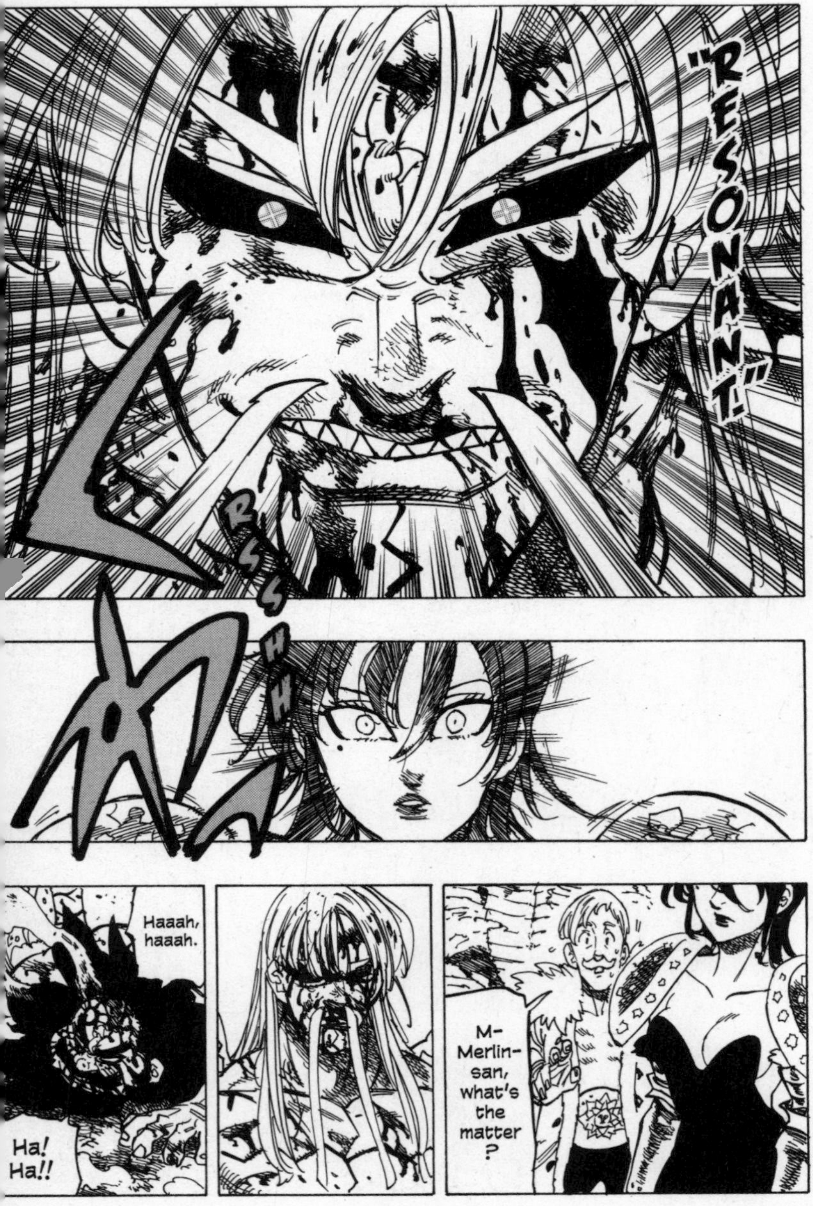
"RESONANT!"
RSSHH
M-Merlin-san, what's the matter?
Haaah, haaah.
Ha! Ha!!

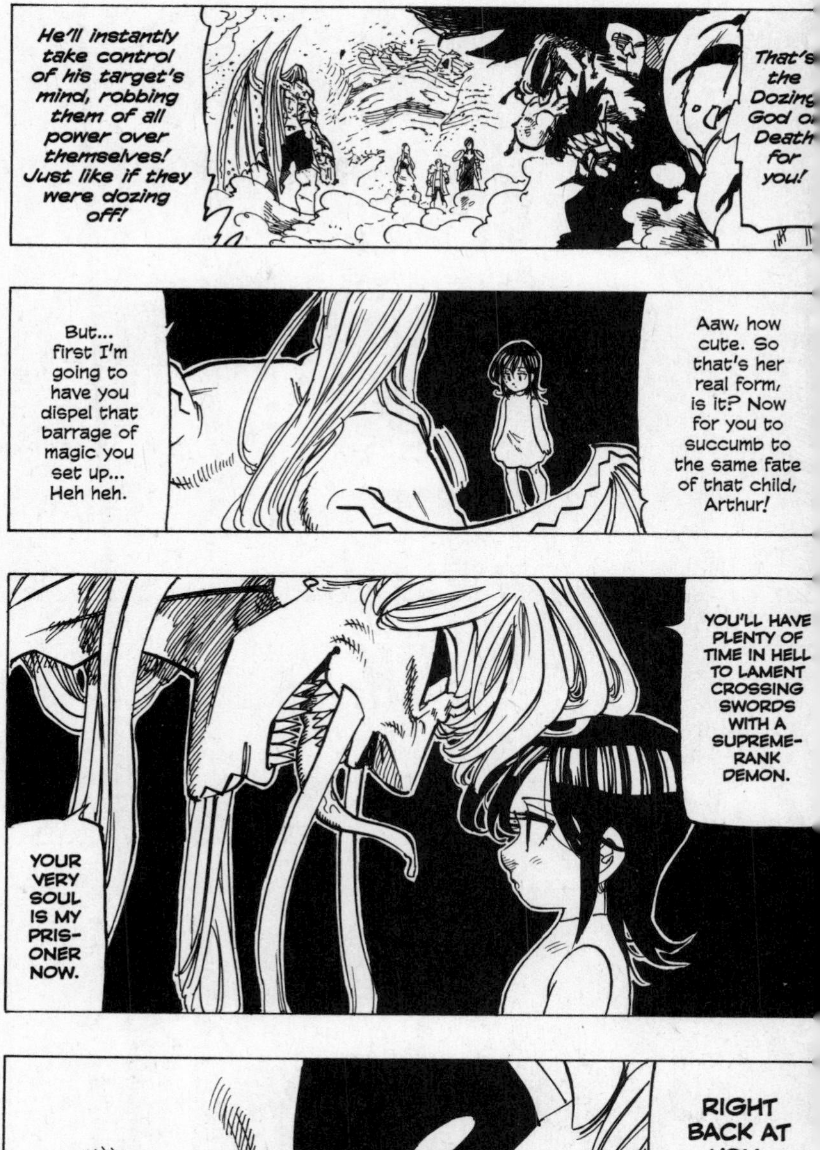
That's the Dozing God o Death for you!
He'll instantly take control of his target's mind, robbing them of all power over themselves! Just like if they were dozing off!
Aaw, how cute. So that's her real form, is it? Now for you to succumb to the same fate of that child, Arthur!
But... first I'm going to have you dispel that barrage of magic you set up... Heh heh.
YOU'LL HAVE PLENTY OF TIME IN HELL TO LAMENT CROSSING SWORDS WITH A SUPREME-RANK DEMON.
YOUR VERY SOUL IS MY PRIS-ONER NOW.
RIGHT BACK AT YOU.

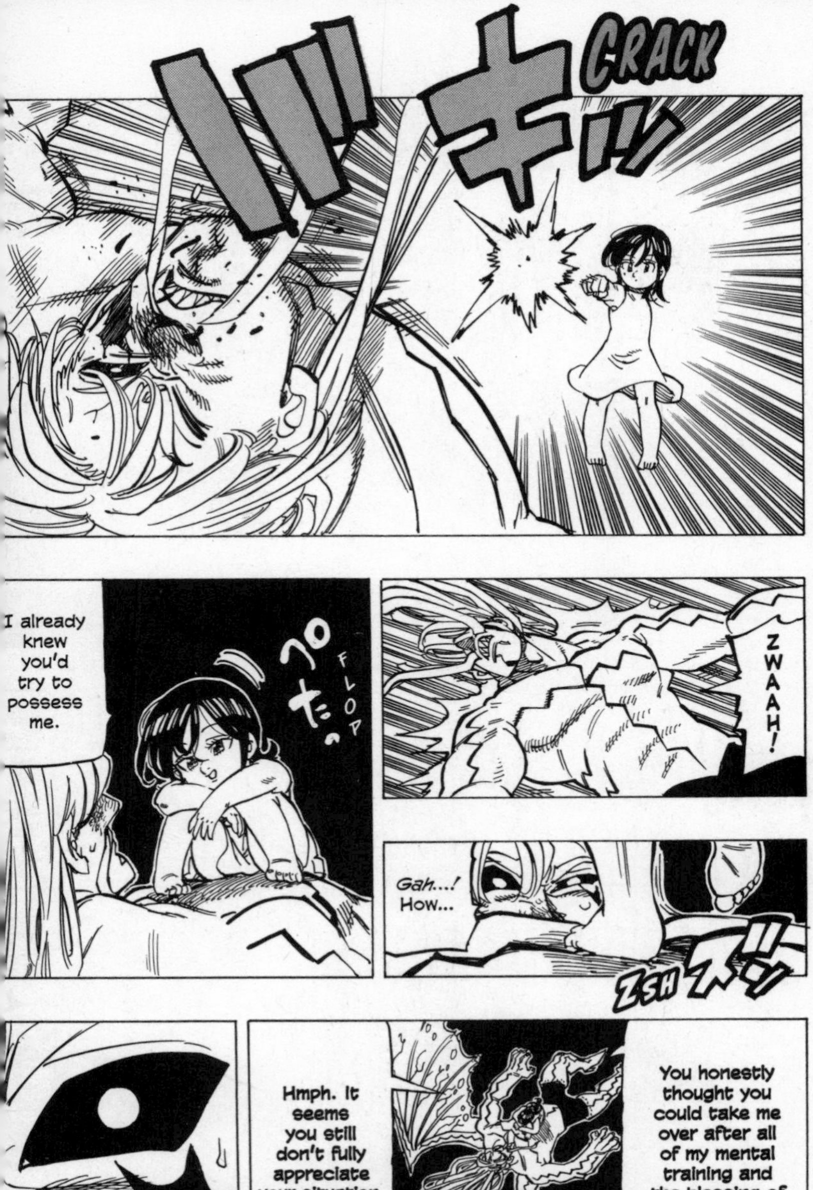
CRACK
ZWAAH!
Gah...! How...
ZSH
FLOP
I already knew you'd try to possess me.
You honestly thought you could take me over after all of my mental training and the blessing of the Supreme Deity?
Hmph. It seems you still don't fully appreciate your situation, You fool.
...!!

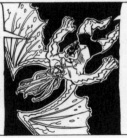

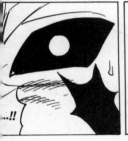

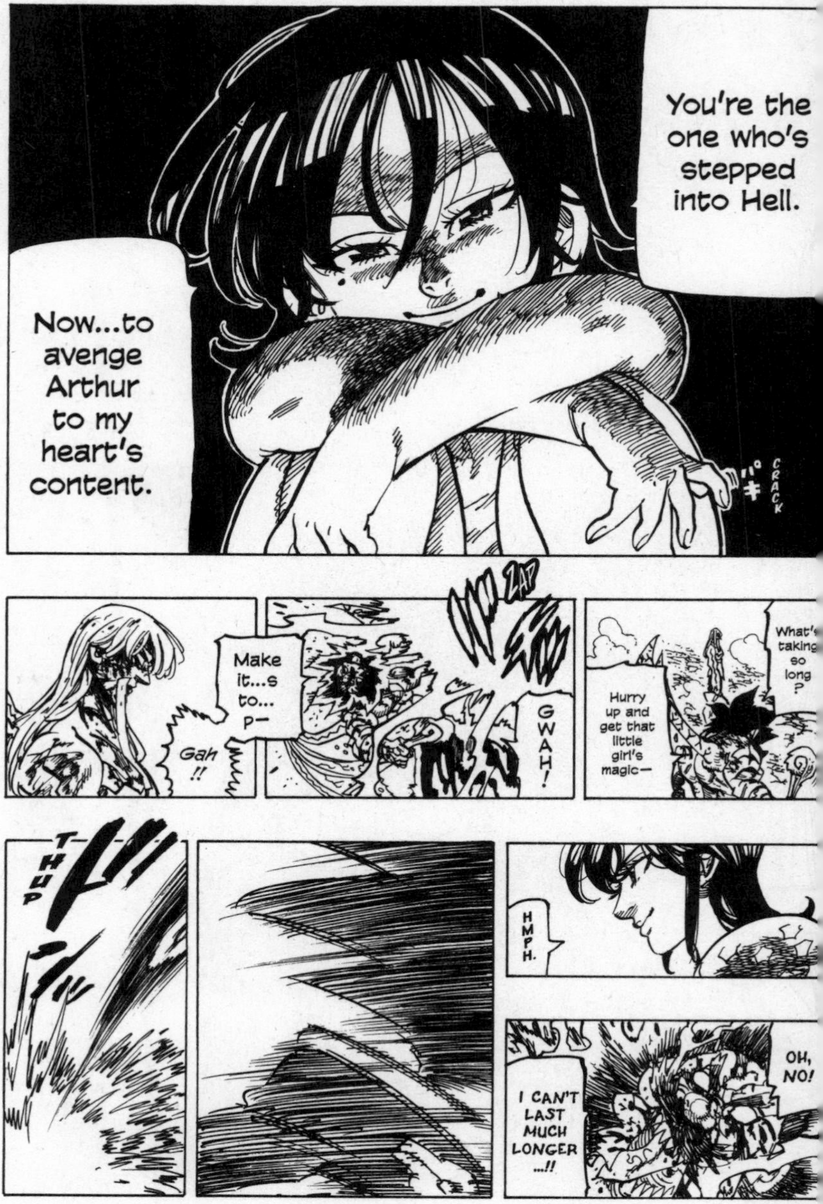

You're the one who's stepped into Hell.
Now...to avenge Arthur to my heart's content.
CRACK
What's taking so long?
Hurry up and get that little girl's magic—
ZAP
GWAH!
Make it...s to... p—
Gah!!
HMPH.
OH, NO!
I CAN'T LAST MUCH LONGER...!!
THUP

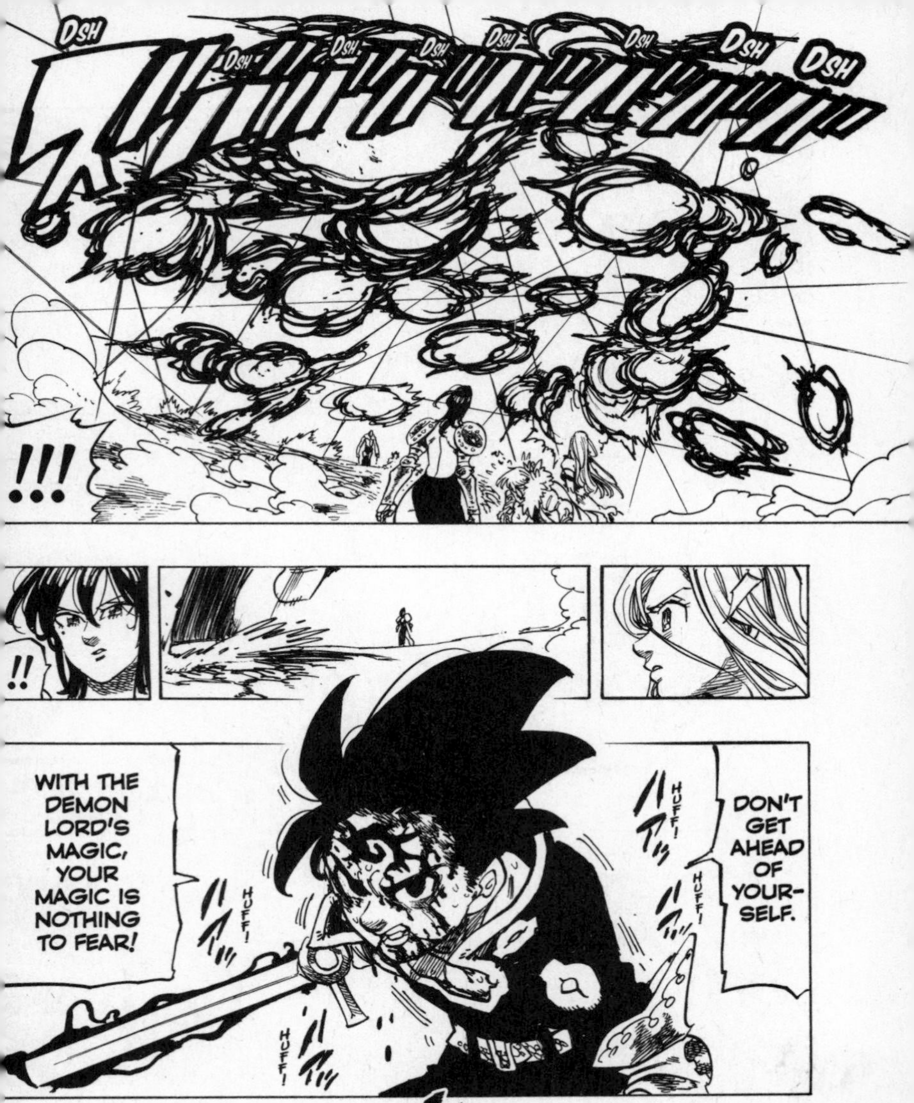
DSH
DSH
DSH
DSH
DSH
DSH
DSH
DSH
!!!
!!
DON'T GET AHEAD OF YOURSELF.
HUFF!
HUFF!
HUFF!
HUFF!
WITH THE DEMON LORD'S MAGIC, YOUR MAGIC IS NOTHING TO FEAR!
SWAY
ZSH
Kuh...

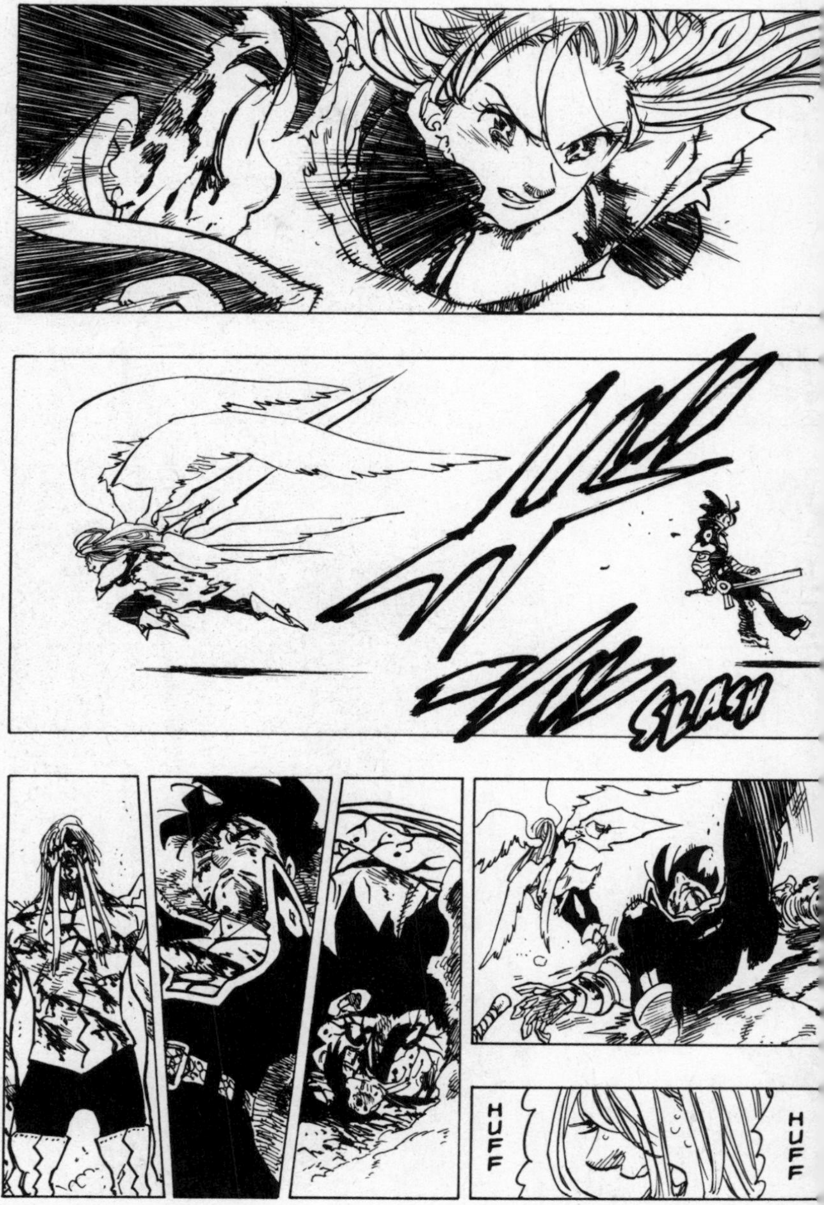
SLASH
HUFF
HUFF

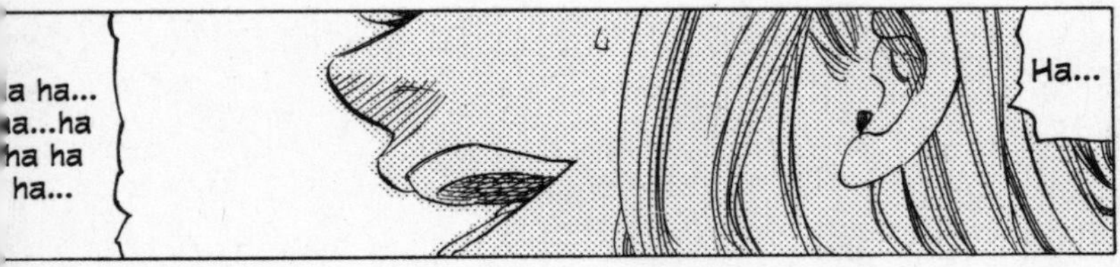
Ha...
a ha...
a...ha
ha ha
ha...

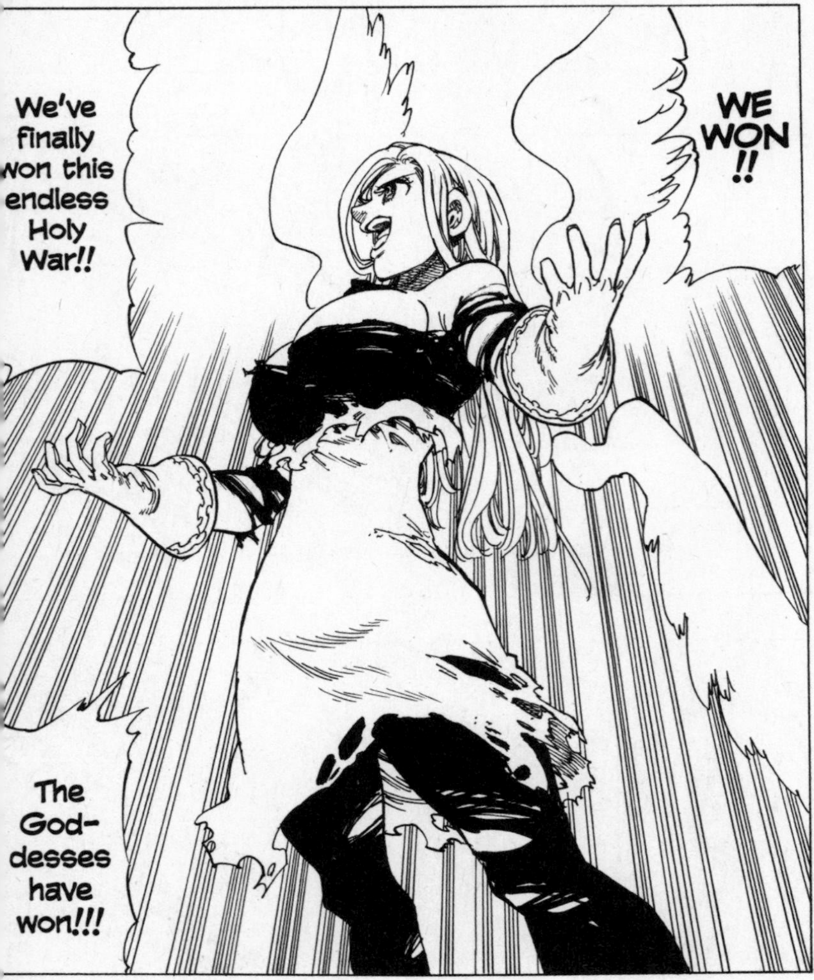
WE WON!!
We've finally won this endless Holy War!!
The God-desses have won!!!

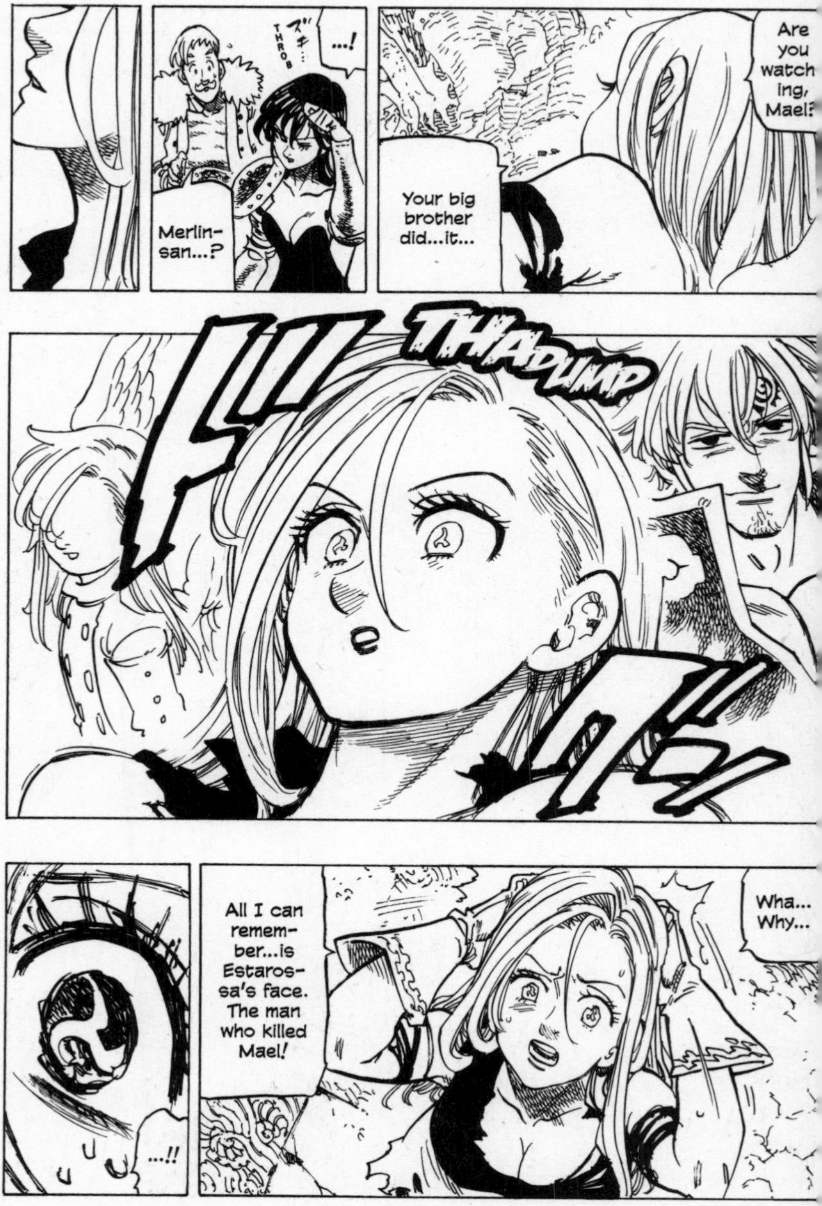
Are you watch ing, Mael?
Your big brother did...it...
...!
ズキ... THROB
Merlin-san...?
THADUMP
Wha... Why...
All I can remem-ber...is Estaros-sa's face. The man who killed Mael!
...!!

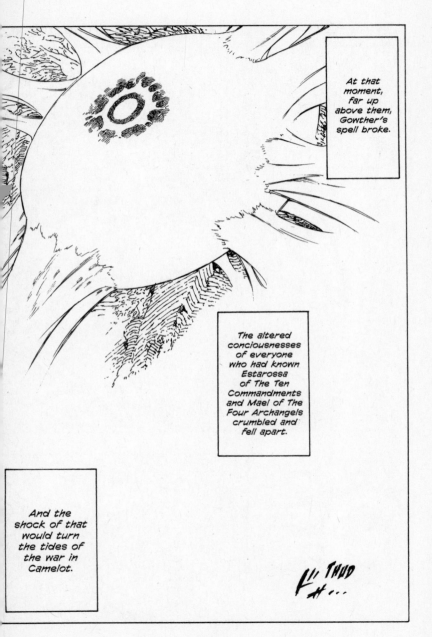

At that moment, far up above them, Gowther's spell broke.

The altered conciousnesses of everyone who had known Estarossa of The Ten Commandments and Mael of The Four Archangels crumbled and fell apart.

And the shock of that would turn the tides of the war in Camelot.

FU THUD
H...

Chapter 292 - The Stuff of Nightmares, The Return of Hope

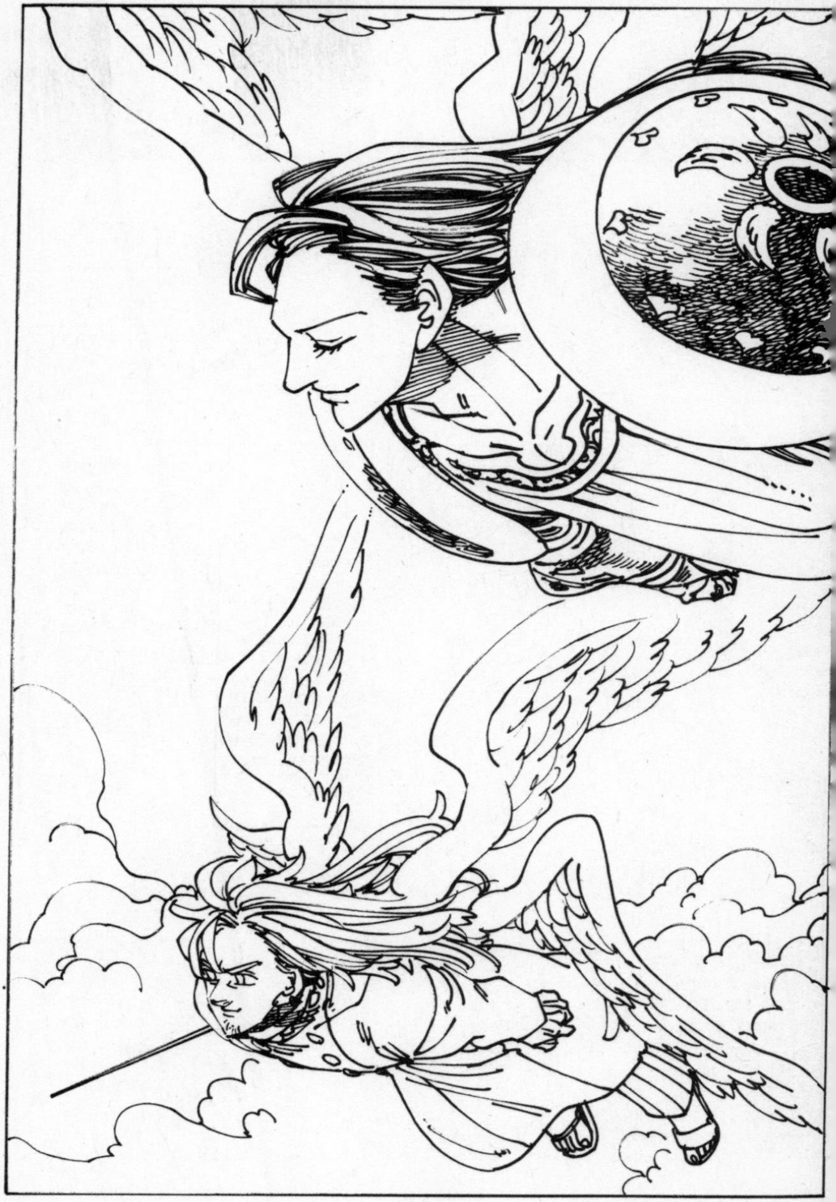

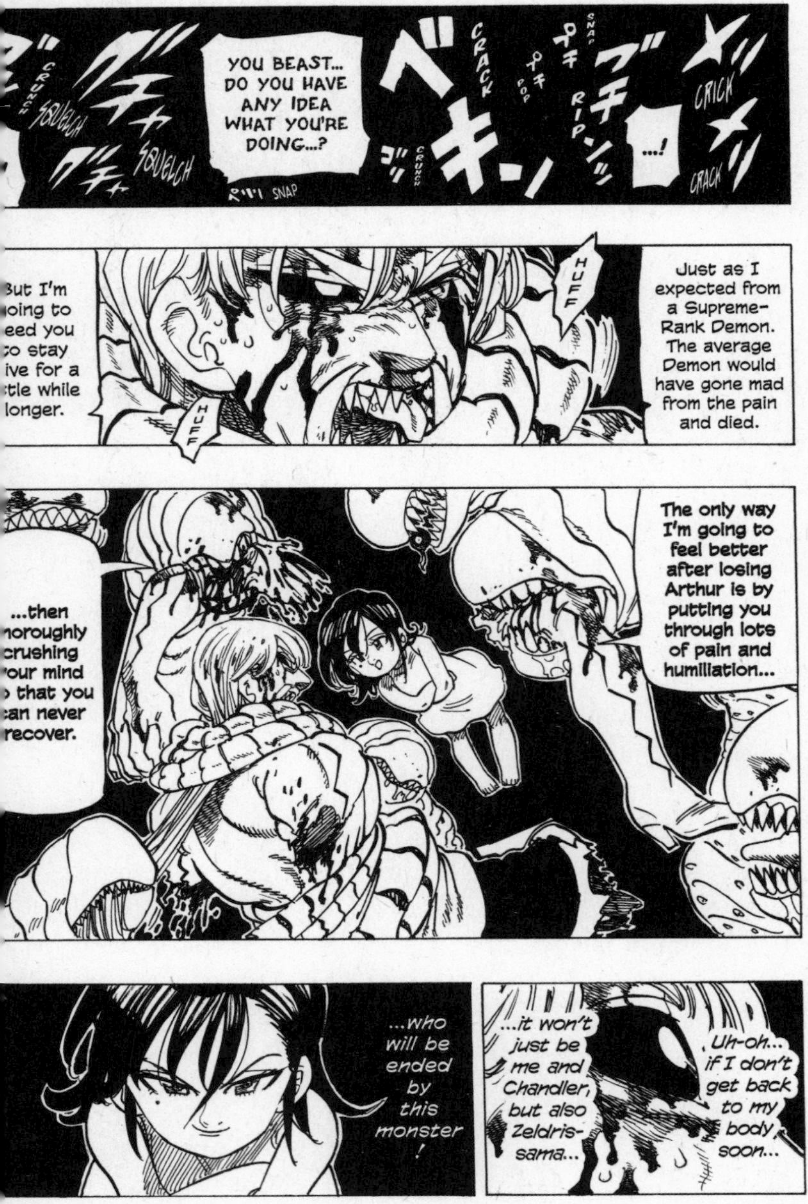
CRICK
CRACK
...!
SNAP
RIP
POP
CRACK
CRUNCH
YOU BEAST... DO YOU HAVE ANY IDEA WHAT YOU'RE DOING...?
SNAP
SQUELCH
SQUELCH
CRUNCH
Just as I expected from a Supreme-Rank Demon. The average Demon would have gone mad from the pain and died.
HUFF
HUFF
But I'm oing to eed you o stay ive for a tle while longer.
The only way I'm going to feel better after losing Arthur is by putting you through lots of pain and humiliation...
...then horoughly crushing our mind that you an never recover.
Uh-oh... if I don't get back to my body soon...
...it won't just be me and Chandler, but also Zeldris-sama...
...who will be ended by this monster!

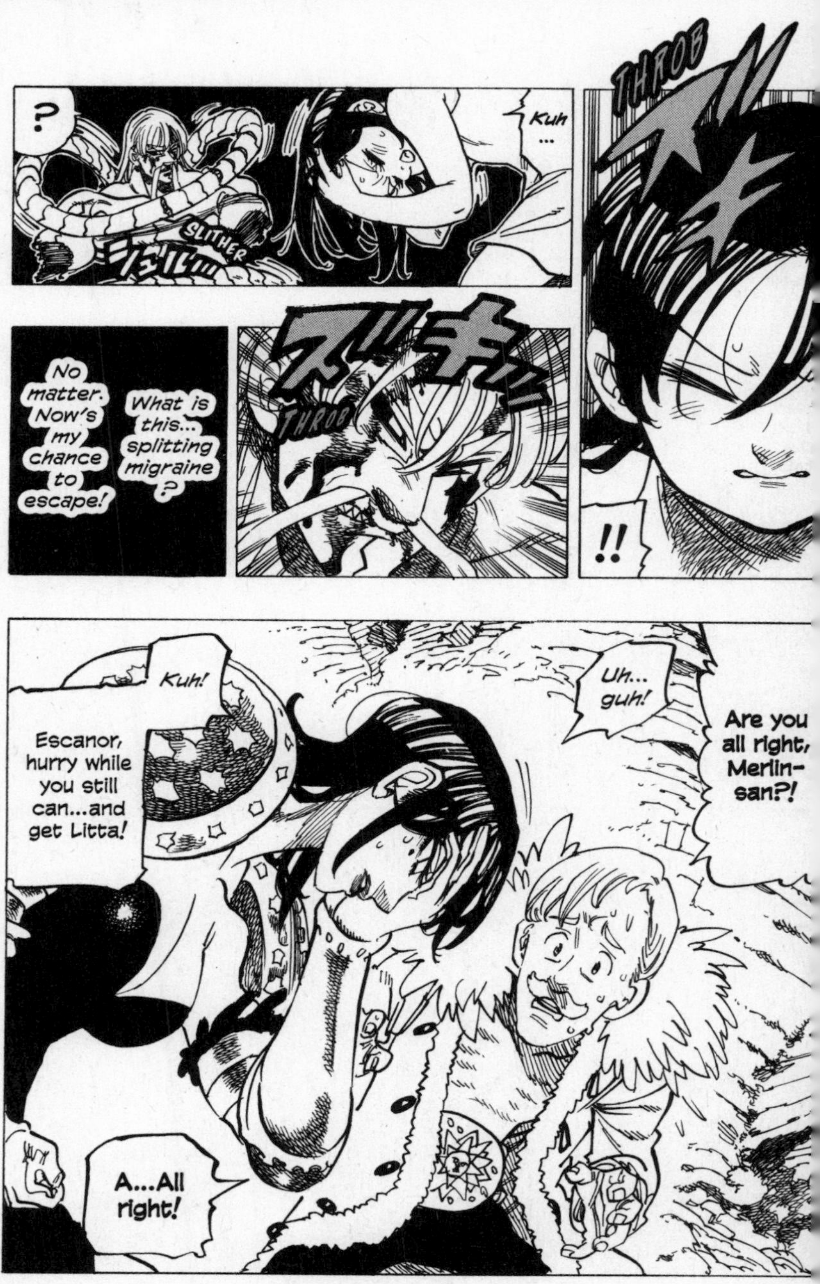

THROB
!!
Kuh
...
?
SLITHER
THROB
What is this... splitting migraine?
No matter. Now's my chance to escape!
Are you all right, Merlin-san?!
Uh... guh!
Kuh!
Escanor, hurry while you still can...and get Litta!
A...All right!

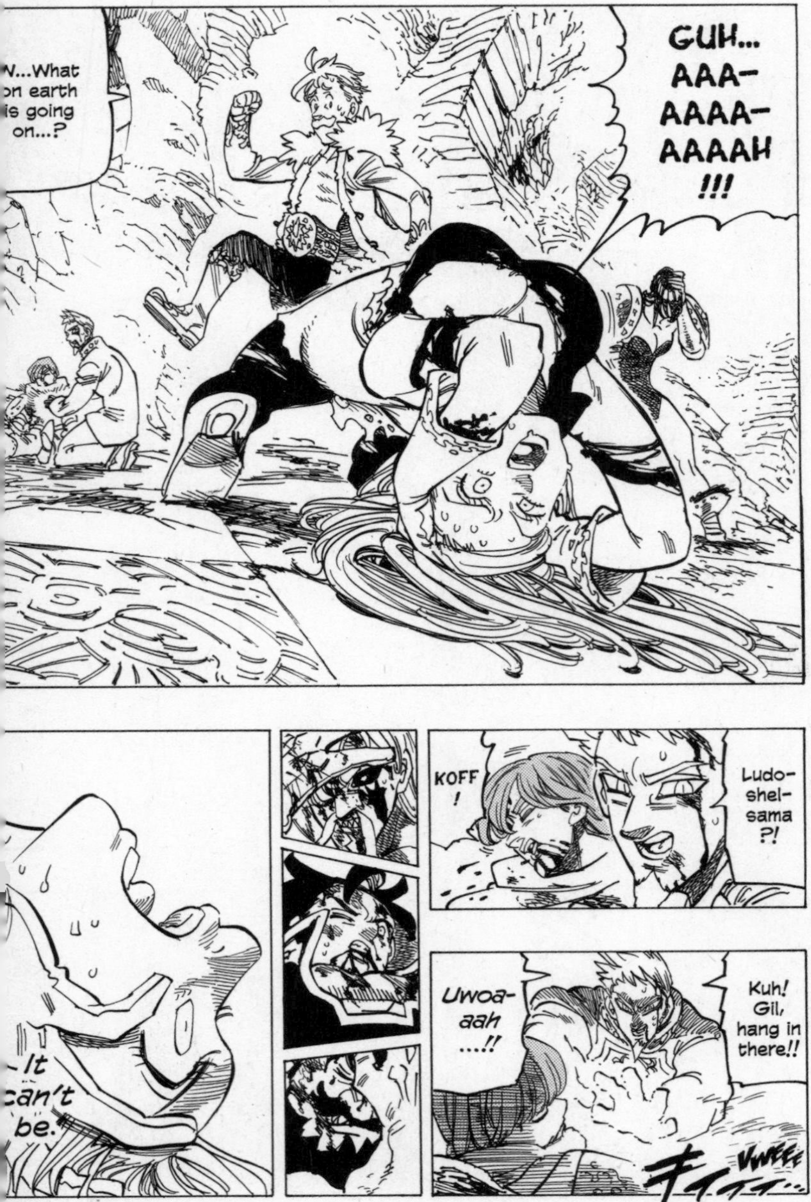
GUH... AAA-AAAA-AAAAH!!!
...What on earth is going on...?
Ludo-shel-sama ?!
KOFF !
Kuh! Gil, hang in there!!
Uwoa-aah ....!!
VWEEE
It can't be.

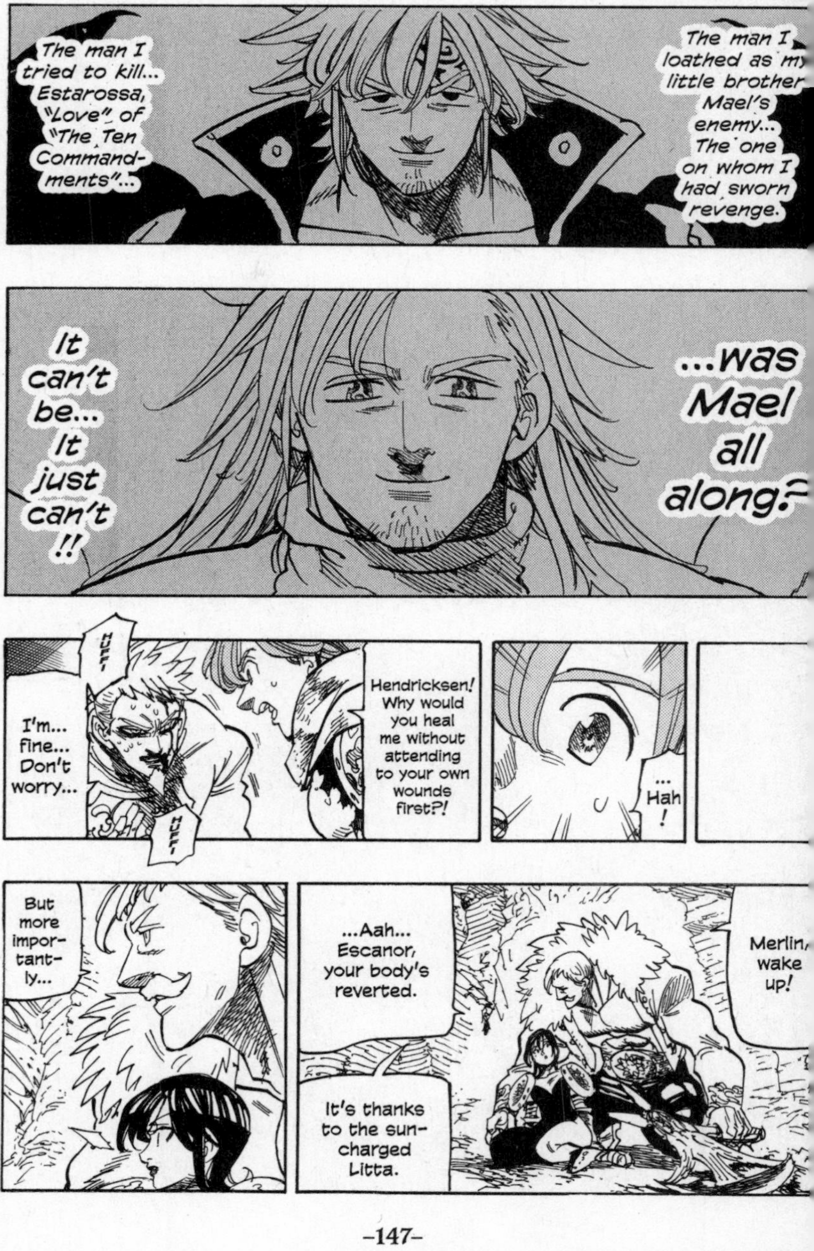

The man I loathed as my little brother Mael's enemy... The one on whom I had sworn revenge.
The man I tried to kill... Estarossa, "Love" of "The Ten Commandments"...
...was Mael all along?
It can't be... It just can't!!
...Hah!
Hendricksen! Why would you heal me without attending to your own wounds first?!
HUFF
I'm... fine... Don't worry...
HUFF
Merlin, wake up!
...Aah... Escanor, your body's reverted.
It's thanks to the sun-charged Litta.
But more importantly...

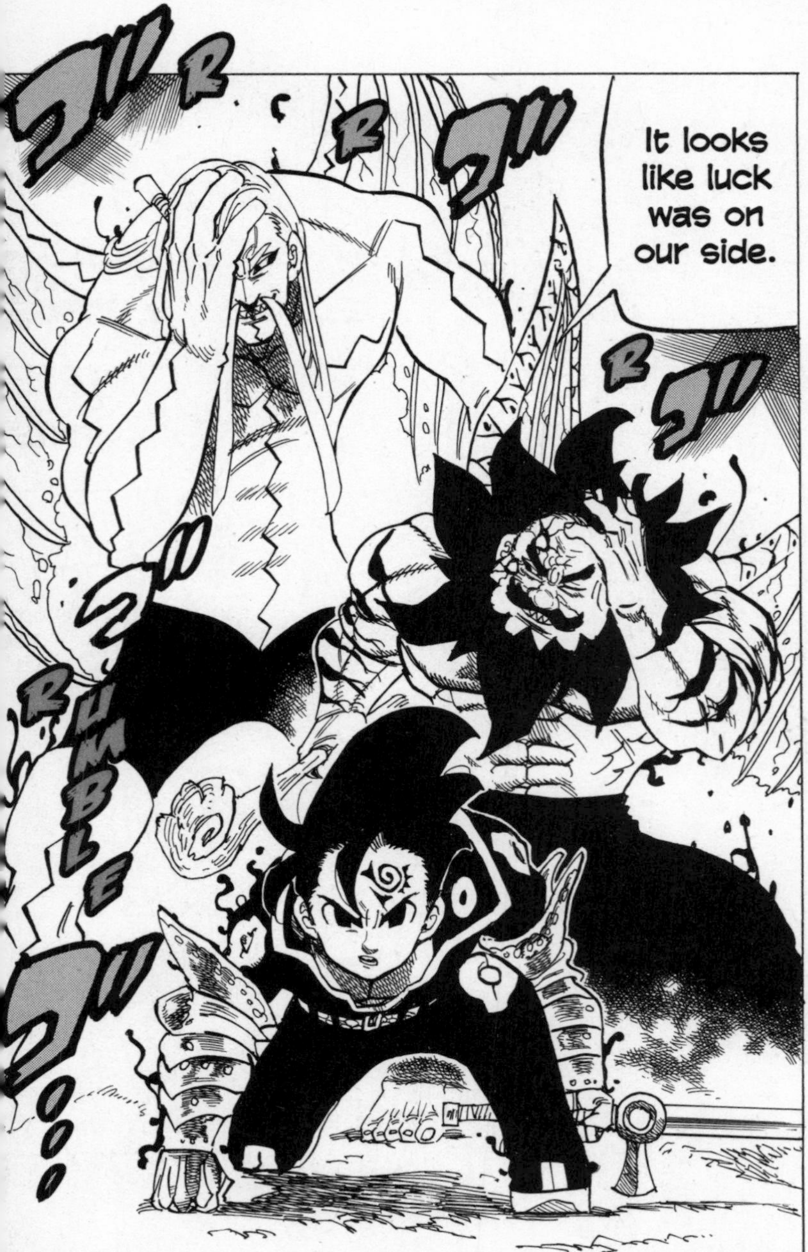
It looks like luck was on our side.
RUMBLE

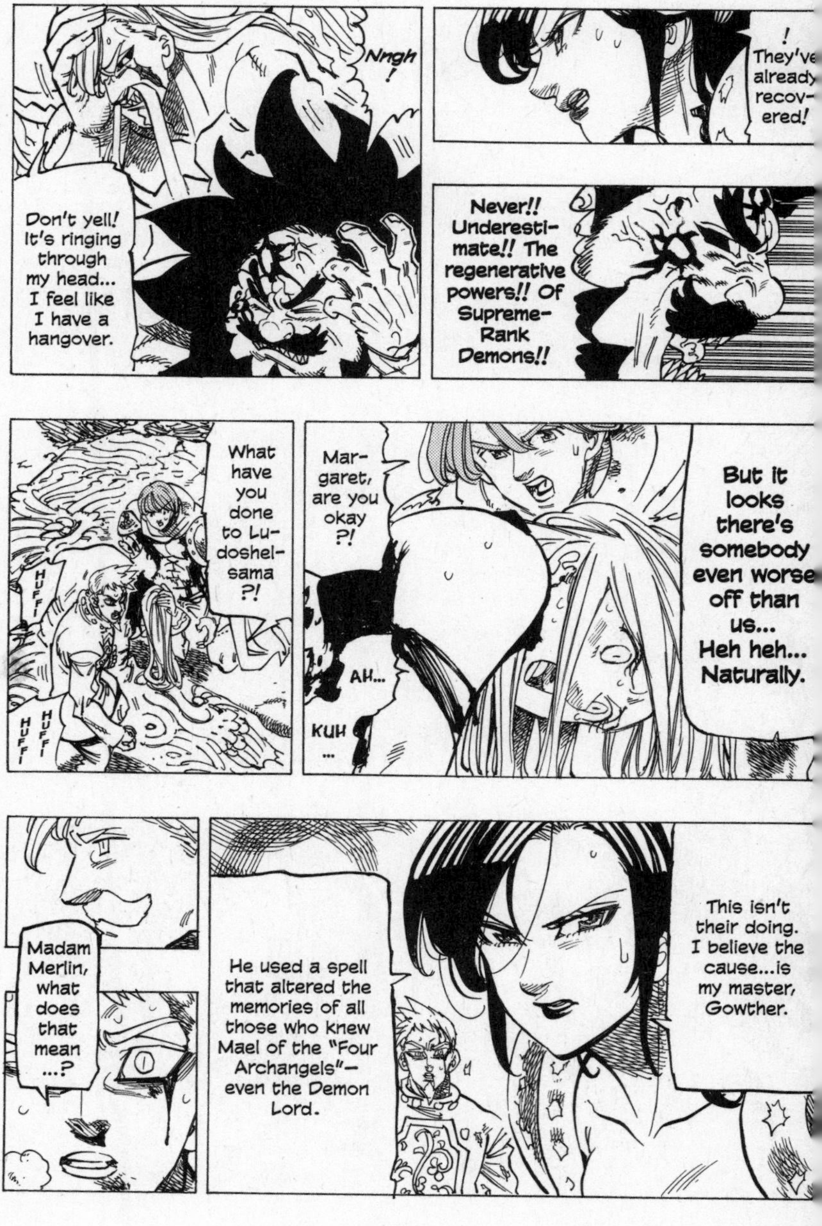

! They've already recovered!
Never!! Underestimate!! The regenerative powers!! Of Supreme-Rank Demons!!
Nngh !
Don't yell! It's ringing through my head... I feel like I have a hangover.
But it looks there's somebody even worse off than us... Heh heh... Naturally.
Margaret, are you okay ?!
AH...
KUH ...
What have you done to Ludoshel-sama ?!
HUFF
HUFF
HUFF
This isn't their doing. I believe the cause...is my master, Gowther.
He used a spell that altered the memories of all those who knew Mael of the "Four Archangels"—even the Demon Lord.
Madam Merlin, what does that mean ...?

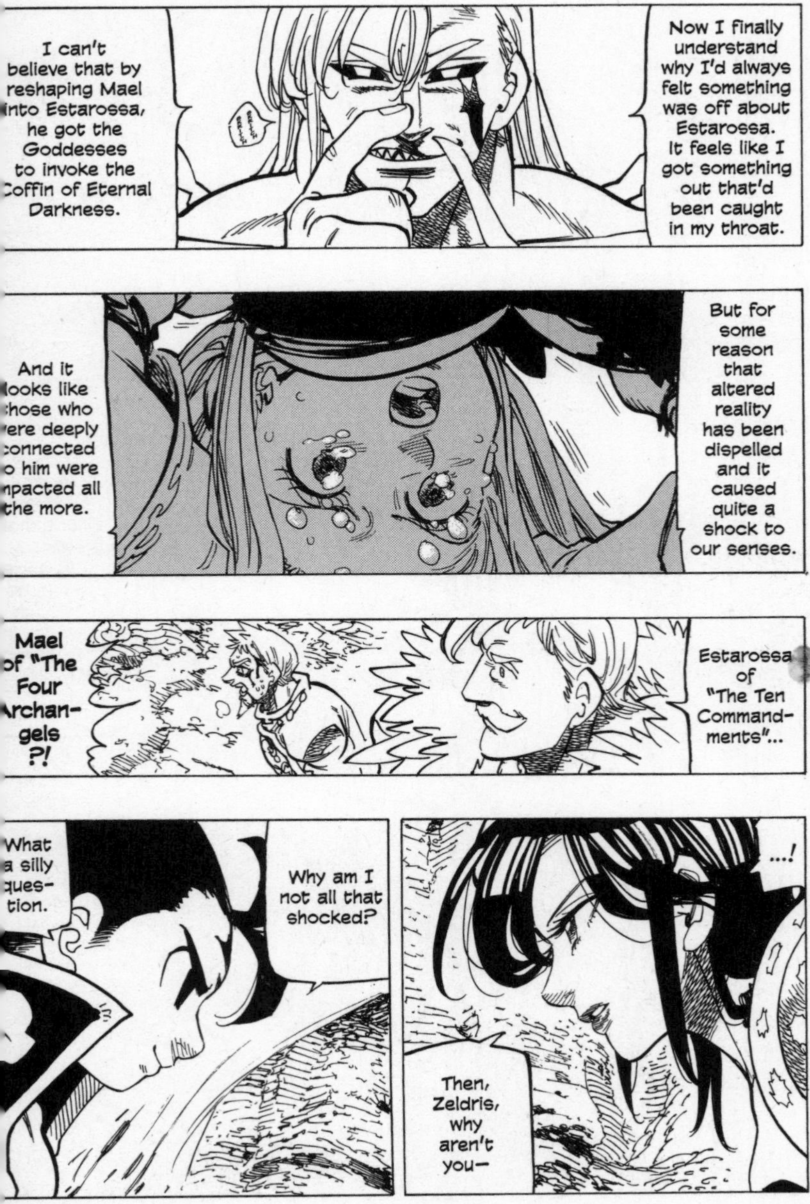

Now I finally understand why I'd always felt something was off about Estarossa. It feels like I got something out that'd been caught in my throat.
I can't believe that by reshaping Mael into Estarossa, he got the Goddesses to invoke the Coffin of Eternal Darkness.
But for some reason that altered reality has been dispelled and it caused quite a shock to our senses.
And it looks like those who were deeply connected to him were impacted all the more.
Estarossa of "The Ten Command- ments"...
Mael of "The Four Archan- gels ?!
...!
Then, Zeldris, why aren't you—
Why am I not all that shocked?
What a silly ques- tion.

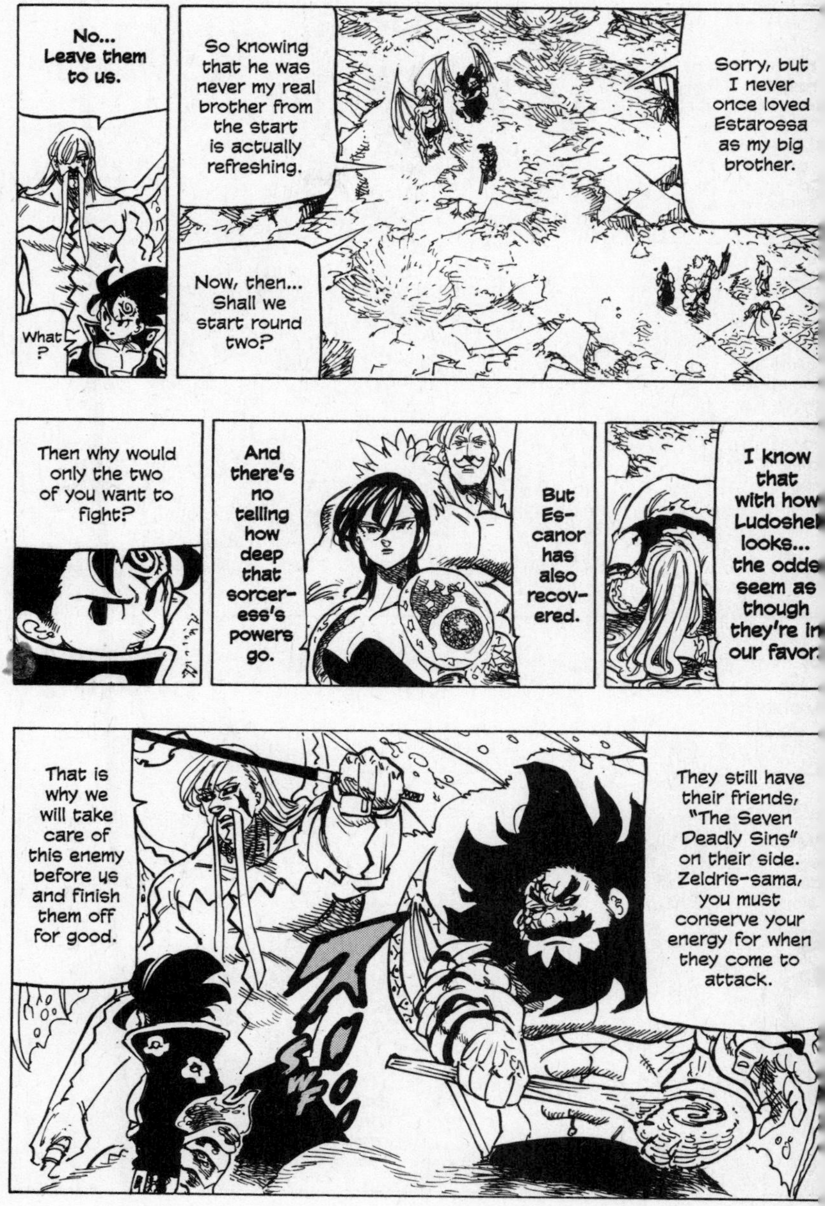
Sorry, but I never once loved Estarossa as my big brother.
So knowing that he was never my real brother from the start is actually refreshing.
Now, then... Shall we start round two?
No... Leave them to us.
What?
I know that with how Ludoshel looks... the odds seem as though they're in our favor.
But Es-canor has also recov-ered.
And there's no telling how deep that sorcer-ess's powers go.
Then why would only the two of you want to fight?
They still have their friends, "The Seven Deadly Sins" on their side. Zeldris-sama, you must conserve your energy for when they come to attack.
That is why we will take care of this enemy before us and finish them off for good.
SWF

This is our task.

IT MUST BE DONE!

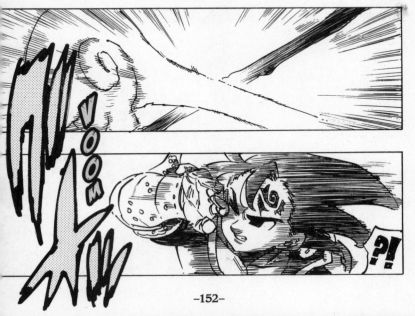

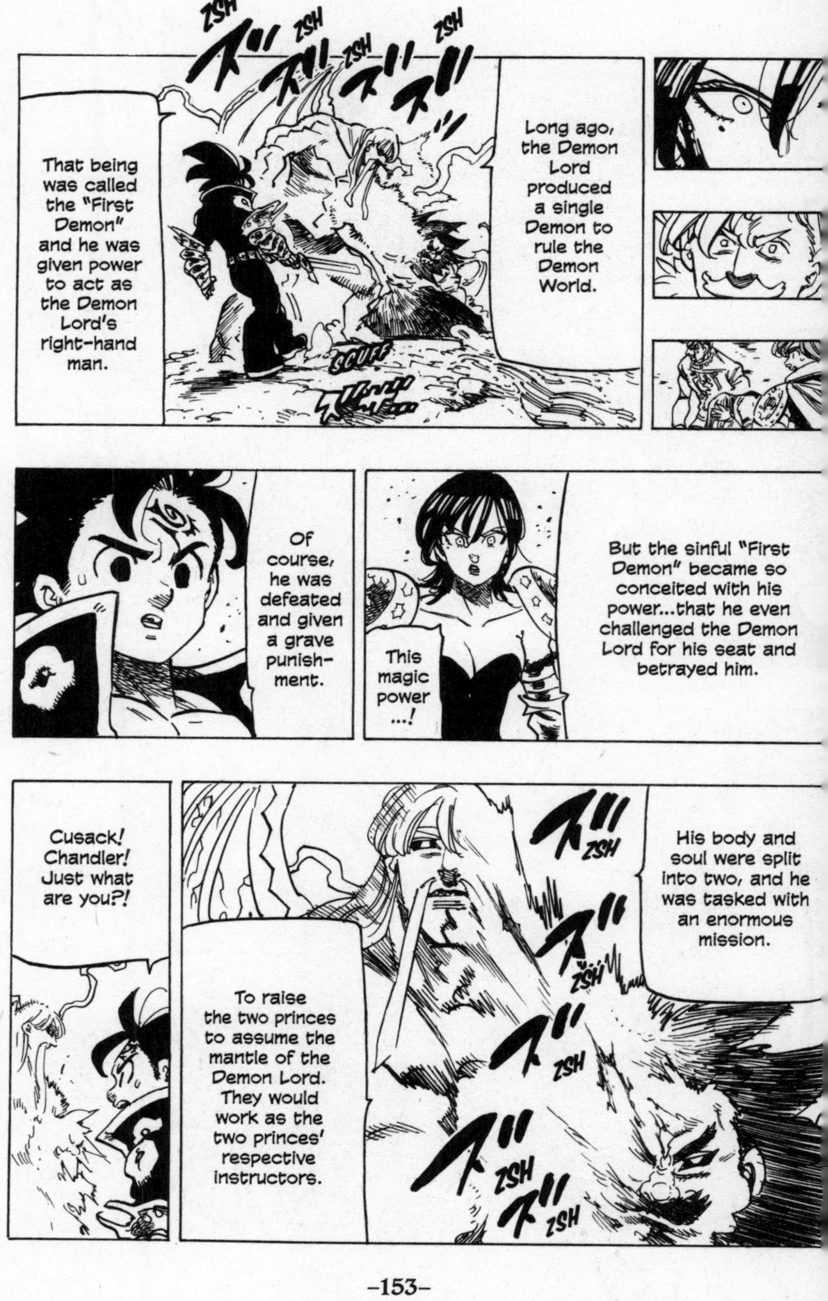
ZSH
ZSH
ZSH
ZSH
Long ago, the Demon Lord produced a single Demon to rule the Demon World.
That being was called the "First Demon" and he was given power to act as the Demon Lord's right-hand man.
SCUFF
But the sinful "First Demon" became so conceited with his power...that he even challenged the Demon Lord for his seat and betrayed him.
This magic power ...!
Of course, he was defeated and given a grave punish-ment.
His body and soul were split into two, and he was tasked with an enormous mission.
ZSH
ZSH
ZSH
ZSH
ZSH
To raise the two princes to assume the mantle of the Demon Lord. They would work as the two princes' respective instructors.
Cusack! Chandler! Just what are you?!

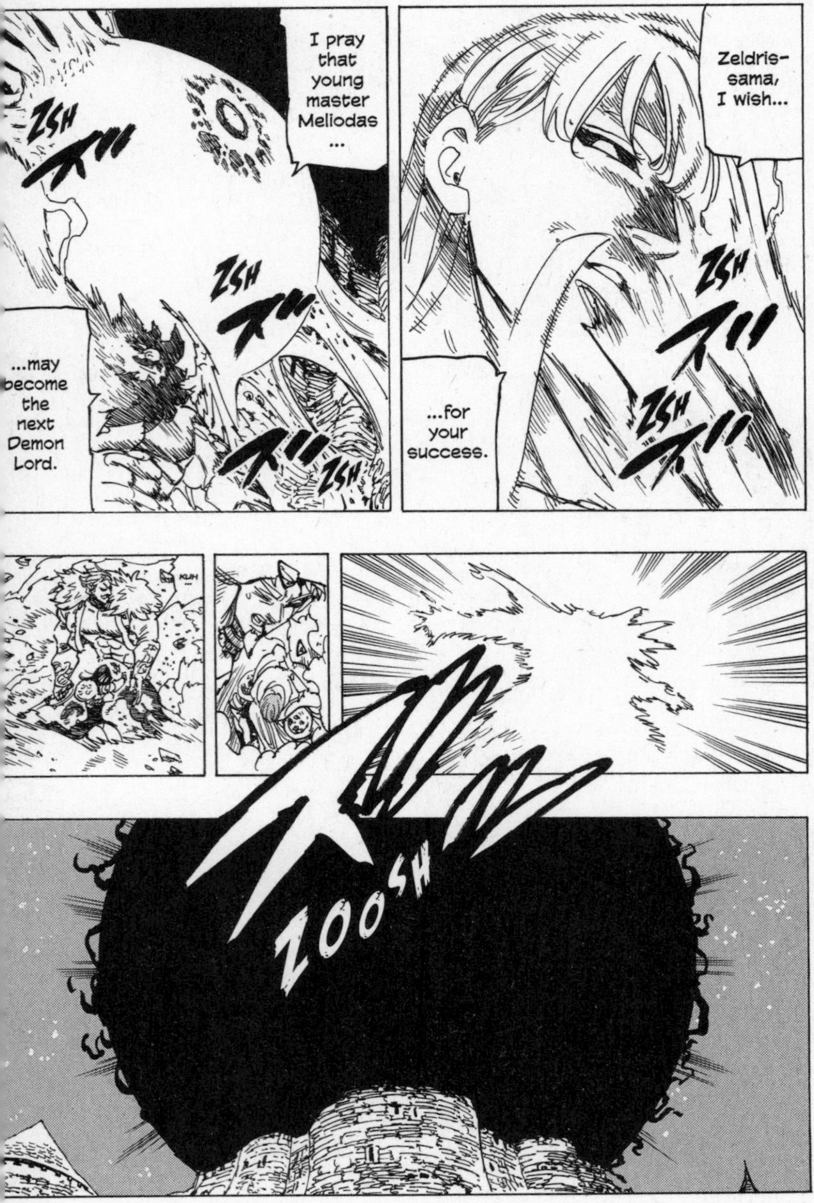
Zeldris-sama, I wish...
ZSH
ZSH
...for your success.
I pray that young master Meliodas ...
ZSH
ZSH
...may become the next Demon Lord.
ZSH
KUH ...
ZOOSH

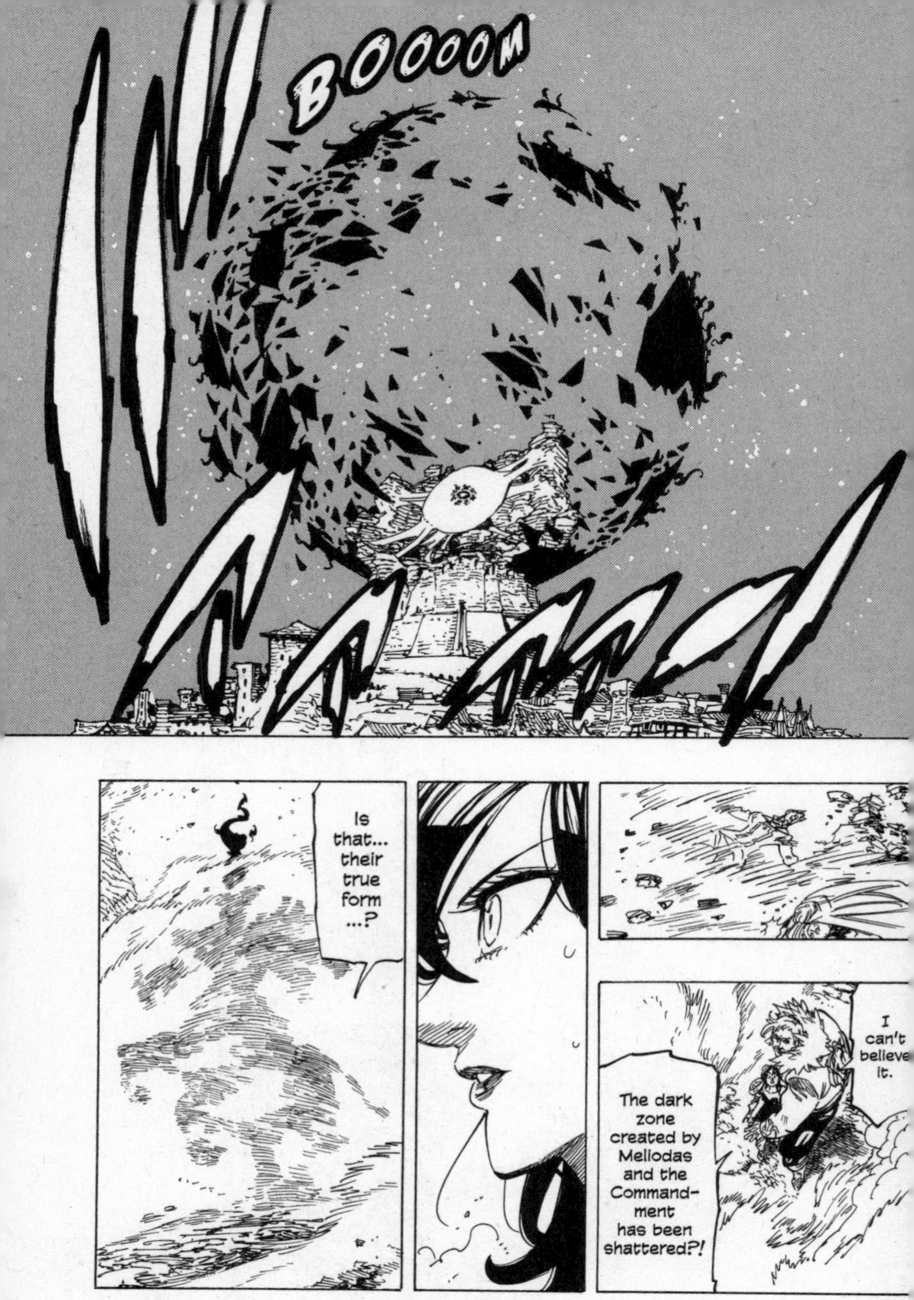
BOOOOM
I can't believe it.
The dark zone created by Meliodas and the Commandment has been shattered?!
Is that... their true form ...?

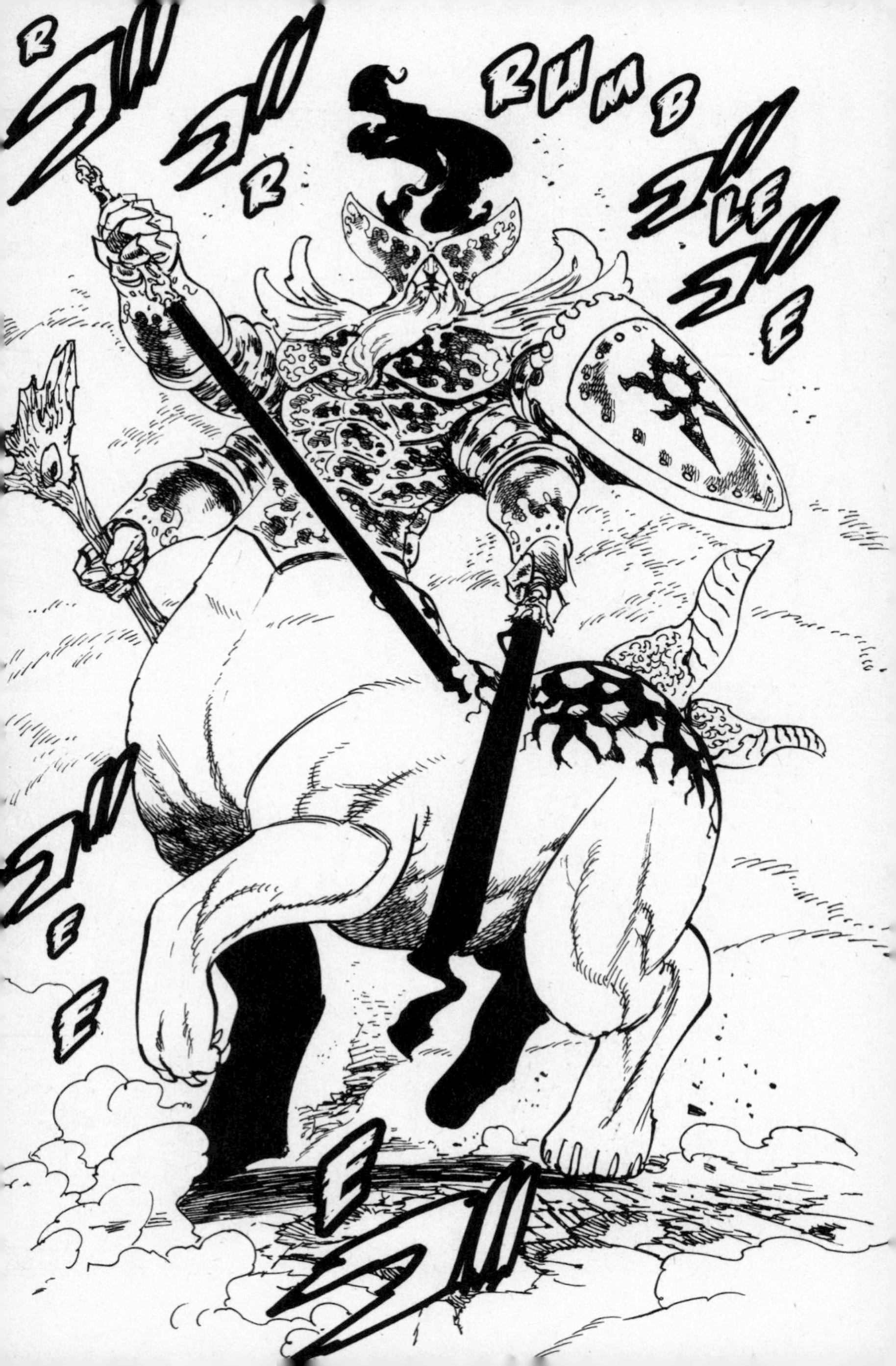
RUMBLE
E
R
R
E
E
E

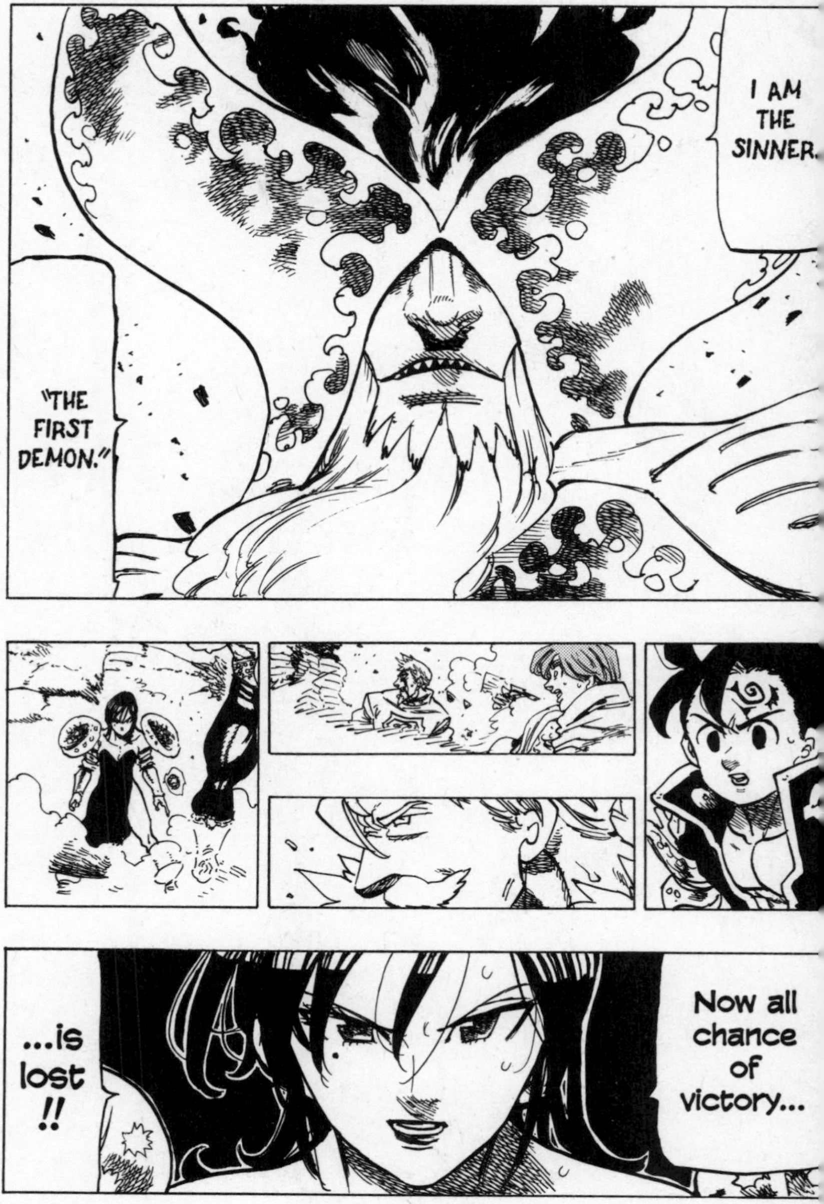
I AM THE SINNER.
"THE FIRST DEMON."
Now all chance of victory...
...is lost !!

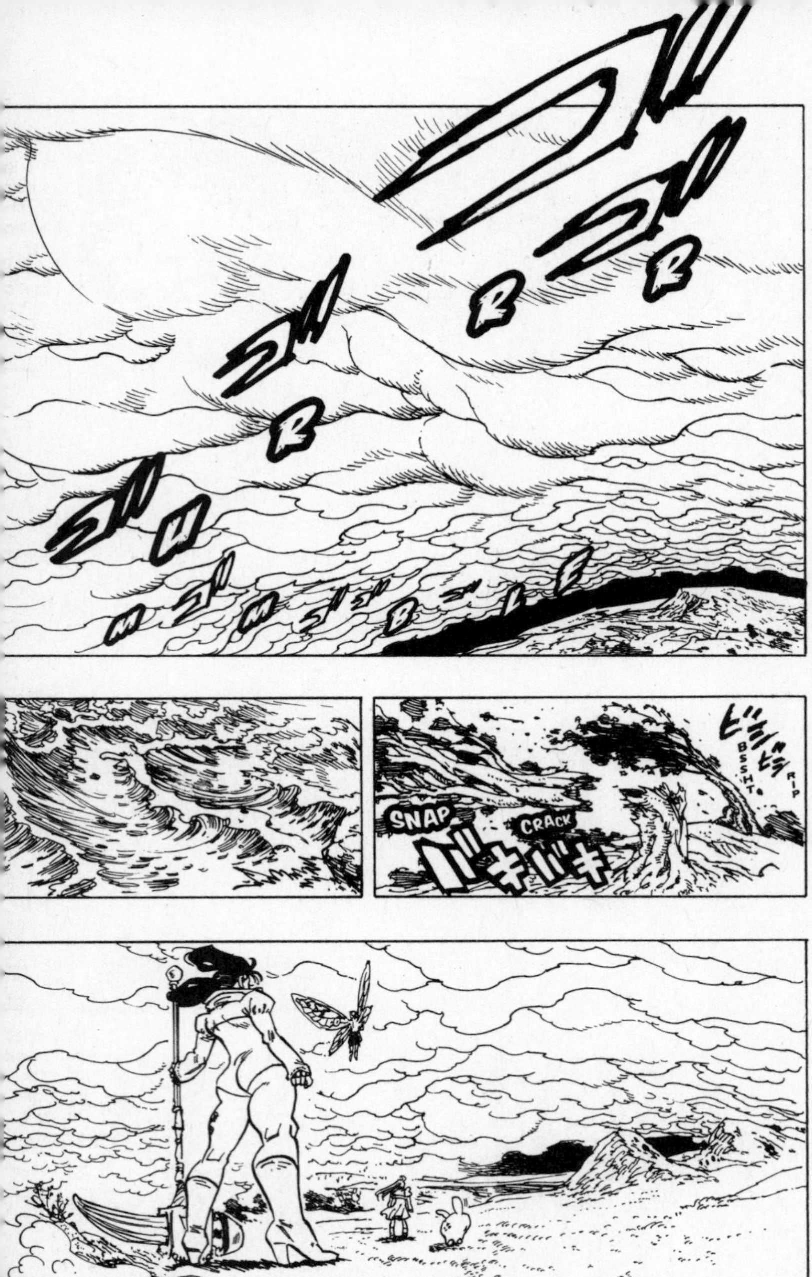
BSSHT
RIP
CRACK
SNAP
バキバキ

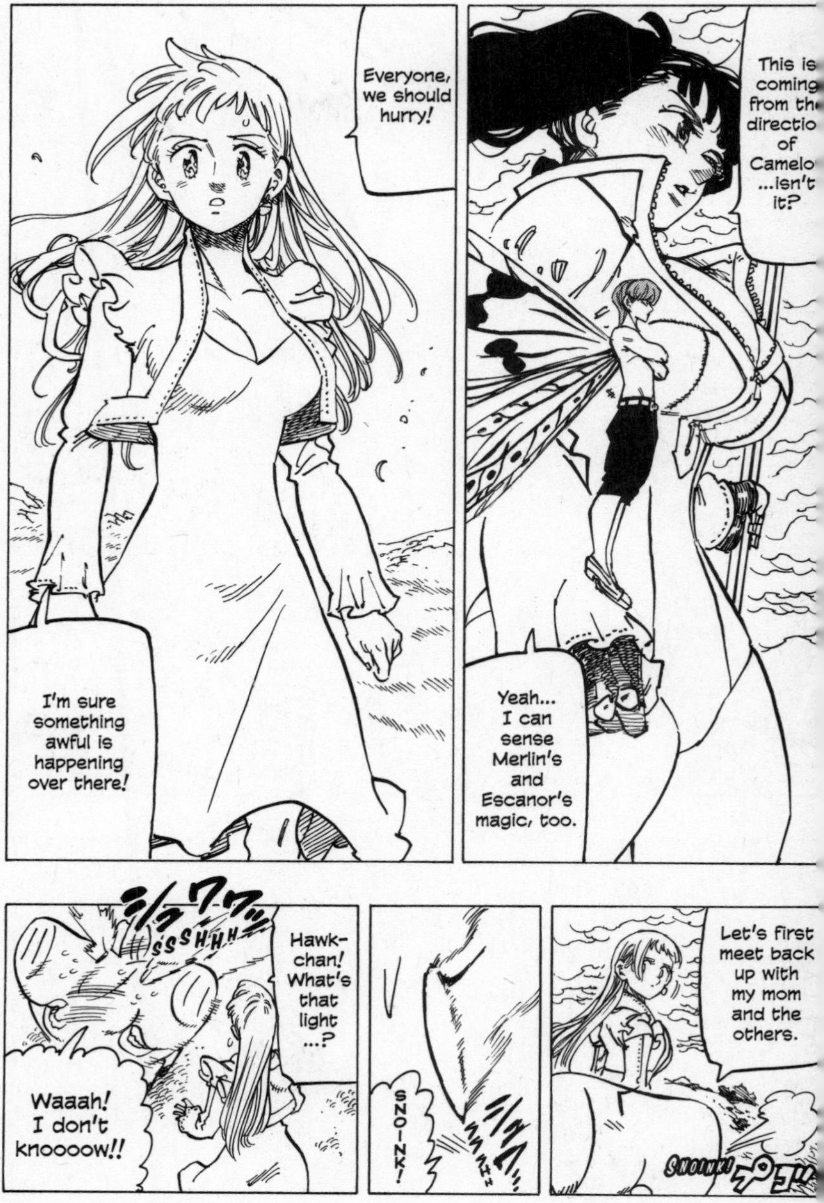
This is coming from th directio of Camelo ...isn't it?
Yeah... I can sense Merlin's and Escanor's magic, too.
Everyone, we should hurry!
I'm sure something awful is happening over there!
Let's first meet back up with my mom and the others.
SNOINK
SNO-INK!
SHH
SSSHHH
Hawk-chan! What's that light ...?
Waaah! I don't knoooow!!

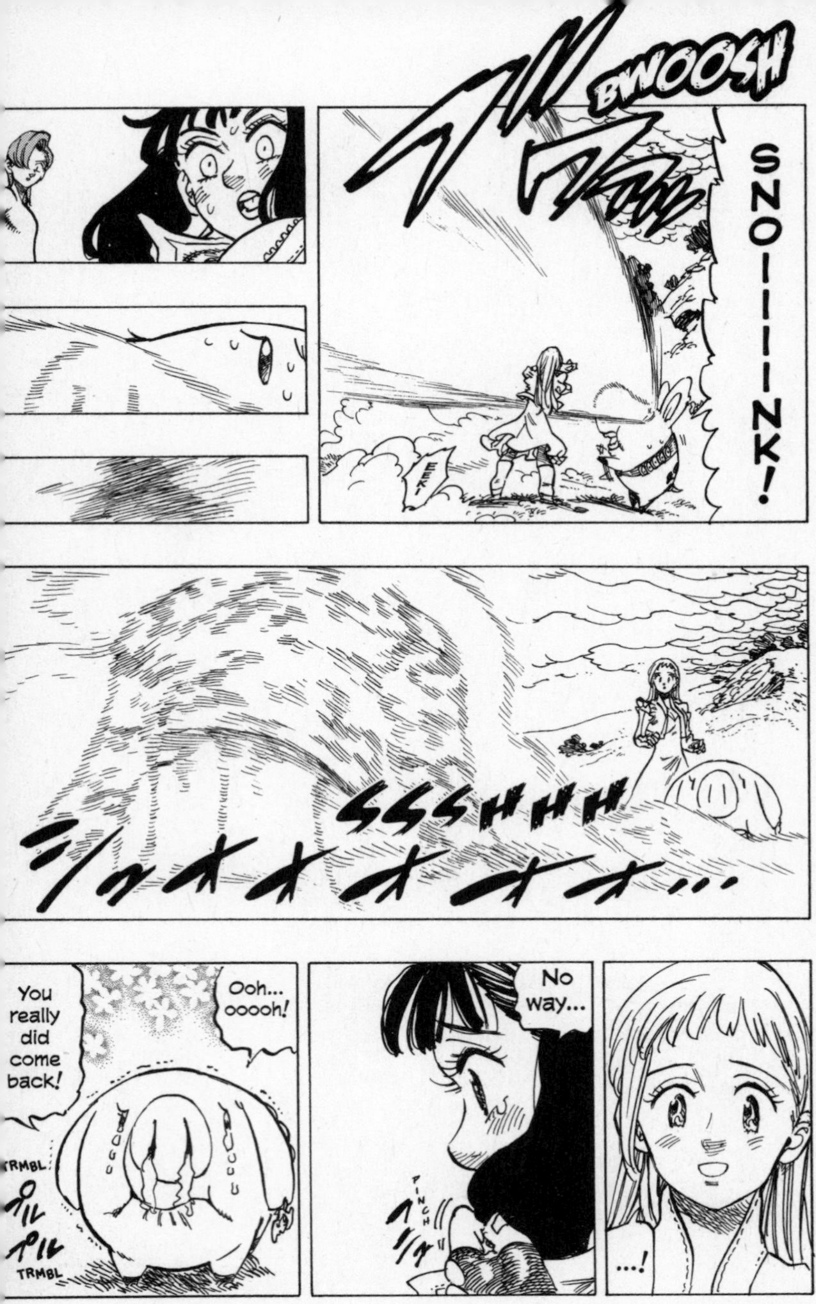
BWOOSH
SNOIIIINK!
EEK!
SSSHHH
シュオオオオオ…
...!
No way...
PINCH
Ooh... ooooh!
You really did come back!
TRMBL
プルプル
TRMBL

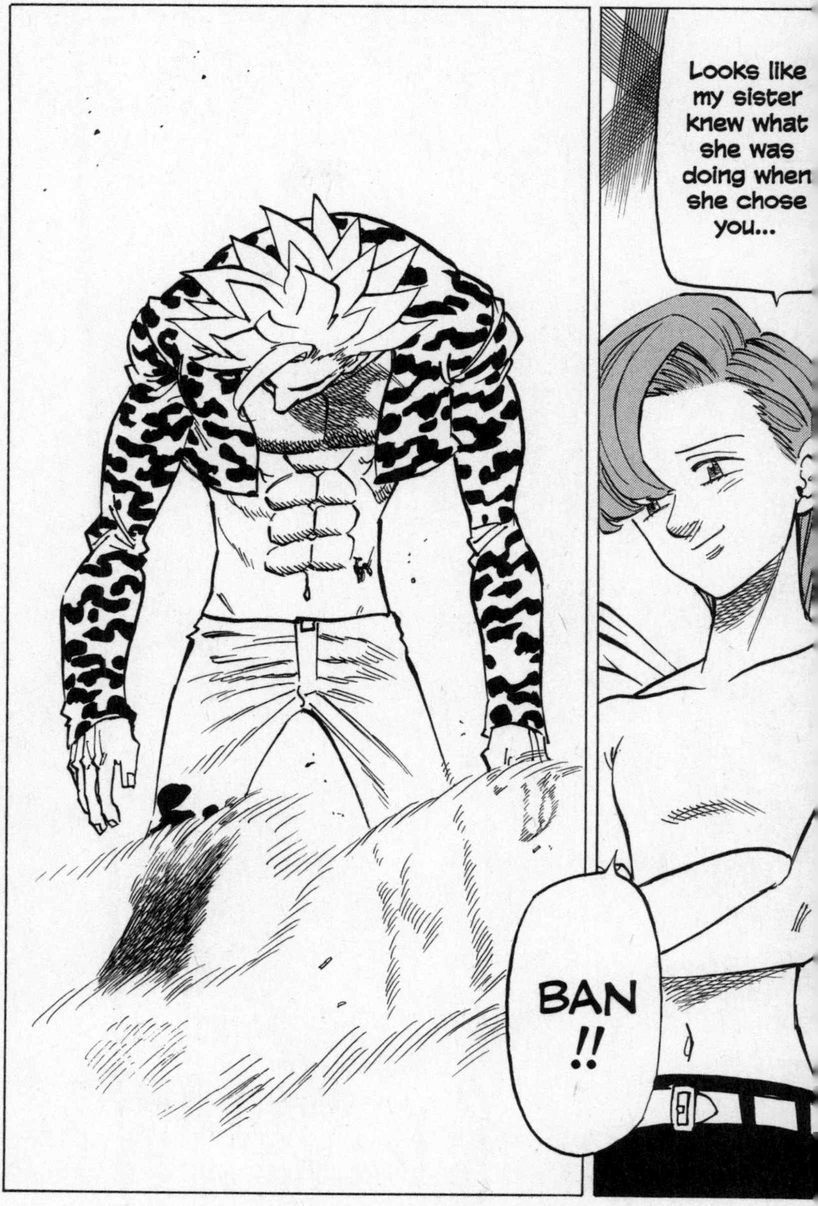
Looks like my sister knew what she was doing when she chose you...
BAN !!

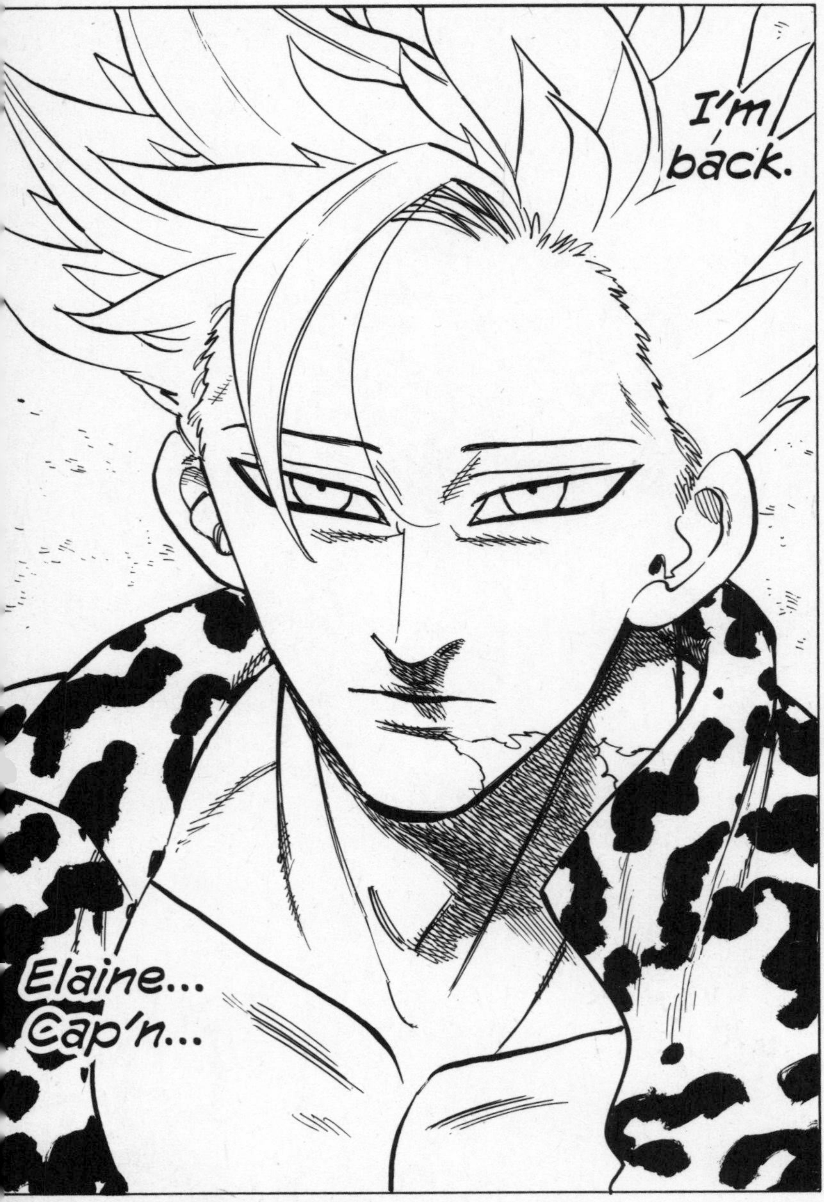
I'm back.
Elaine... Cap'n...

Chapter 293 - When “Someday” Comes Tru

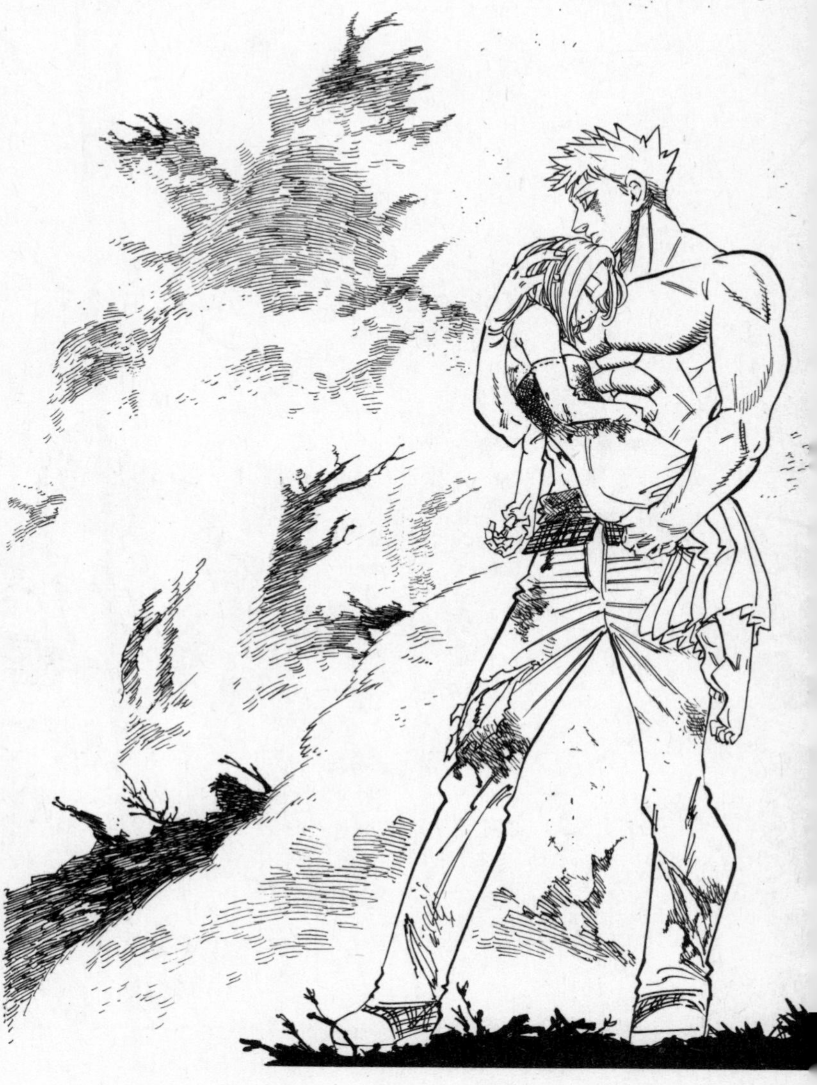

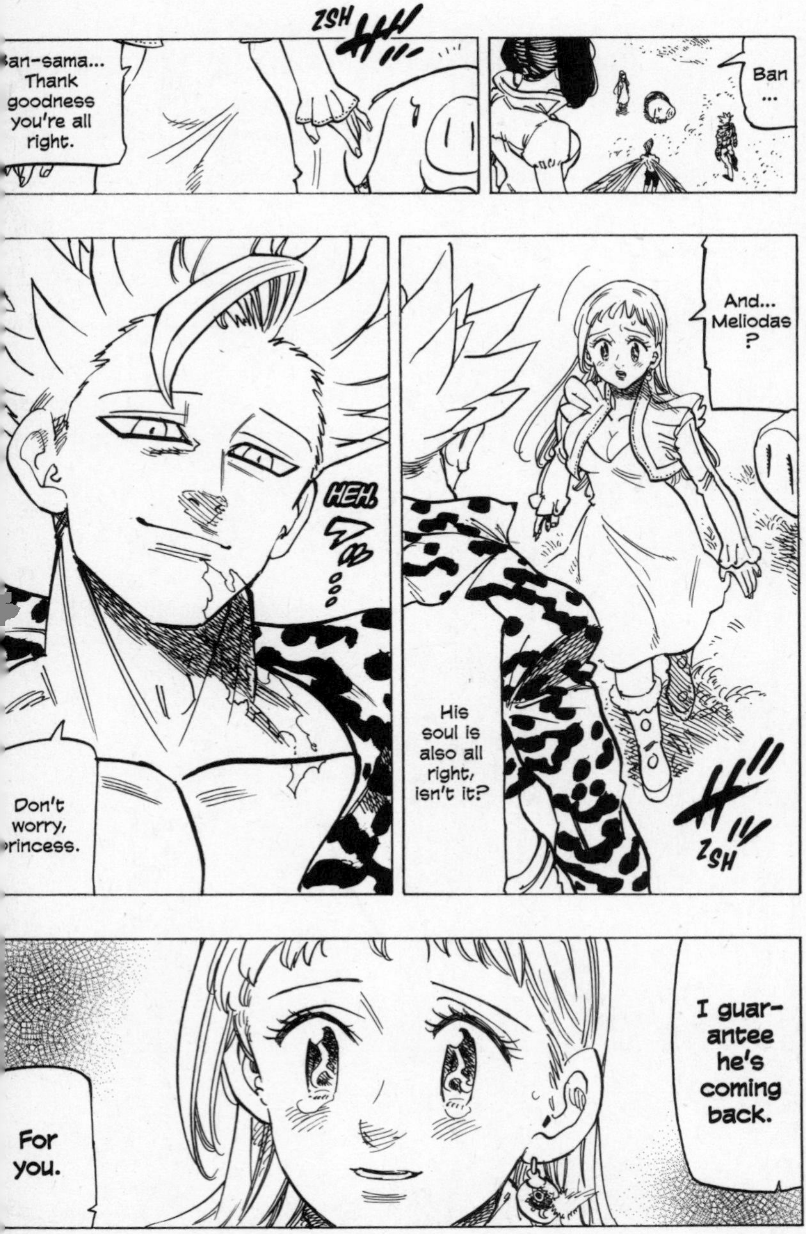
Ban ...
ZSH
an-sama... Thank goodness you're all right.
And... Meliodas ?
His soul is also all right, isn't it?
ZSH
HEH.
Don't worry, rincess.
I guar-antee he's coming back.
For you.

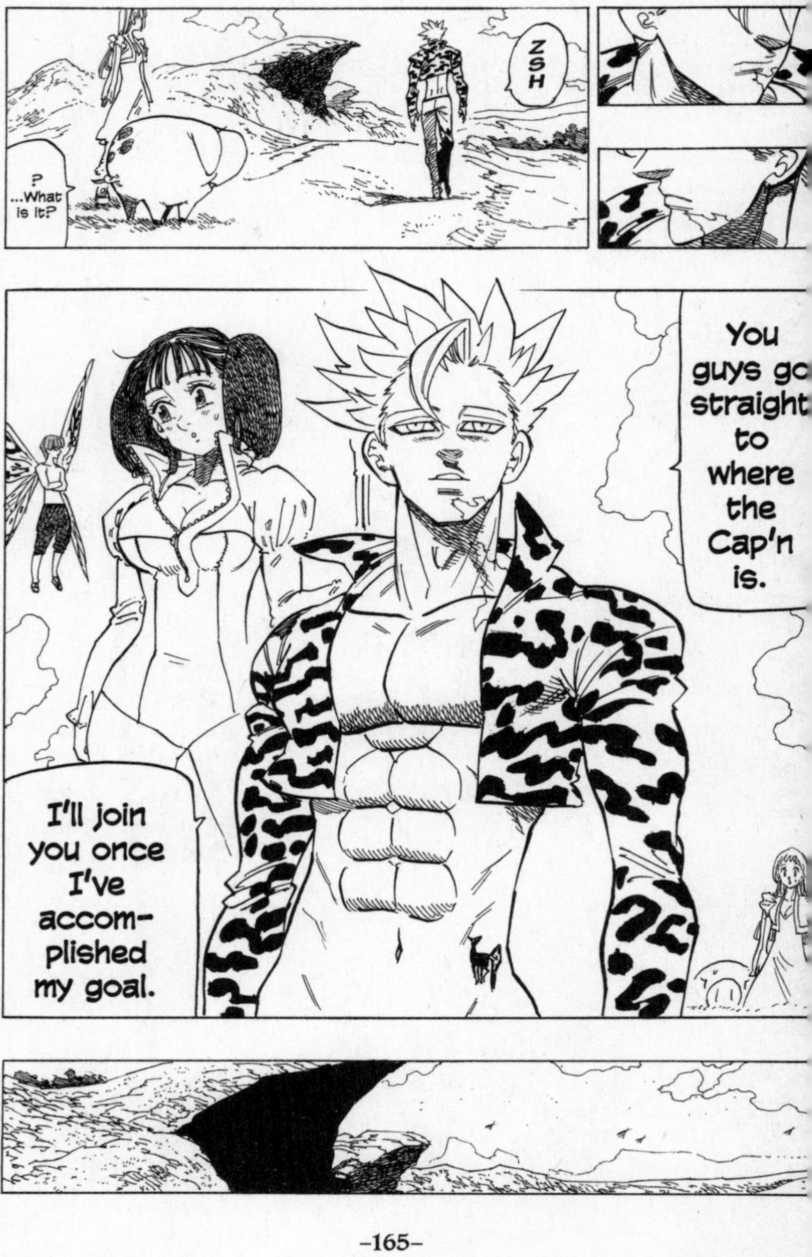
ZSH
? ...What is it?
You guys go straight to where the Cap'n is.
I'll join you once I've accomplished my goal.

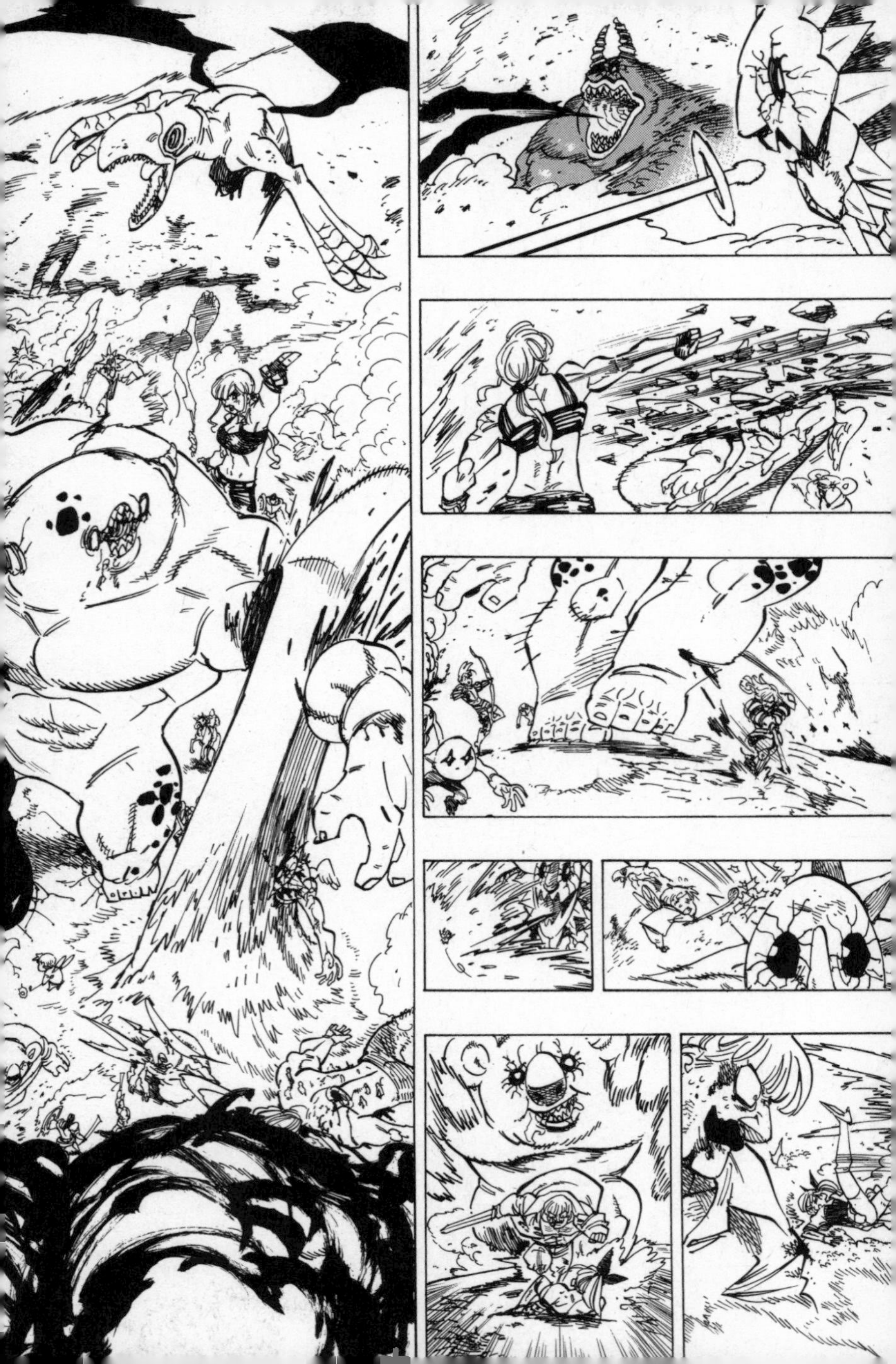

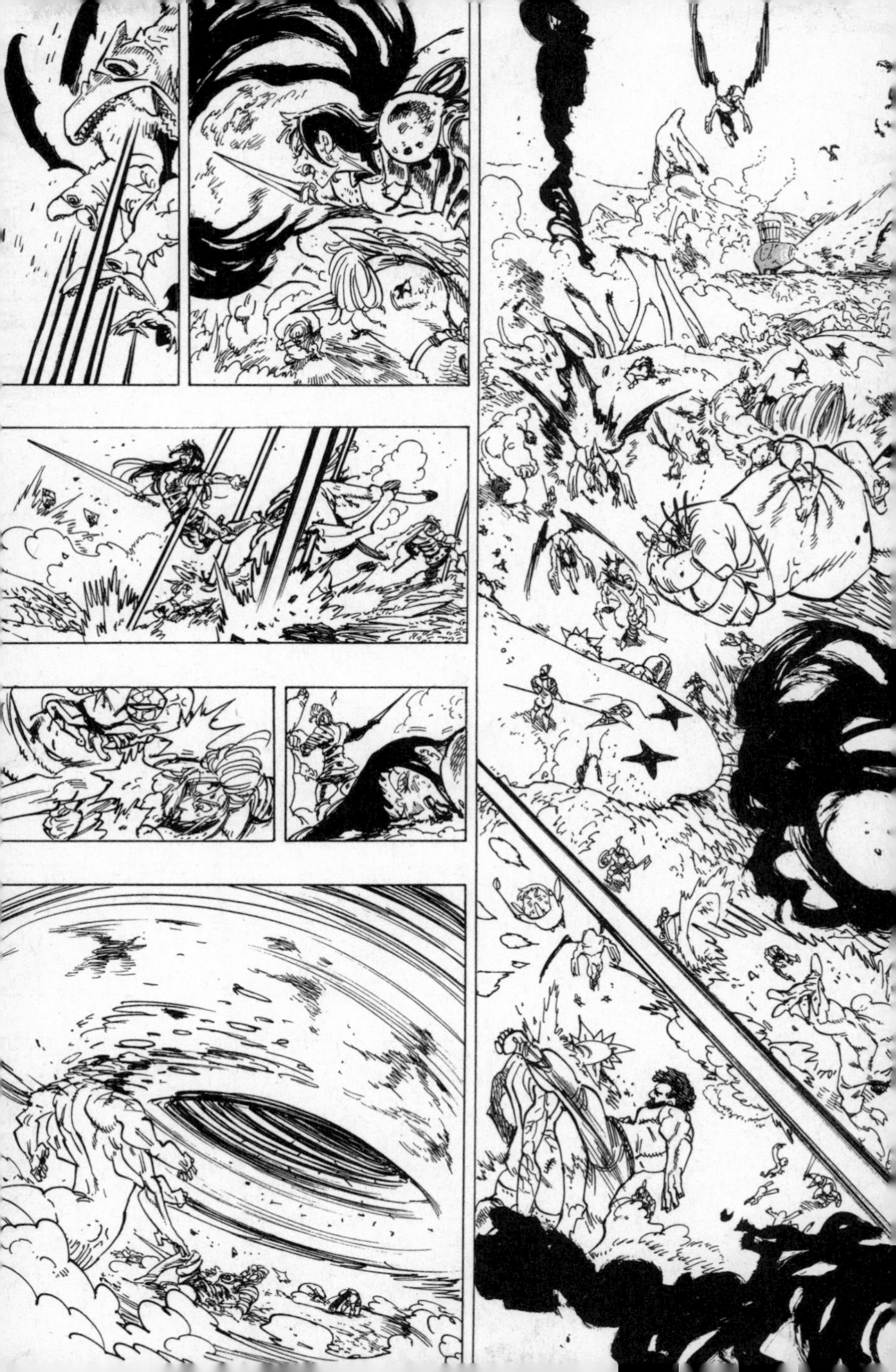

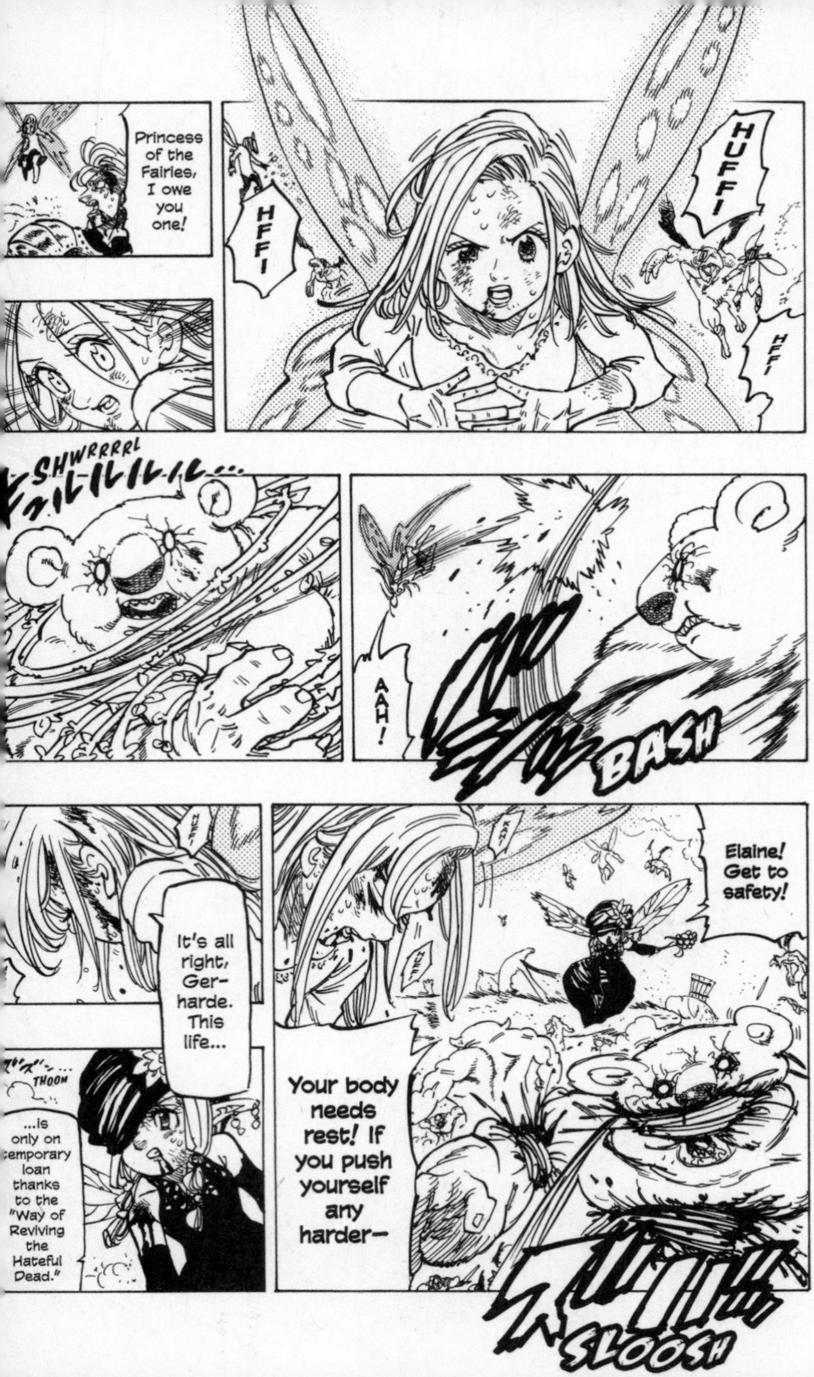
HUFF!
HFF!
HFF!
Princess of the Fairies, I owe you one!
AAH!
BASH
SHWRRRRL
Elaine! Get to safety!
Your body needs rest! If you push yourself any harder—
SLOOSH
It's all right, Gerharde. This life...
THOOM
...is only on temporary loan thanks to the "Way of Reviving the Hateful Dead."

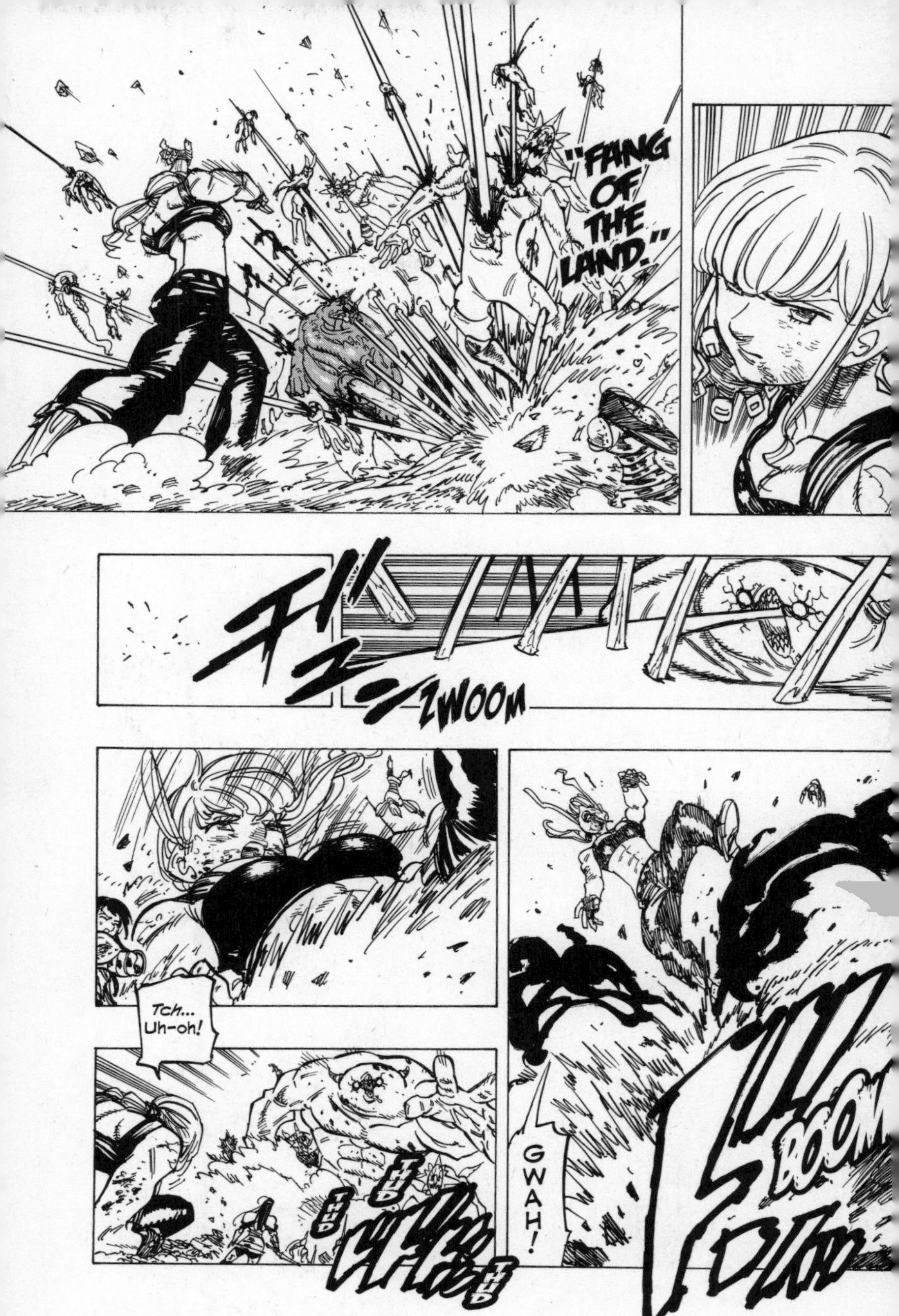
"FANG OF THE LAND."
ZWOOM
GWAH!
BOOM
Tch... Uh-oh!
THUD
THUD
THUD

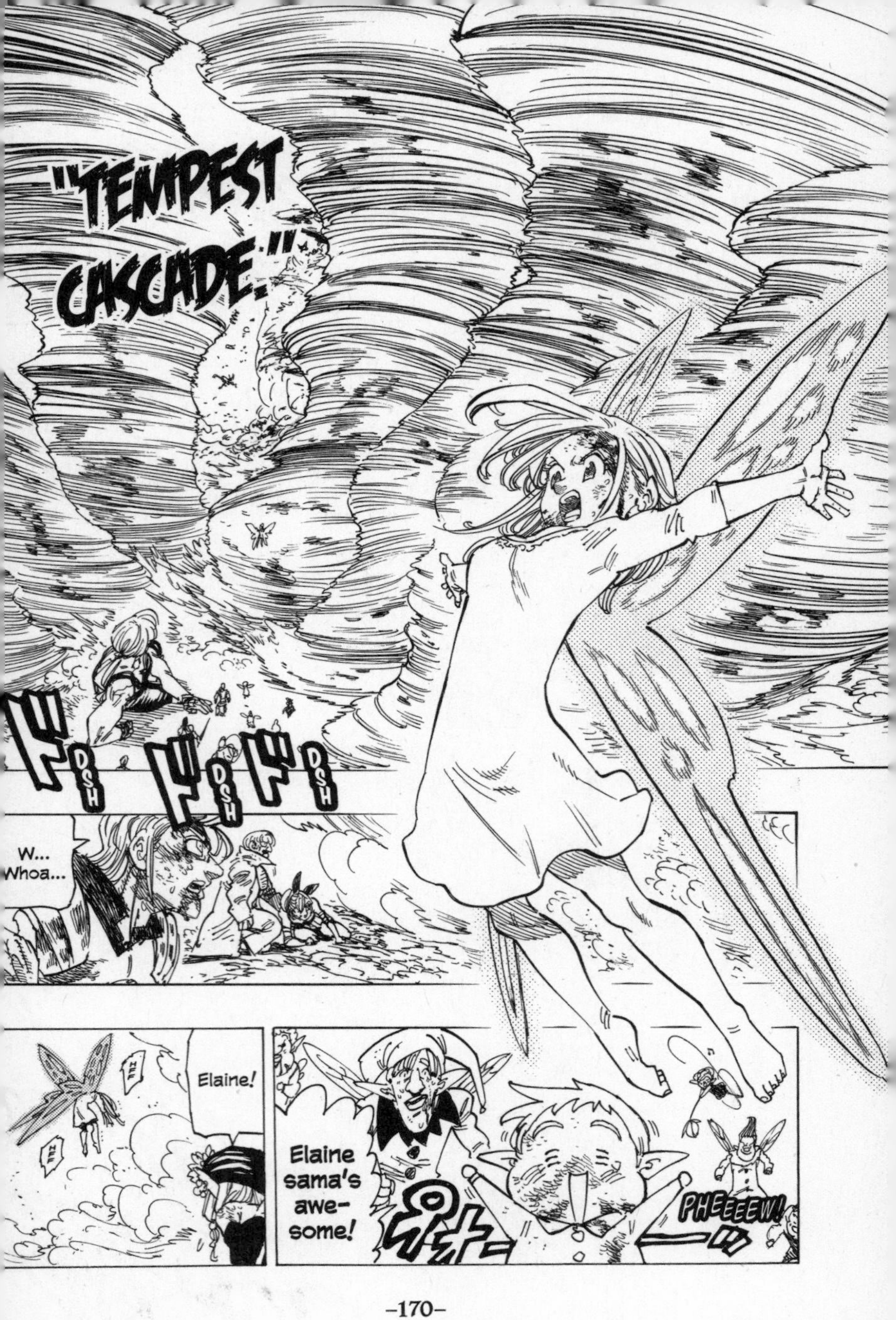
"TEMPEST CASCADE."
DSH
DSH
DSH
W... Whoa...
Elaine sama's awe-some!
PHEEEEW!
Elaine!
HEF
HEF

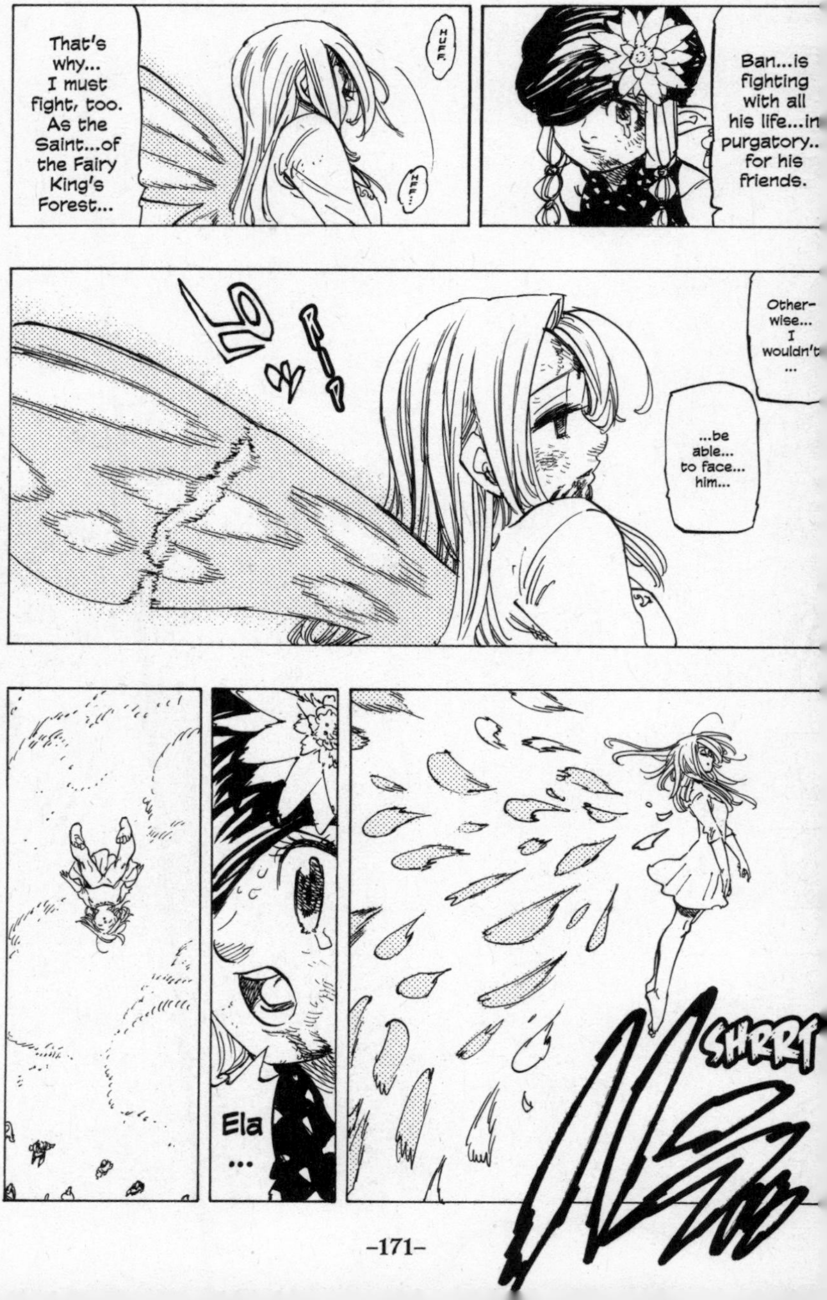
Ban...is fighting with all his life...in purgatory.. for his friends.
HUFF
HFF...
That's why... I must fight, too. As the Saint...of the Fairy King's Forest...
Other-wise... I wouldn't ...
...be able... to face... him...
RIP
SHRRT
Ela ...

CRICK
コキ

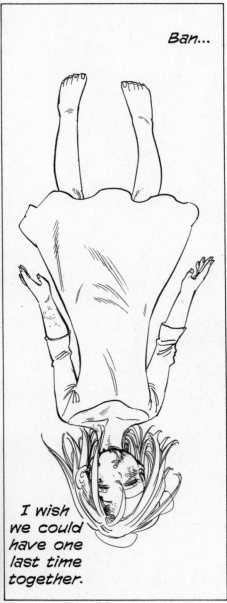

Ban...

I wish
we could
have one
last time
together.

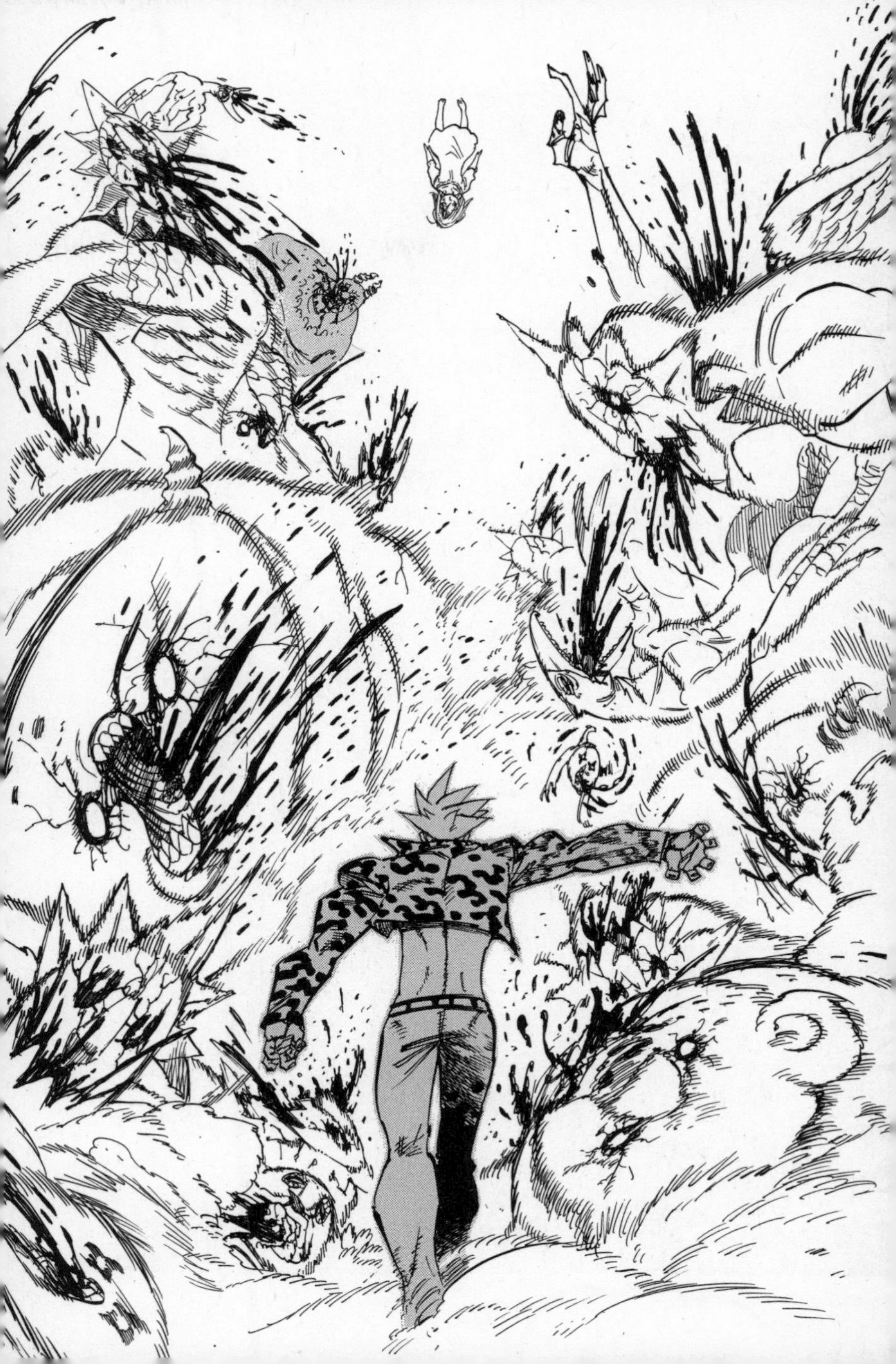

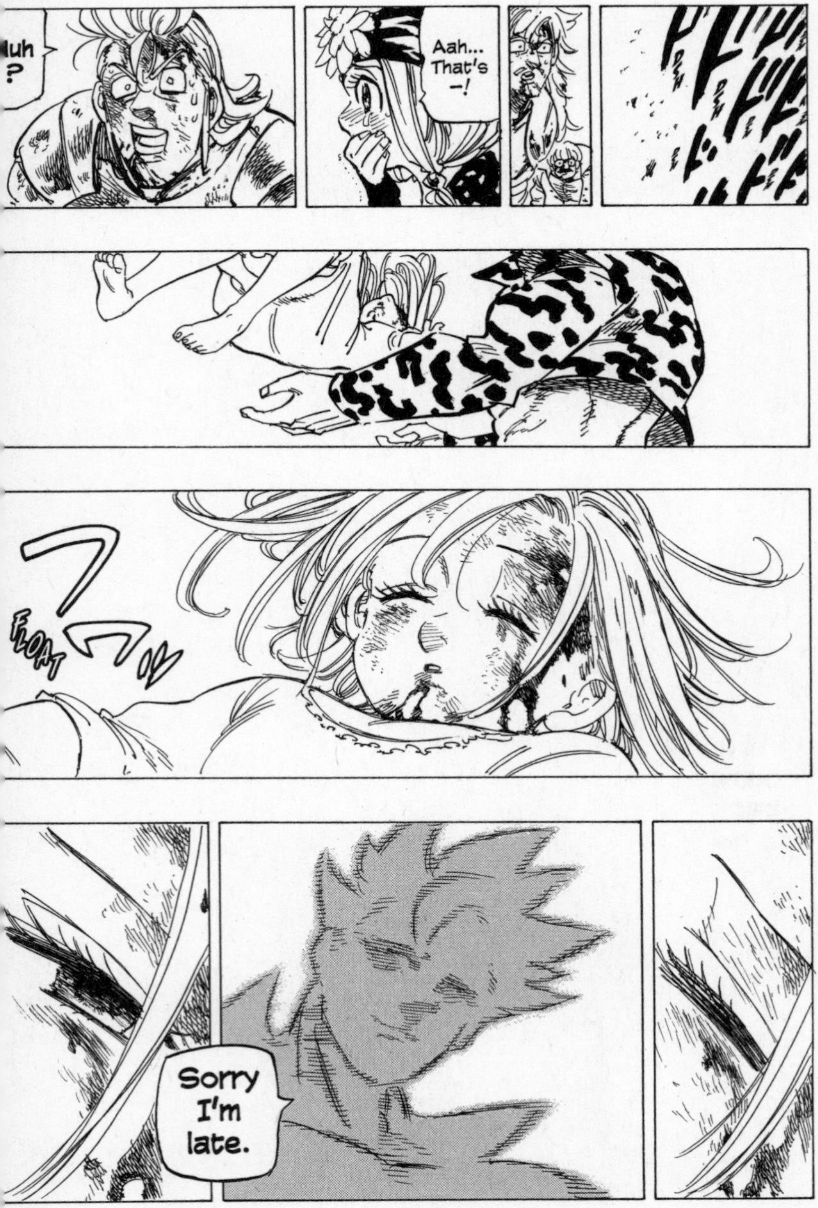
Aah... That's —!
Huh?
FLOAT
Sorry I'm late.

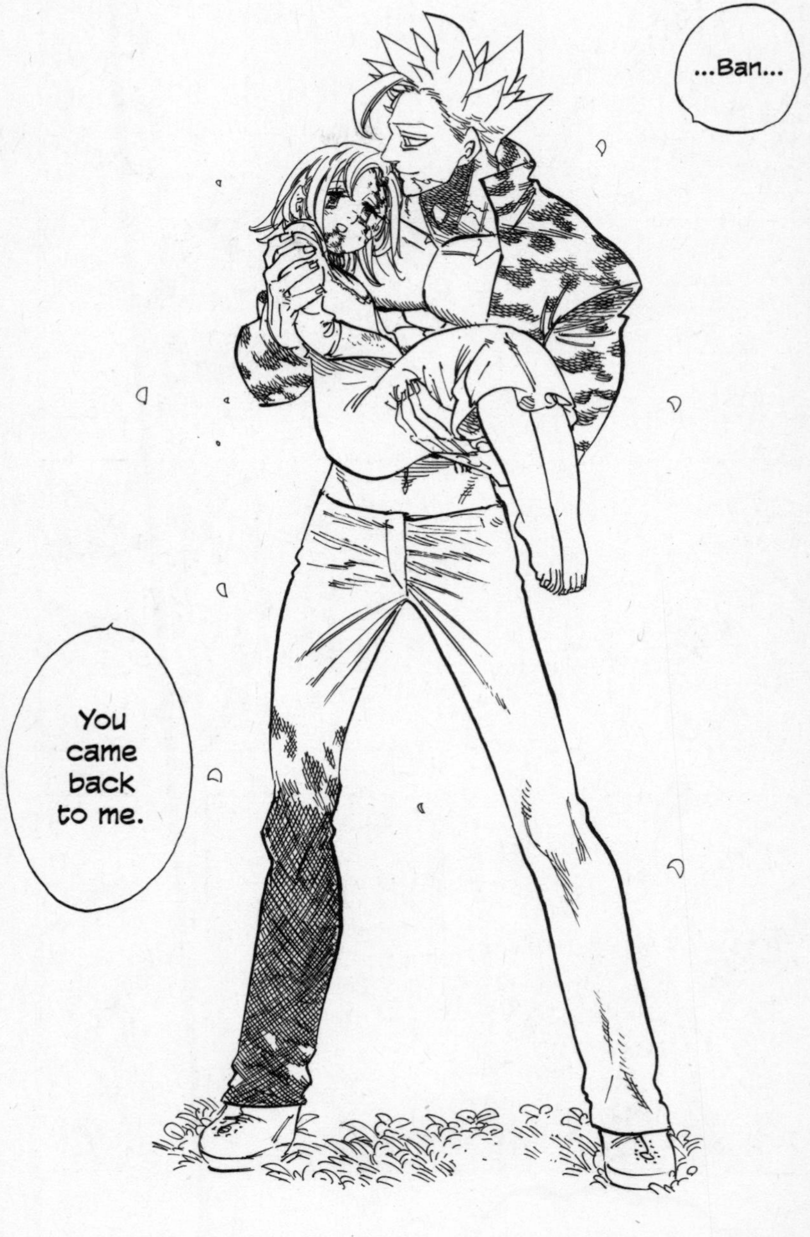
...Ban...
You came back to me.

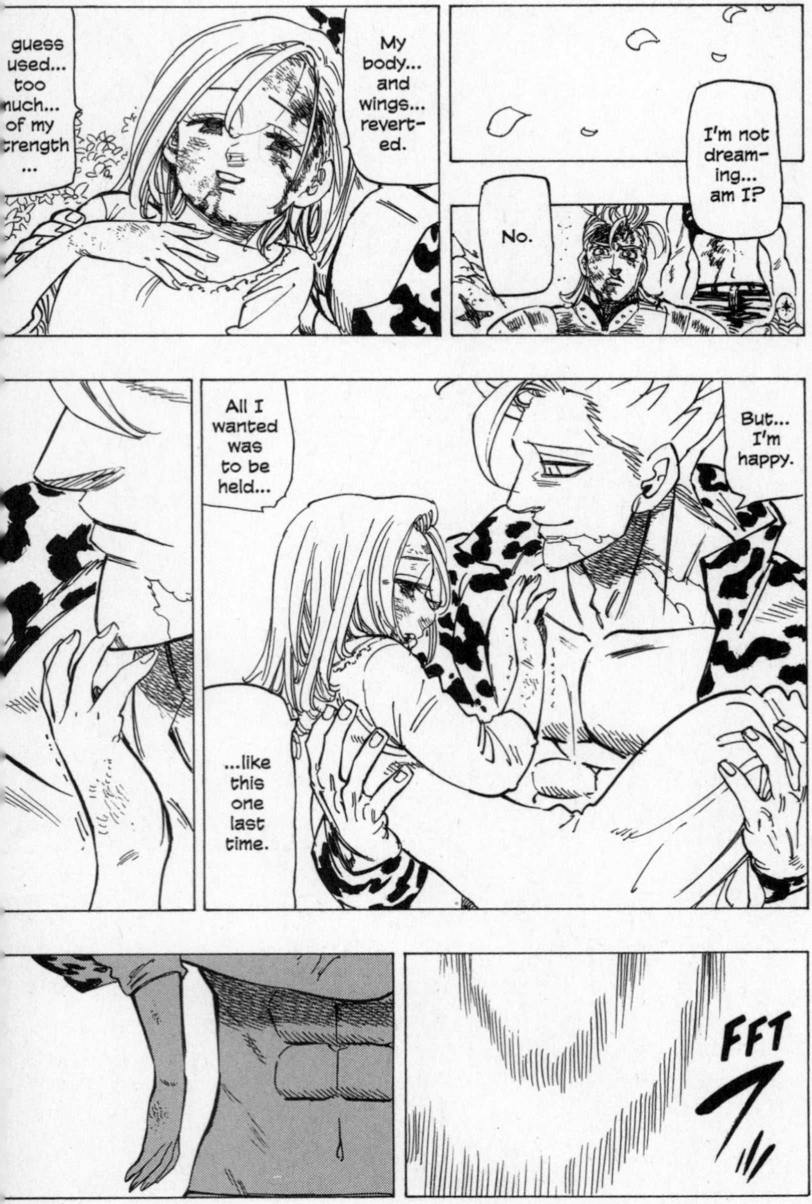
I'm not dreaming... am I?
No.
My body... and wings... reverted.
guess used... too nuch... of my trength ...
But... I'm happy.
All I wanted was to be held...
...like this one last time.
FFT

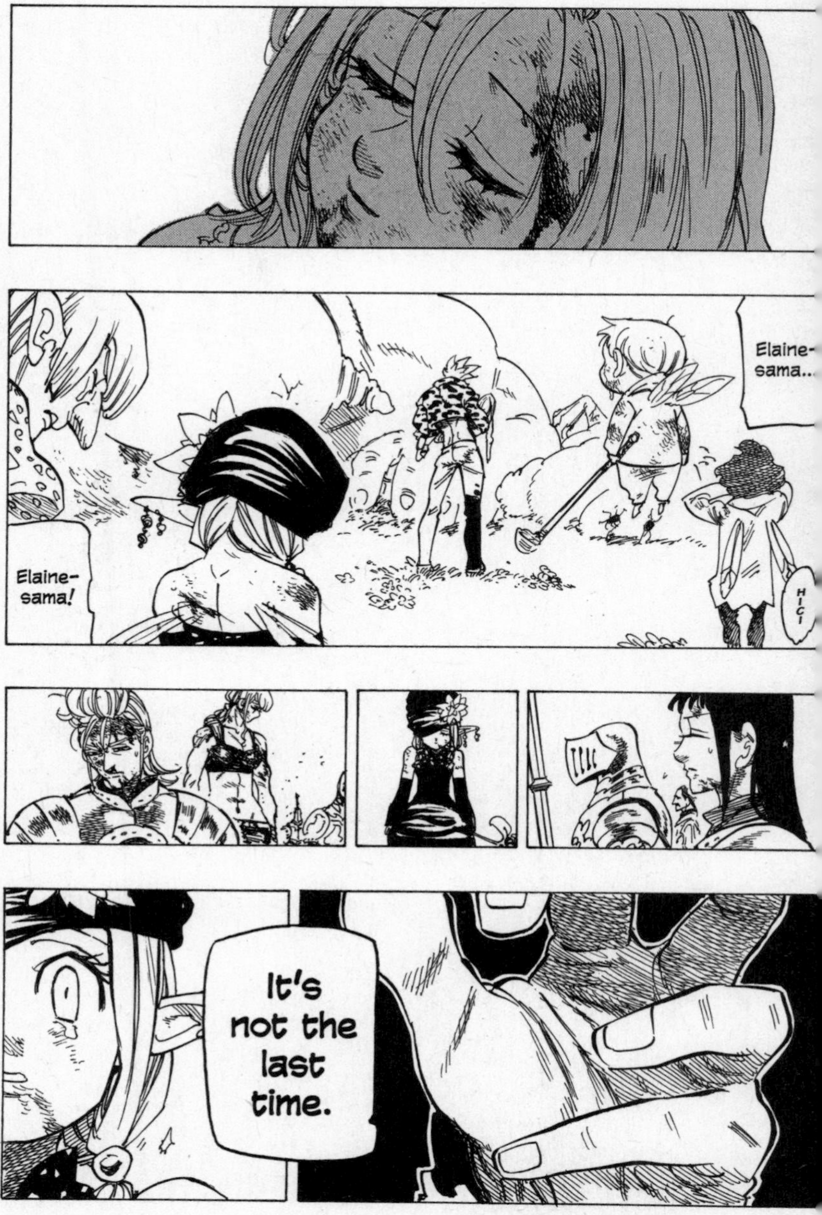
Elaine-sama...
HICI
Elaine-sama!
It's not the last time.

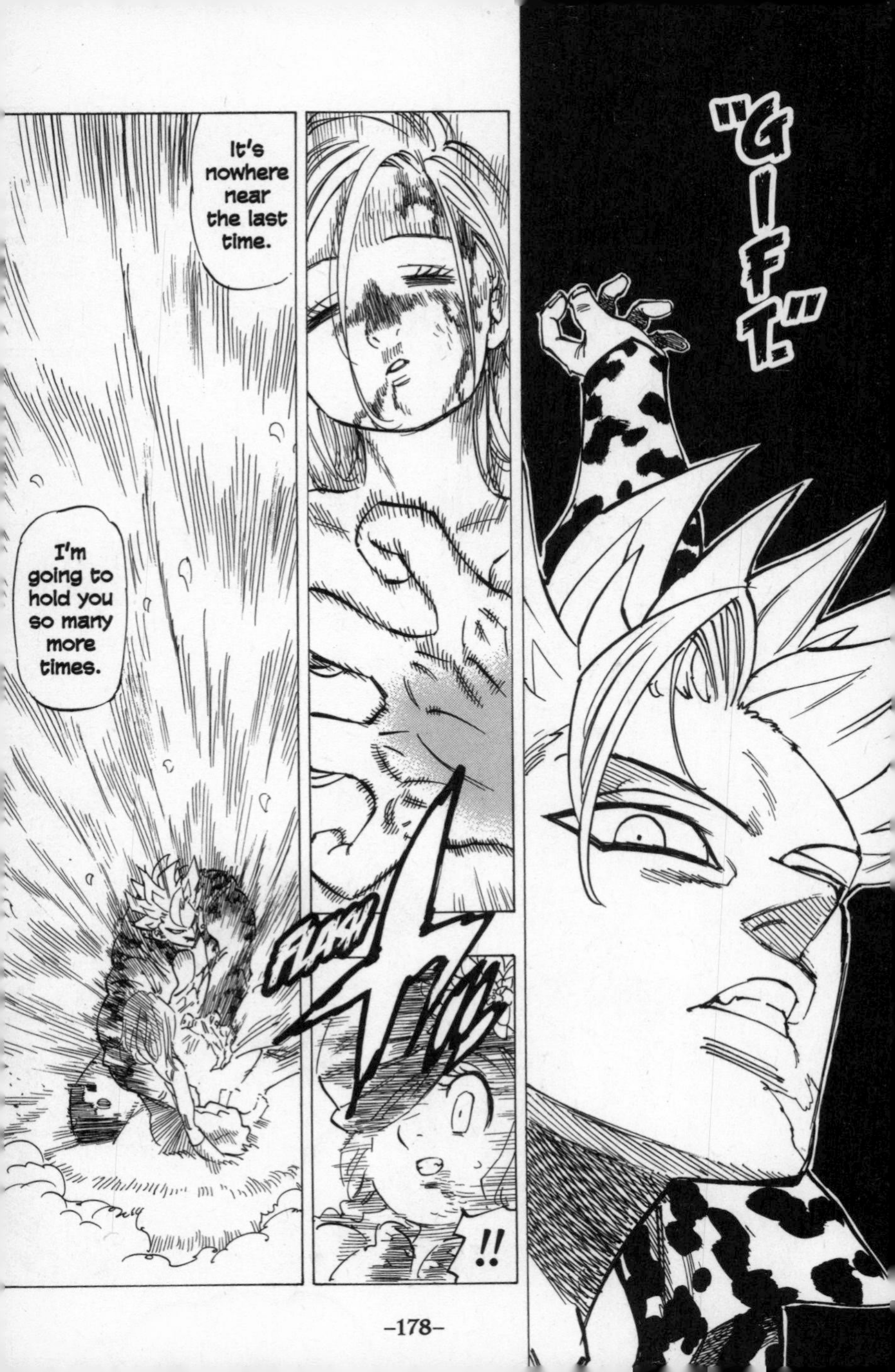
"GIFT."
It's nowhere near the last time.
!!
I'm going to hold you so many more times.

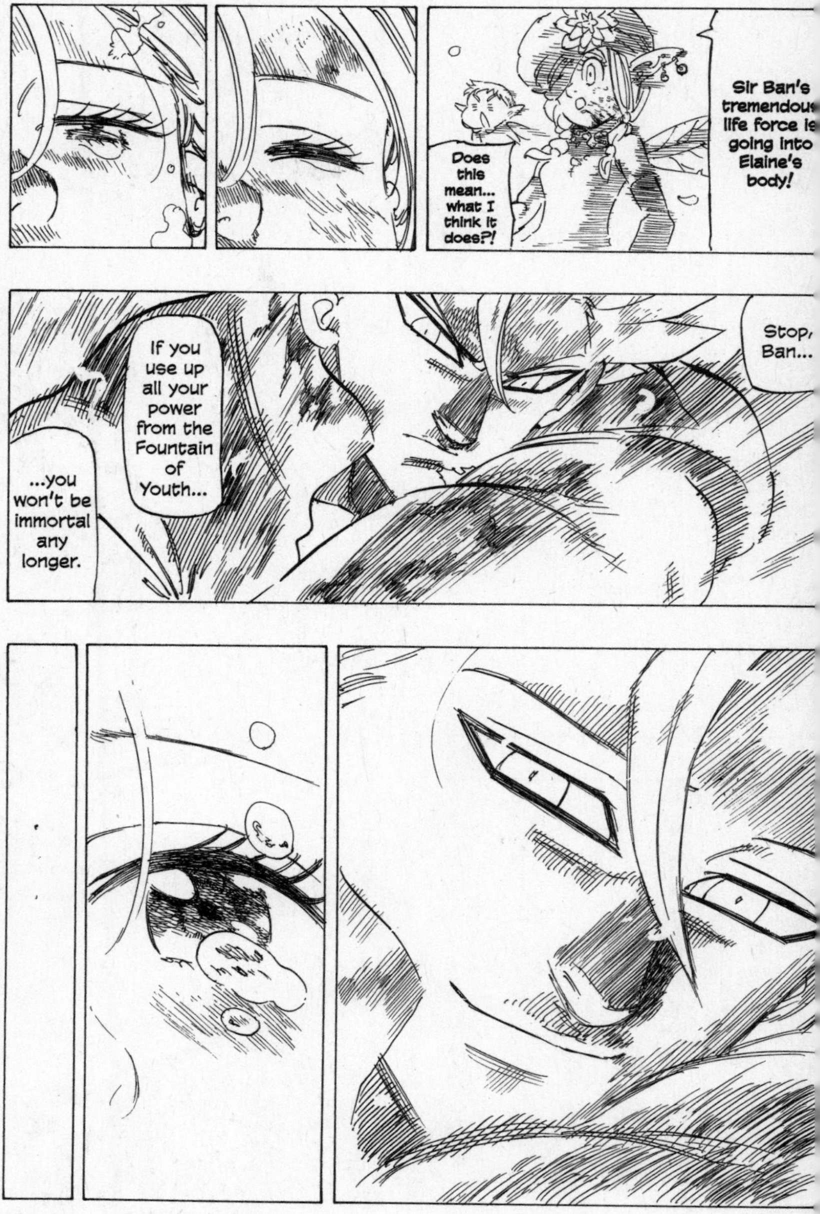
Sir Ban's tremendous life force is going into Elaine's body!
Does this mean... what I think it does?!
Stop, Ban...
If you use up all your power from the Fountain of Youth...
...you won't be immortal any longer.

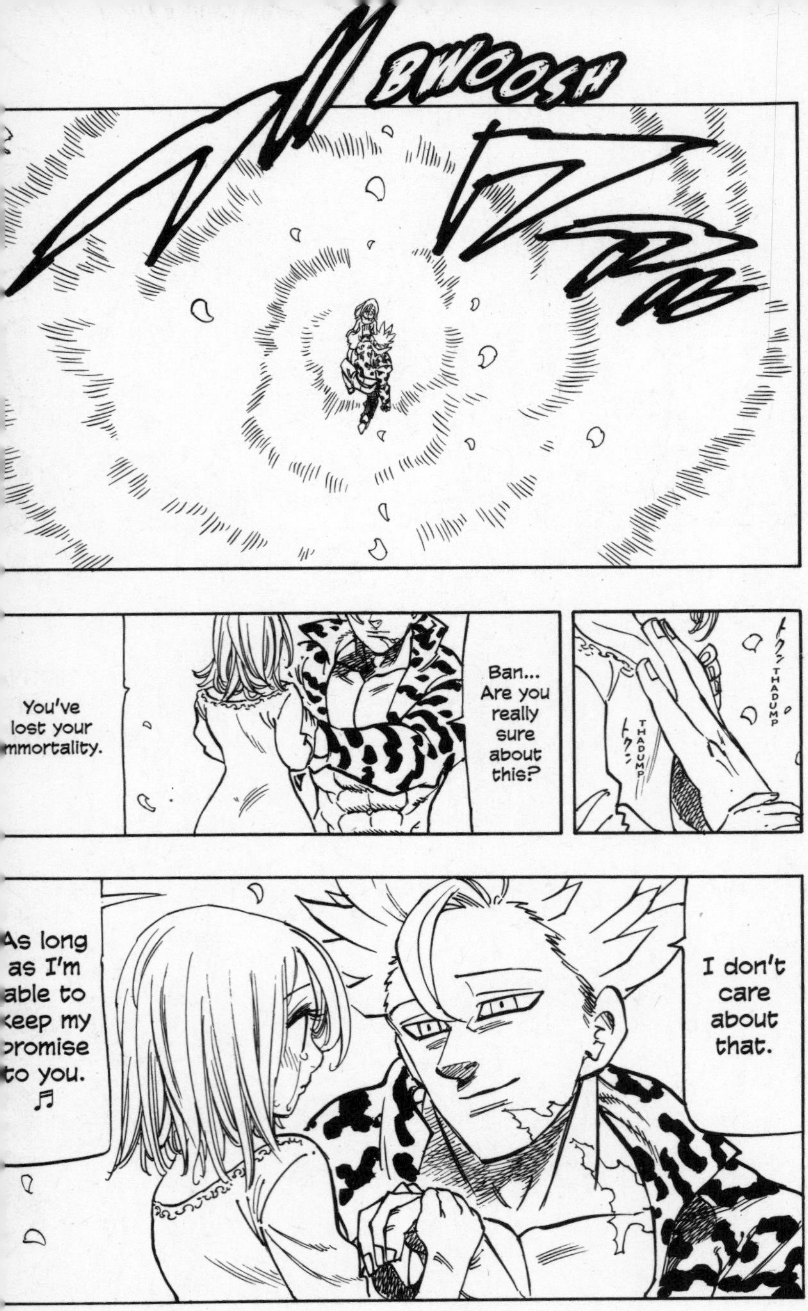
BWOOSH
THADUMP
THADUMP
Ban... Are you really sure about this?
You've lost your mmortality.
I don't care about that.
As long as I'm able to ceep my oromise to you. ♬

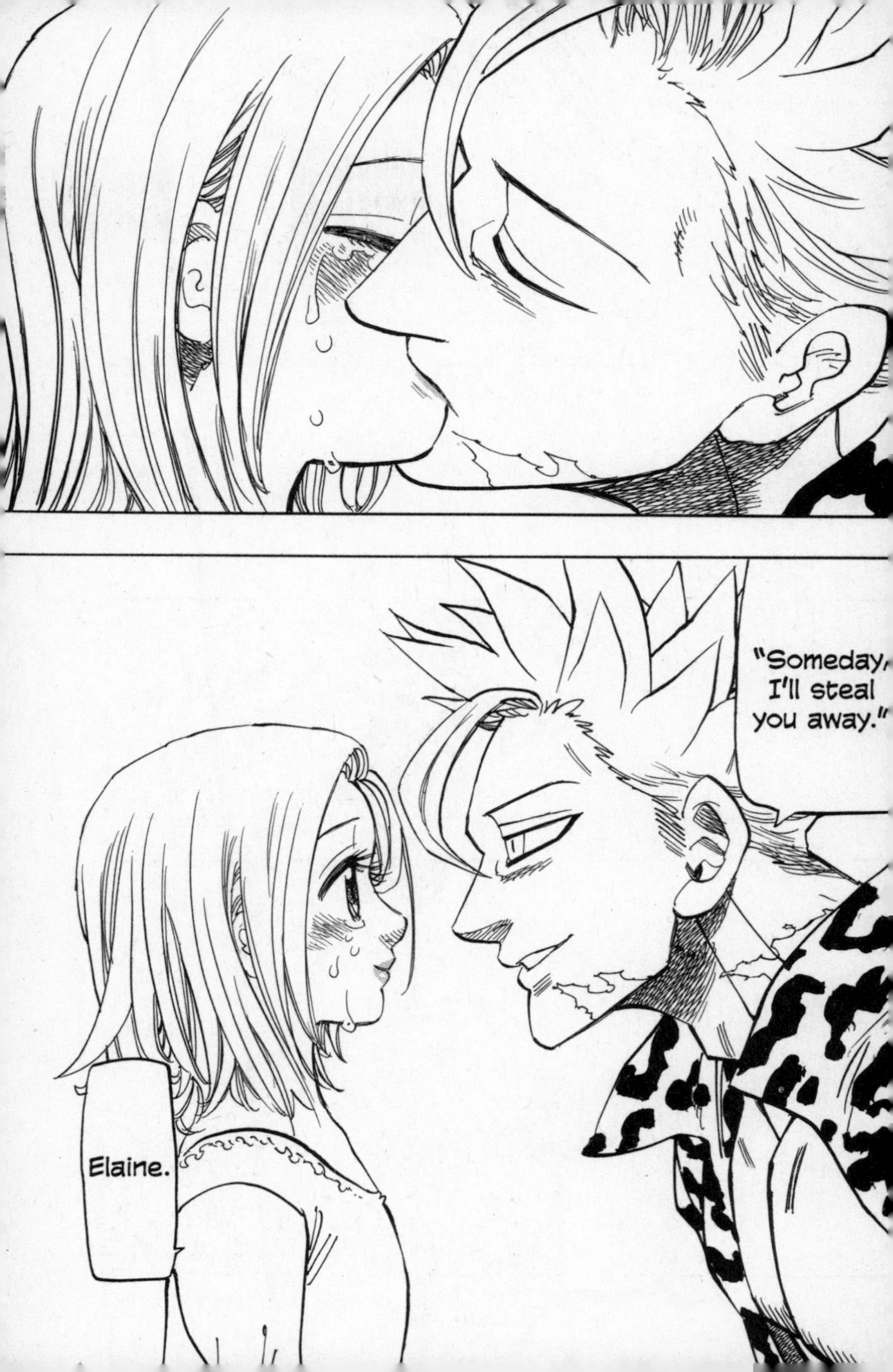
"Someday, I'll steal you away."
Elaine.

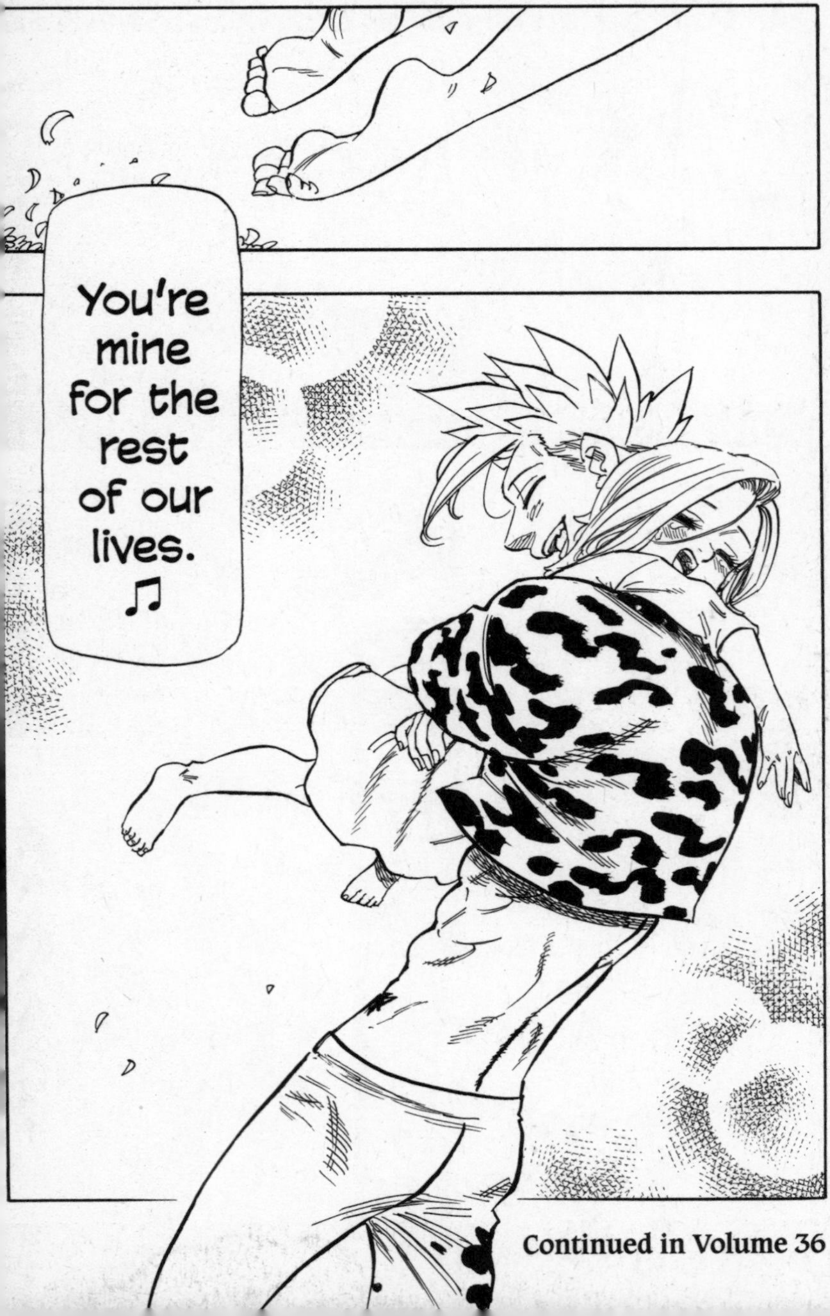
You're mine for the rest of our lives. ♫

Continued in Volume 36

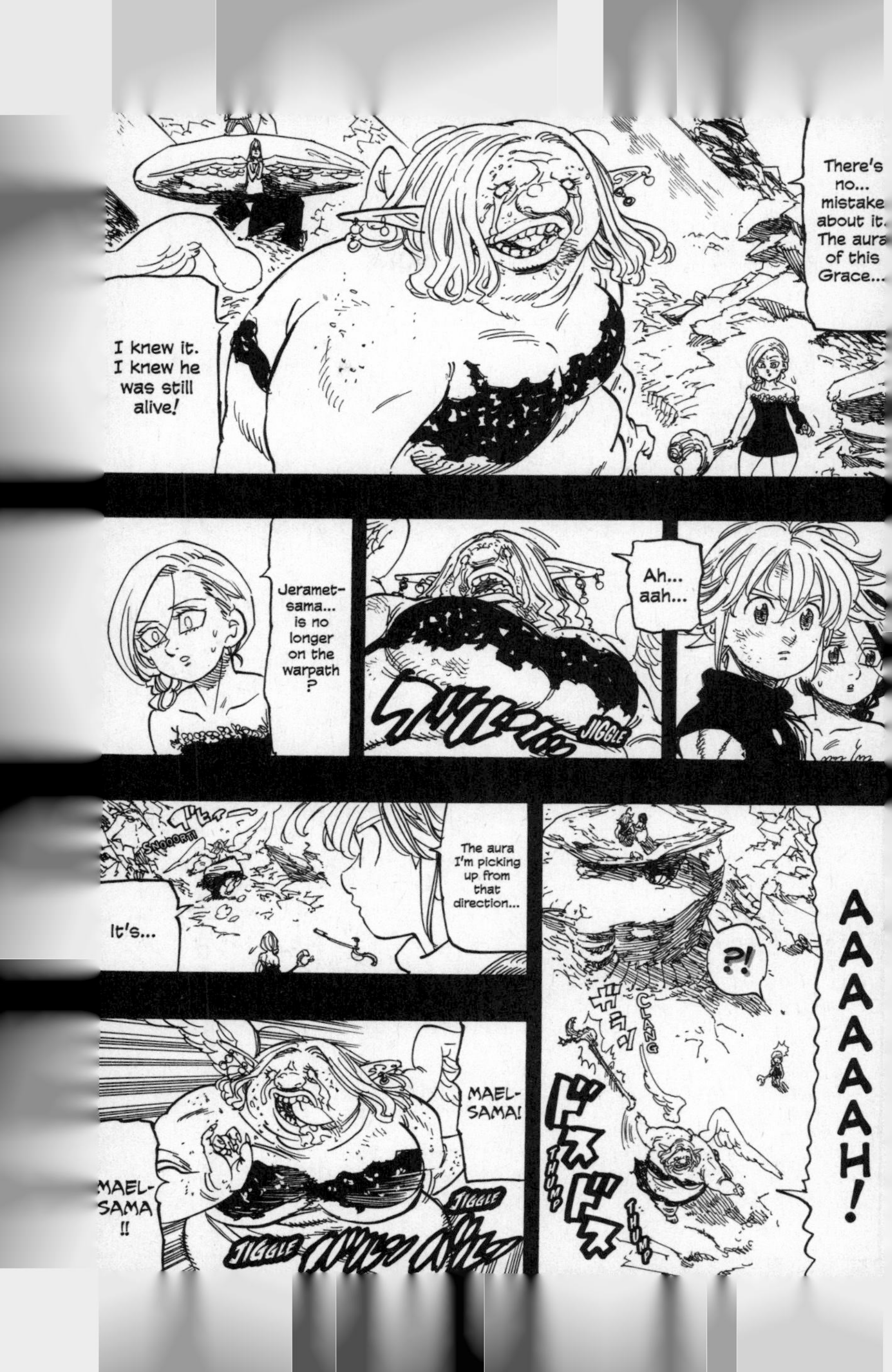
There's no... mistake about it. The aura of this Grace...
I knew it. I knew he was still alive!
Ah... aah...
JIGGLE
Jeramet-sama... is no longer on the warpath?
AAAAAAH!
?!
CLANG
THUMP
THUMP
The aura I'm picking up from that direction...
SNOOORT!
It's...
MAEL-SAMA!
JIGGLE
MAEL-SAMA!!
JIGGLE

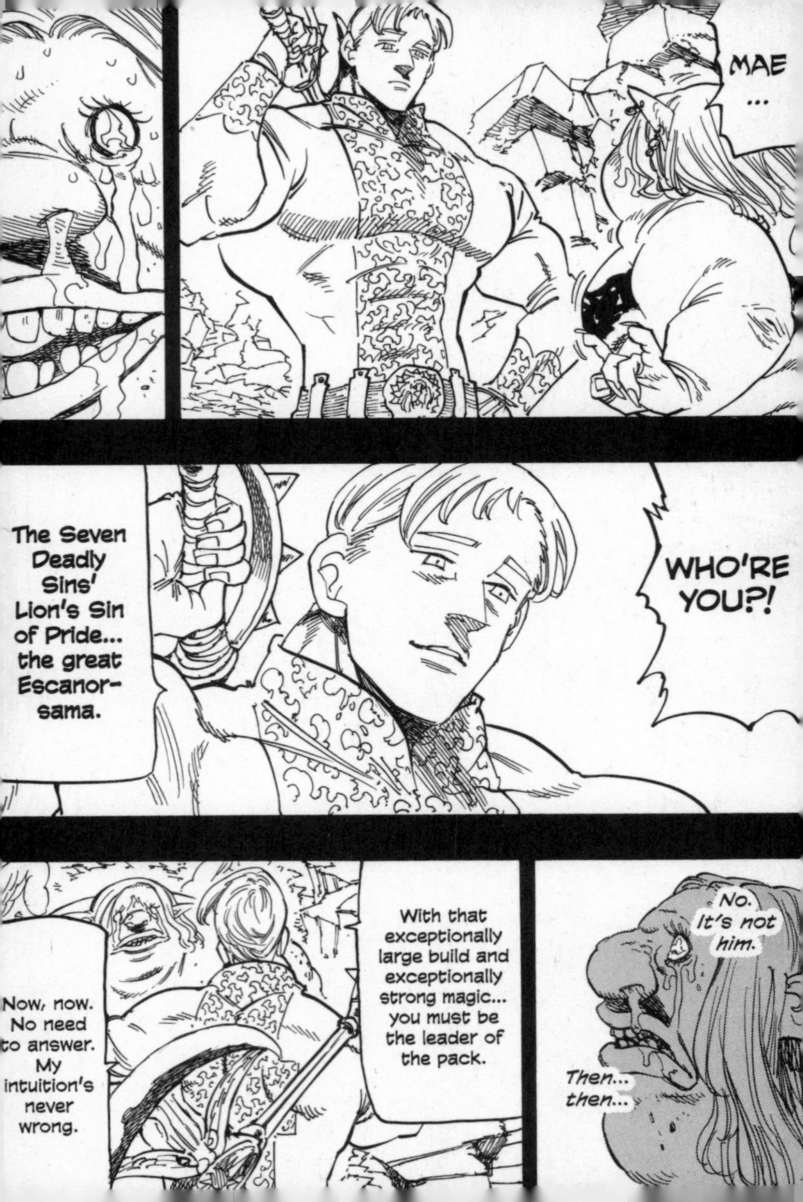
MAE ...
WHO'RE YOU?!
The Seven Deadly Sins' Lion's Sin of Pride... the great Escanor-sama.
No. It's not him.
Then... then...
With that exceptionally large build and exceptionally strong magic... you must be the leader of the pack.
Now, now. No need to answer. My intuition's never wrong.

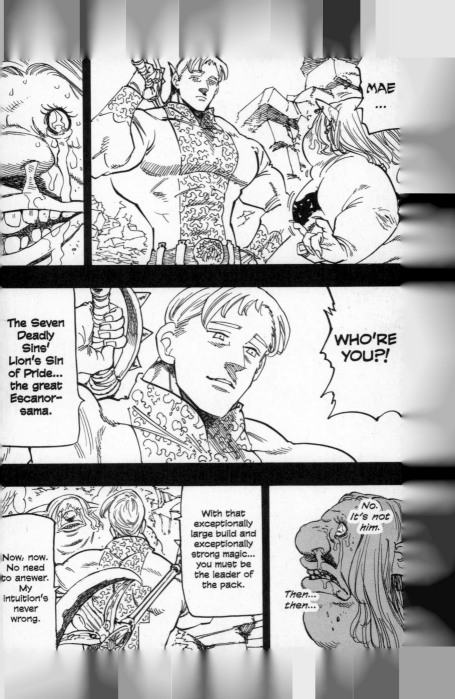

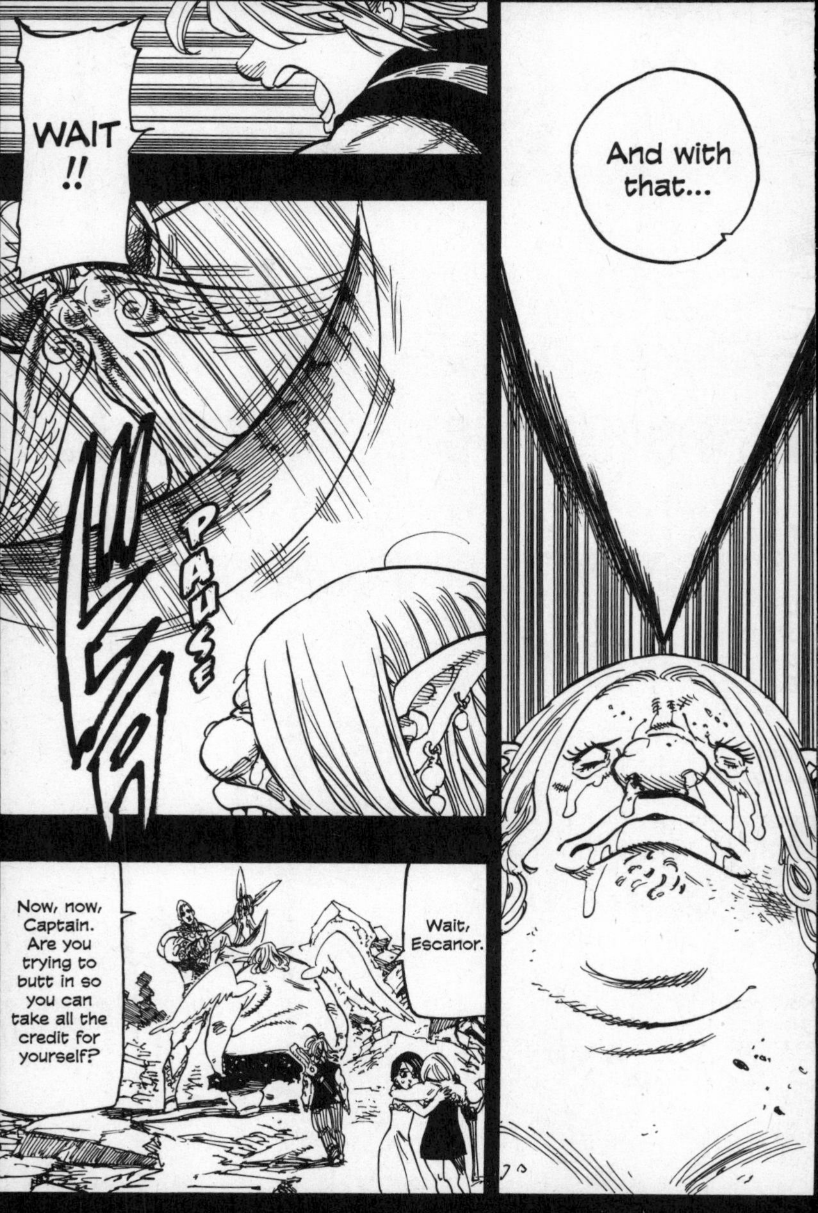
And with that...
WAIT!!
PAUSE
Wait, Escanor.
Now, now, Captain. Are you trying to butt in so you can take all the credit for yourself?

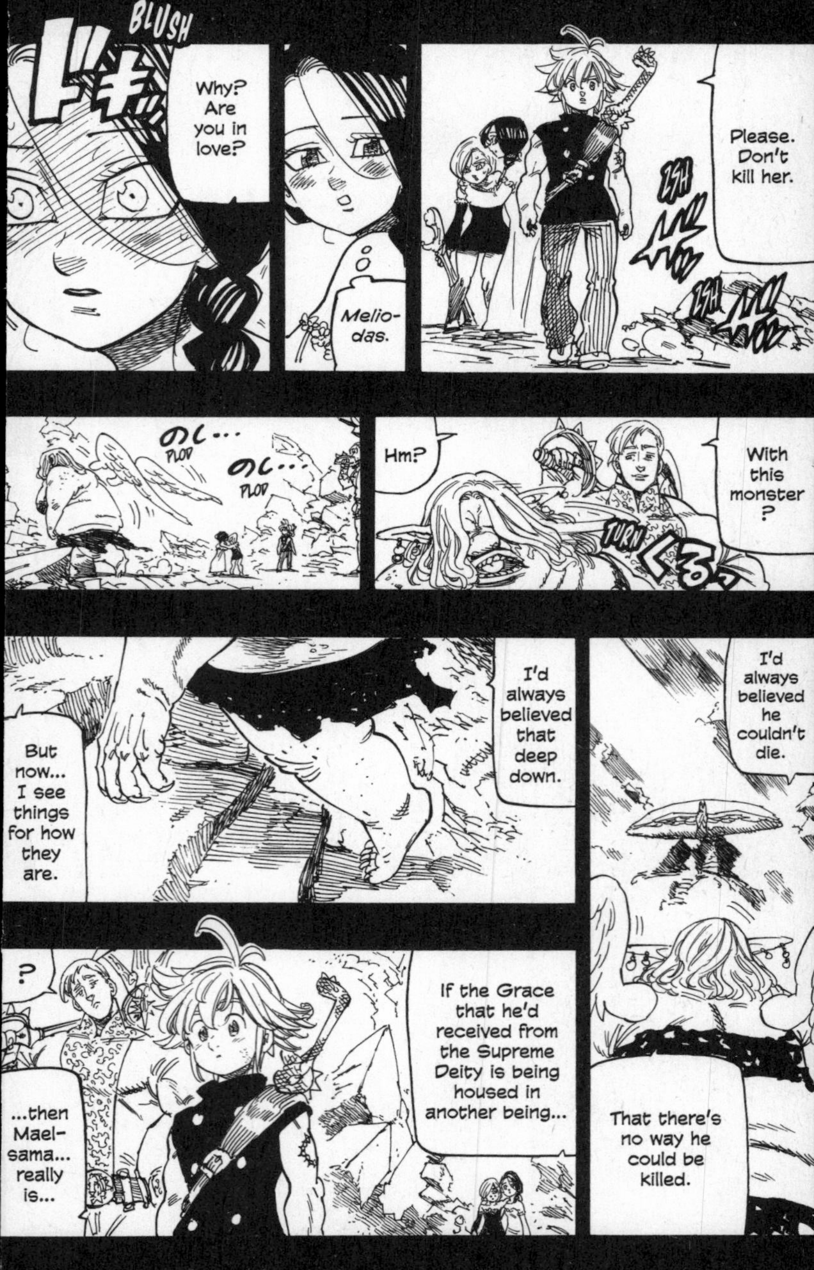
Please. Don't kill her.
ISH
ISH
Melio-das.
BLUSH
Why? Are you in love?
With this monster?
TURN
Hm?
PLOD
PLOD
I'd always believed he couldn't die.
That there's no way he could be killed.
I'd always believed that deep down.
But now... I see things for how they are.
If the Grace that he'd received from the Supreme Deity is being housed in another being...
...then Mael-sama... really is...
?

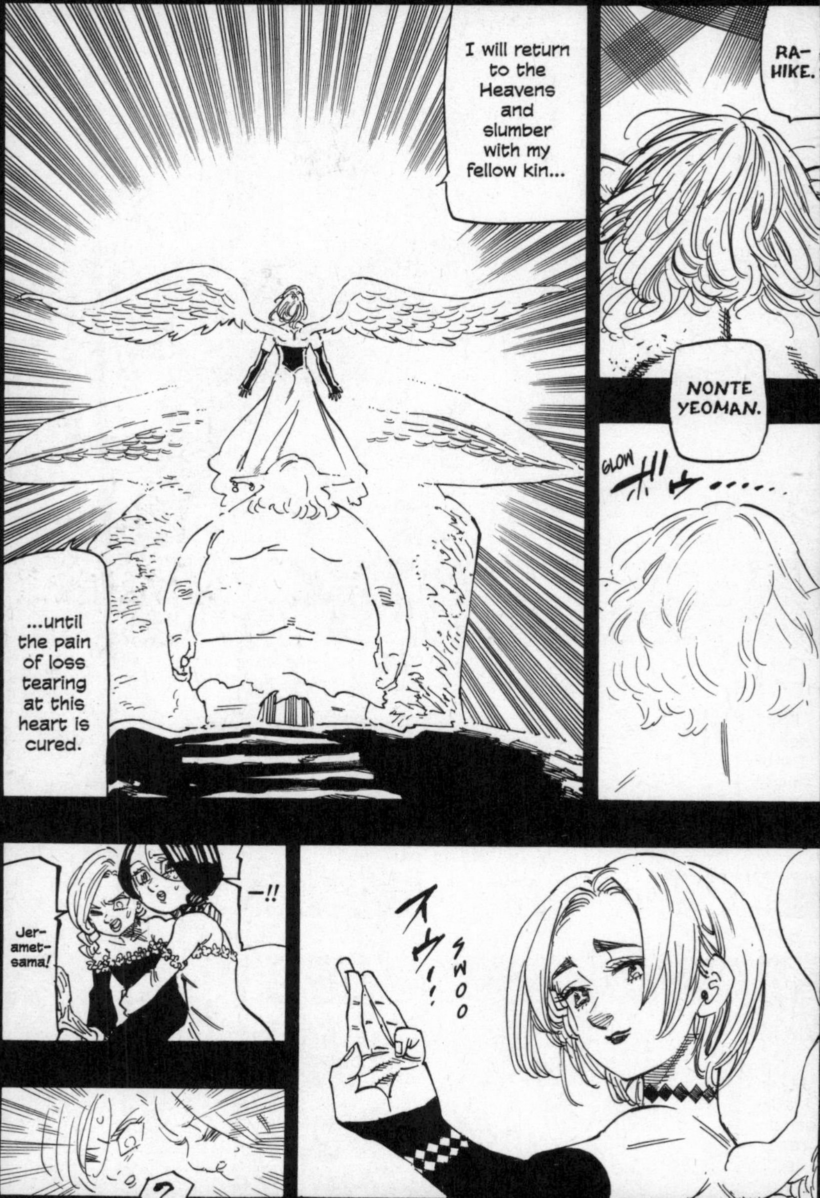
RA-
HIKE.
NONTE
YEOMAN.
GLOW
I will return to the Heavens and slumber with my fellow kin...
...until the pain of loss tearing at this heart is cured.
SWOOO
—!!
Jer-amet-sama!
?

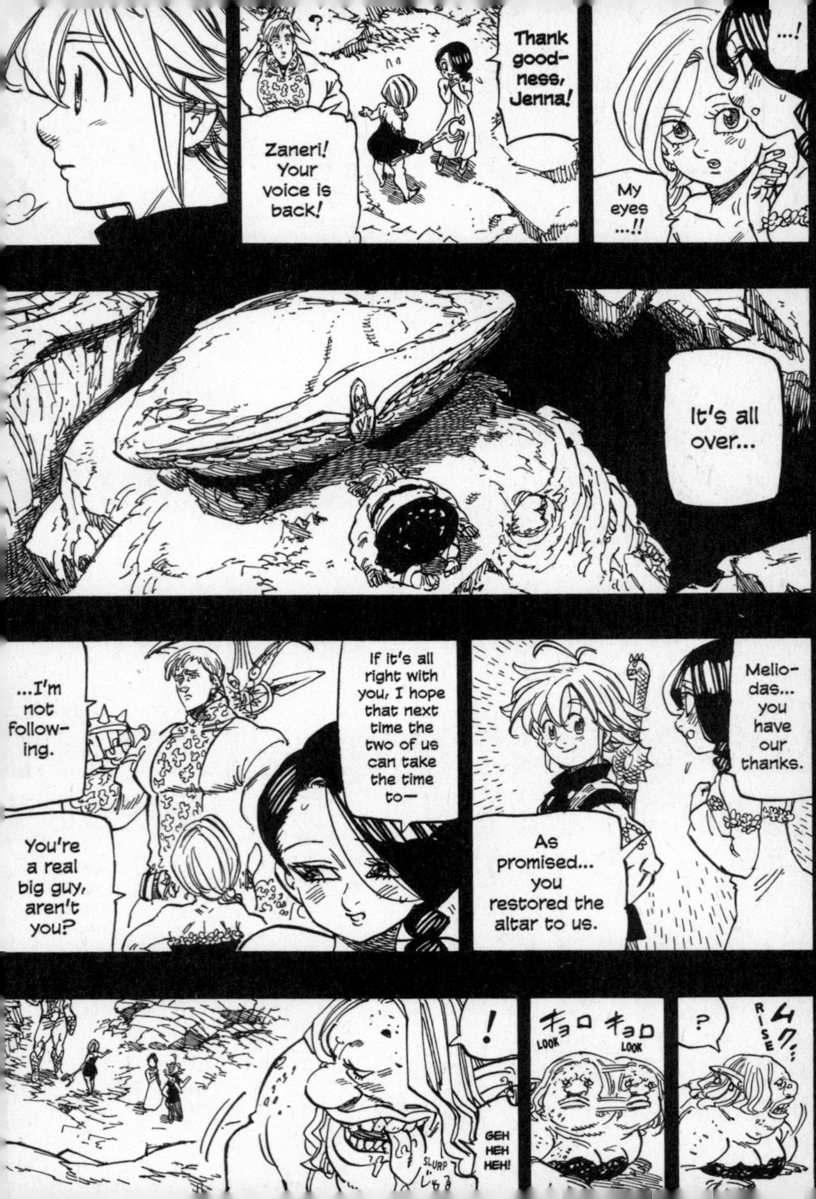
...!
My eyes ...!!
Thank goodness, Jenna!
?
Zaneri! Your voice is back!
It's all over...
Melio-das... you have our thanks.
As promised... you restored the altar to us.
If it's all right with you, I hope that next time the two of us can take the time to—
...I'm not follow-ing.
You're a real big guy, aren't you?
?
RISE
ムク
キョロ キョロ
LOOK LOOK
!
GEH HEH HEH!
SLURP
じゅる

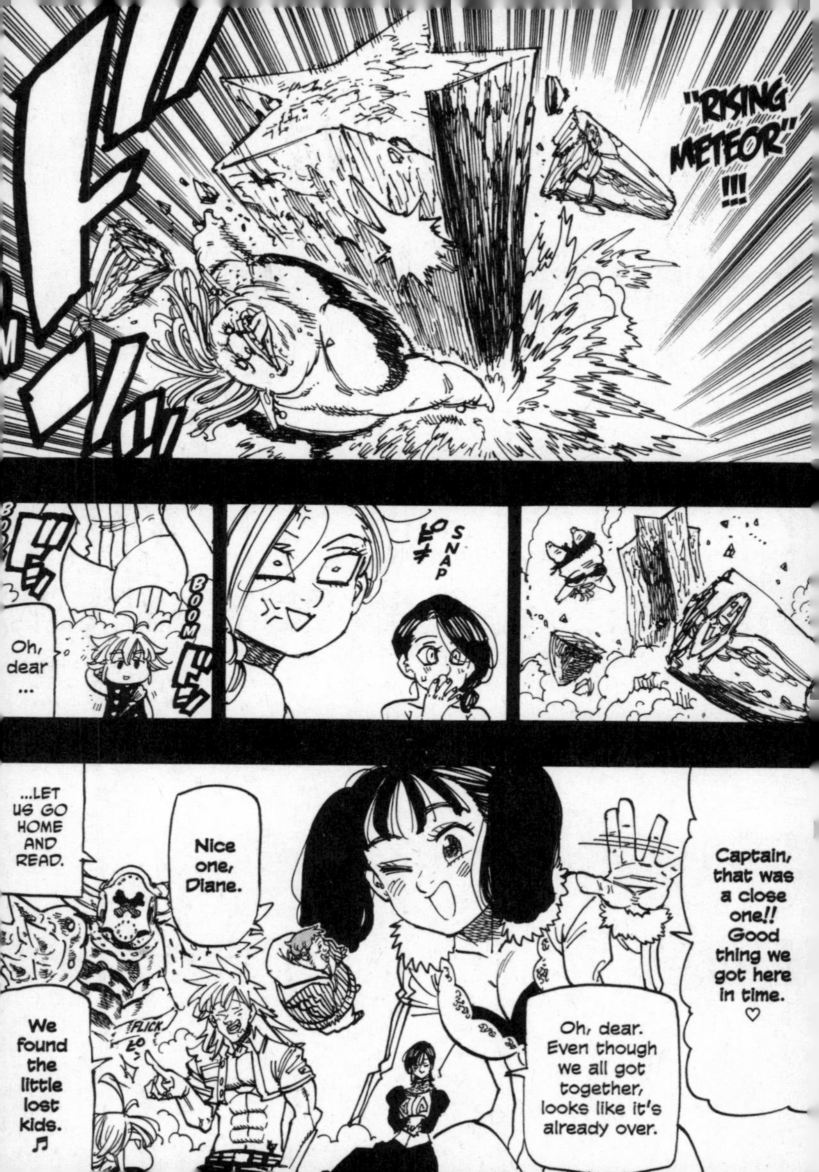
"RISING METEOR"!!!
SNAP
BOOM
Oh, dear ...
Captain, that was a close one!! Good thing we got here in time. ♡
Nice one, Diane.
...LET US GO HOME AND READ.
Oh, dear. Even though we all got together, looks like it's already over.
FLICK
We found the little lost kids. ♫

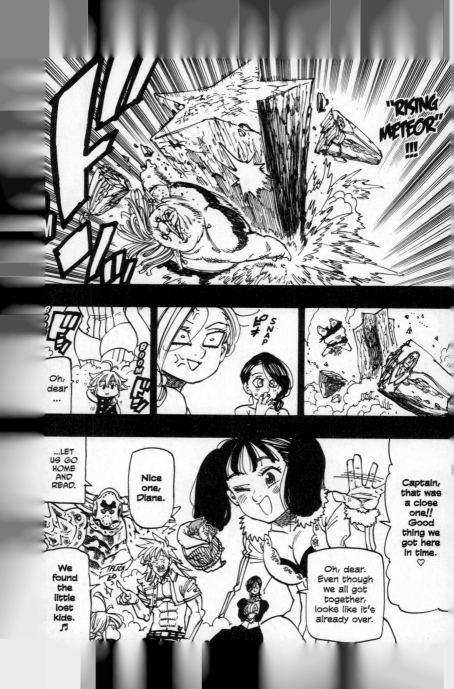

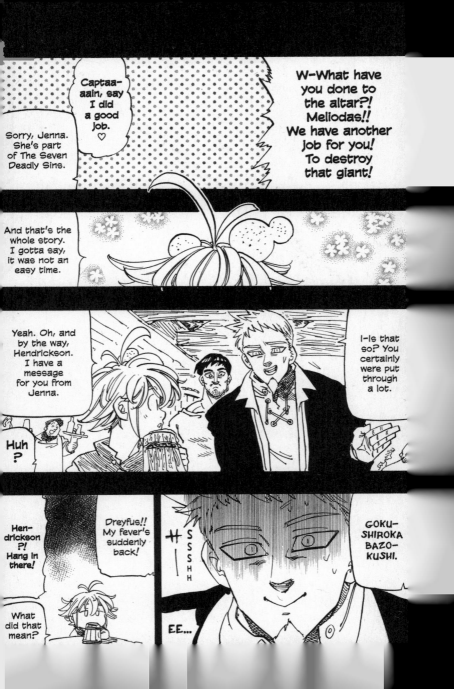

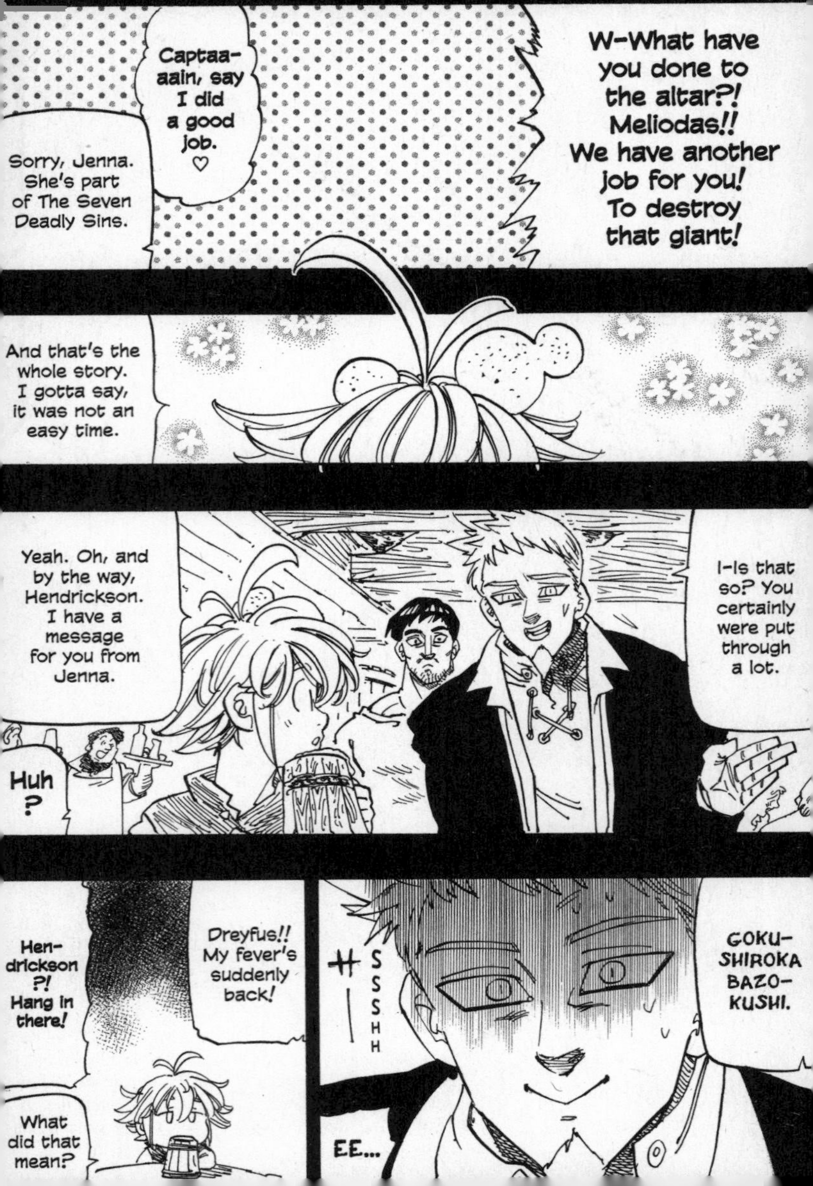
W-What have you done to the altar?! Meliodas!! We have another job for you! To destroy that giant!
Captaa-aain, say I did a good job. ♡
Sorry, Jenna. She's part of The Seven Deadly Sins.
And that's the whole story. I gotta say, it was not an easy time.
I-Is that so? You certainly were put through a lot.
Yeah. Oh, and by the way, Hendrickson. I have a message for you from Jenna.
Huh?
GOKU-SHIROKA BAZO-KUSHI.
SSSHH
EE...
Dreyfus!! My fever's suddenly back!
Hendrickson?! Hang in there!
What did that mean?

· KAMOME
SHIRAHAMA ·

Witch Hat Atelier

A magical manga adventure for fans of Disney and Studio Ghibli!

Witch Hat Atelier © Kamome Shirahama/Kodansha

The magical adventure that took Japan by storm is finally here, from acclaimed DC and Marvel cover artist Kamome Shirahama!

In a world where everyone takes wonders like magic spells and dragons for granted, Coco is a girl with a simple dream: She wants to be a witch. But everybody knows magicians are born, not made, and Coco was not born with a gift for magic. Resigned to her un-magical life, Coco is about to give up on her dream to become a witch...until the day she meets Qifrey, a mysterious, traveling magician. After secretly seeing Qifrey perform magic in a way she's never seen before, Coco soon learns what everybody "knows" might not be the truth, and discovers that her magical dream may not be as far away as it may seem...

KC
KODANSHA
COMICS

MRAC

The Seven Deadly Sins volume 35 is a work of fiction. Names, characters, places, and incidents are the products of the author's imagination or are used fictitiously. Any resemblance to actual events, locales, or persons, living or dead, is entirely coincidental.

A Kodansha Comics Trade Paperback Original.

Published in the United States by Kodansha Comics, an imprint of Kodansha USA Publishing, LLC, New York.

Publication rights for this English edition arranged through Kodansha Ltd., Tokyo.

First published in Japan in 2019 by Kodansha Ltd., Tokyo.

ISBN 978-1-63236-873-7

Printed in the United States of America.

www.kodanshacomics.com

9 8 7 6 5 4 3 2 1

Translation: Christine Dashiell
Lettering: James Dashiell
Kodansha Comics edition cover design: Phil Balsman